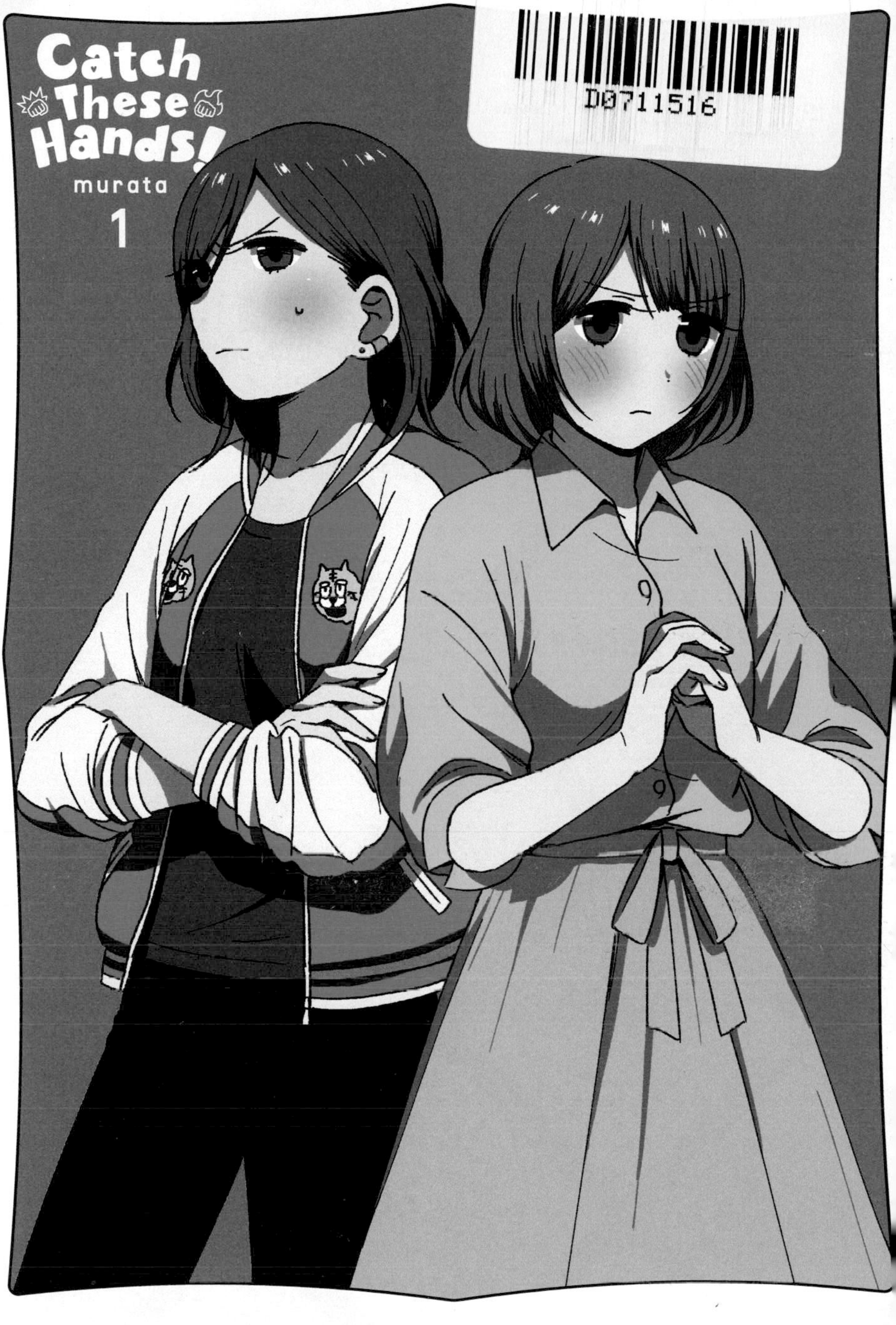
Catch These Hands!
murata
1

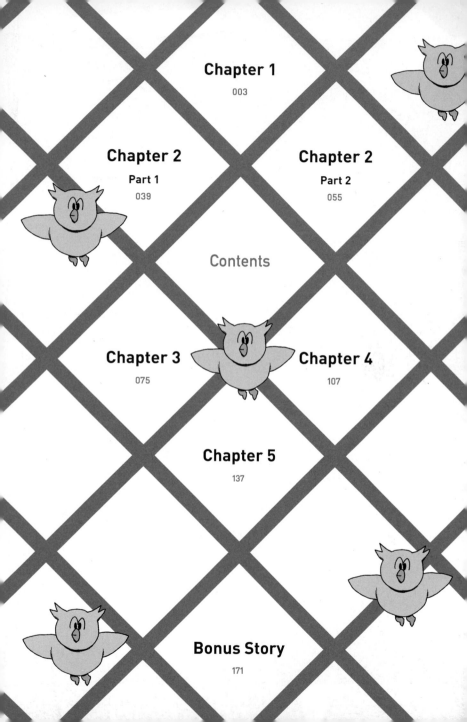

Contents

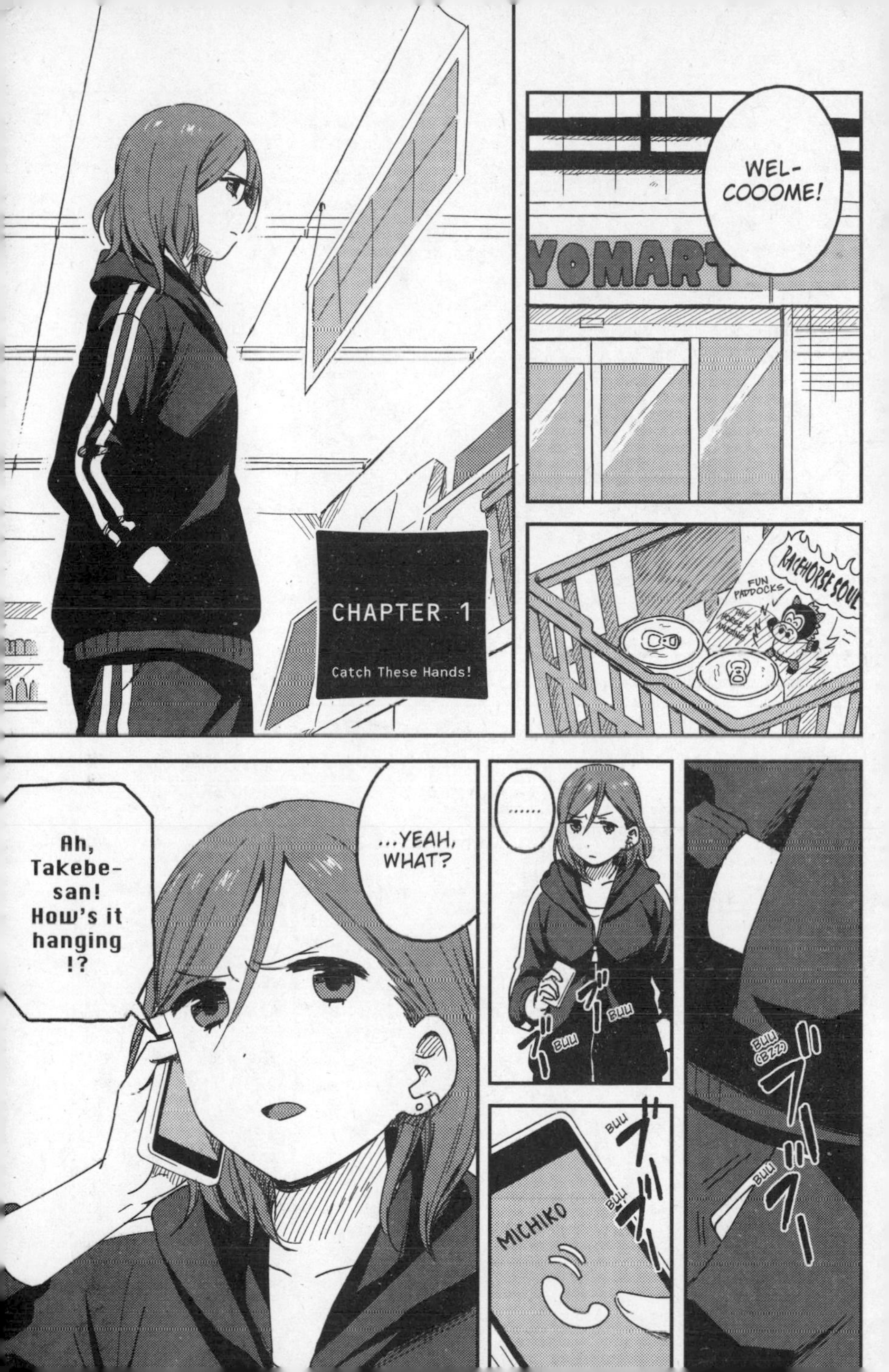

WEL-COOOME!
YOMART
RACEHORSE SOUL
FUN PADDOCKS
THIS HORSE IS AMAZING!
CHAPTER 1
Catch These Hands!
BUU (BZZZ)
BUU
......
BUU
BUU
BUU
BUU
BUU
MICHIKO
...YEAH, WHAT?
Ah, Takebe-san! How's it hanging!?

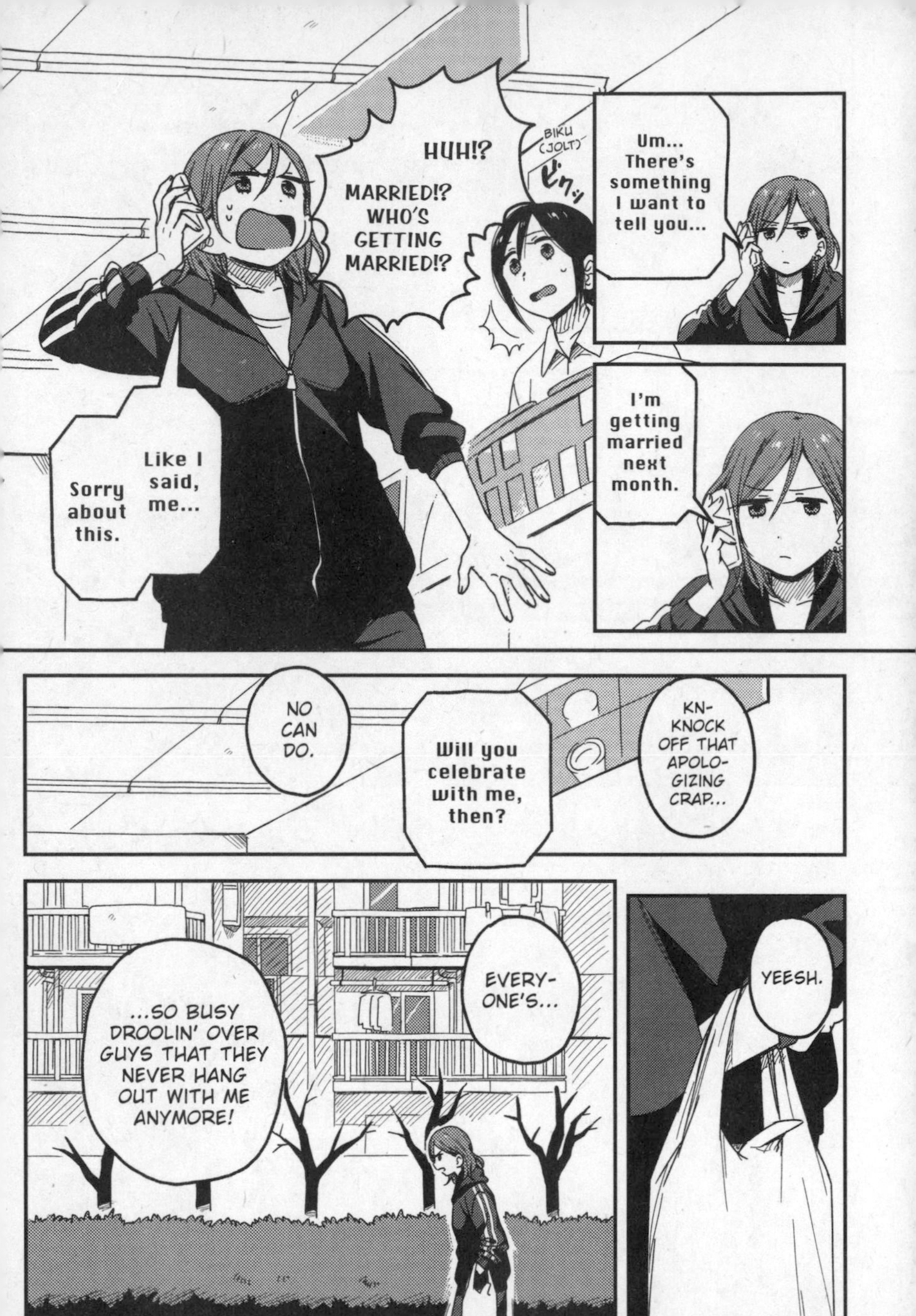
Um... There's something I want to tell you...
I'm getting married next month.
BIKU (JOLT)
ビクッ
HUH!?
MARRIED!? WHO'S GETTING MARRIED!?
Like I said, me...
Sorry about this.
KN-KNOCK OFF THAT APOLOGIZING CRAP...
Will you celebrate with me, then?
NO CAN DO.
YEESH.
EVERYONE'S...
...SO BUSY DROOLIN' OVER GUYS THAT THEY NEVER HANG OUT WITH ME ANYMORE!

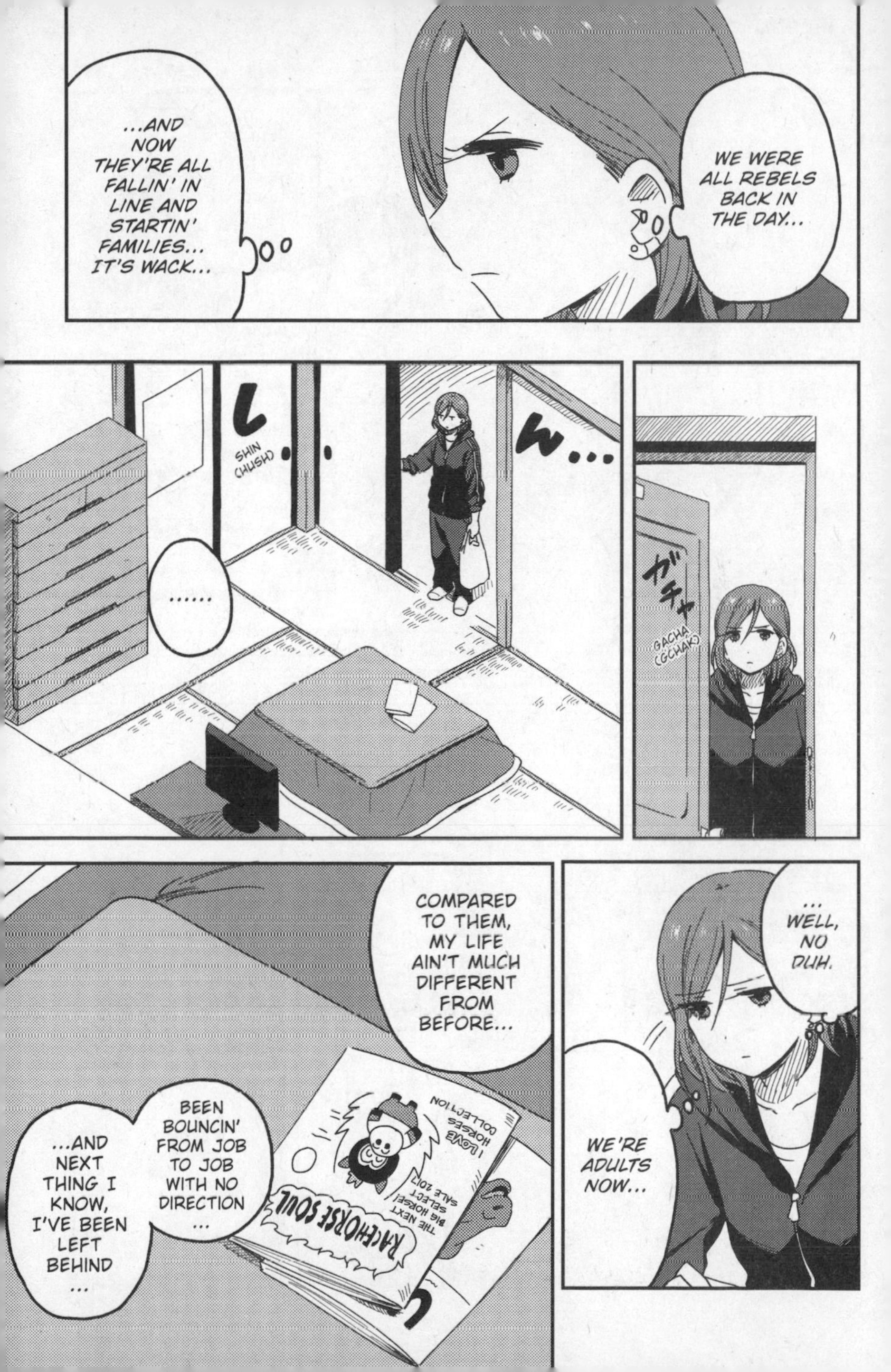
WE WERE ALL REBELS BACK IN THE DAY...
...AND NOW THEY'RE ALL FALLIN' IN LINE AND STARTIN' FAMILIES... IT'S WACK...
ガチャ
GACHA (GCHAK)
L...
SHIN (HUSH)
W...
......
...WELL, NO DUH.
WE'RE ADULTS NOW...
COMPARED TO THEM, MY LIFE AIN'T MUCH DIFFERENT FROM BEFORE...
BEEN BOUNCIN' FROM JOB TO JOB WITH NO DIRECTION...
...AND NEXT THING I KNOW, I'VE BEEN LEFT BEHIND...
RACEHORSE SOUL
THE NEXT BIG HORSE! SELECT SALE 2017
I LOVE HORSES COLLECTION

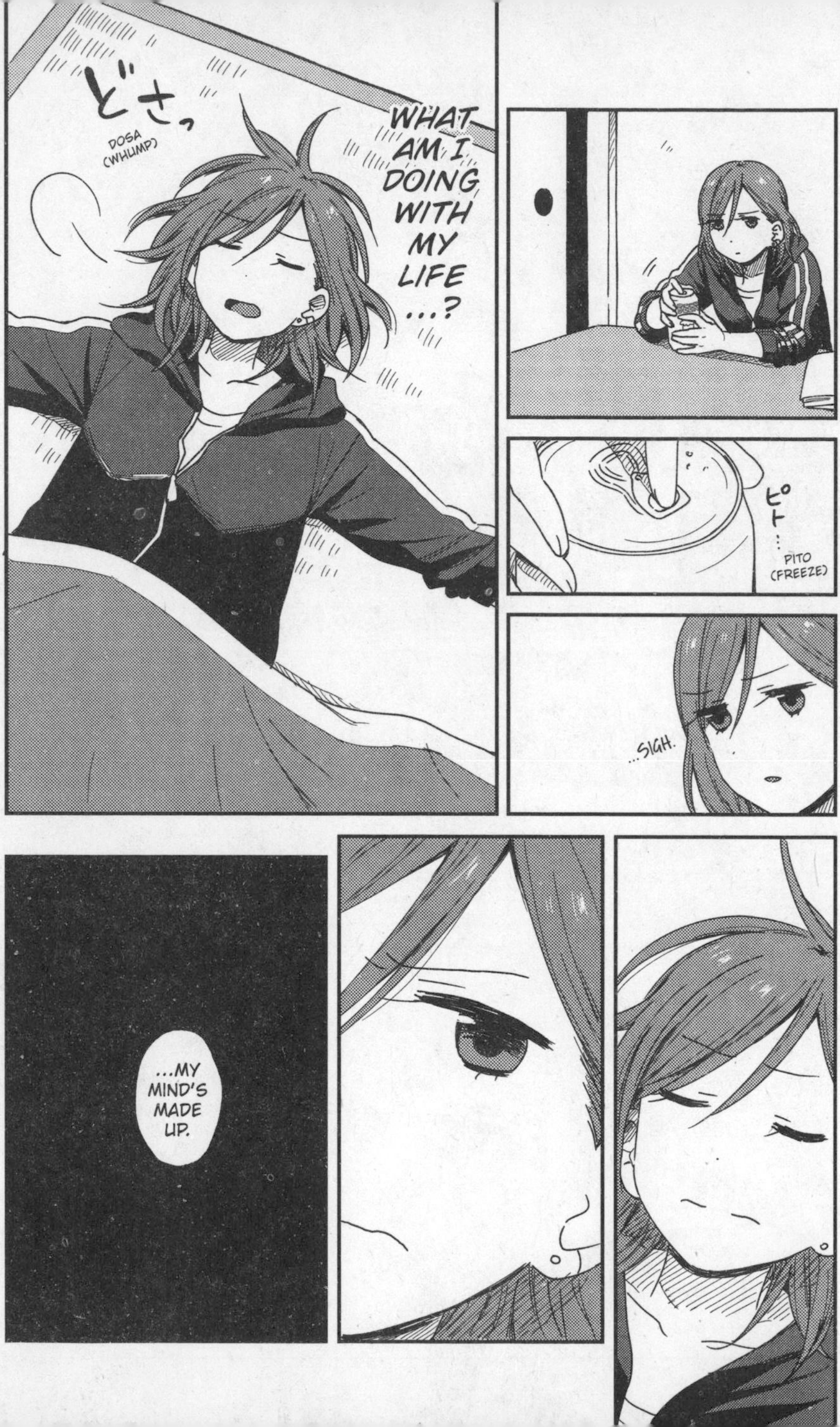
ピト…
PITO (FREEZE)
...SIGH.
WHAT AM I DOING WITH MY LIFE ...?
どさっ
DOSA (WHUMP)
...MY MIND'S MADE UP.

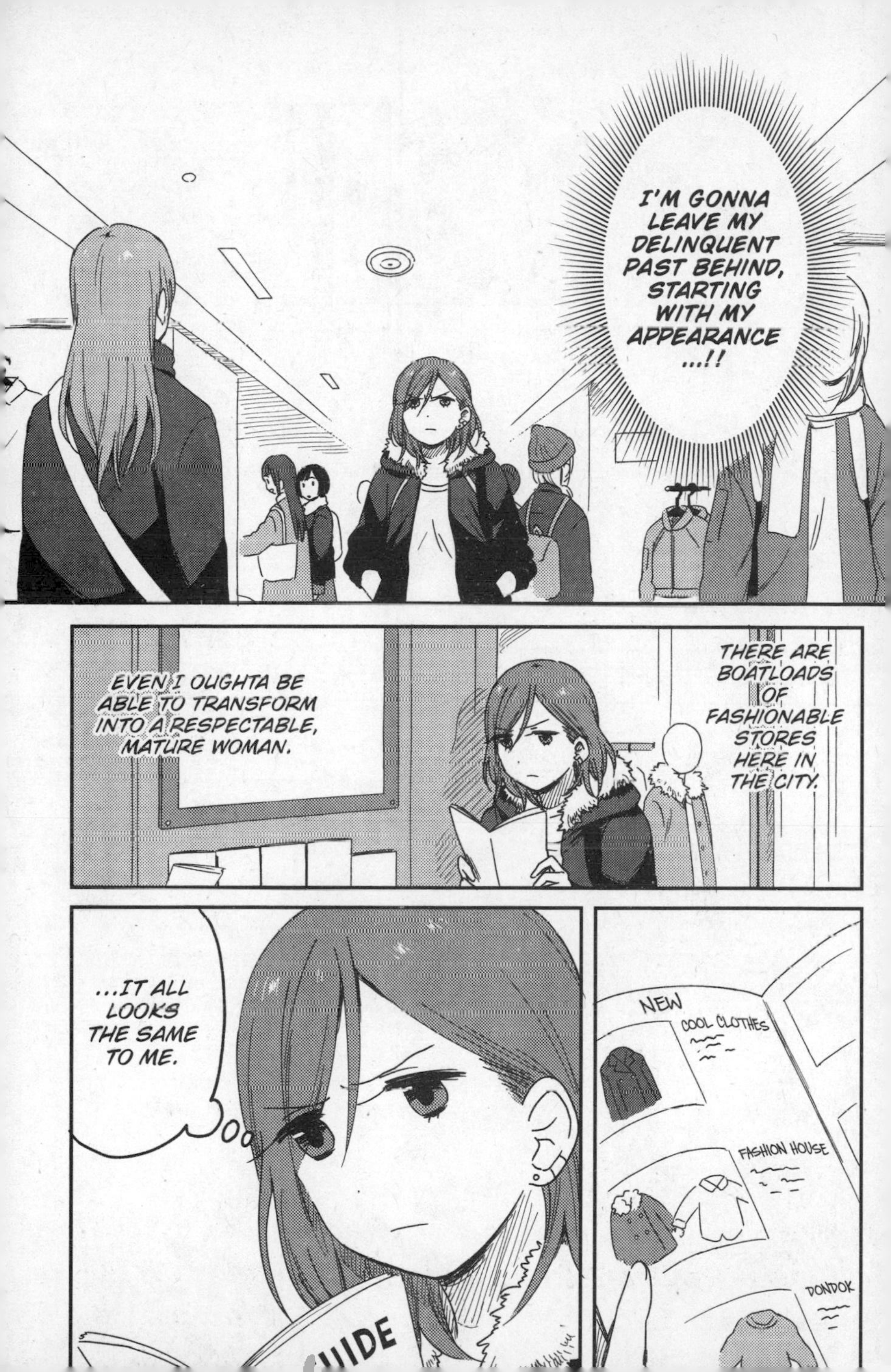
I'M GONNA LEAVE MY DELINQUENT PAST BEHIND, STARTING WITH MY APPEARANCE ...!!
THERE ARE BOATLOADS OF FASHIONABLE STORES HERE IN THE CITY.
EVEN I OUGHTA BE ABLE TO TRANSFORM INTO A RESPECTABLE, MATURE WOMAN.
NEW
COOL CLOTHES
FASHION HOUSE
DONDOK
...IT ALL LOOKS THE SAME TO ME.

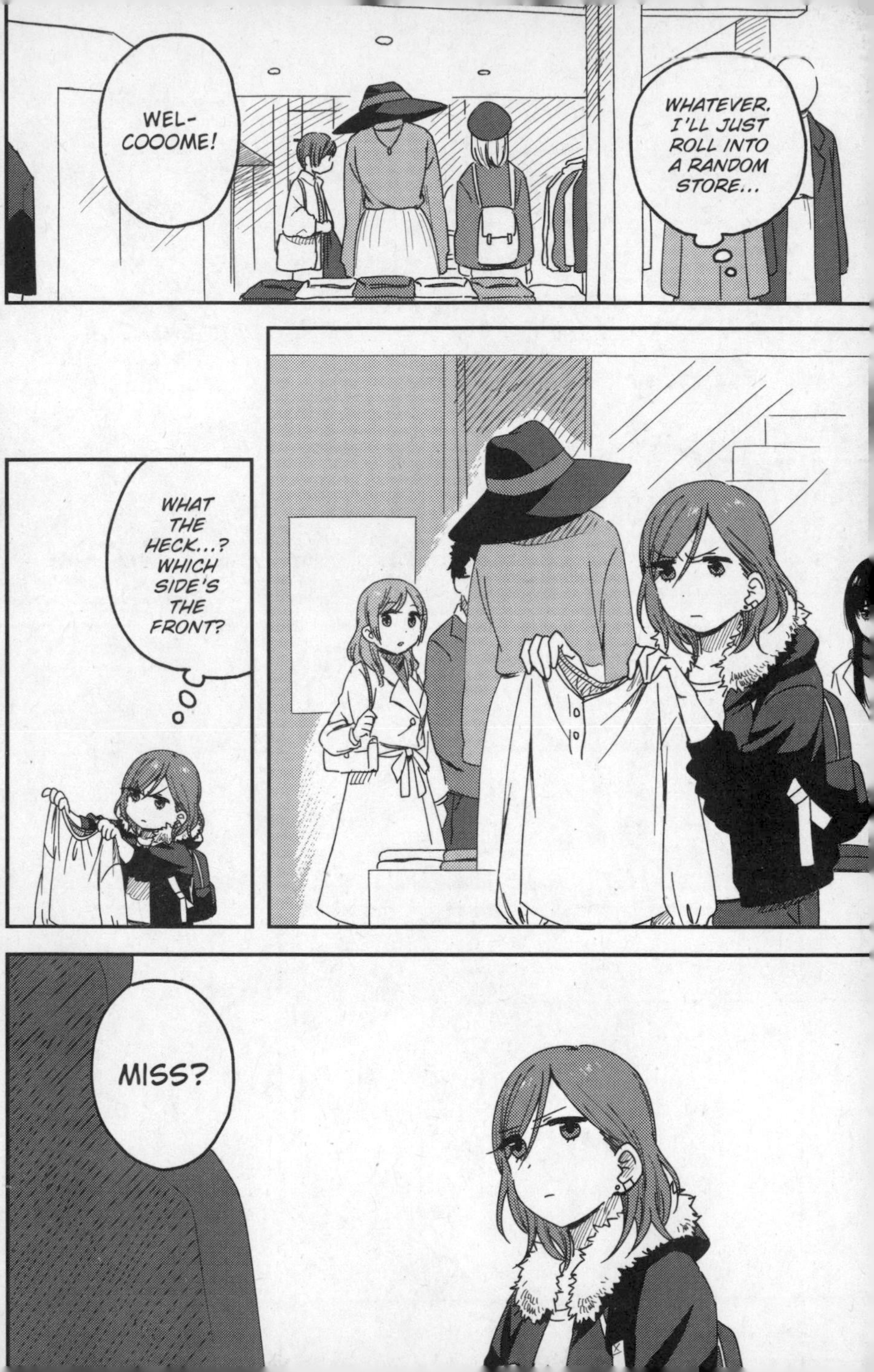
WHATEVER. I'LL JUST ROLL INTO A RANDOM STORE...
WEL-COOOME!
WHAT THE HECK...? WHICH SIDE'S THE FRONT?
MISS?

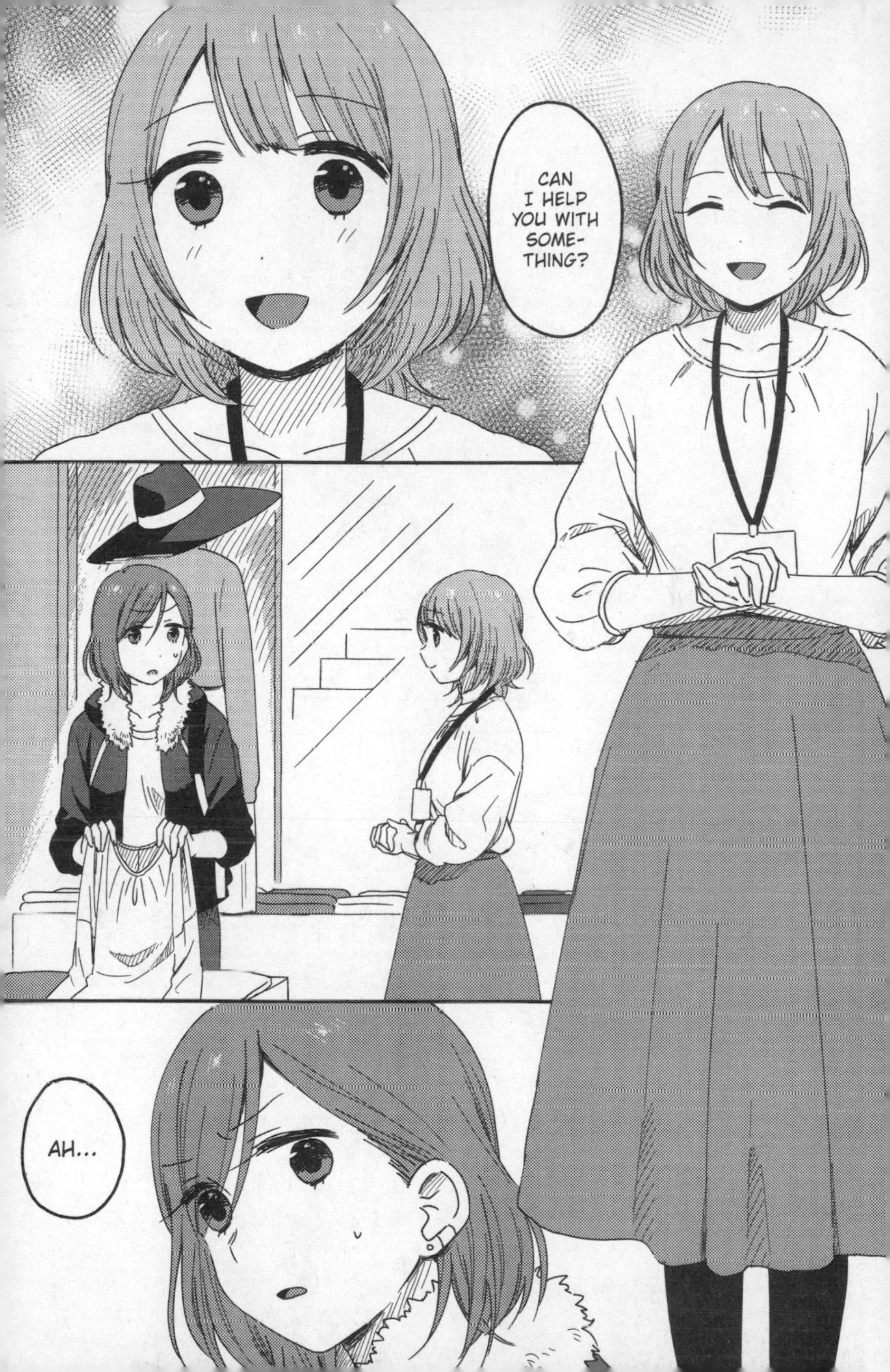
CAN I HELP YOU WITH SOME-THING?
AH...

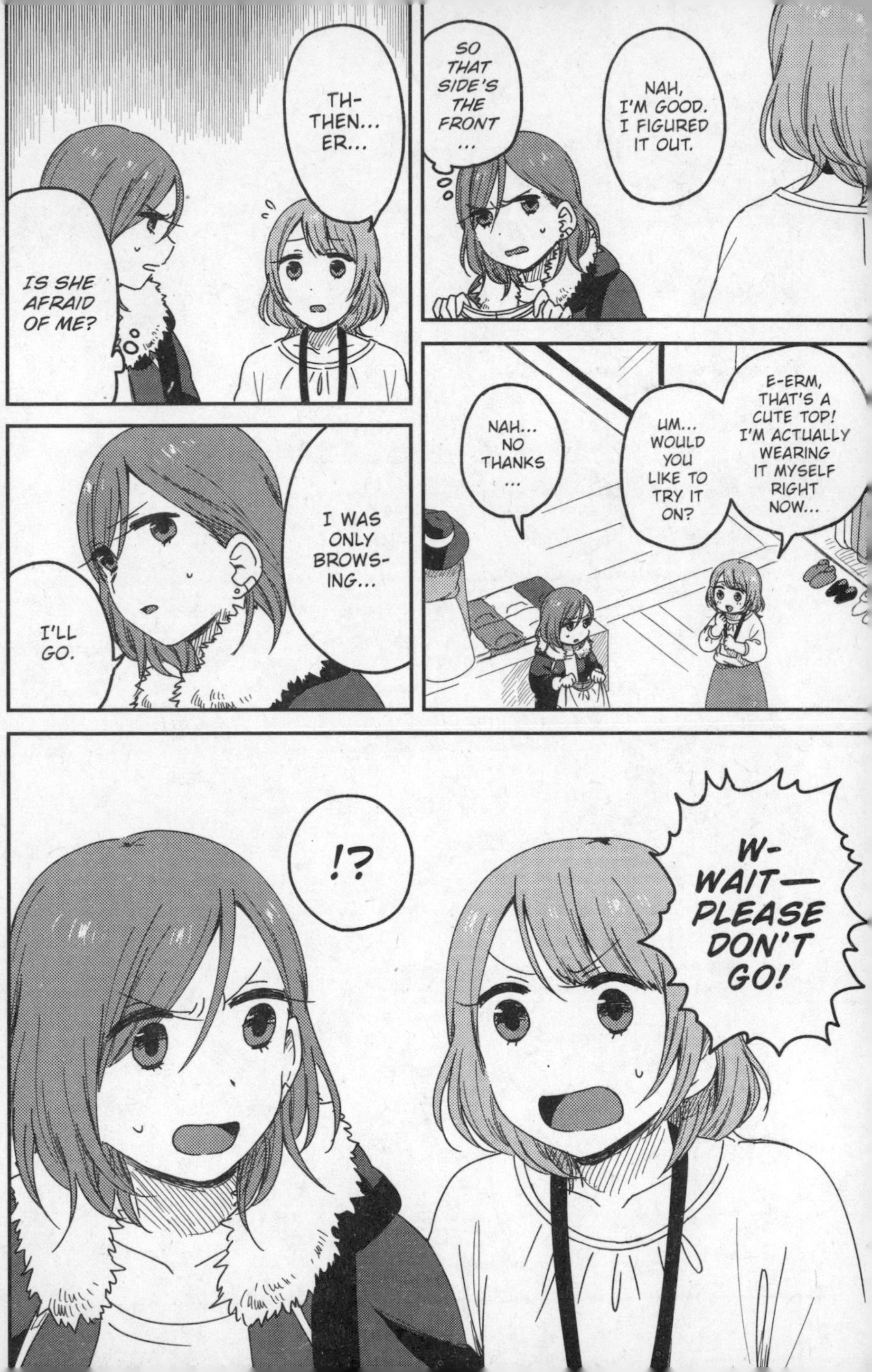
NAH, I'M GOOD. I FIGURED IT OUT.
SO THAT SIDE'S THE FRONT ...
TH-THEN... ER...
IS SHE AFRAID OF ME?
E-ERM, THAT'S A CUTE TOP! I'M ACTUALLY WEARING IT MYSELF RIGHT NOW...
UM... WOULD YOU LIKE TO TRY IT ON?
NAH... NO THANKS ...
I WAS ONLY BROWSING...
I'LL GO.
W-WAIT—PLEASE DON'T GO!
!?

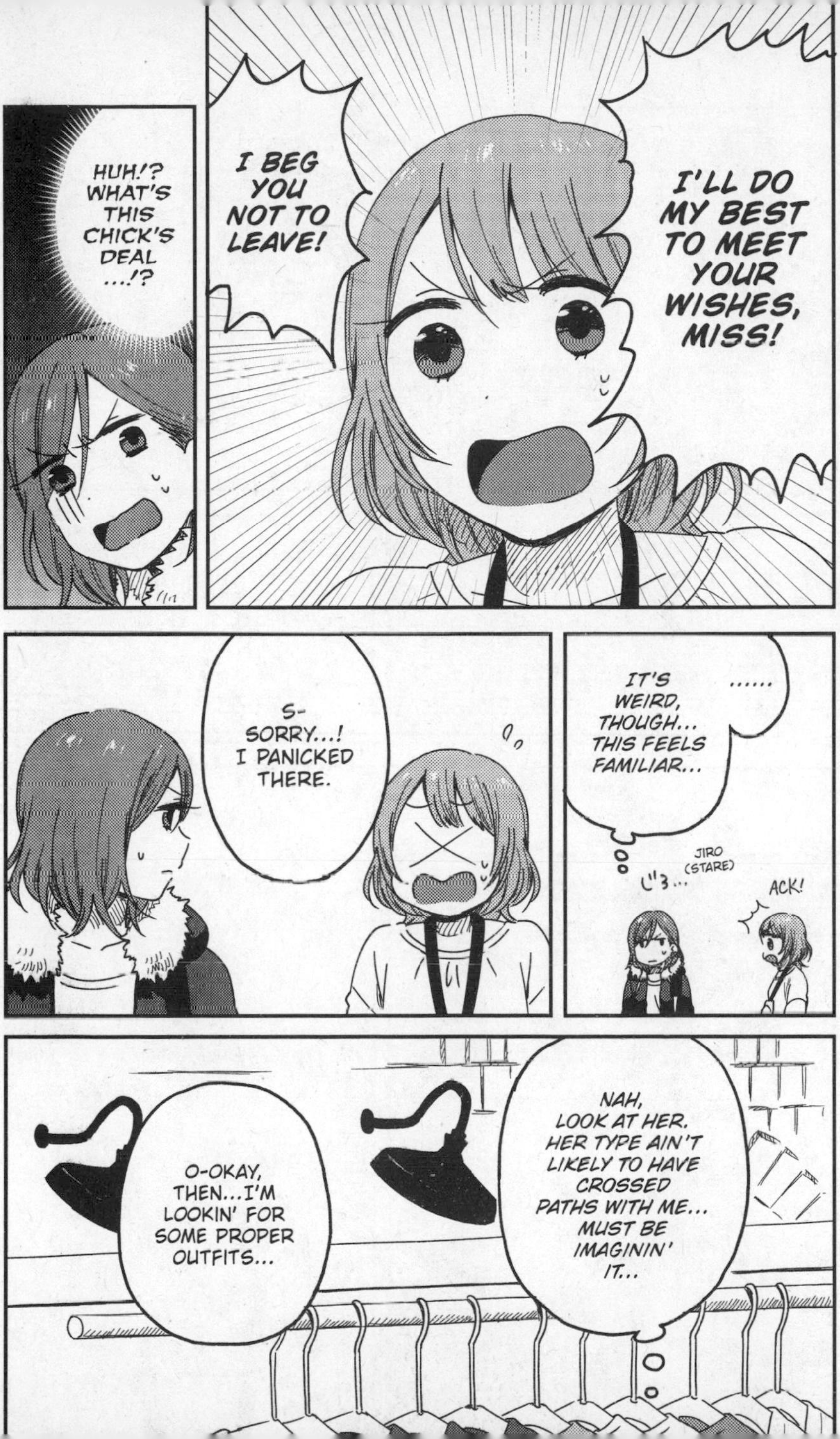
I'LL DO MY BEST TO MEET YOUR WISHES, MISS!
I BEG YOU NOT TO LEAVE!
HUH!? WHAT'S THIS CHICK'S DEAL ...!?
......
IT'S WEIRD, THOUGH... THIS FEELS FAMILIAR...
じー...
JIRO (STARE)
ACK!
S-SORRY...! I PANICKED THERE.
NAH, LOOK AT HER. HER TYPE AIN'T LIKELY TO HAVE CROSSED PATHS WITH ME... MUST BE IMAGININ' IT...
O-OKAY, THEN...I'M LOOKIN' FOR SOME PROPER OUTFITS...

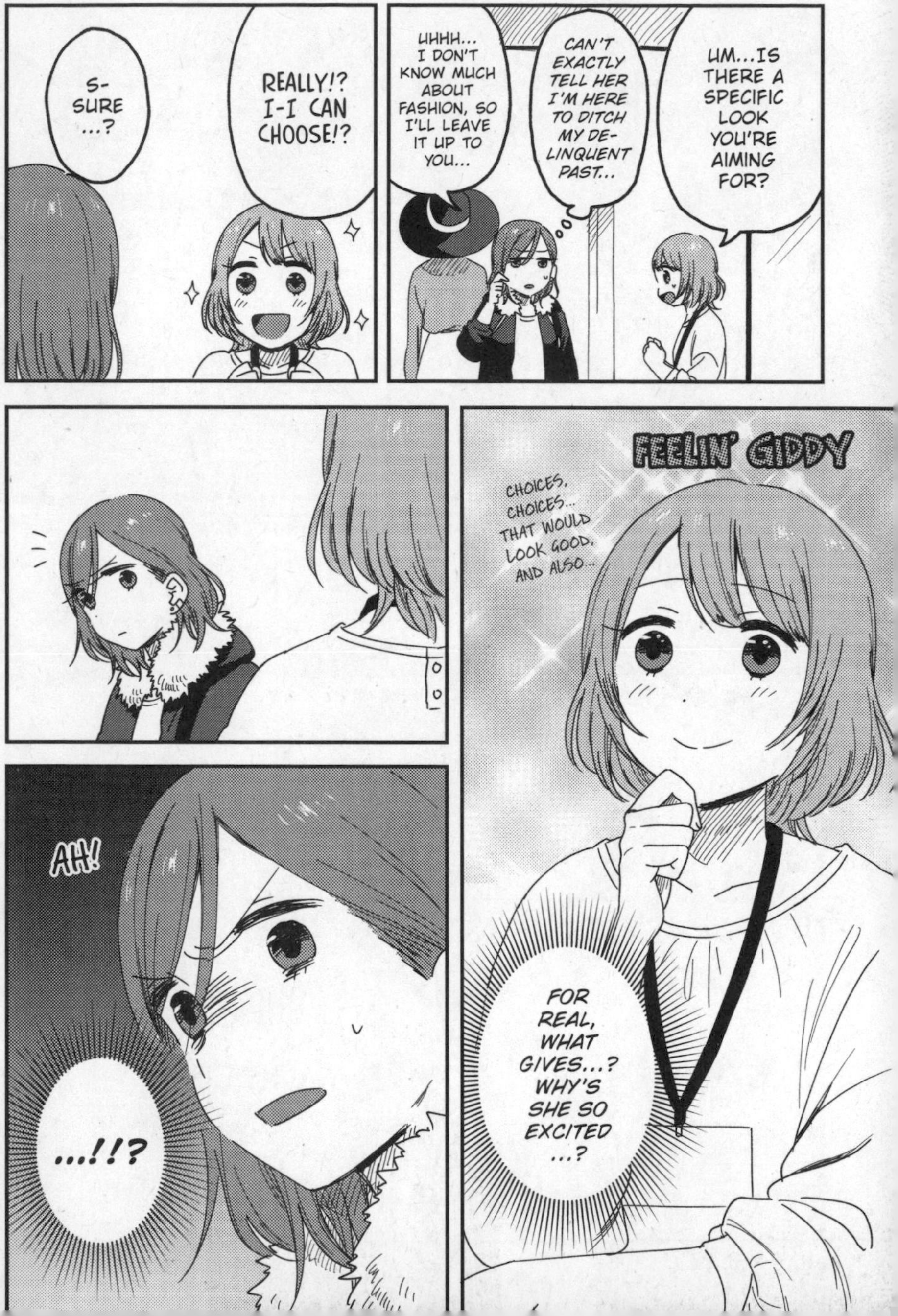
UM...IS THERE A SPECIFIC LOOK YOU'RE AIMING FOR?
CAN'T EXACTLY TELL HER I'M HERE TO DITCH MY DE-LINQUENT PAST...
UHHH... I DON'T KNOW MUCH ABOUT FASHION, SO I'LL LEAVE IT UP TO YOU...
REALLY!? I-I CAN CHOOSE!?
S-SURE ...?
FEELIN' GIDDY
CHOICES, CHOICES... THAT WOULD LOOK GOOD, AND ALSO...
FOR REAL, WHAT GIVES...? WHY'S SHE SO EXCITED ...?
AH!
...!!?

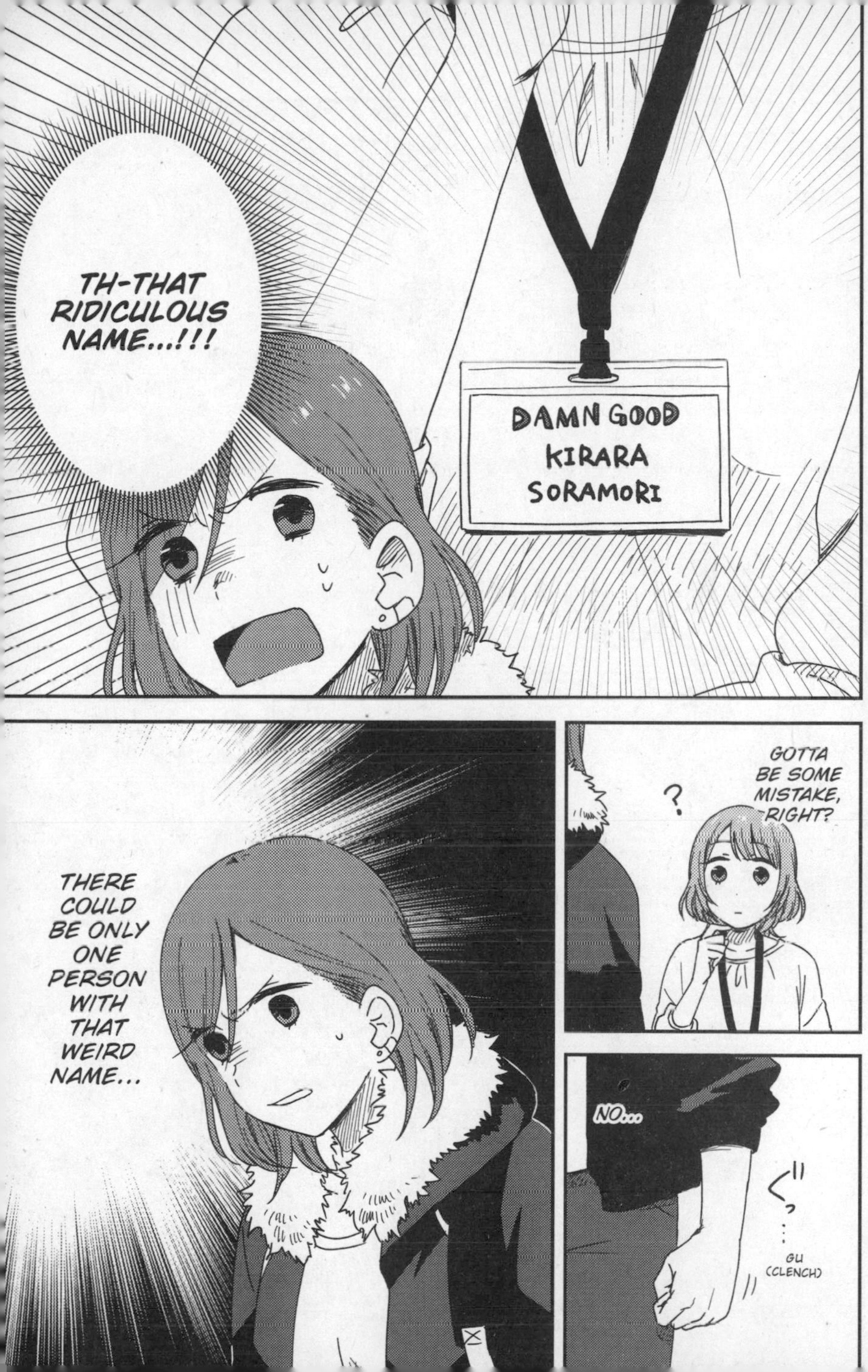
DAMN GOOD
KIRARA
SORAMORI
TH-THAT RIDICULOUS NAME...!!!
?
GOTTA BE SOME MISTAKE, RIGHT?
NO...
GU (CLENCH)
THERE COULD BE ONLY ONE PERSON WITH THAT WEIRD NAME...

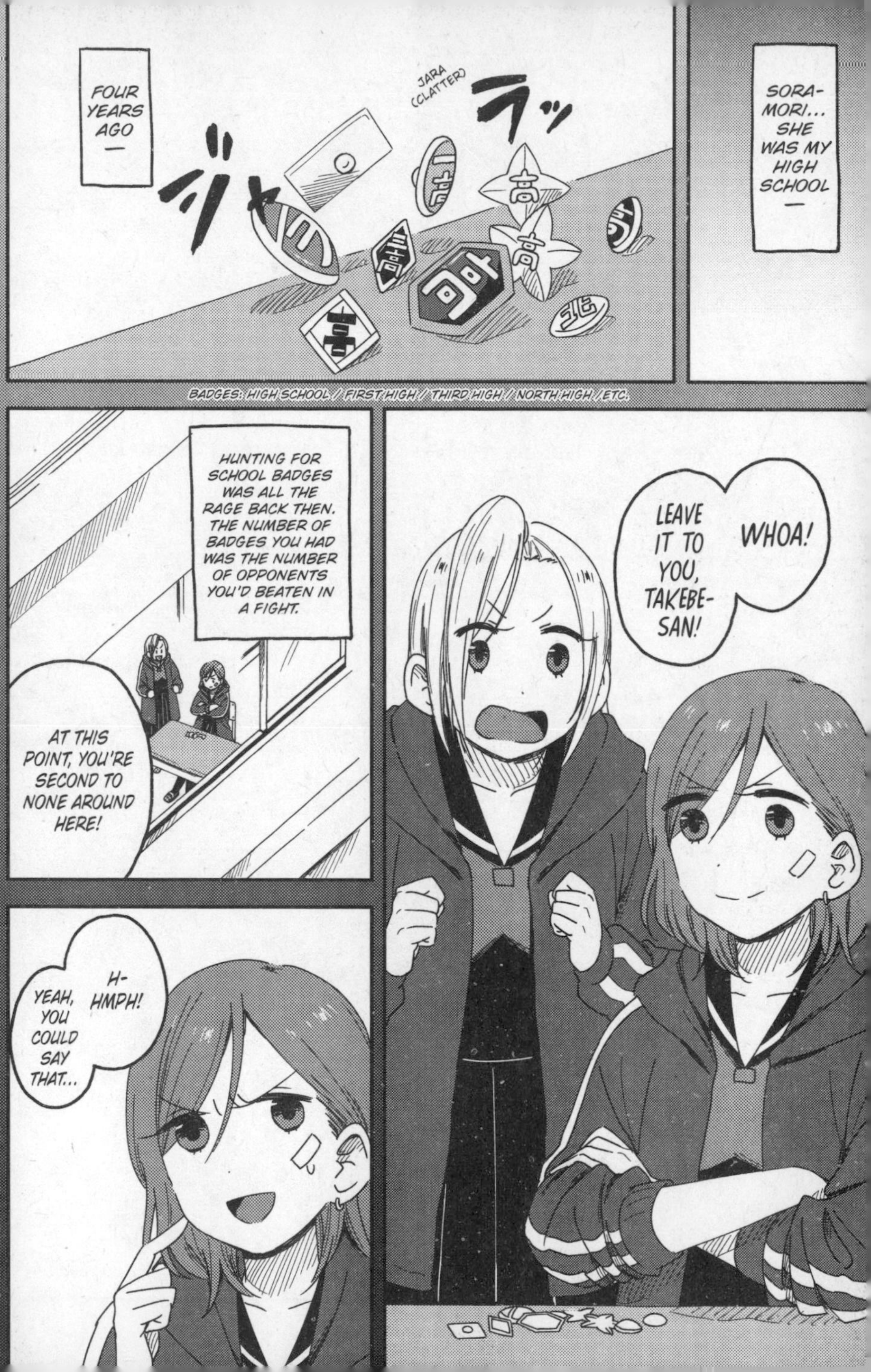
SORA-MORI... SHE WAS MY HIGH SCHOOL —
FOUR YEARS AGO —
JARA (CLATTER)
ジャラッ
BADGES: HIGH SCHOOL / FIRST HIGH / THIRD HIGH / NORTH HIGH / ETC.
WHOA!
LEAVE IT TO YOU, TAKEBE-SAN!
HUNTING FOR SCHOOL BADGES WAS ALL THE RAGE BACK THEN. THE NUMBER OF BADGES YOU HAD WAS THE NUMBER OF OPPONENTS YOU'D BEATEN IN A FIGHT.
AT THIS POINT, YOU'RE SECOND TO NONE AROUND HERE!
H-HMPH!
YEAH, YOU COULD SAY THAT...

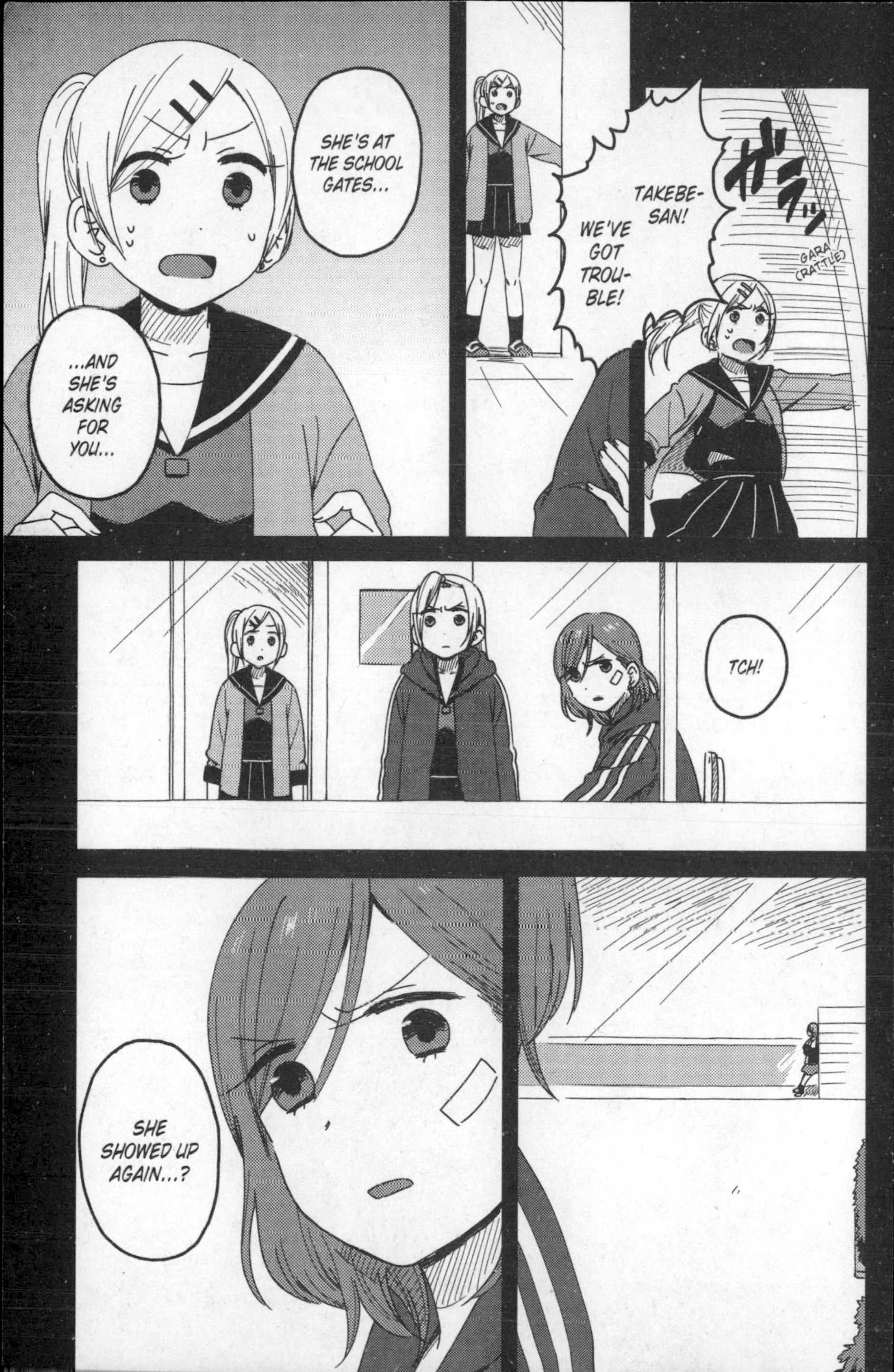
ガラッ
GARA (RATTLE)
TAKEBE-SAN!
WE'VE GOT TROUBLE!
SHE'S AT THE SCHOOL GATES...
...AND SHE'S ASKING FOR YOU...
TCH!
SHE SHOWED UP AGAIN...?

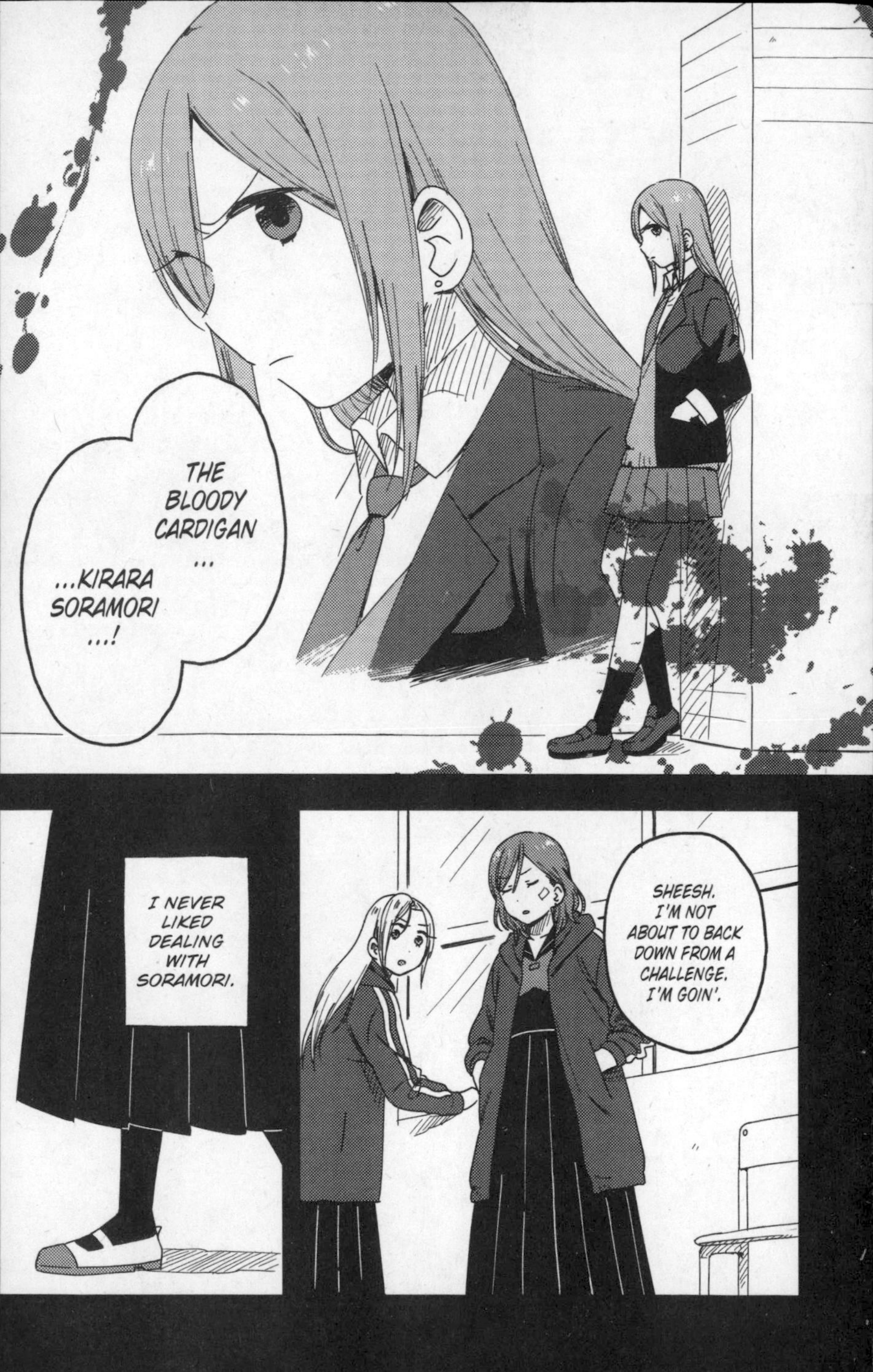
THE BLOODY CARDIGAN ...
...KIRARA SORAMORI ...!
SHEESH. I'M NOT ABOUT TO BACK DOWN FROM A CHALLENGE. I'M GOIN'.
I NEVER LIKED DEALING WITH SORAMORI.

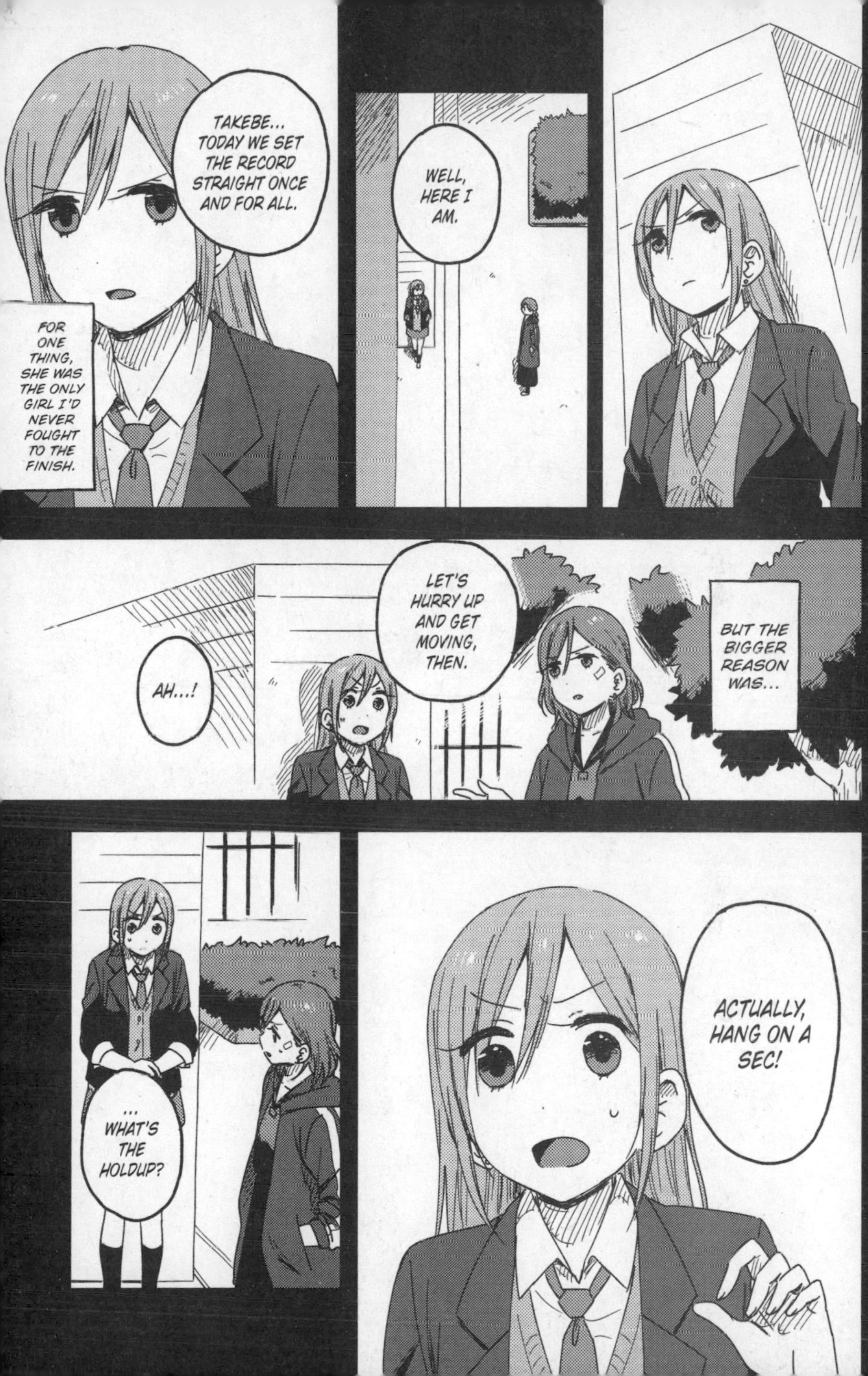
WELL, HERE I AM.
TAKEBE... TODAY WE SET THE RECORD STRAIGHT ONCE AND FOR ALL.
FOR ONE THING, SHE WAS THE ONLY GIRL I'D NEVER FOUGHT TO THE FINISH.
BUT THE BIGGER REASON WAS...
LET'S HURRY UP AND GET MOVING, THEN.
AH...!
ACTUALLY, HANG ON A SEC!
... WHAT'S THE HOLDUP?

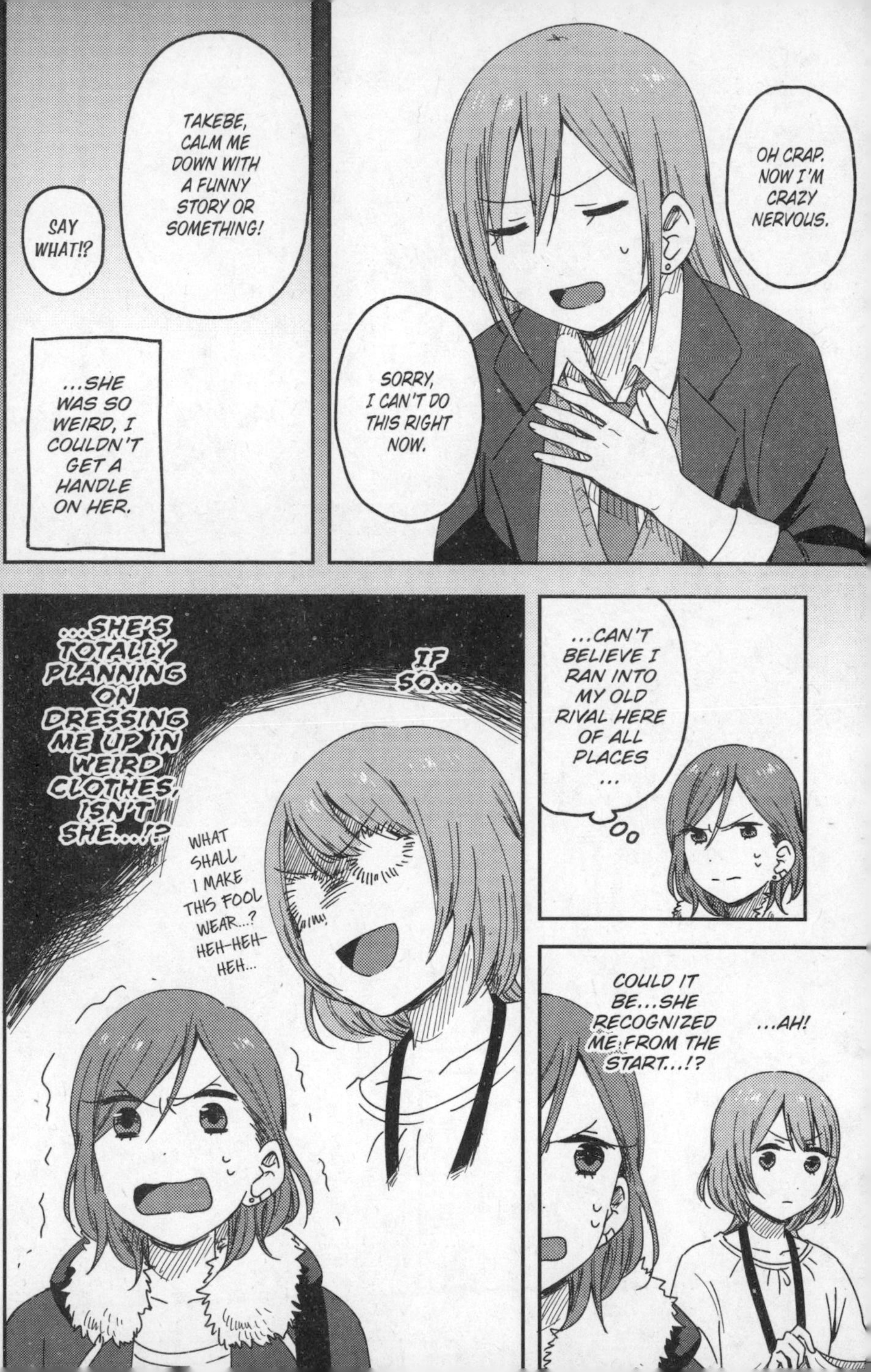
OH CRAP. NOW I'M CRAZY NERVOUS.
SORRY, I CAN'T DO THIS RIGHT NOW.
TAKEBE, CALM ME DOWN WITH A FUNNY STORY OR SOMETHING!
SAY WHAT!?
...SHE WAS SO WEIRD, I COULDN'T GET A HANDLE ON HER.
...CAN'T BELIEVE I RAN INTO MY OLD RIVAL HERE OF ALL PLACES...
...AH!
COULD IT BE...SHE RECOGNIZED ME FROM THE START...!?
IF SO...
...SHE'S TOTALLY PLANNING ON DRESSING ME UP IN WEIRD CLOTHES, ISN'T SHE...!?
WHAT SHALL I MAKE THIS FOOL WEAR...? HEH-HEH-HEH...

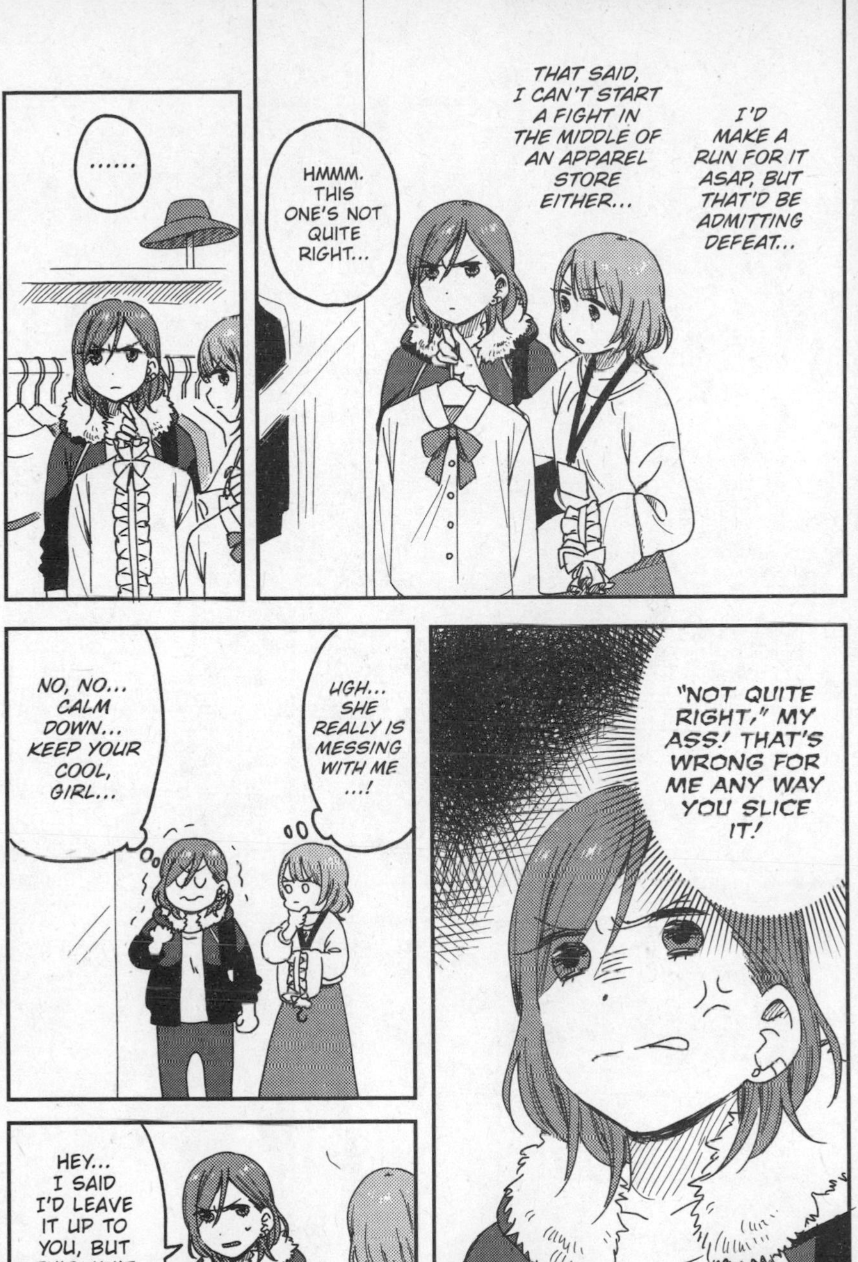
I'D MAKE A RUN FOR IT ASAP, BUT THAT'D BE ADMITTING DEFEAT...
THAT SAID, I CAN'T START A FIGHT IN THE MIDDLE OF AN APPAREL STORE EITHER...
HMMM. THIS ONE'S NOT QUITE RIGHT...
......
"NOT QUITE RIGHT," MY ASS! THAT'S WRONG FOR ME ANY WAY YOU SLICE IT!
UGH... SHE REALLY IS MESSING WITH ME ...!
NO, NO... CALM DOWN... KEEP YOUR COOL, GIRL...
HEY... I SAID I'D LEAVE IT UP TO YOU, BUT THIS AIN'T GONNA FLY...

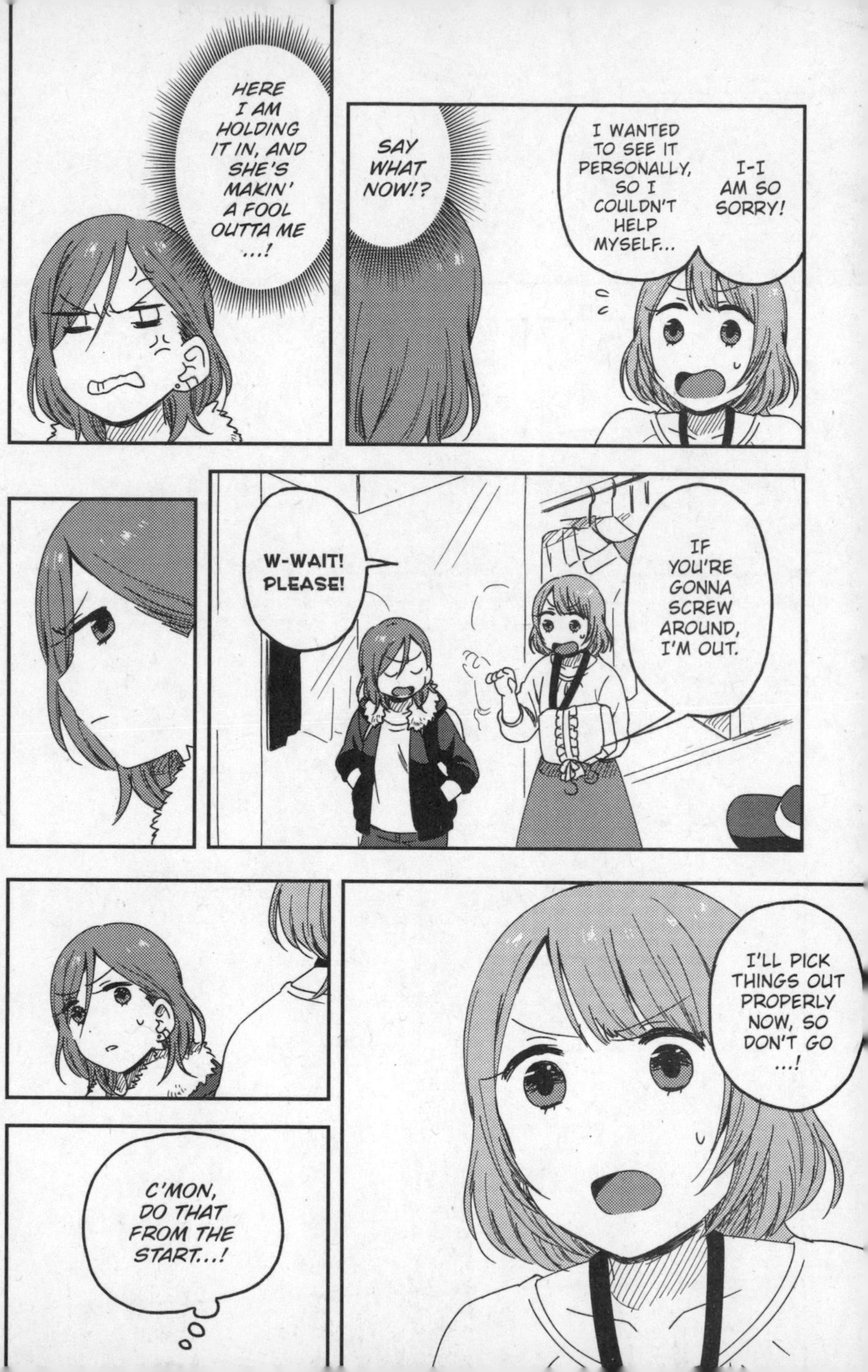
I-I AM SO SORRY!
I WANTED TO SEE IT PERSONALLY, SO I COULDN'T HELP MYSELF...
SAY WHAT NOW!?
HERE I AM HOLDING IT IN, AND SHE'S MAKIN' A FOOL OUTTA ME ...!
IF YOU'RE GONNA SCREW AROUND, I'M OUT.
W-WAIT! PLEASE!
I'LL PICK THINGS OUT PROPERLY NOW, SO DON'T GO ...!
C'MON, DO THAT FROM THE START...!

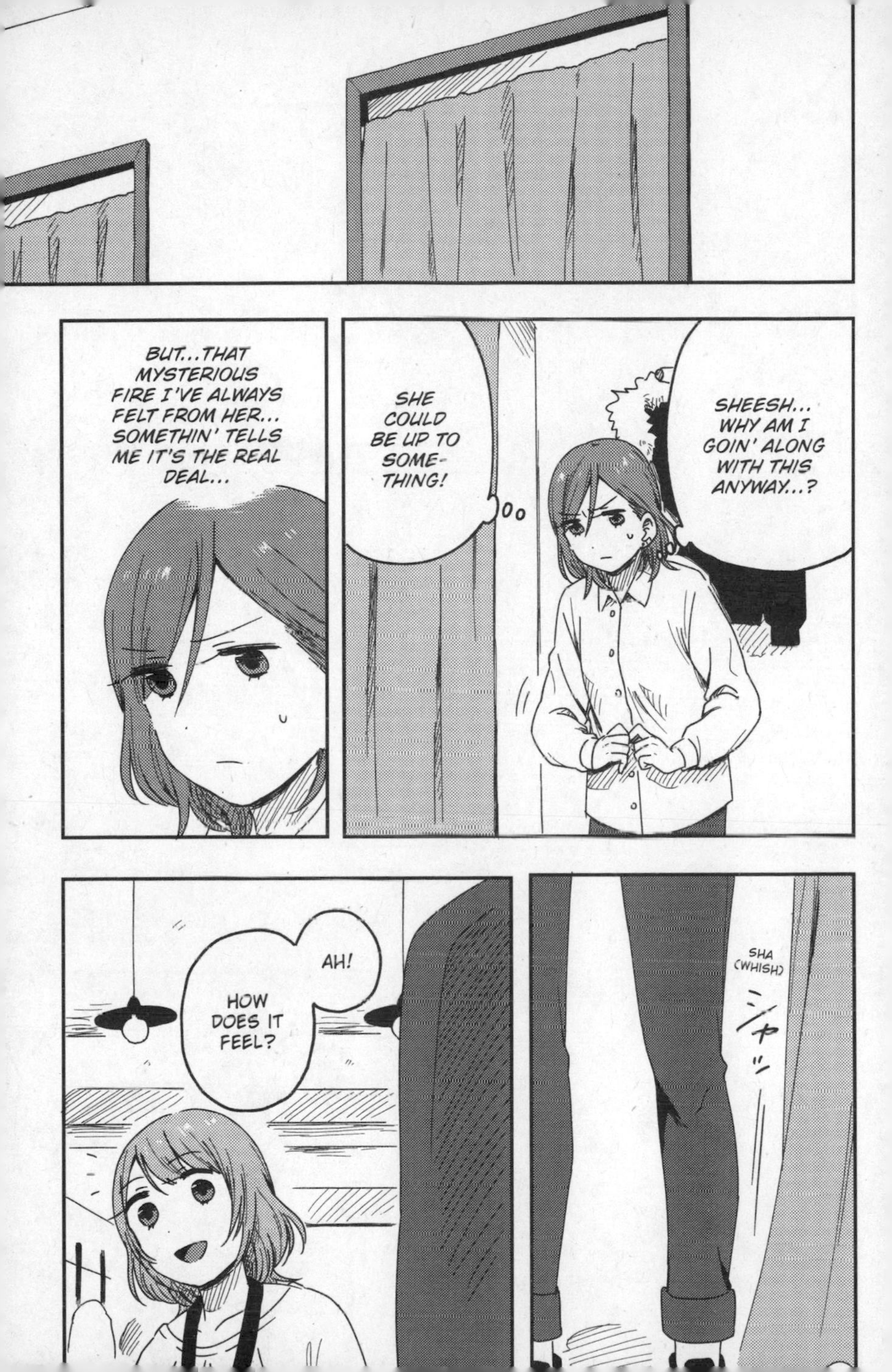
SHEESH... WHY AM I GOIN' ALONG WITH THIS ANYWAY...?
SHE COULD BE UP TO SOME-THING!
BUT...THAT MYSTERIOUS FIRE I'VE ALWAYS FELT FROM HER... SOMETHIN' TELLS ME IT'S THE REAL DEAL...
SHA (WHISH)
シャッ
AH!
HOW DOES IT FEEL?

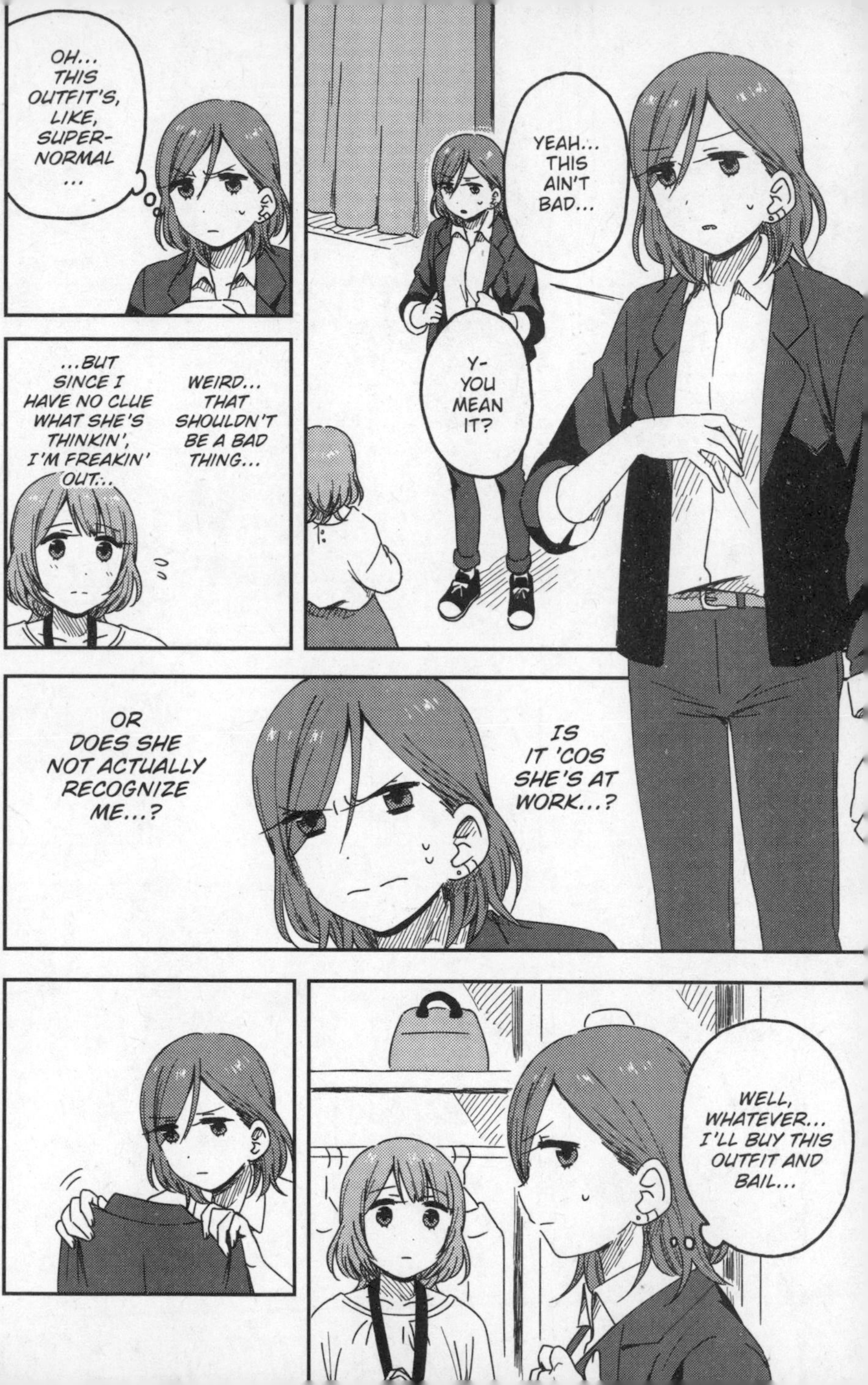
YEAH... THIS AIN'T BAD...
Y-YOU MEAN IT?
OH... THIS OUTFIT'S, LIKE, SUPER-NORMAL...
WEIRD... THAT SHOULDN'T BE A BAD THING...
...BUT SINCE I HAVE NO CLUE WHAT SHE'S THINKIN', I'M FREAKIN' OUT...
IS IT 'COS SHE'S AT WORK...?
OR DOES SHE NOT ACTUALLY RECOGNIZE ME...?
WELL, WHATEVER... I'LL BUY THIS OUTFIT AND BAIL...

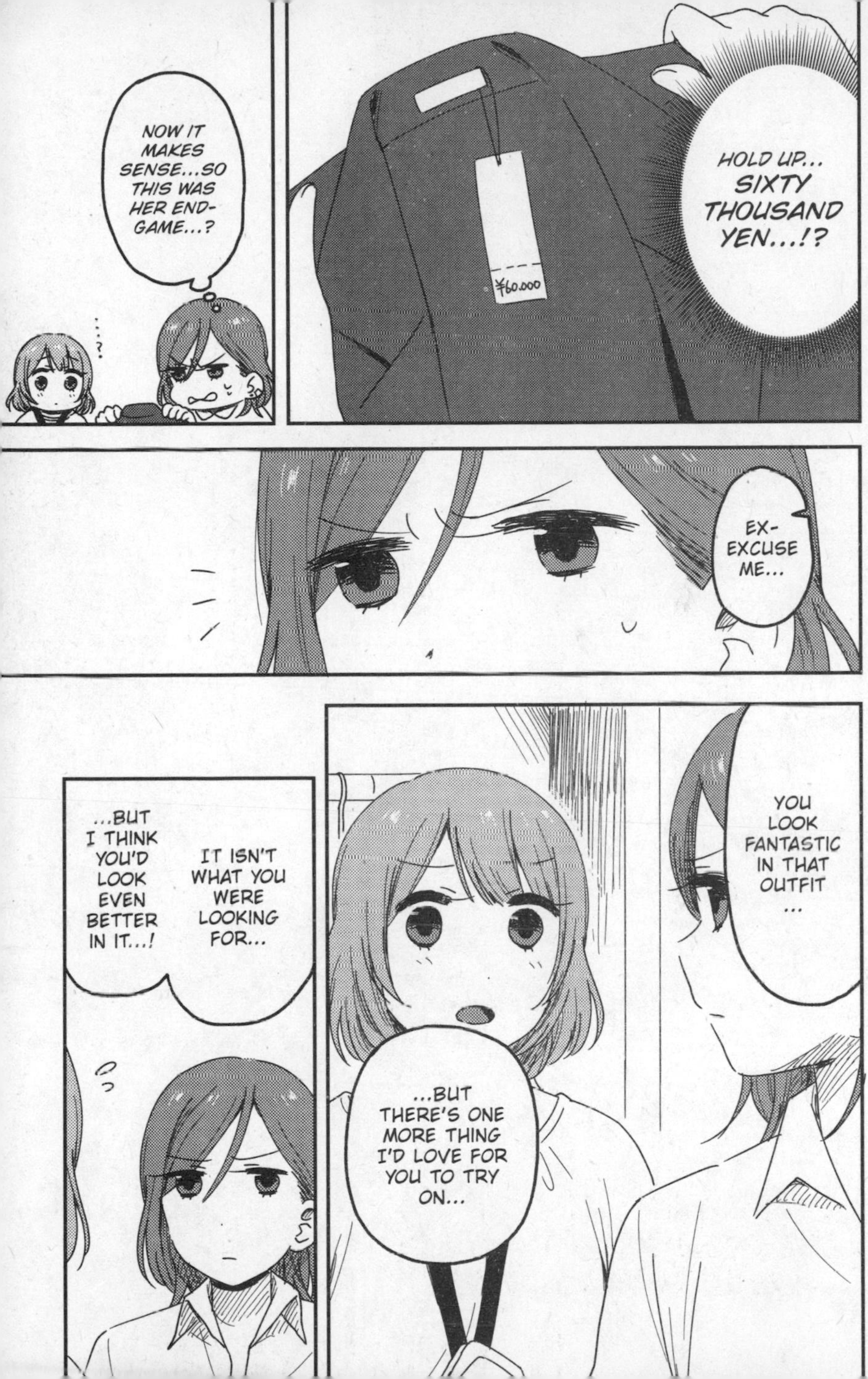
HOLD UP... SIXTY THOUSAND YEN...!?
¥60.000
NOW IT MAKES SENSE...SO THIS WAS HER END-GAME...?
...?
EX- EXCUSE ME...
YOU LOOK FANTASTIC IN THAT OUTFIT ...
...BUT THERE'S ONE MORE THING I'D LOVE FOR YOU TO TRY ON...
IT ISN'T WHAT YOU WERE LOOKING FOR...
...BUT I THINK YOU'D LOOK EVEN BETTER IN IT...!

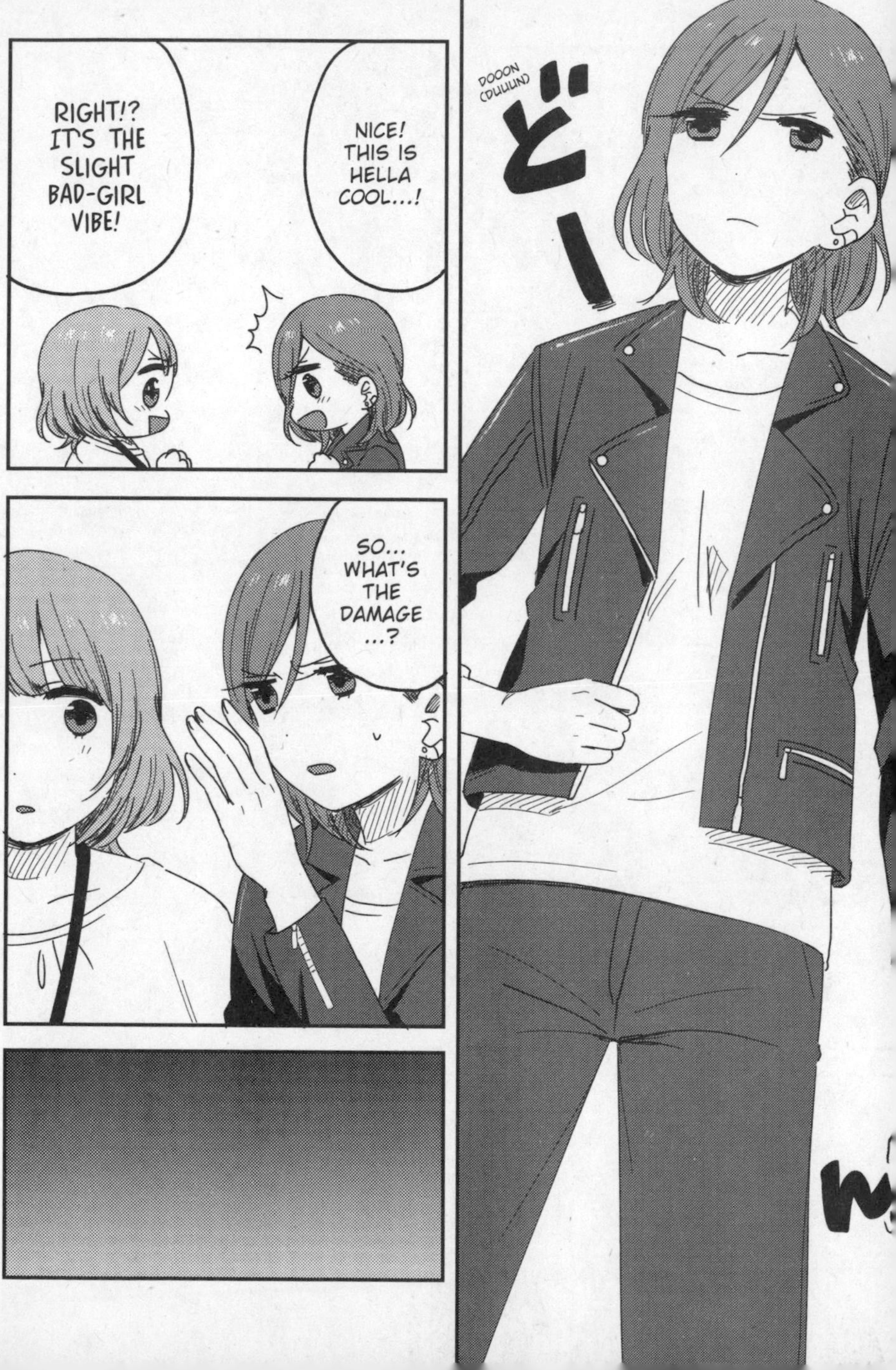
DOOON (DUUUN)
NICE! THIS IS HELLA COOL...!
RIGHT!? IT'S THE SLIGHT BAD-GIRL VIBE!
SO... WHAT'S THE DAMAGE ...?

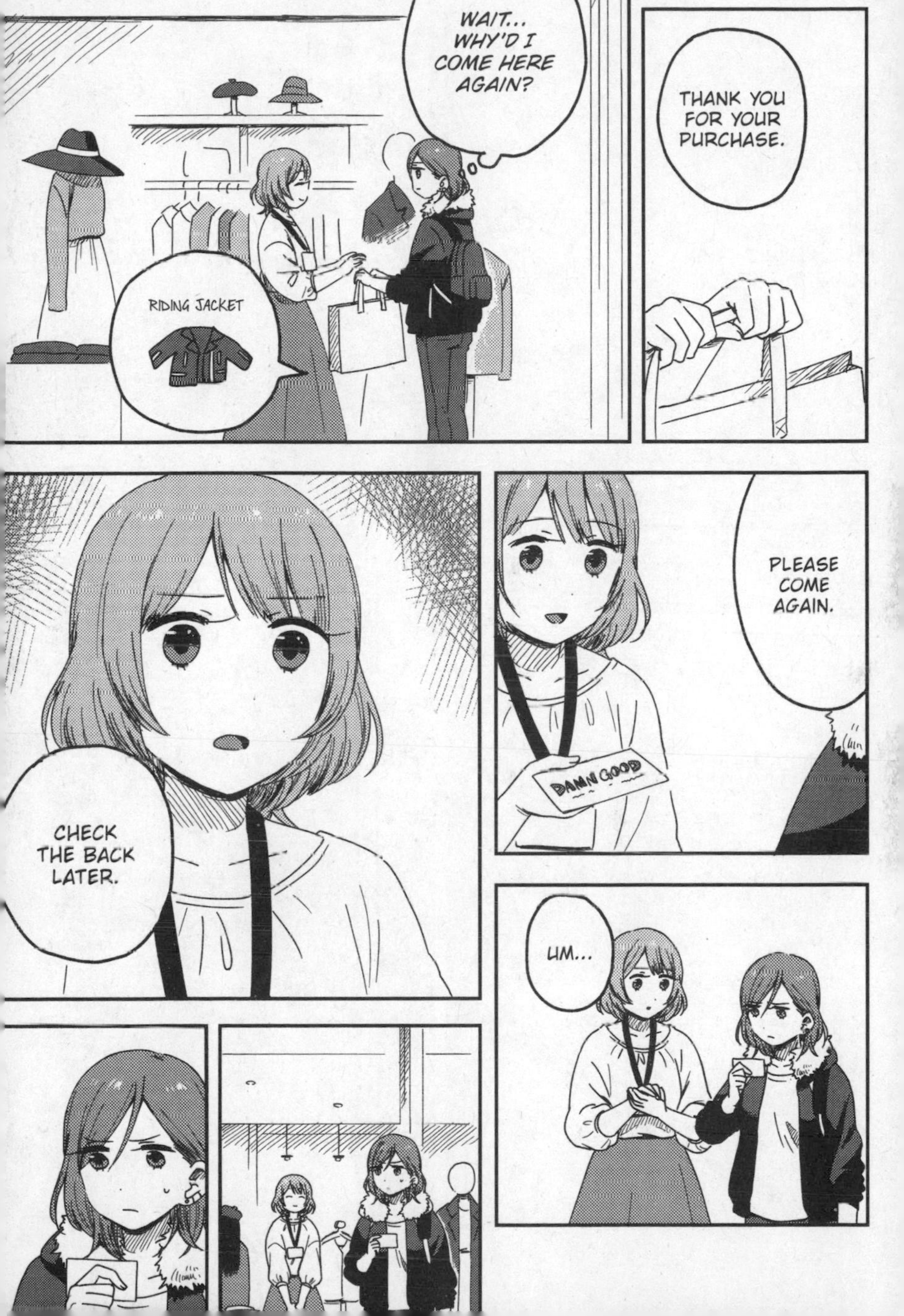
THANK YOU FOR YOUR PURCHASE.
WAIT... WHY'D I COME HERE AGAIN?
RIDING JACKET
PLEASE COME AGAIN.
DAMN GOOD
CHECK THE BACK LATER.
UM...

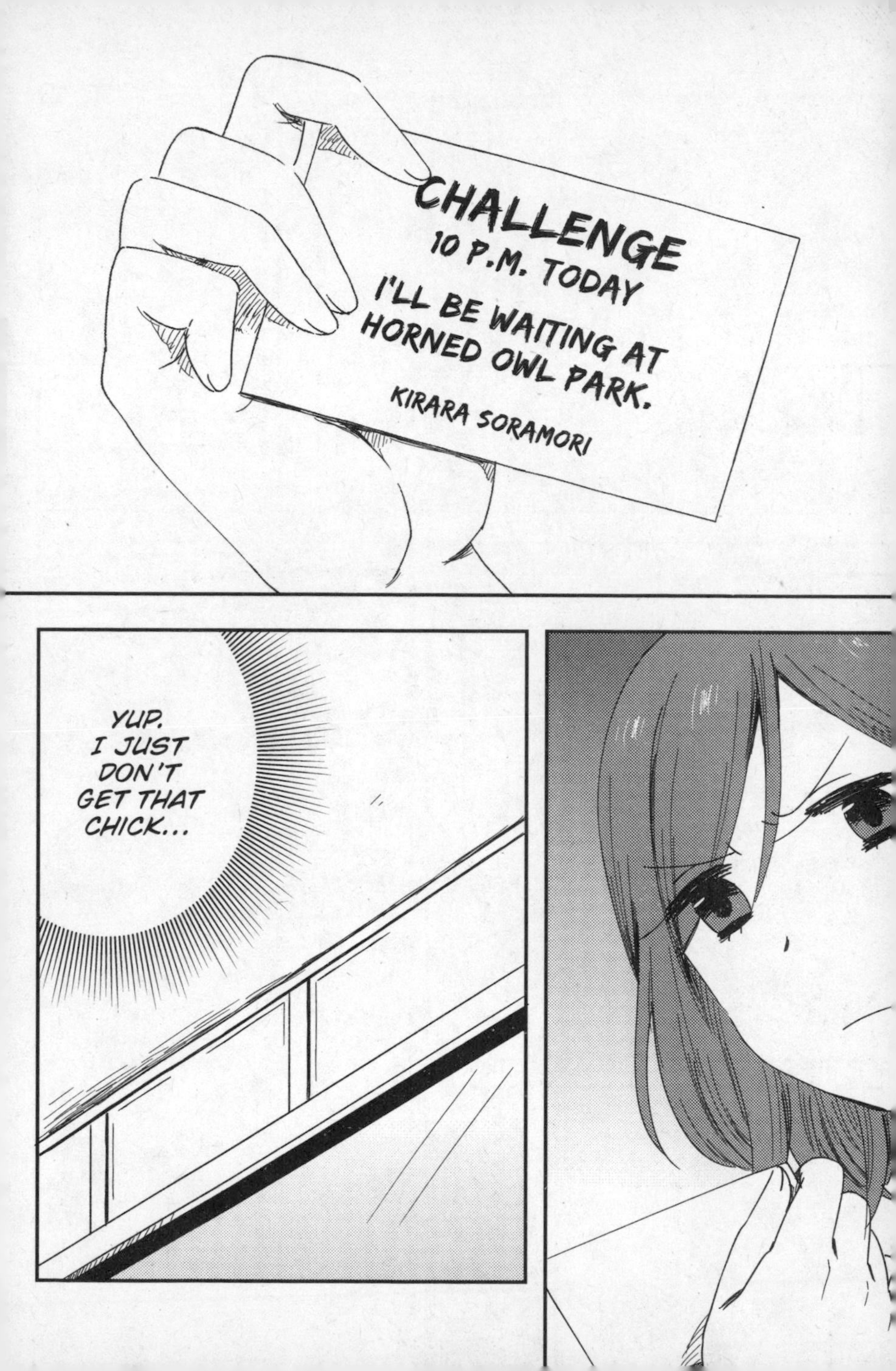
CHALLENGE
10 P.M. TODAY
I'LL BE WAITING AT HORNED OWL PARK.
KIRARA SORAMORI
YUP. I JUST DON'T GET THAT CHICK...

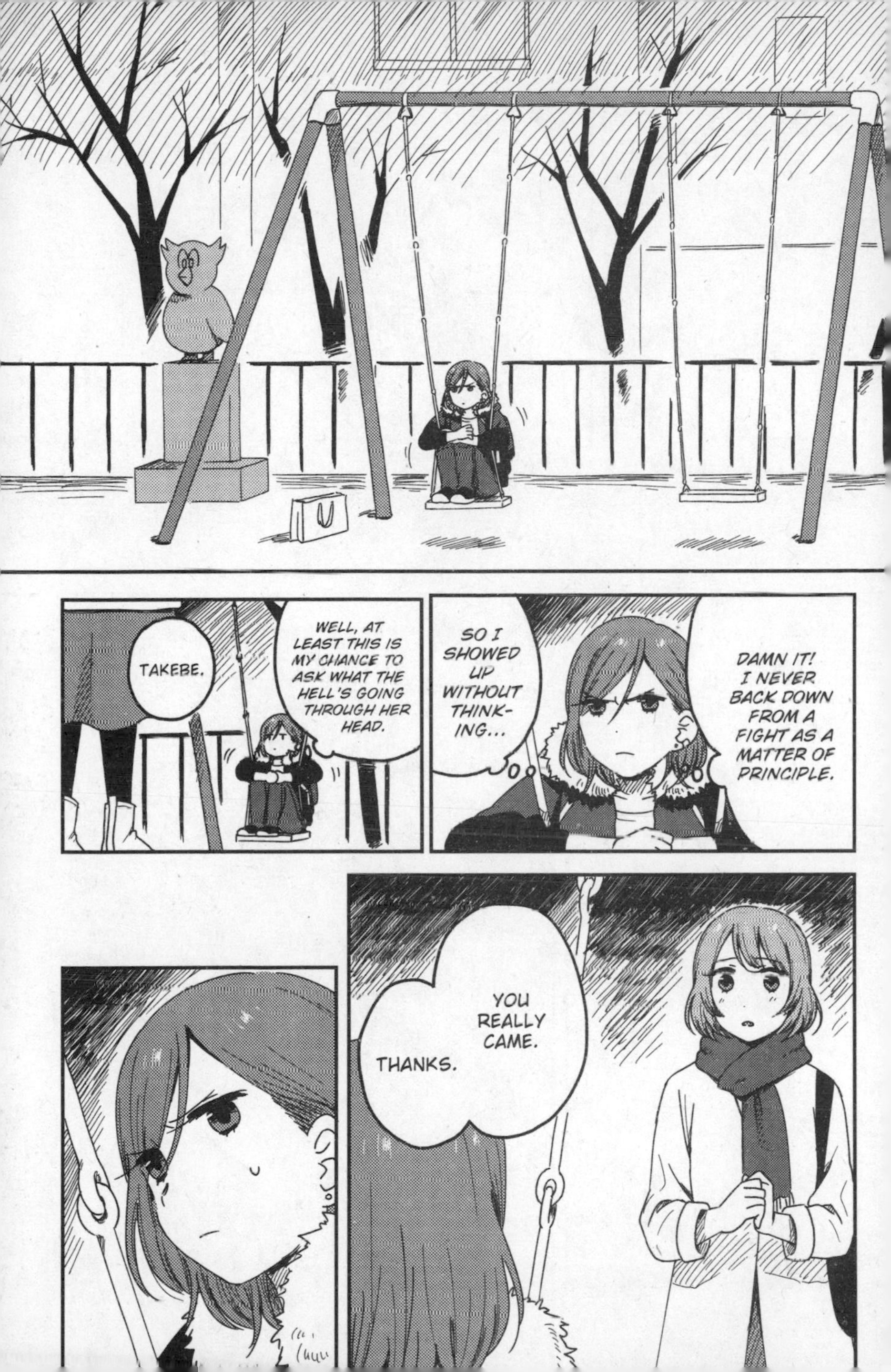
DAMN IT! I NEVER BACK DOWN FROM A FIGHT AS A MATTER OF PRINCIPLE.
SO I SHOWED UP WITHOUT THINK-ING...
WELL, AT LEAST THIS IS MY CHANCE TO ASK WHAT THE HELL'S GOING THROUGH HER HEAD.
TAKEBE.
YOU REALLY CAME.
THANKS.

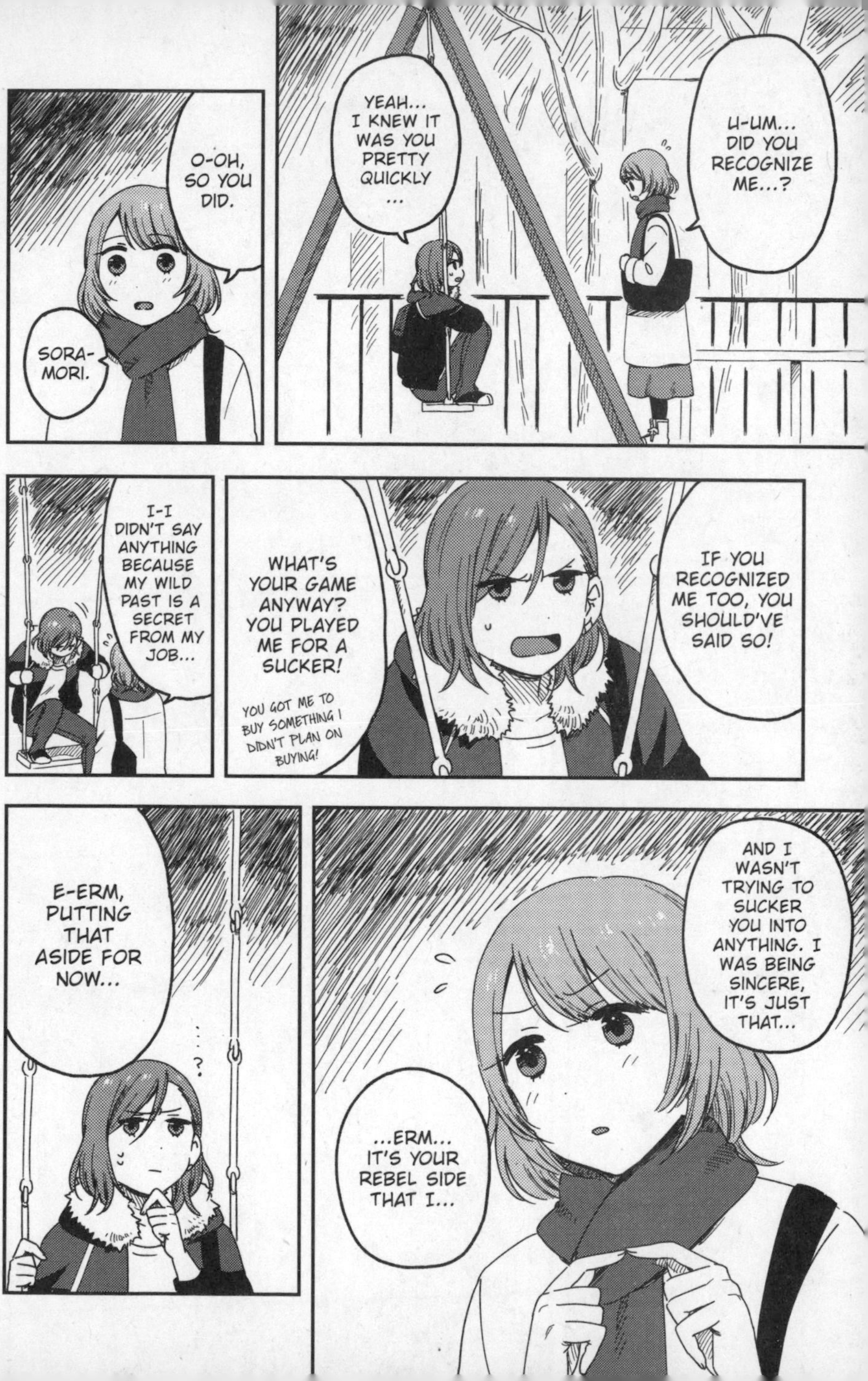
U-UM... DID YOU RECOGNIZE ME...?
YEAH... I KNEW IT WAS YOU PRETTY QUICKLY ...
O-OH, SO YOU DID.
SORA-MORI.
IF YOU RECOGNIZED ME TOO, YOU SHOULD'VE SAID SO!
WHAT'S YOUR GAME ANYWAY? YOU PLAYED ME FOR A SUCKER!
YOU GOT ME TO BUY SOMETHING I DIDN'T PLAN ON BUYING!
I-I DIDN'T SAY ANYTHING BECAUSE MY WILD PAST IS A SECRET FROM MY JOB...
AND I WASN'T TRYING TO SUCKER YOU INTO ANYTHING. I WAS BEING SINCERE, IT'S JUST THAT...
...ERM... IT'S YOUR REBEL SIDE THAT I...
E-ERM, PUTTING THAT ASIDE FOR NOW...
...?

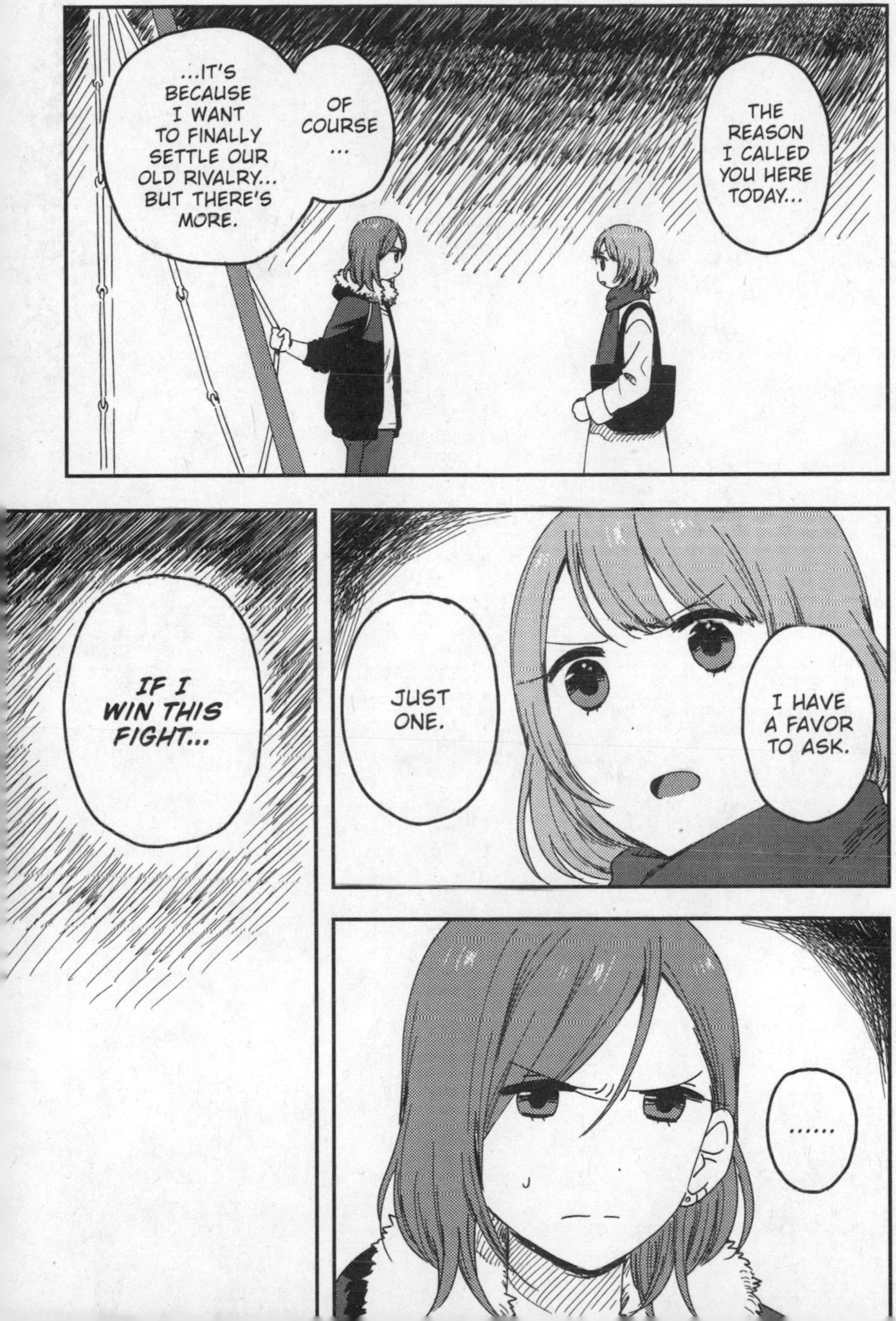
THE REASON I CALLED YOU HERE TODAY...
OF COURSE...
...IT'S BECAUSE I WANT TO FINALLY SETTLE OUR OLD RIVALRY... BUT THERE'S MORE.
I HAVE A FAVOR TO ASK.
JUST ONE.
......
IF I WIN THIS FIGHT...

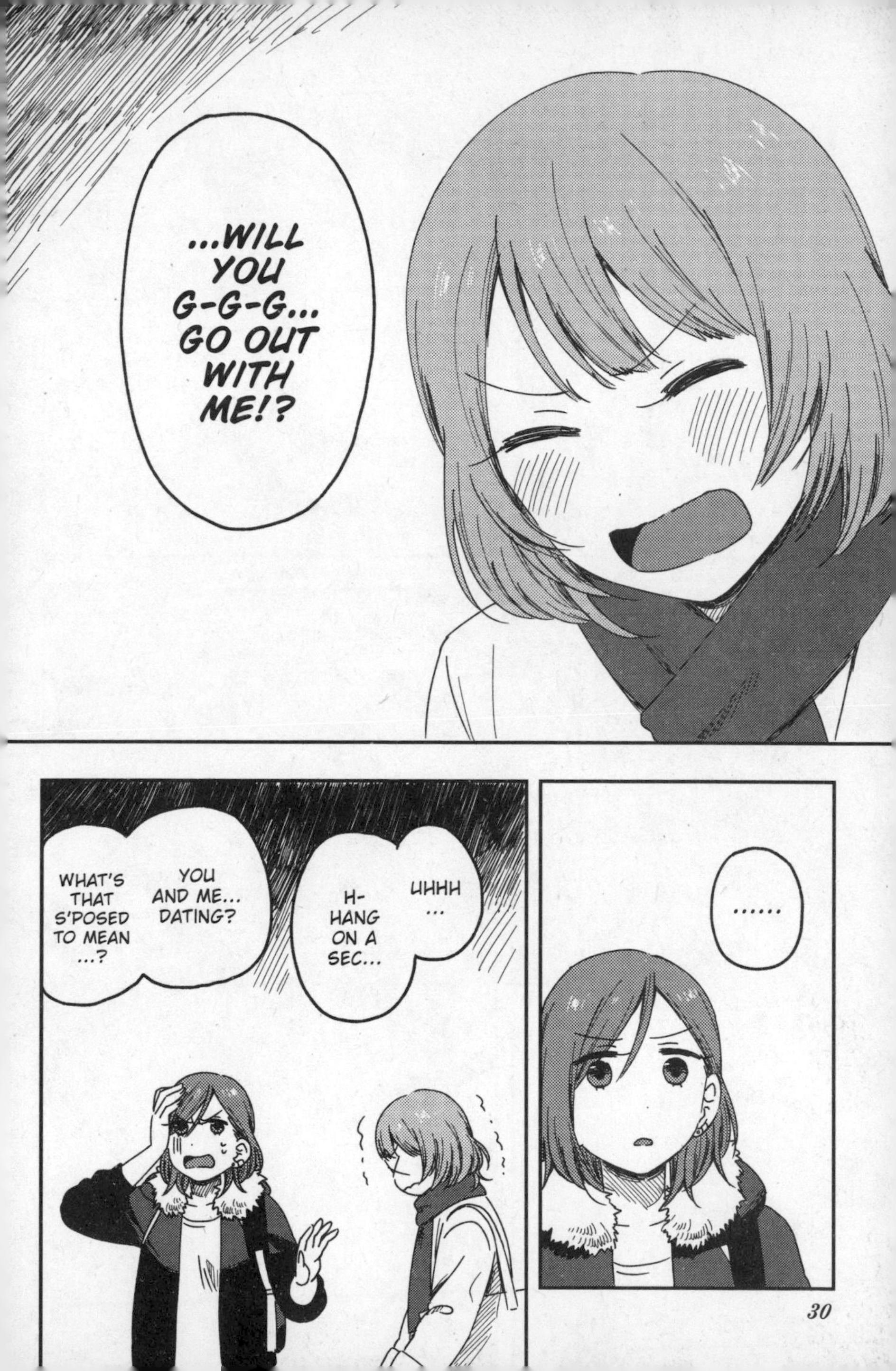
...WILL YOU G-G-G... GO OUT WITH ME!?
......
UHHH...
H-HANG ON A SEC...
YOU AND ME... DATING?
WHAT'S THAT S'POSED TO MEAN...?

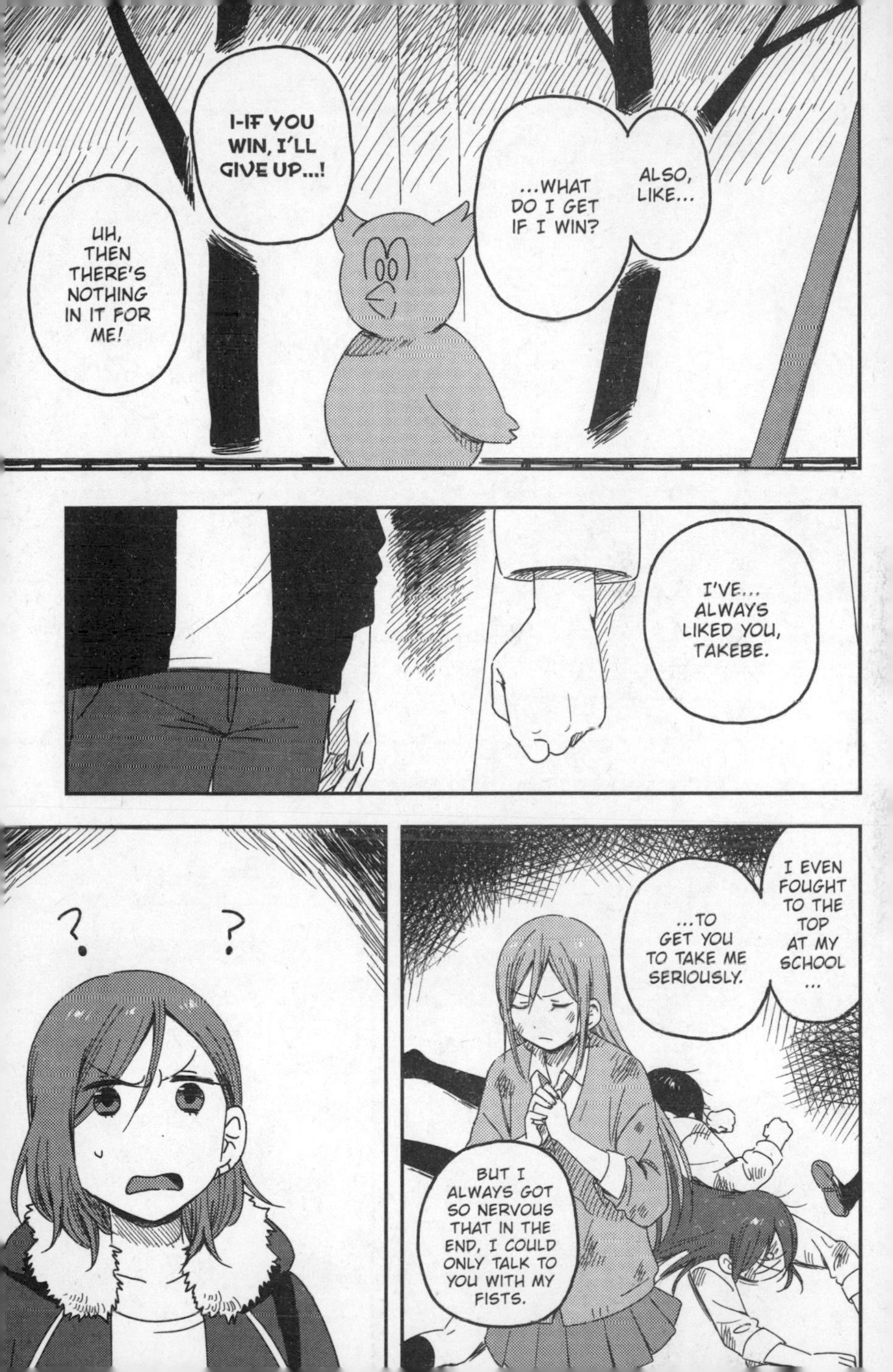
ALSO, LIKE...
...WHAT DO I GET IF I WIN?
I-IF YOU WIN, I'LL GIVE UP...!
UH, THEN THERE'S NOTHING IN IT FOR ME!
I'VE... ALWAYS LIKED YOU, TAKEBE.
I EVEN FOUGHT TO THE TOP AT MY SCHOOL ...
...TO GET YOU TO TAKE ME SERIOUSLY.
BUT I ALWAYS GOT SO NERVOUS THAT IN THE END, I COULD ONLY TALK TO YOU WITH MY FISTS.

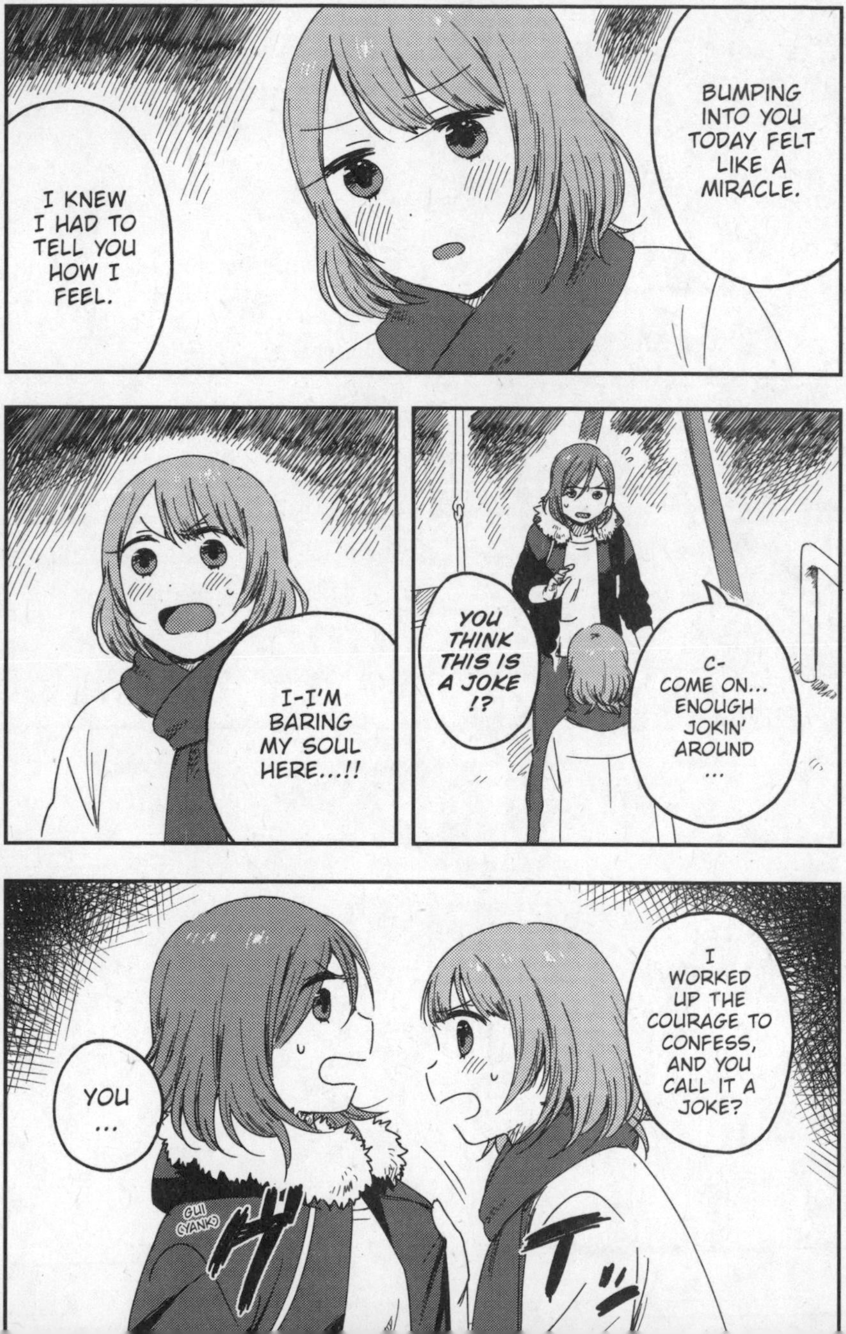
BUMPING INTO YOU TODAY FELT LIKE A MIRACLE.
I KNEW I HAD TO TELL YOU HOW I FEEL.
C- COME ON... ENOUGH JOKIN' AROUND ...
YOU THINK THIS IS A JOKE !?
I-I'M BARING MY SOUL HERE...!!
I WORKED UP THE COURAGE TO CONFESS, AND YOU CALL IT A JOKE?
YOU ...
GUI (YANK)

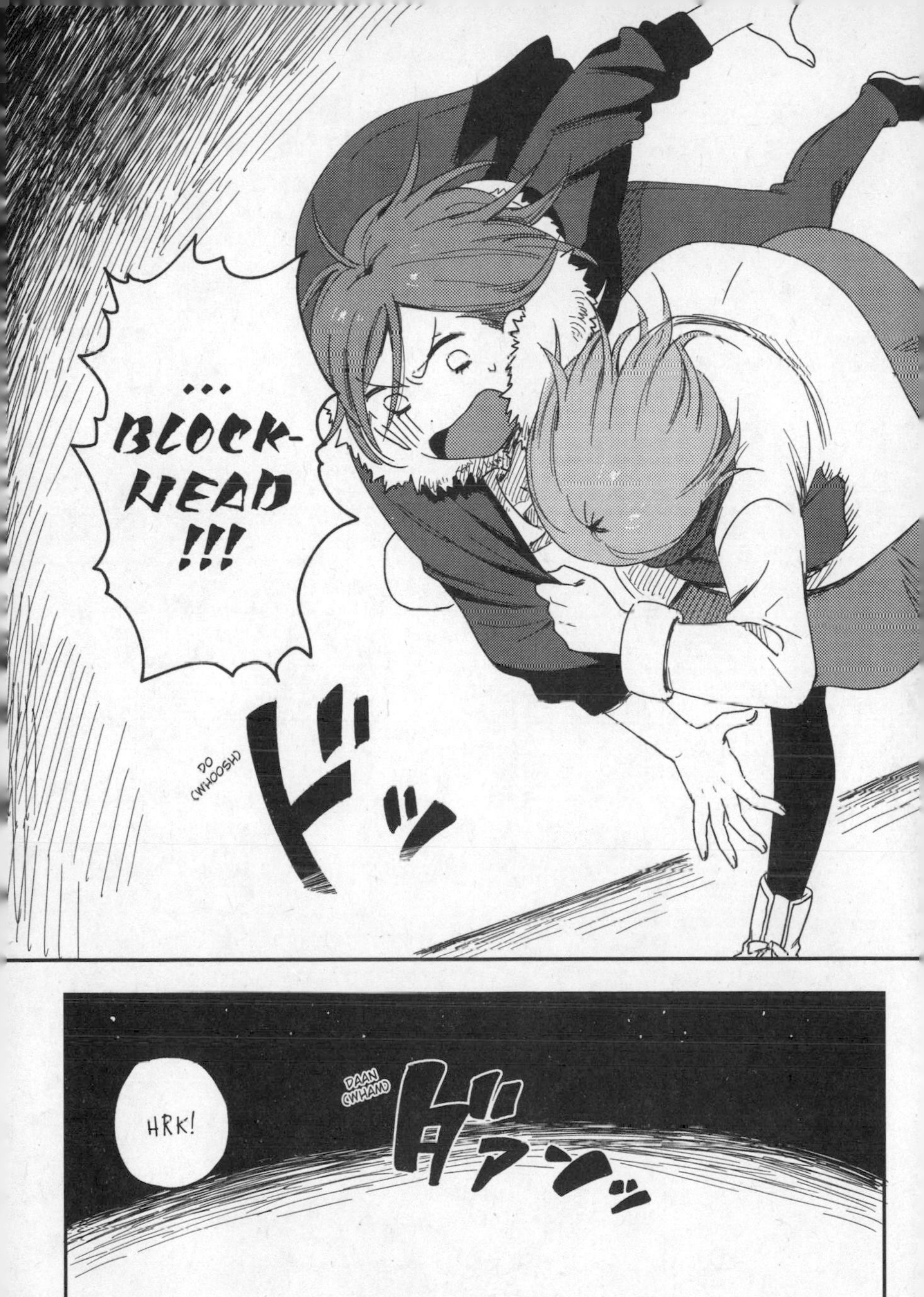
...BLOCK-HEAD!!!
DO (WHOOSH)
DAAN (WHAM)
HRK!

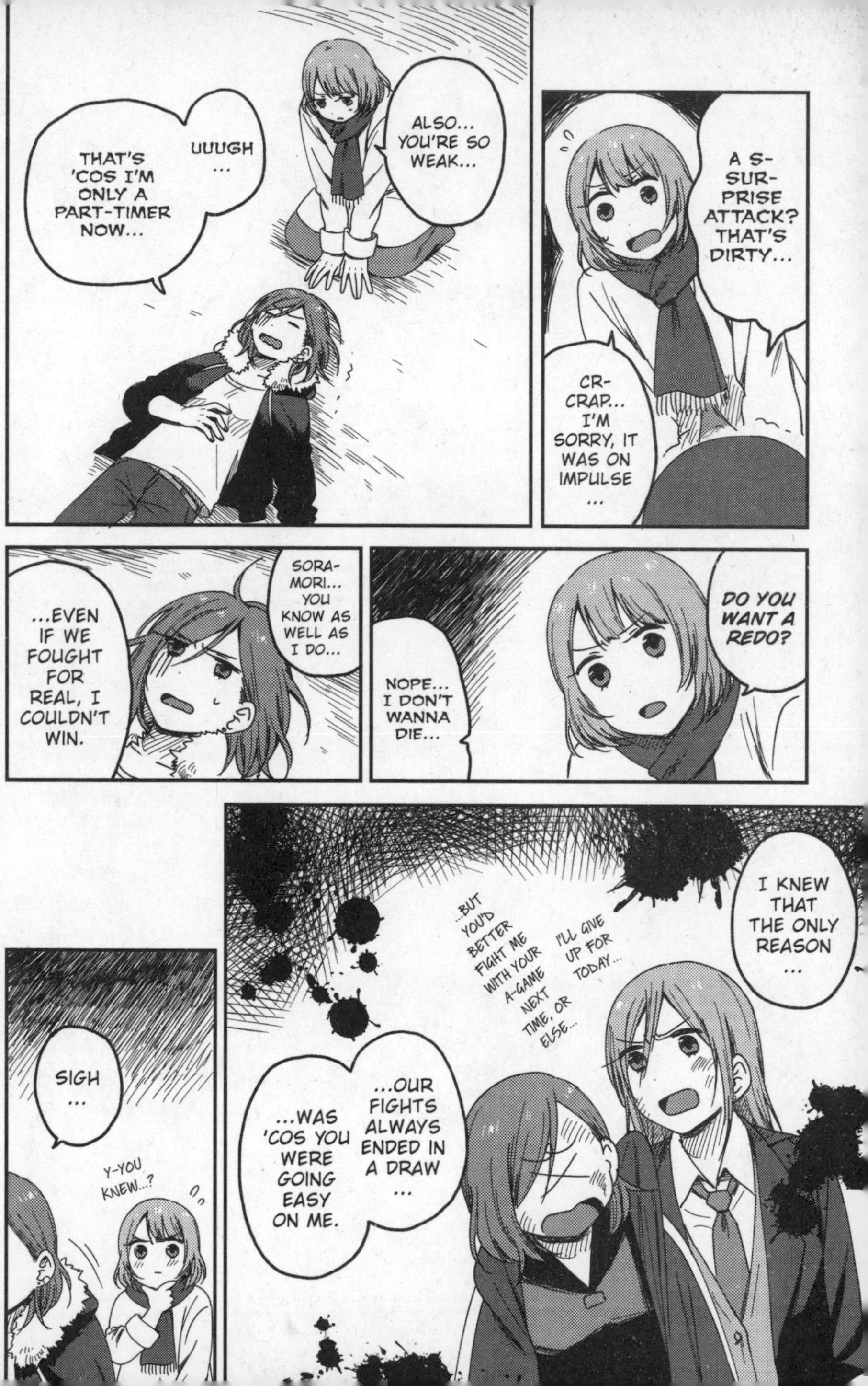
A S-SURPRISE ATTACK? THAT'S DIRTY...
CR-CRAP... I'M SORRY, IT WAS ON IMPULSE...
ALSO... YOU'RE SO WEAK...
UUUGH...
THAT'S 'COS I'M ONLY A PART-TIMER NOW...
DO YOU WANT A REDO?
NOPE... I DON'T WANNA DIE...
SORAMORI... YOU KNOW AS WELL AS I DO...
...EVEN IF WE FOUGHT FOR REAL, I COULDN'T WIN.
I KNEW THAT THE ONLY REASON...
I'LL GIVE UP FOR TODAY...
...BUT YOU'D BETTER FIGHT ME WITH YOUR A-GAME NEXT TIME, OR ELSE...
...OUR FIGHTS ALWAYS ENDED IN A DRAW...
...WAS 'COS YOU WERE GOING EASY ON ME.
SIGH...
Y-YOU KNEW...?

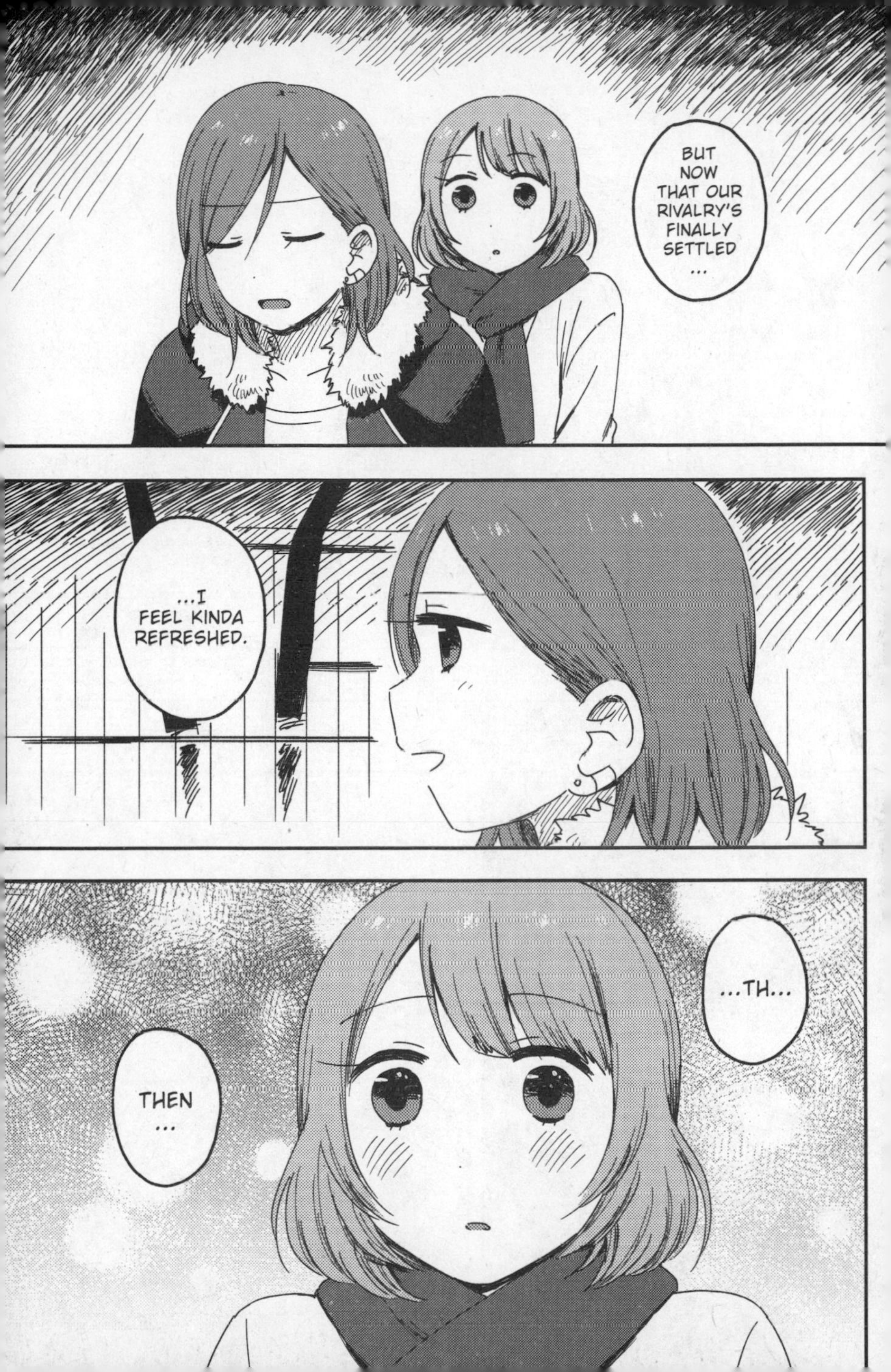
BUT NOW THAT OUR RIVALRY'S FINALLY SETTLED ...
...I FEEL KINDA REFRESHED.
...TH...
THEN ...

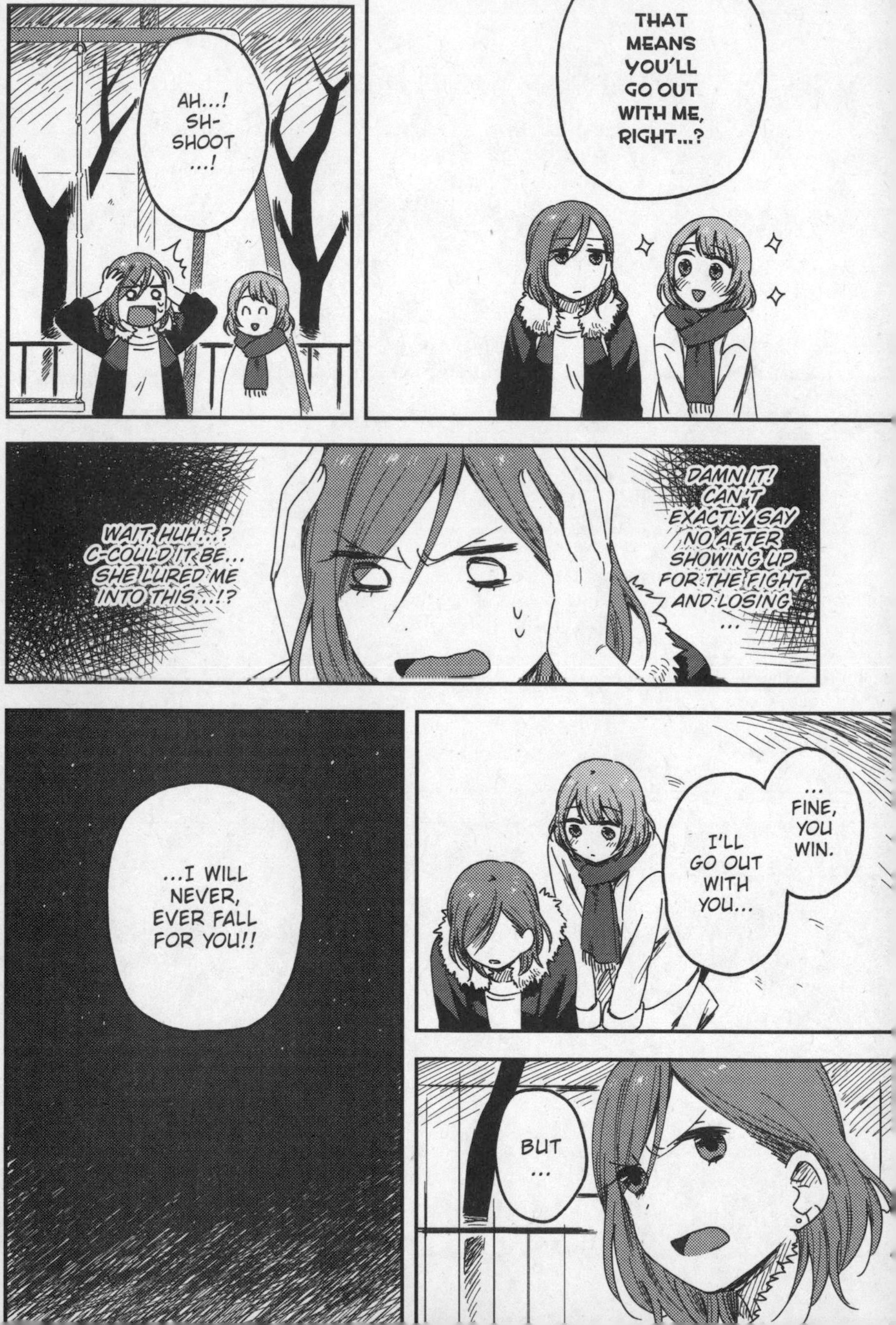
THAT MEANS YOU'LL GO OUT WITH ME, RIGHT...?
AH...! SH-SHOOT...!
DAMN IT! CAN'T EXACTLY SAY NO AFTER SHOWING UP FOR THE FIGHT AND LOSING...
WAIT, HUH...? C-COULD IT BE... SHE LURED ME INTO THIS...!?
...FINE, YOU WIN.
I'LL GO OUT WITH YOU...
BUT...
...I WILL NEVER, EVER FALL FOR YOU!!

Catch These Hands!

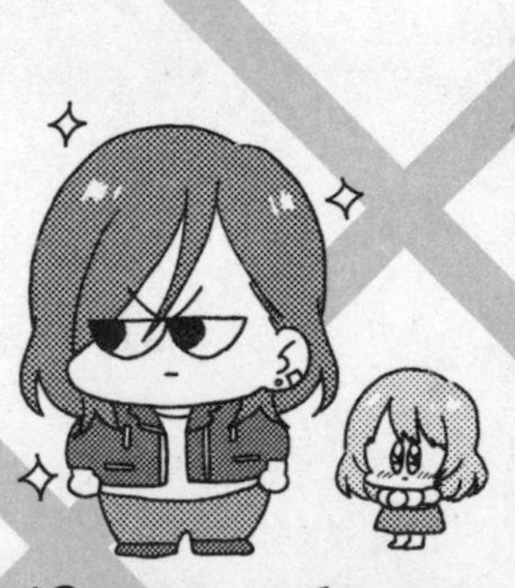

Catch These Hands!

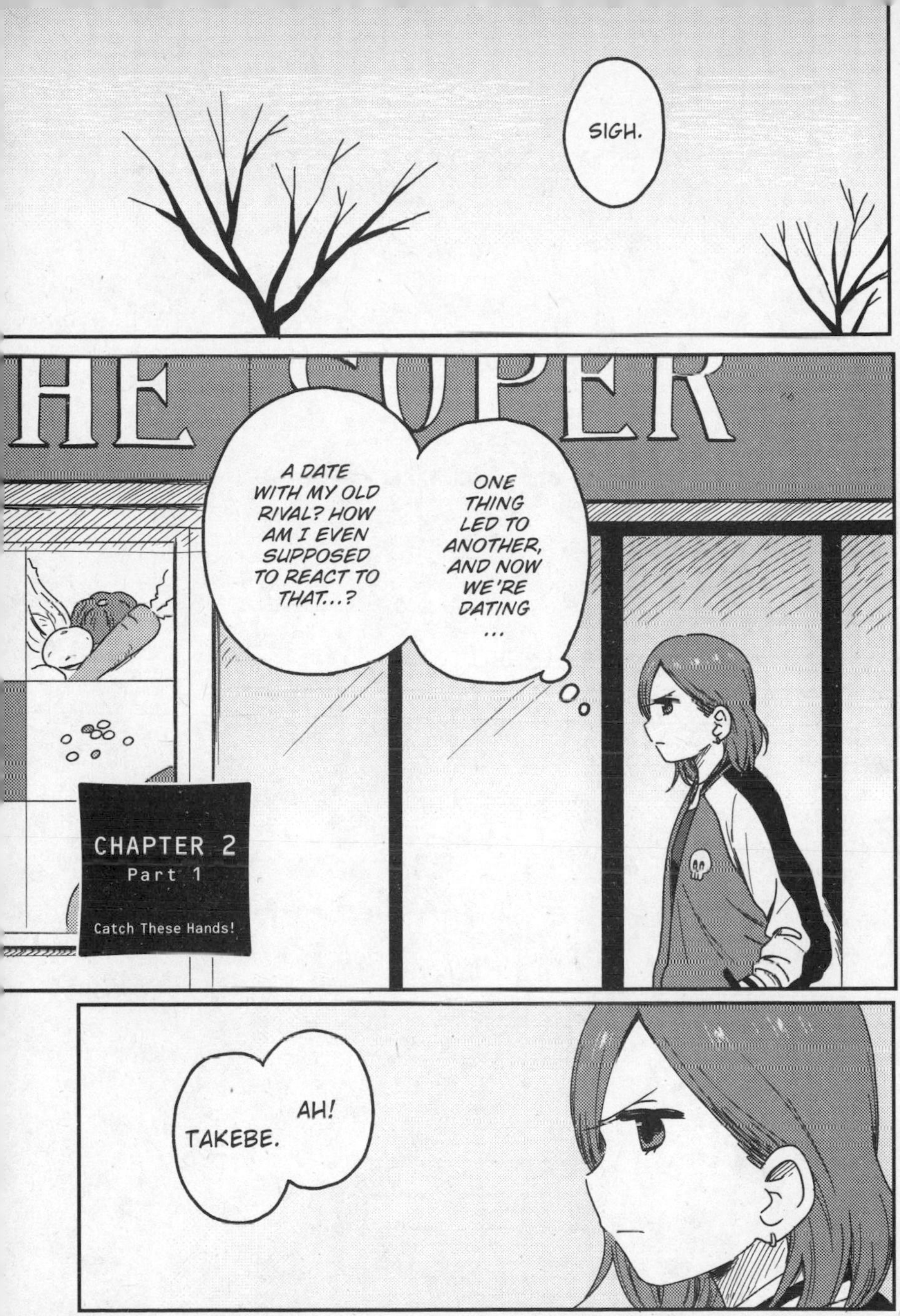
SIGH.
ONE THING LED TO ANOTHER, AND NOW WE'RE DATING ...
A DATE WITH MY OLD RIVAL? HOW AM I EVEN SUPPOSED TO REACT TO THAT...?
CHAPTER 2
Part 1
Catch These Hands!
AH! TAKEBE.

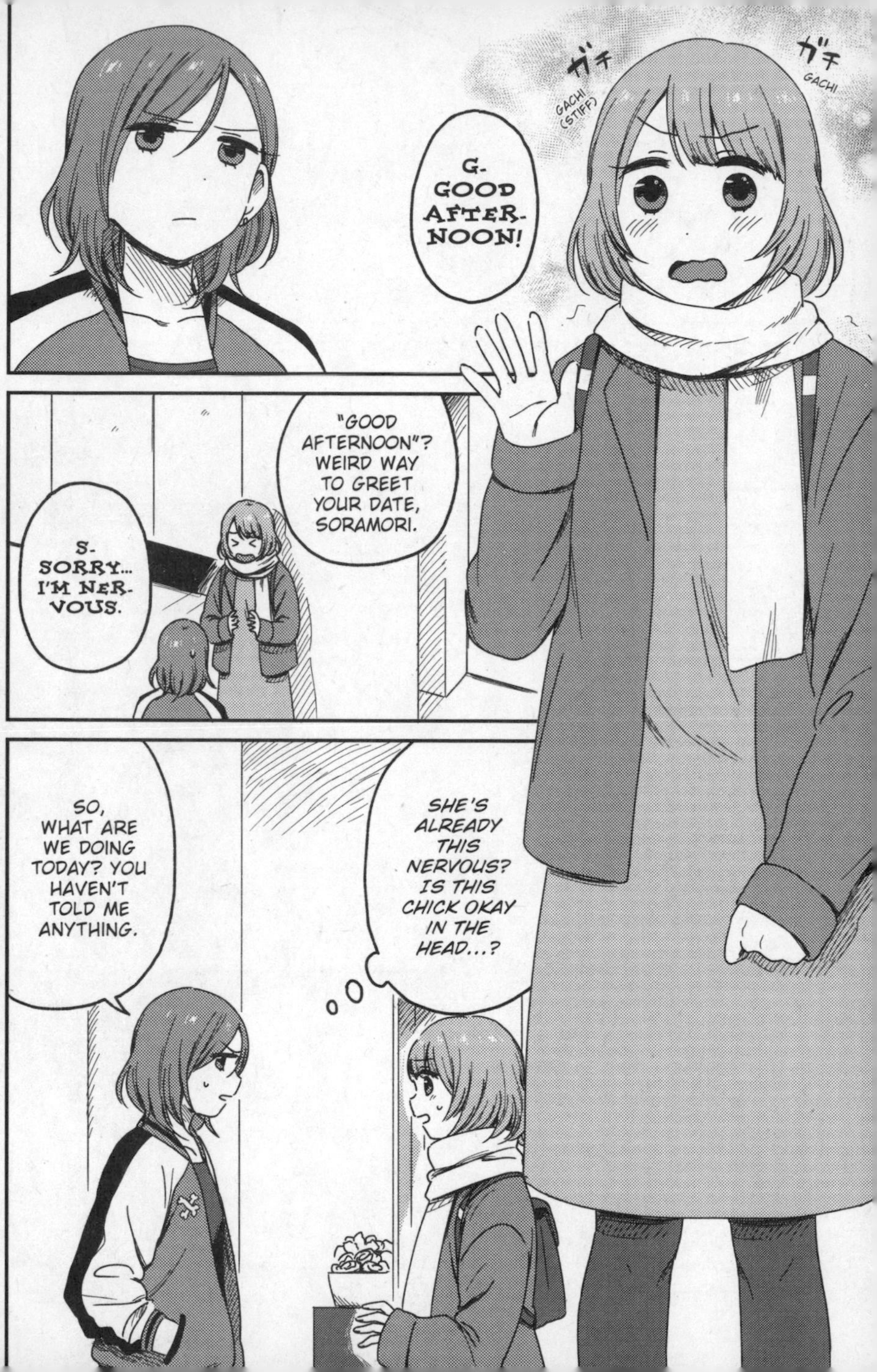

ガチ
GACHI
ガチ
GACHI (STIFF)
G-GOOD AFTERNOON!
"GOOD AFTERNOON"? WEIRD WAY TO GREET YOUR DATE, SORAMORI.
S-SORRY... I'M NERVOUS.
SHE'S ALREADY THIS NERVOUS? IS THIS CHICK OKAY IN THE HEAD...?
SO, WHAT ARE WE DOING TODAY? YOU HAVEN'T TOLD ME ANYTHING.

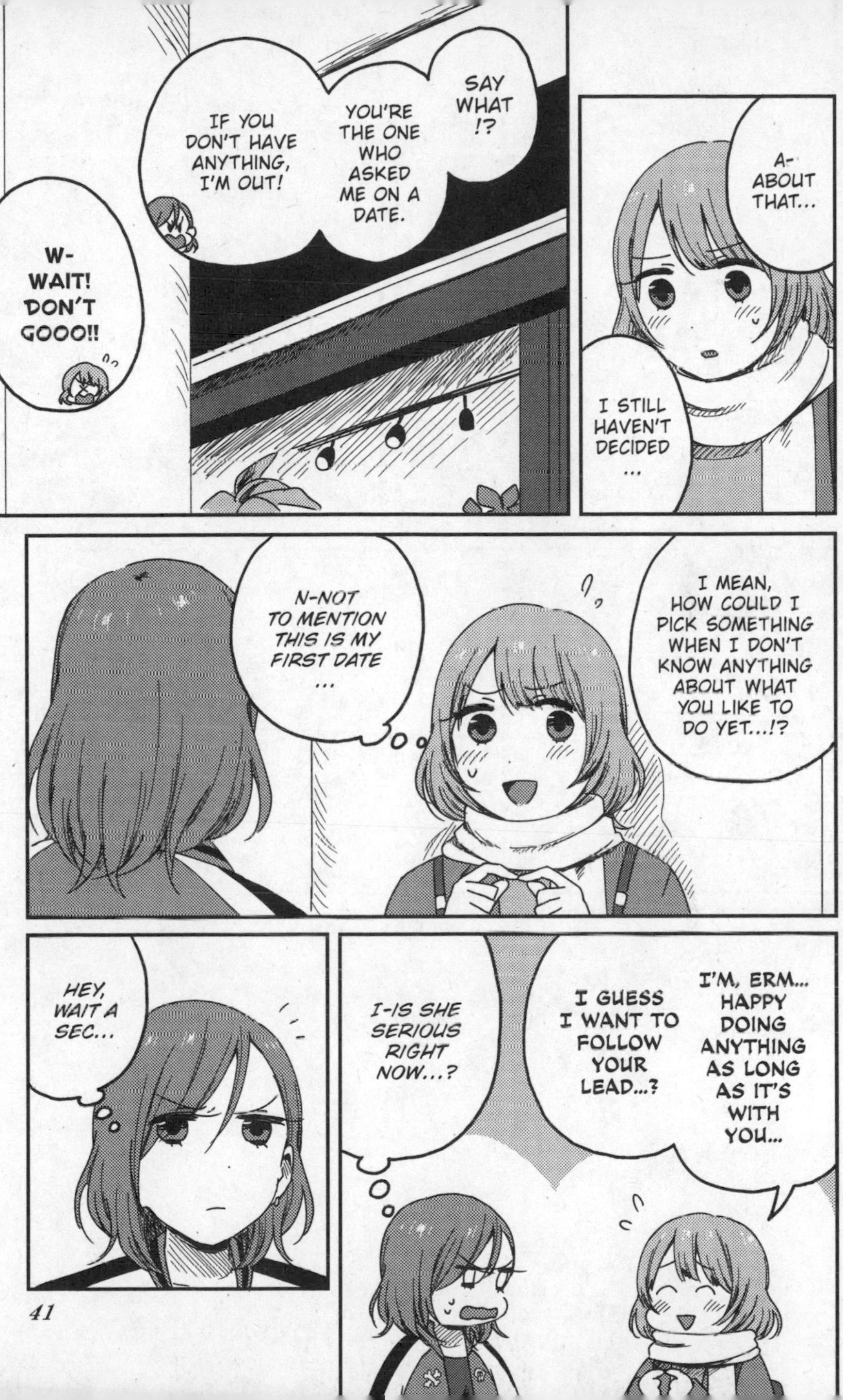
A- ABOUT THAT...
I STILL HAVEN'T DECIDED ...
SAY WHAT !?
YOU'RE THE ONE WHO ASKED ME ON A DATE.
IF YOU DON'T HAVE ANYTHING, I'M OUT!
W- WAIT! DON'T GOOO!!
I MEAN, HOW COULD I PICK SOMETHING WHEN I DON'T KNOW ANYTHING ABOUT WHAT YOU LIKE TO DO YET...!?
N-NOT TO MENTION THIS IS MY FIRST DATE ...
I'M, ERM... HAPPY DOING ANYTHING AS LONG AS IT'S WITH YOU...
I GUESS I WANT TO FOLLOW YOUR LEAD...?
I-IS SHE SERIOUS RIGHT NOW...?
HEY, WAIT A SEC...

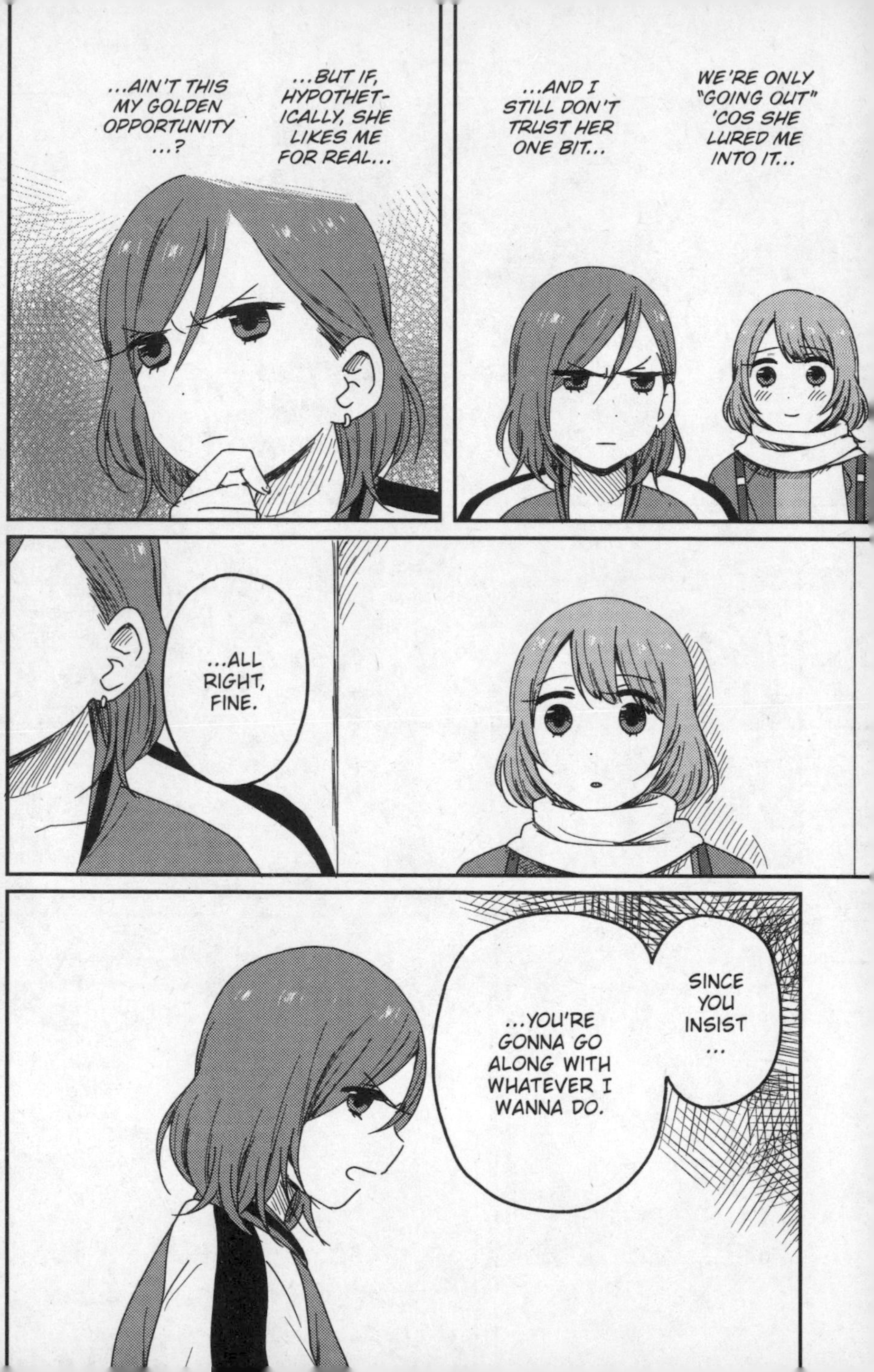
WE'RE ONLY "GOING OUT" 'COS SHE LURED ME INTO IT...
...AND I STILL DON'T TRUST HER ONE BIT...
...BUT IF, HYPOTHETICALLY, SHE LIKES ME FOR REAL...
...AIN'T THIS MY GOLDEN OPPORTUNITY...?
...ALL RIGHT, FINE.
SINCE YOU INSIST...
...YOU'RE GONNA GO ALONG WITH WHATEVER I WANNA DO.

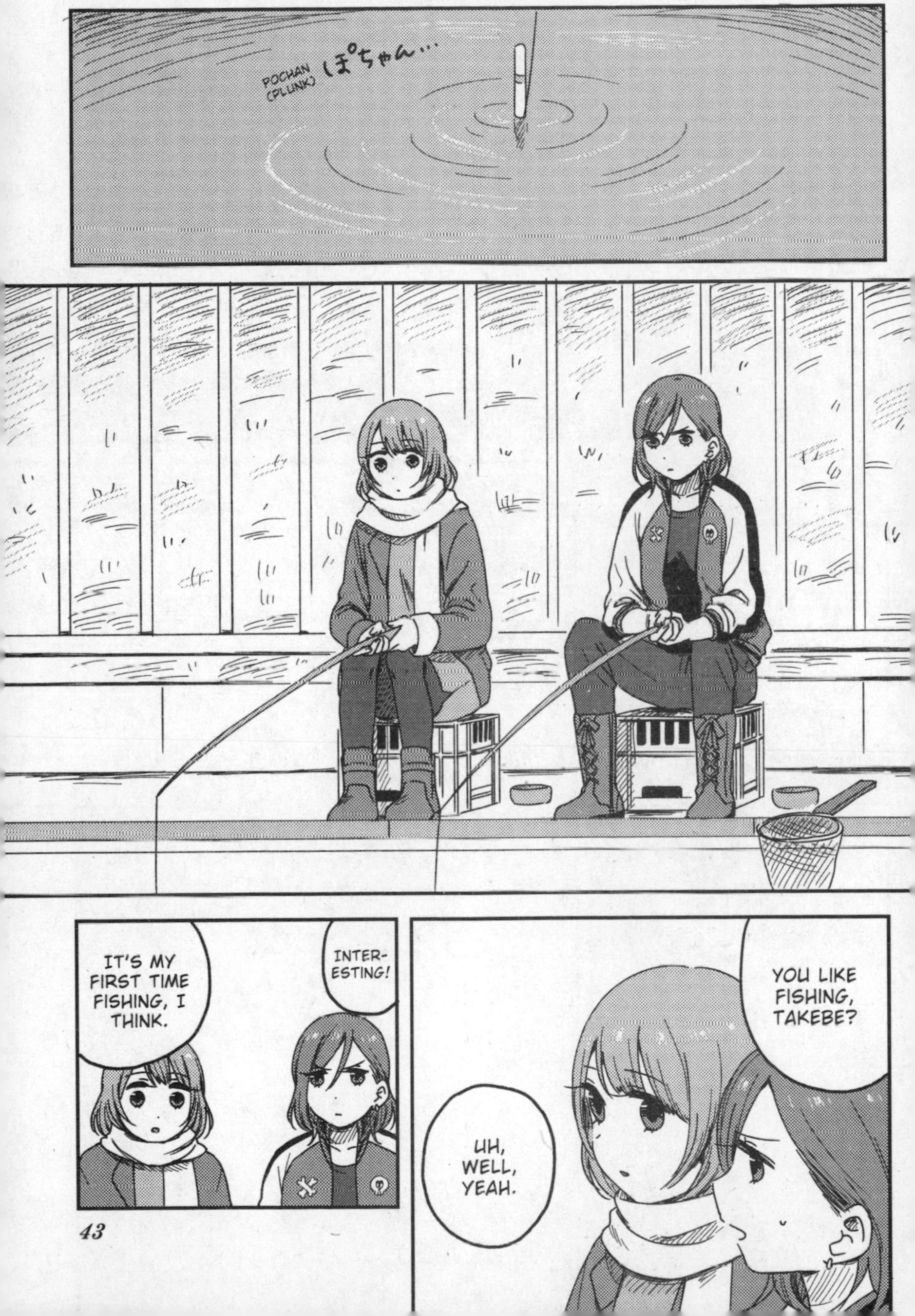
POCHAN (PLUNK)
ぽちゃん…
YOU LIKE FISHING, TAKEBE?
UH, WELL, YEAH.
INTER-ESTING!
IT'S MY FIRST TIME FISHING, I THINK.

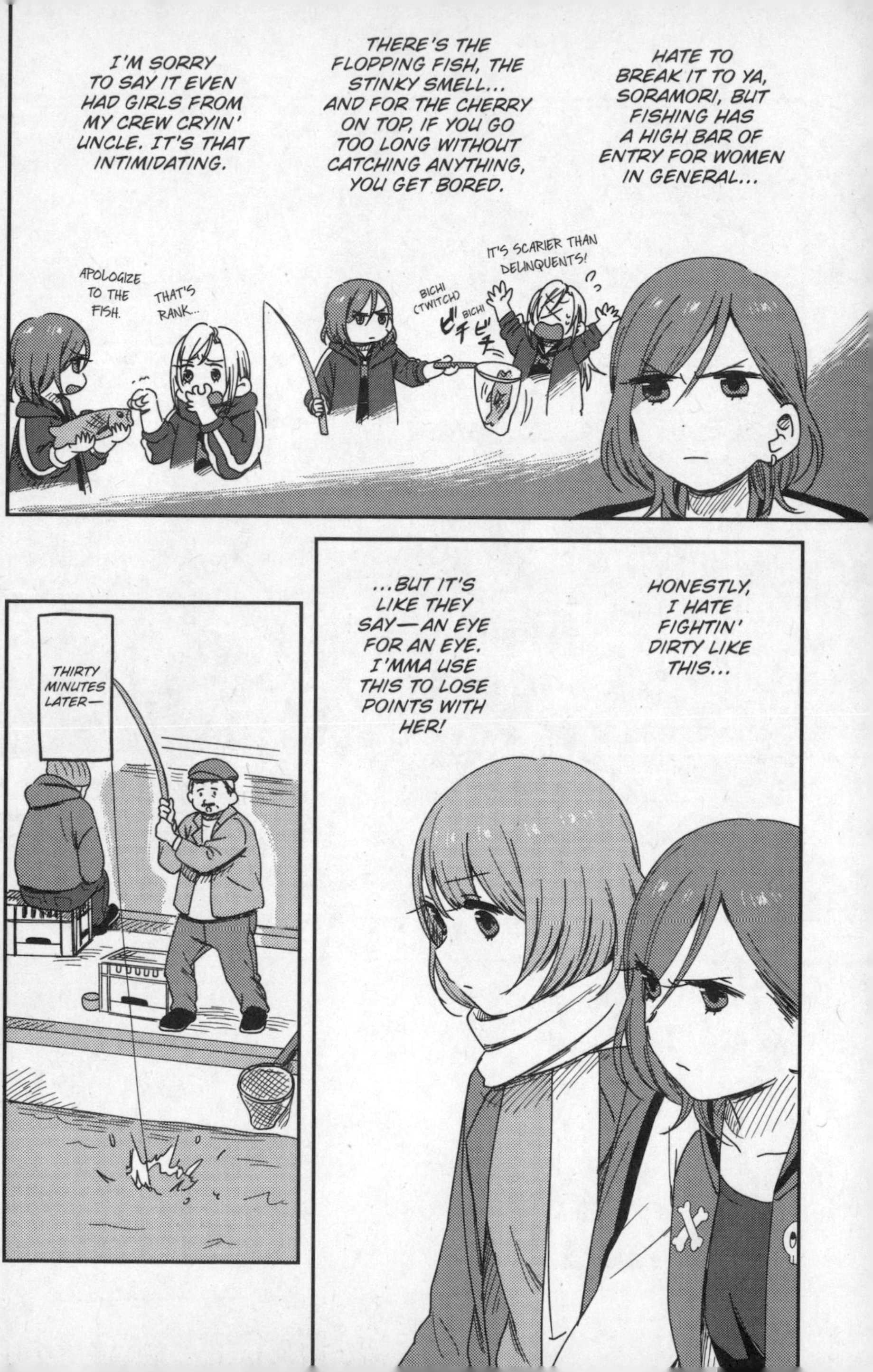
HATE TO BREAK IT TO YA, SORAMORI, BUT FISHING HAS A HIGH BAR OF ENTRY FOR WOMEN IN GENERAL...
THERE'S THE FLOPPING FISH, THE STINKY SMELL... AND FOR THE CHERRY ON TOP, IF YOU GO TOO LONG WITHOUT CATCHING ANYTHING, YOU GET BORED.
I'M SORRY TO SAY IT EVEN HAD GIRLS FROM MY CREW CRYIN' UNCLE. IT'S THAT INTIMIDATING.
IT'S SCARIER THAN DELINQUENTS!
BICHI (TWITCH) BICHI
THAT'S RANK...
APOLOGIZE TO THE FISH.
HONESTLY, I HATE FIGHTIN' DIRTY LIKE THIS...
...BUT IT'S LIKE THEY SAY—AN EYE FOR AN EYE. I'MMA USE THIS TO LOSE POINTS WITH HER!
THIRTY MINUTES LATER—

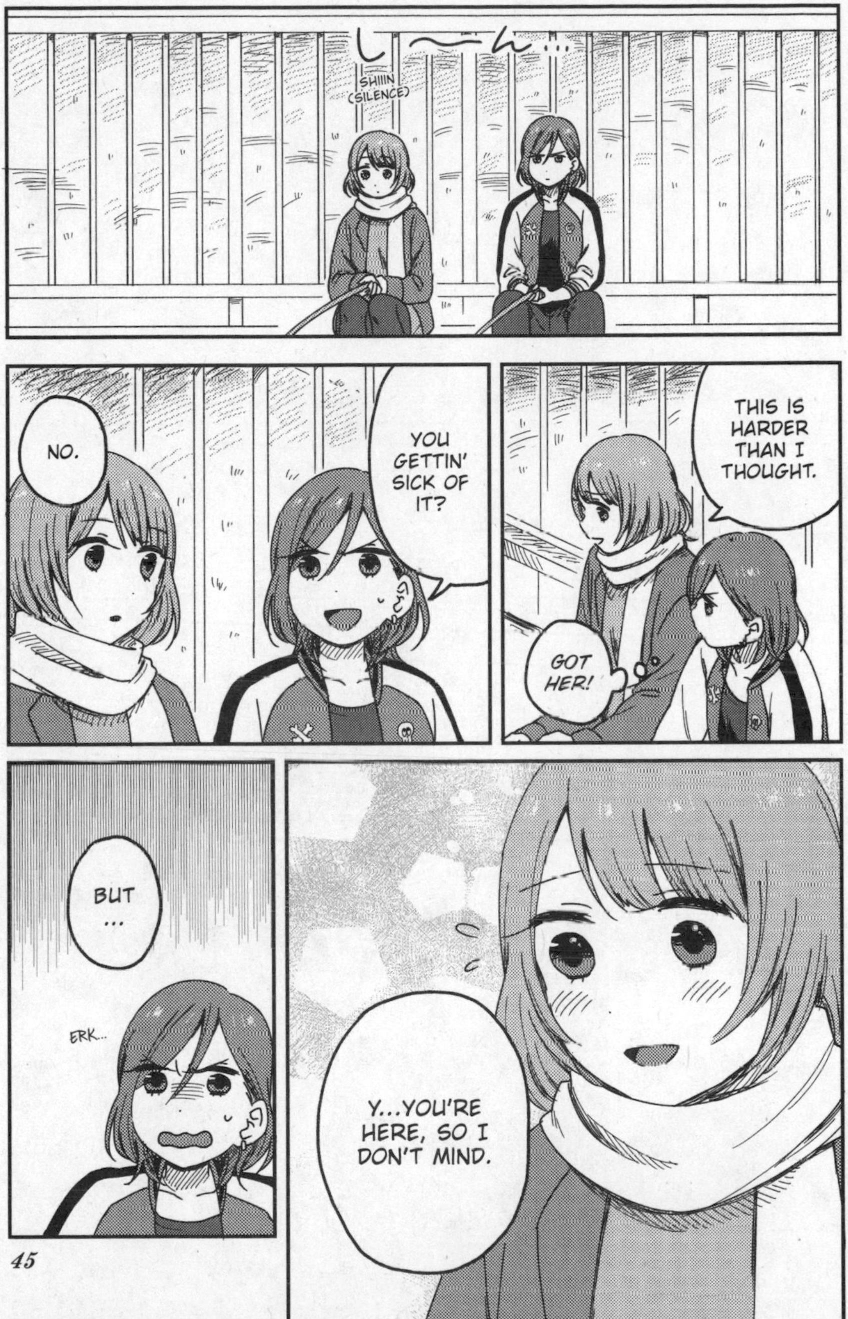
しーん…
SHIIIN (SILENCE)
THIS IS HARDER THAN I THOUGHT.
GOT HER!
YOU GETTIN' SICK OF IT?
NO.
Y...YOU'RE HERE, SO I DON'T MIND.
BUT ...
ERK...

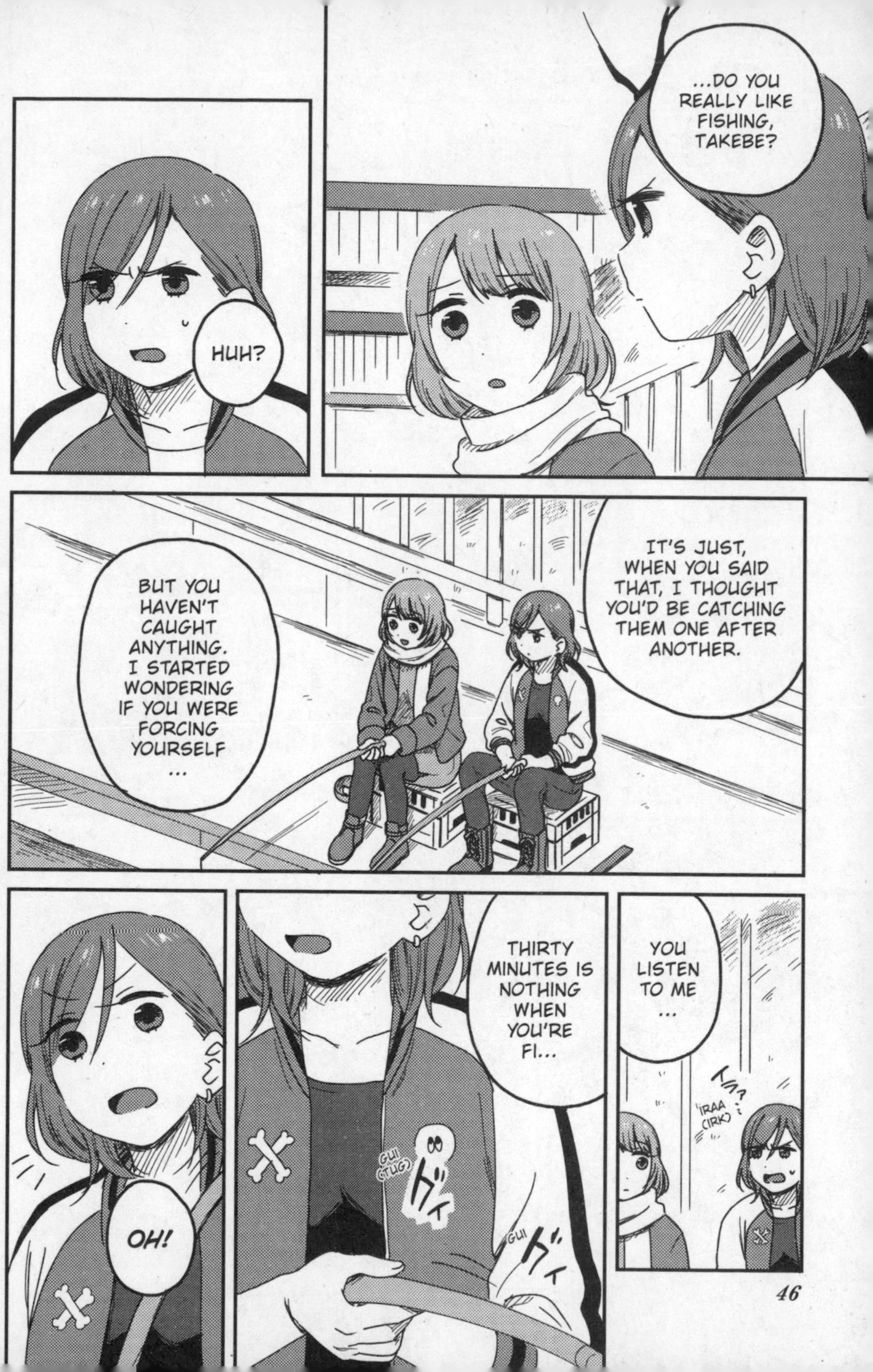
...DO YOU REALLY LIKE FISHING, TAKEBE?
HUH?
IT'S JUST, WHEN YOU SAID THAT, I THOUGHT YOU'D BE CATCHING THEM ONE AFTER ANOTHER.
BUT YOU HAVEN'T CAUGHT ANYTHING. I STARTED WONDERING IF YOU WERE FORCING YOURSELF ...
YOU LISTEN TO ME ...
IRAA (IRK)
THIRTY MINUTES IS NOTHING WHEN YOU'RE FI...
GUI (TUG)
GUI
OH!

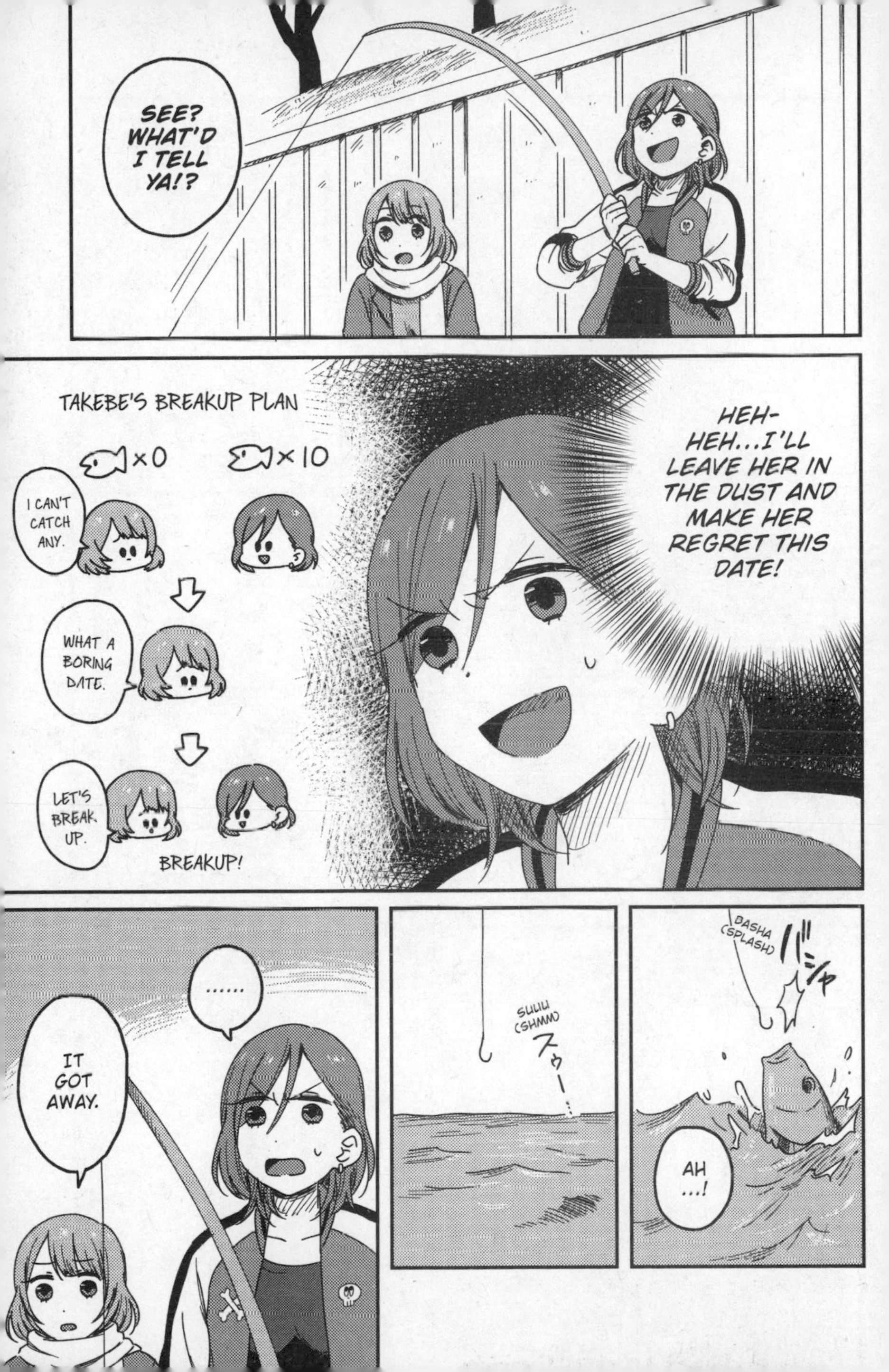
SEE? WHAT'D I TELL YA!?
HEH-HEH...I'LL LEAVE HER IN THE DUST AND MAKE HER REGRET THIS DATE!
TAKEBE'S BREAKUP PLAN
×0
×10
I CAN'T CATCH ANY.
WHAT A BORING DATE.
LET'S BREAK UP.
BREAKUP!
BASHA (SPLASH)
AH ...!
SULUU (SHMM)
......
IT GOT AWAY.

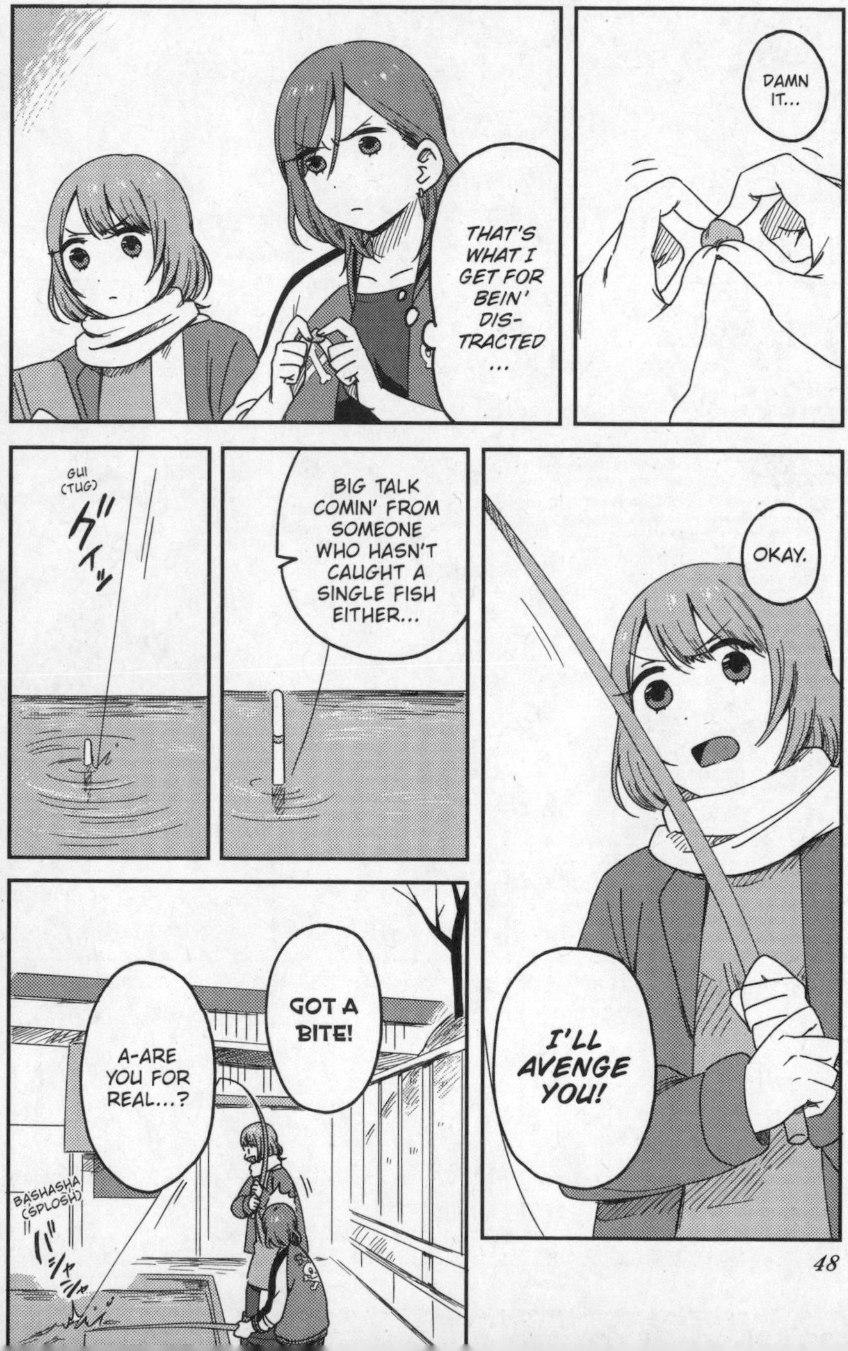
DAMN IT...
THAT'S WHAT I GET FOR BEIN' DIS-TRACTED ...
OKAY.
I'LL AVENGE YOU!
BIG TALK COMIN' FROM SOMEONE WHO HASN'T CAUGHT A SINGLE FISH EITHER...
GUI (TUG)
グイッ
GOT A BITE!
A-ARE YOU FOR REAL...?
BASHASHA (SPLOSH)

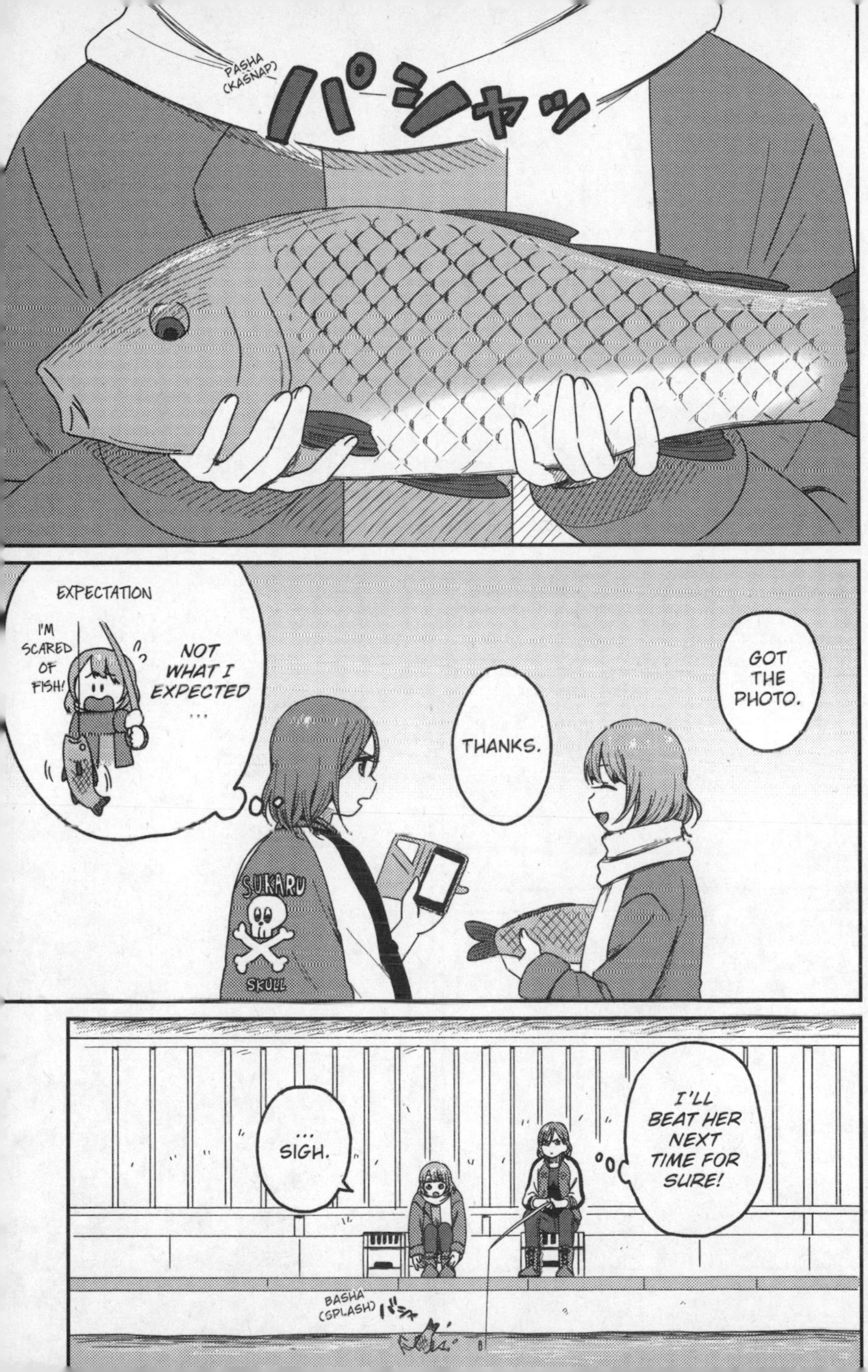
PASHA (KASNAP)
パシャッ
GOT THE PHOTO.
THANKS.
NOT WHAT I EXPECTED ...
EXPECTATION
I'M SCARED OF FISH!
SUKARU
SKULL
I'LL BEAT HER NEXT TIME FOR SURE!
... SIGH.
BASHA (SPLASH)

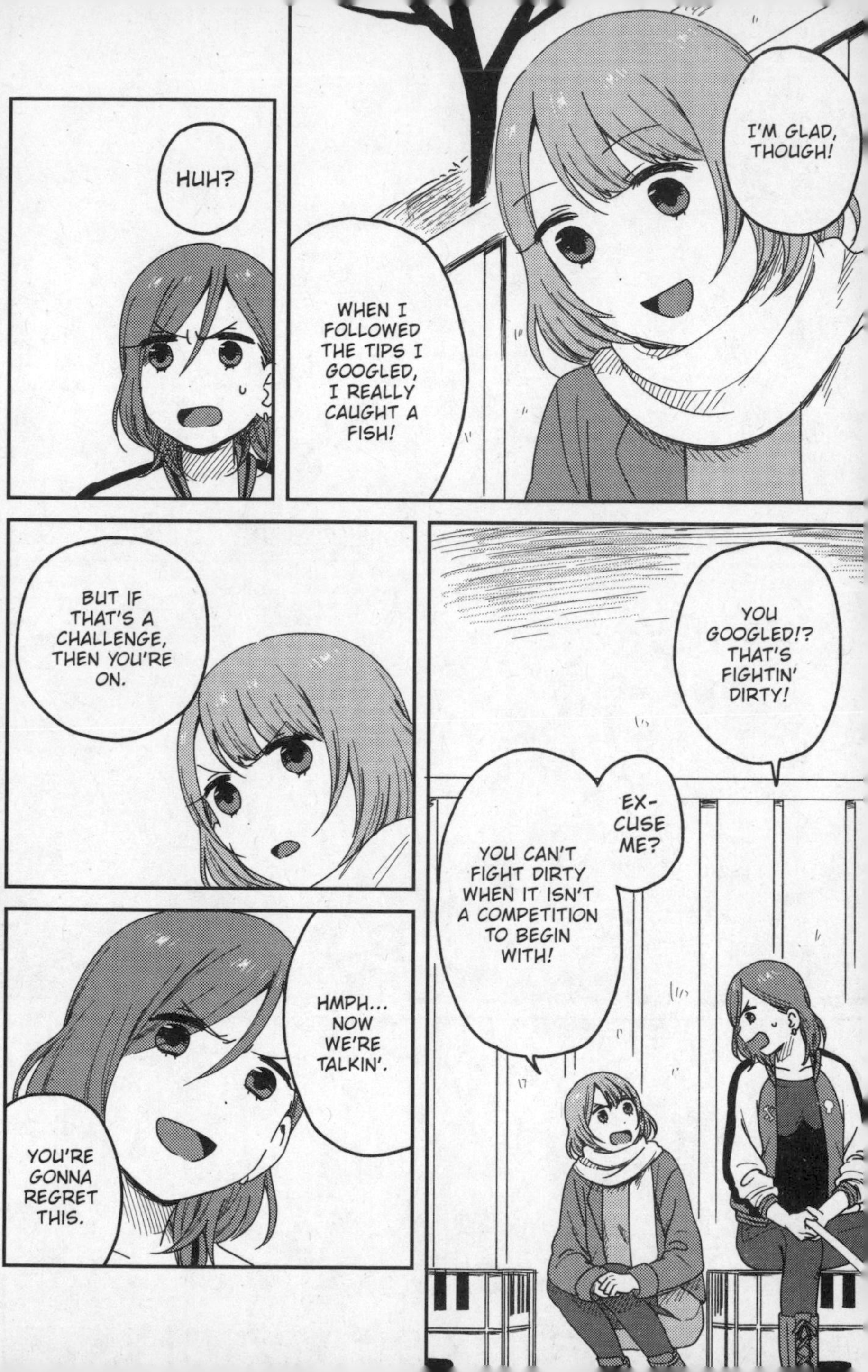
I'M GLAD, THOUGH!
WHEN I FOLLOWED THE TIPS I GOOGLED, I REALLY CAUGHT A FISH!
HUH?
YOU GOOGLED!? THAT'S FIGHTIN' DIRTY!
EX-CUSE ME?
YOU CAN'T FIGHT DIRTY WHEN IT ISN'T A COMPETITION TO BEGIN WITH!
BUT IF THAT'S A CHALLENGE, THEN YOU'RE ON.
HMPH... NOW WE'RE TALKIN'.
YOU'RE GONNA REGRET THIS.

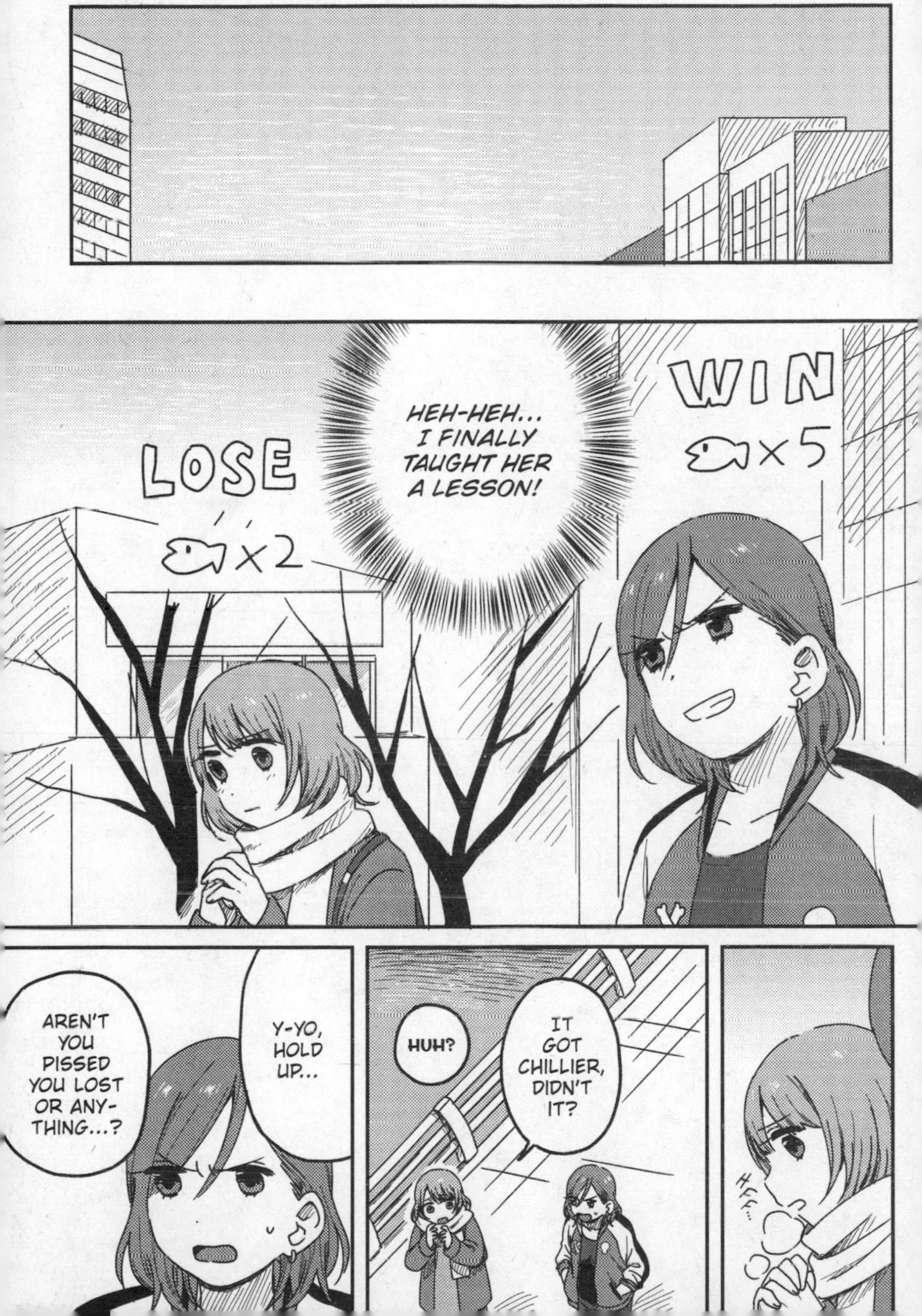
WIN
×5
HEH-HEH... I FINALLY TAUGHT HER A LESSON!
LOSE
×2
HFF...
IT GOT CHILLIER, DIDN'T IT?
HUH?
Y-YO, HOLD UP...
AREN'T YOU PISSED YOU LOST OR ANY-THING...?

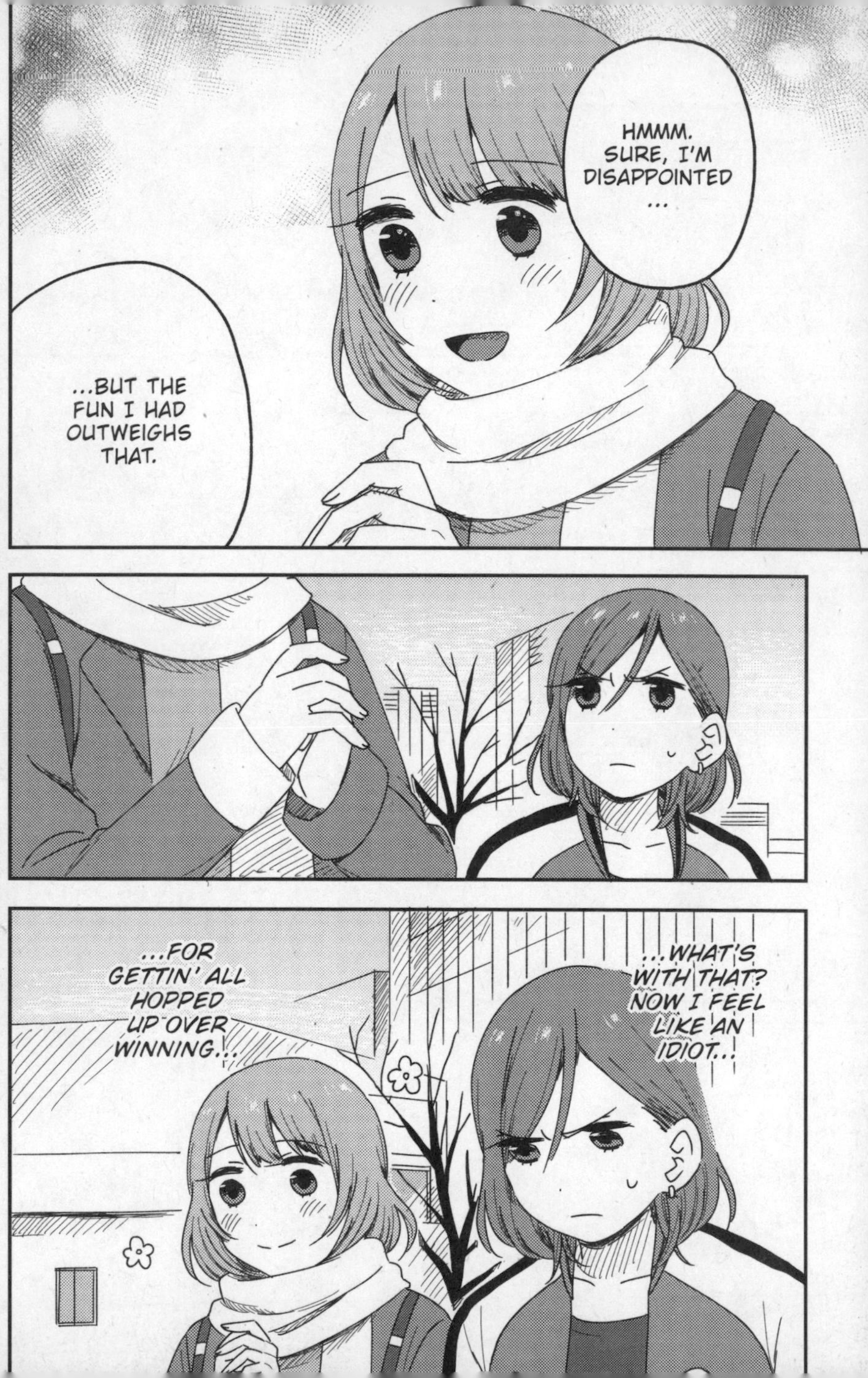
HMMM. SURE, I'M DISAPPOINTED ...
...BUT THE FUN I HAD OUTWEIGHS THAT.
...WHAT'S WITH THAT? NOW I FEEL LIKE AN IDIOT...
...FOR GETTIN' ALL HOPPED UP OVER WINNING...

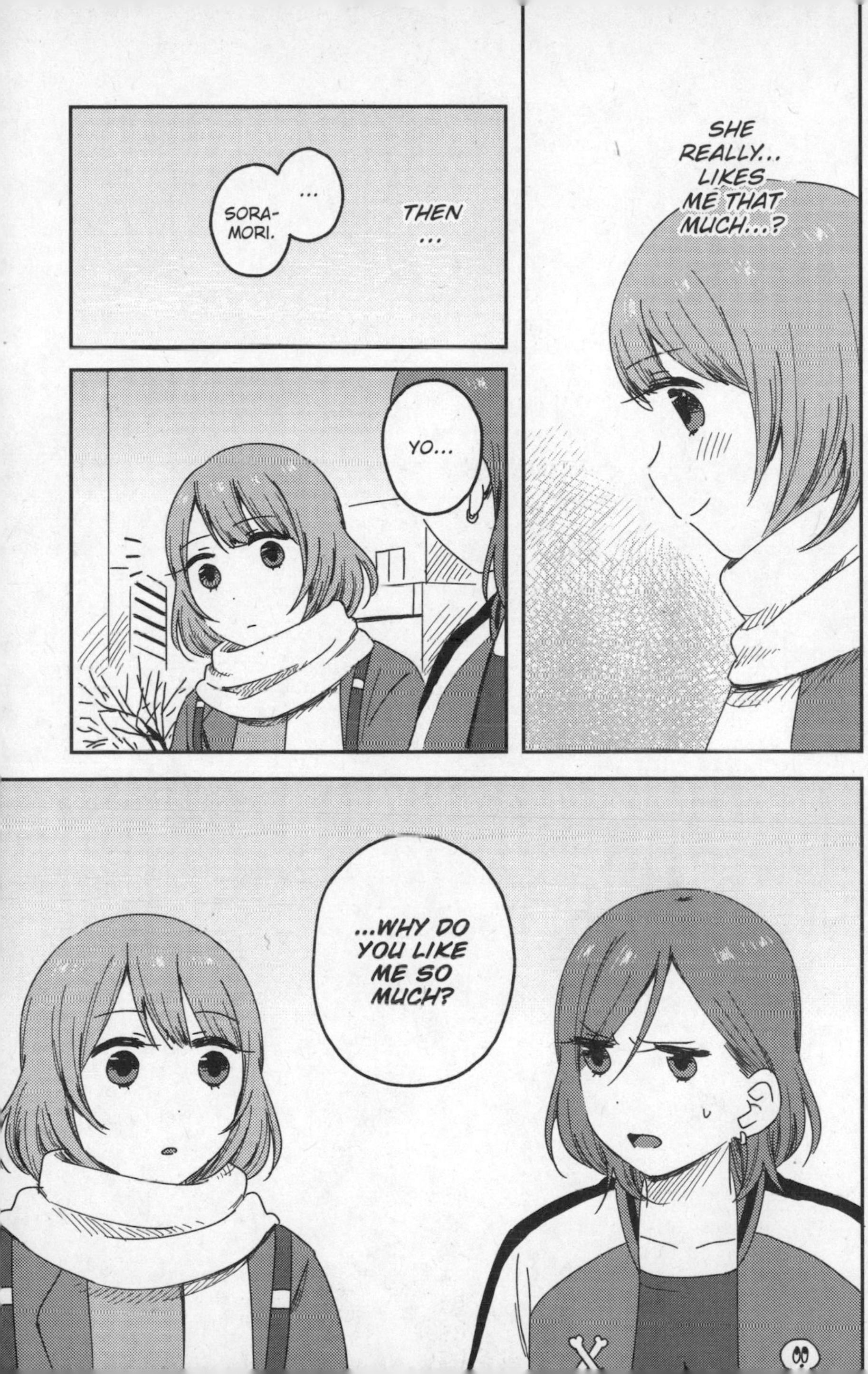
SHE REALLY... LIKES ME THAT MUCH...?
THEN ...
... SORA-MORI.
YO...
...WHY DO YOU LIKE ME SO MUCH?

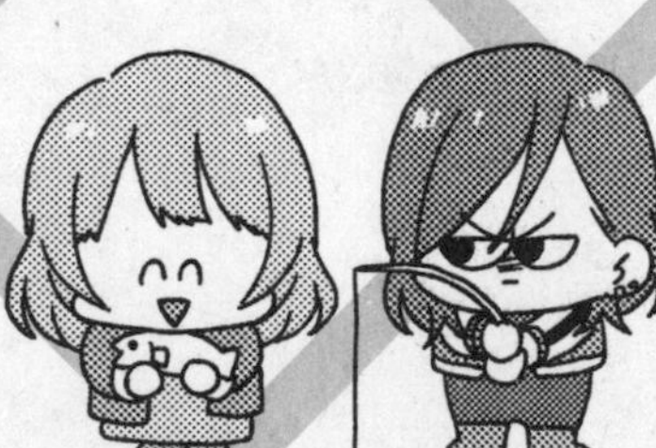

Catch These Hands!

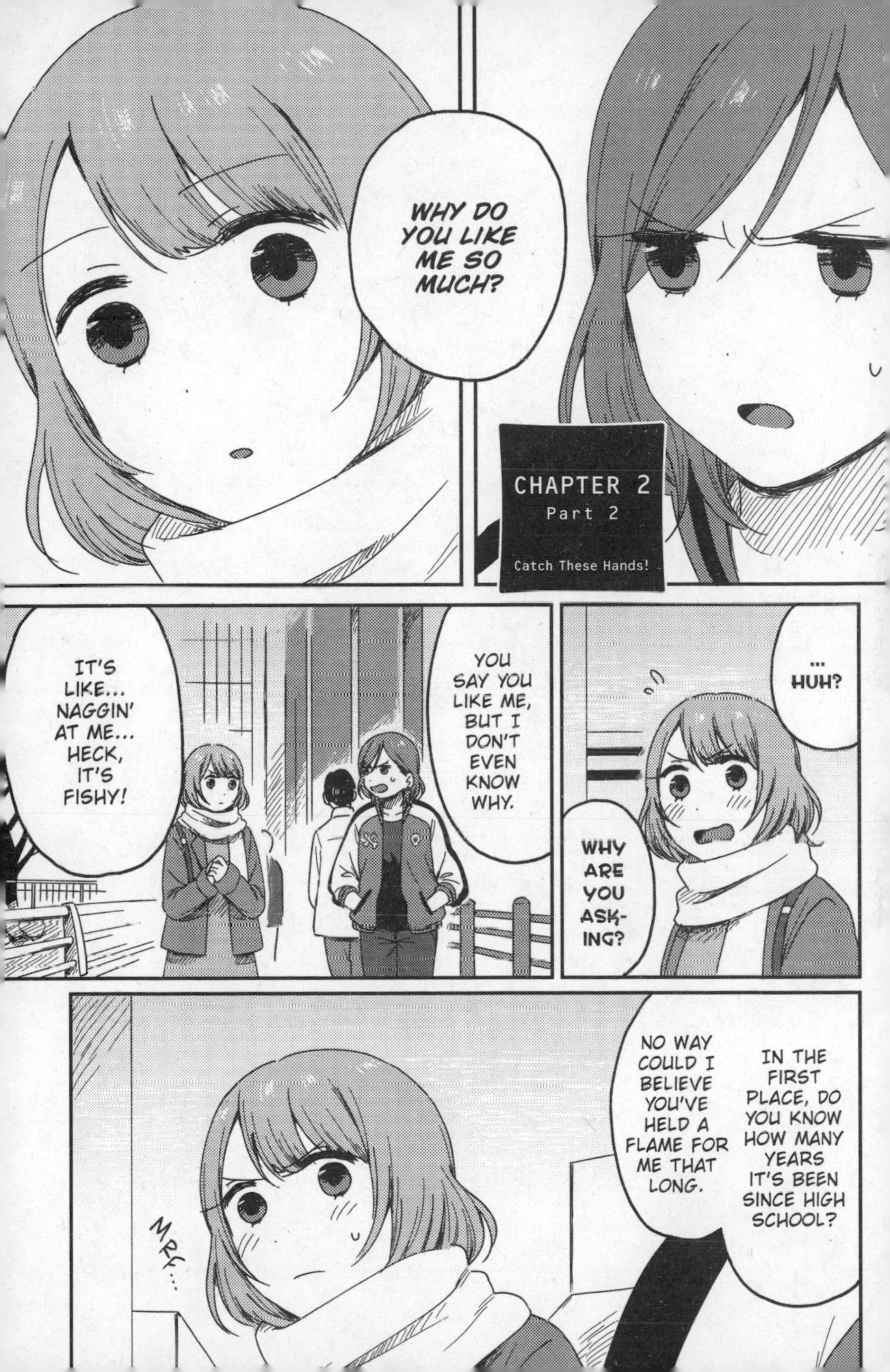
CHAPTER 2
Part 2
Catch These Hands!
WHY DO YOU LIKE ME SO MUCH?
... HUH?
WHY ARE YOU ASKING?
YOU SAY YOU LIKE ME, BUT I DON'T EVEN KNOW WHY.
IT'S LIKE... NAGGIN' AT ME... HECK, IT'S FISHY!
IN THE FIRST PLACE, DO YOU KNOW HOW MANY YEARS IT'S BEEN SINCE HIGH SCHOOL?
NO WAY COULD I BELIEVE YOU'VE HELD A FLAME FOR ME THAT LONG.
MRF...

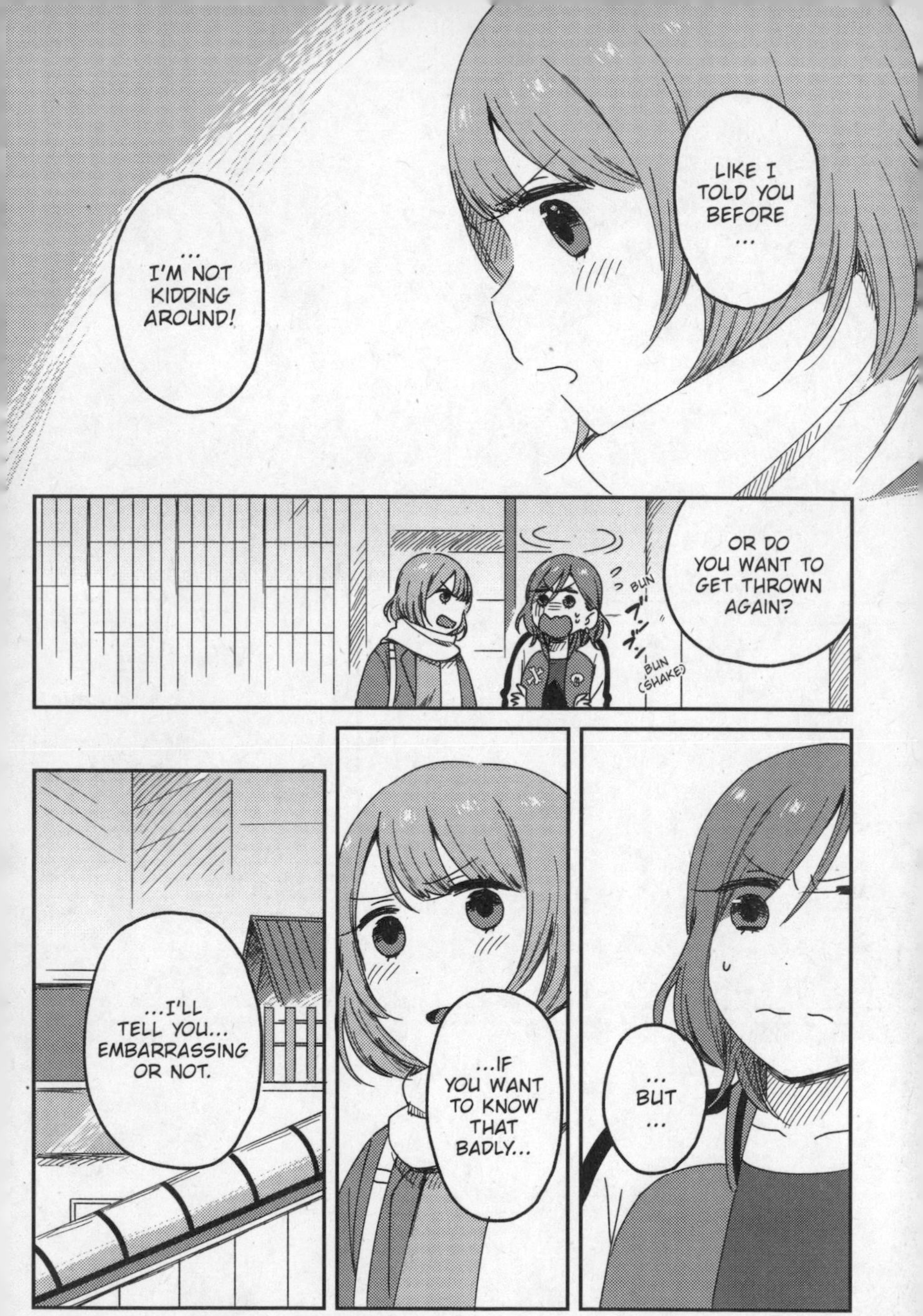
LIKE I TOLD YOU BEFORE ...
... I'M NOT KIDDING AROUND!
OR DO YOU WANT TO GET THROWN AGAIN?
BUN
BUN (SHAKE)
... BUT ...
...IF YOU WANT TO KNOW THAT BADLY...
...I'LL TELL YOU... EMBARRASSING OR NOT.

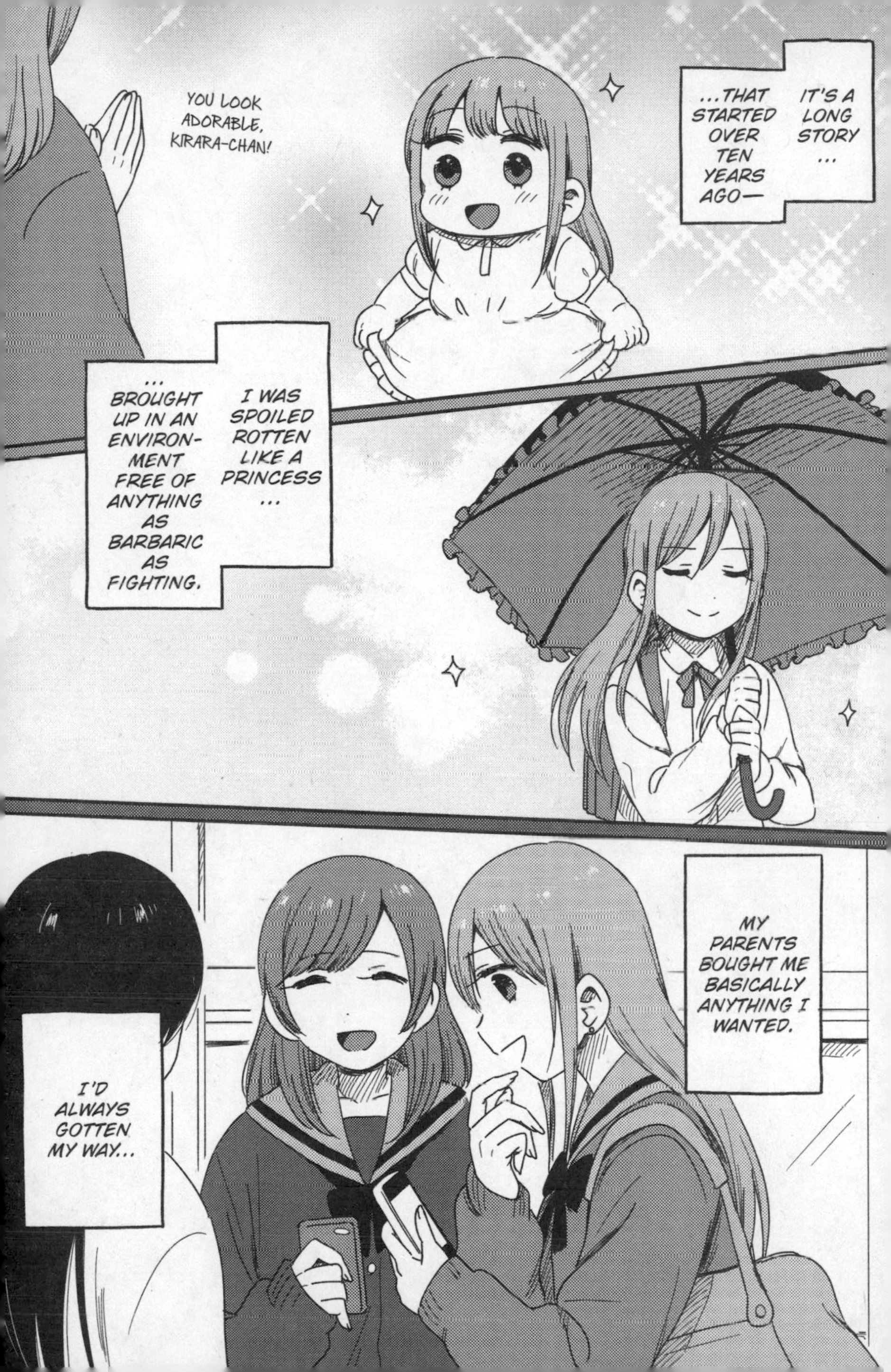
IT'S A LONG STORY ...
...THAT STARTED OVER TEN YEARS AGO—
YOU LOOK ADORABLE, KIRARA-CHAN!
I WAS SPOILED ROTTEN LIKE A PRINCESS ...
... BROUGHT UP IN AN ENVIRON-MENT FREE OF ANYTHING AS BARBARIC AS FIGHTING.
MY PARENTS BOUGHT ME BASICALLY ANYTHING I WANTED.
I'D ALWAYS GOTTEN MY WAY...

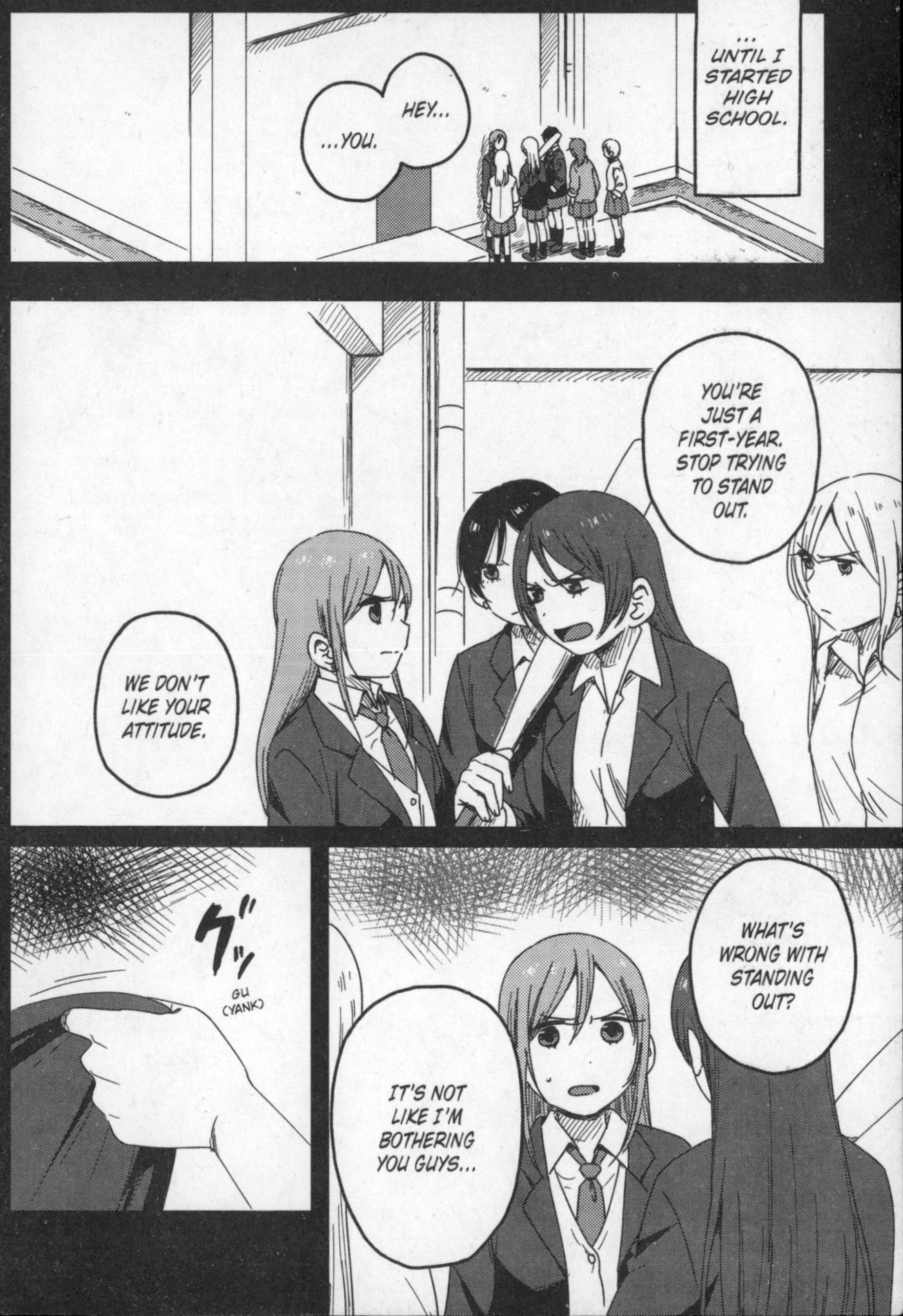
...UNTIL I STARTED HIGH SCHOOL.
HEY... ...YOU.
YOU'RE JUST A FIRST-YEAR. STOP TRYING TO STAND OUT.
WE DON'T LIKE YOUR ATTITUDE.
WHAT'S WRONG WITH STANDING OUT?
IT'S NOT LIKE I'M BOTHERING YOU GUYS...
グッ
GU (YANK)

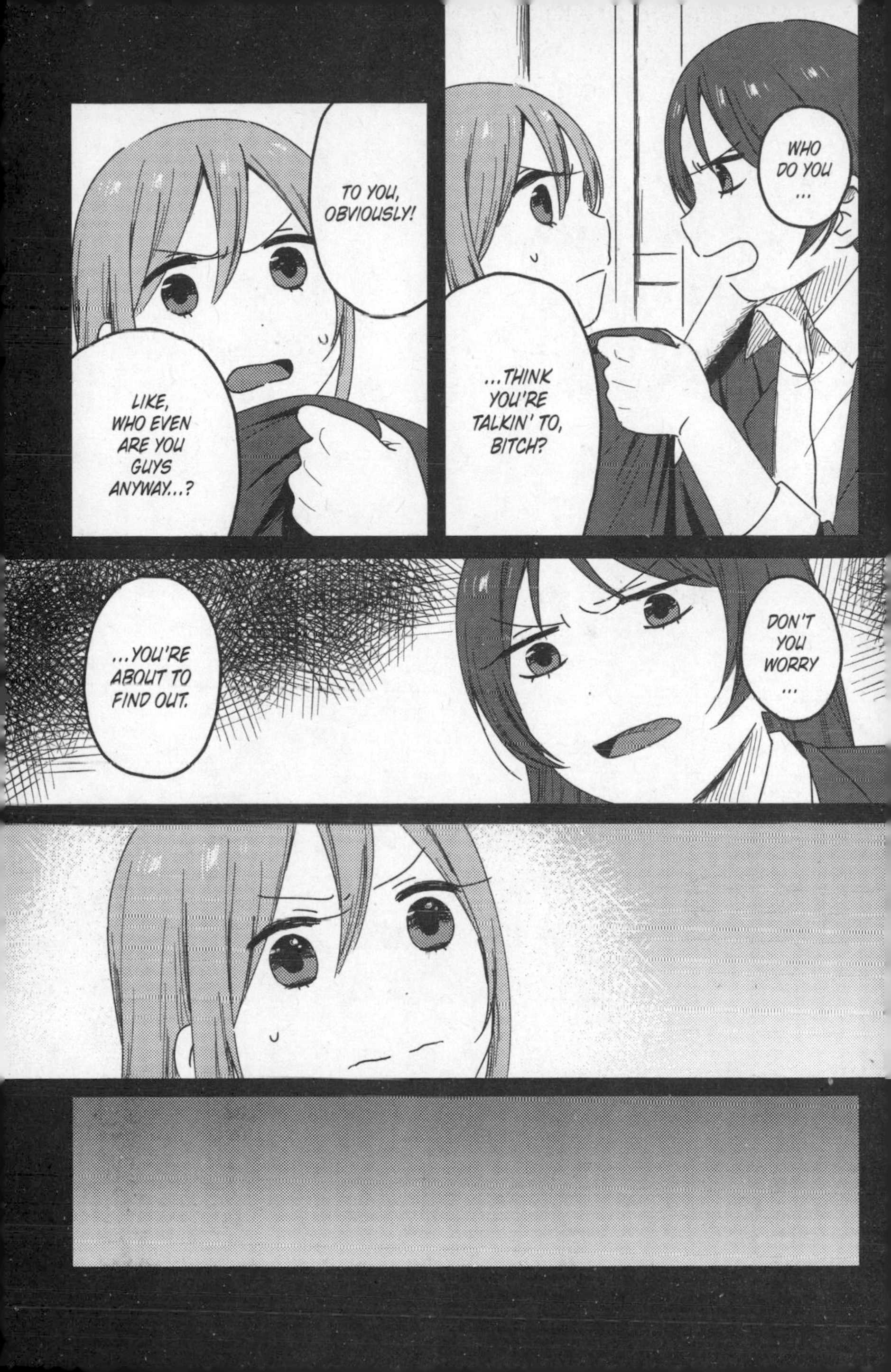
WHO DO YOU ...
...THINK YOU'RE TALKIN' TO, BITCH?
TO YOU, OBVIOUSLY!
LIKE, WHO EVEN ARE YOU GUYS ANYWAY...?
DON'T YOU WORRY ...
...YOU'RE ABOUT TO FIND OUT.

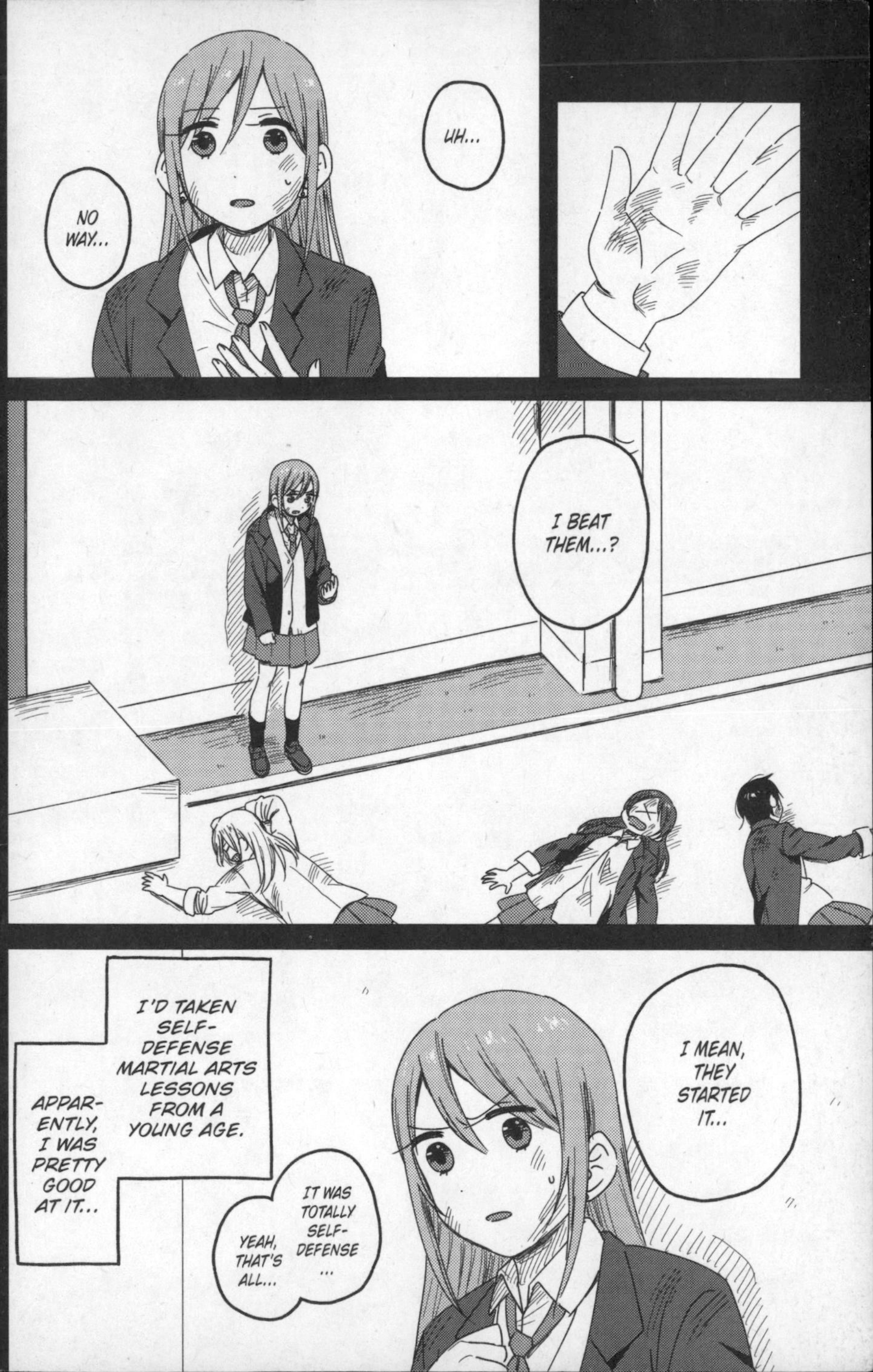
UH...
NO WAY...
I BEAT THEM...?
I MEAN, THEY STARTED IT...
IT WAS TOTALLY SELF-DEFENSE...
YEAH, THAT'S ALL...
I'D TAKEN SELF-DEFENSE MARTIAL ARTS LESSONS FROM A YOUNG AGE.
APPARENTLY, I WAS PRETTY GOOD AT IT...

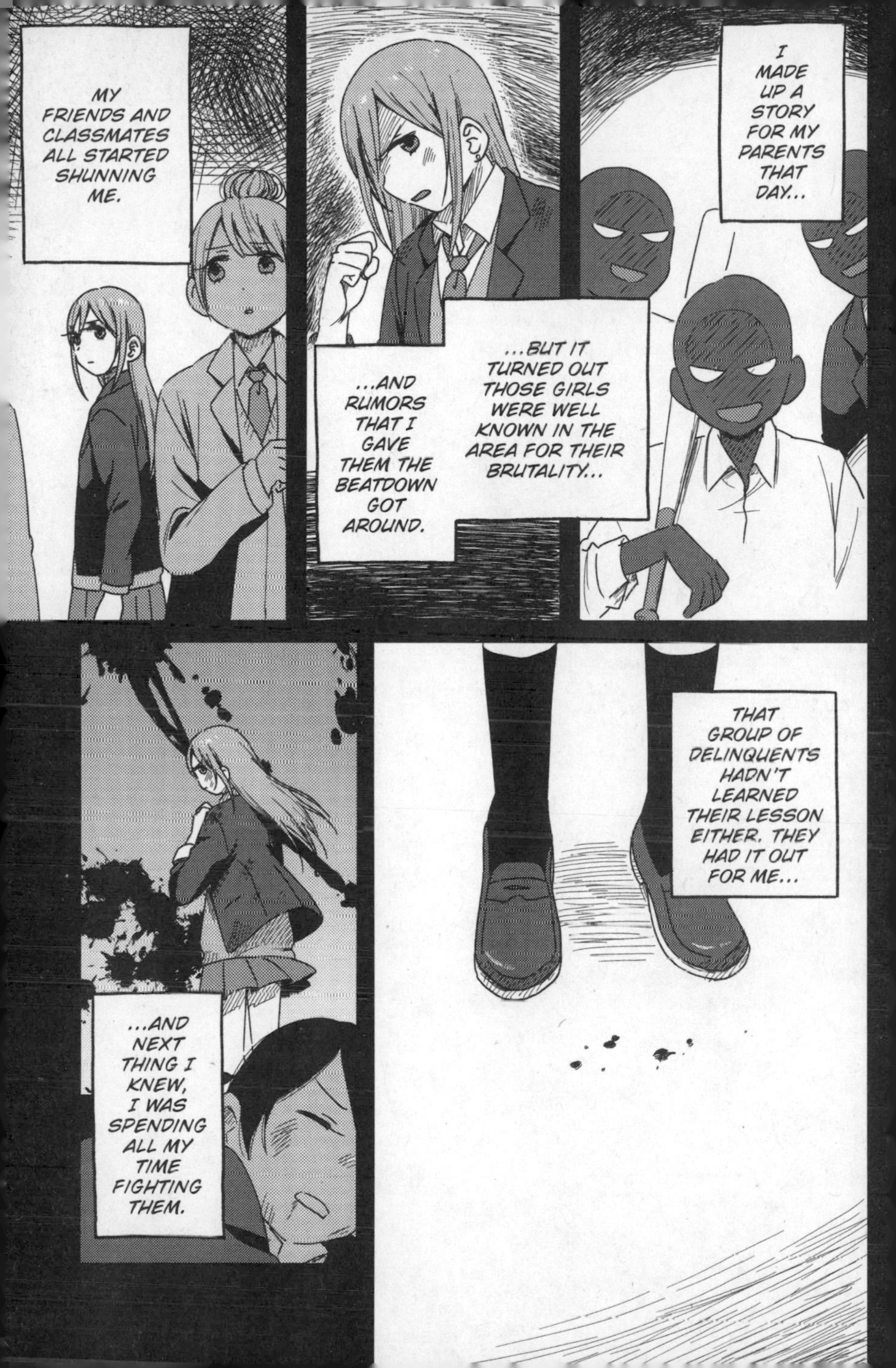
I MADE UP A STORY FOR MY PARENTS THAT DAY...
...BUT IT TURNED OUT THOSE GIRLS WERE WELL KNOWN IN THE AREA FOR THEIR BRUTALITY...
...AND RUMORS THAT I GAVE THEM THE BEATDOWN GOT AROUND.
MY FRIENDS AND CLASSMATES ALL STARTED SHUNNING ME.
THAT GROUP OF DELINQUENTS HADN'T LEARNED THEIR LESSON EITHER. THEY HAD IT OUT FOR ME...
...AND NEXT THING I KNEW, I WAS SPENDING ALL MY TIME FIGHTING THEM.

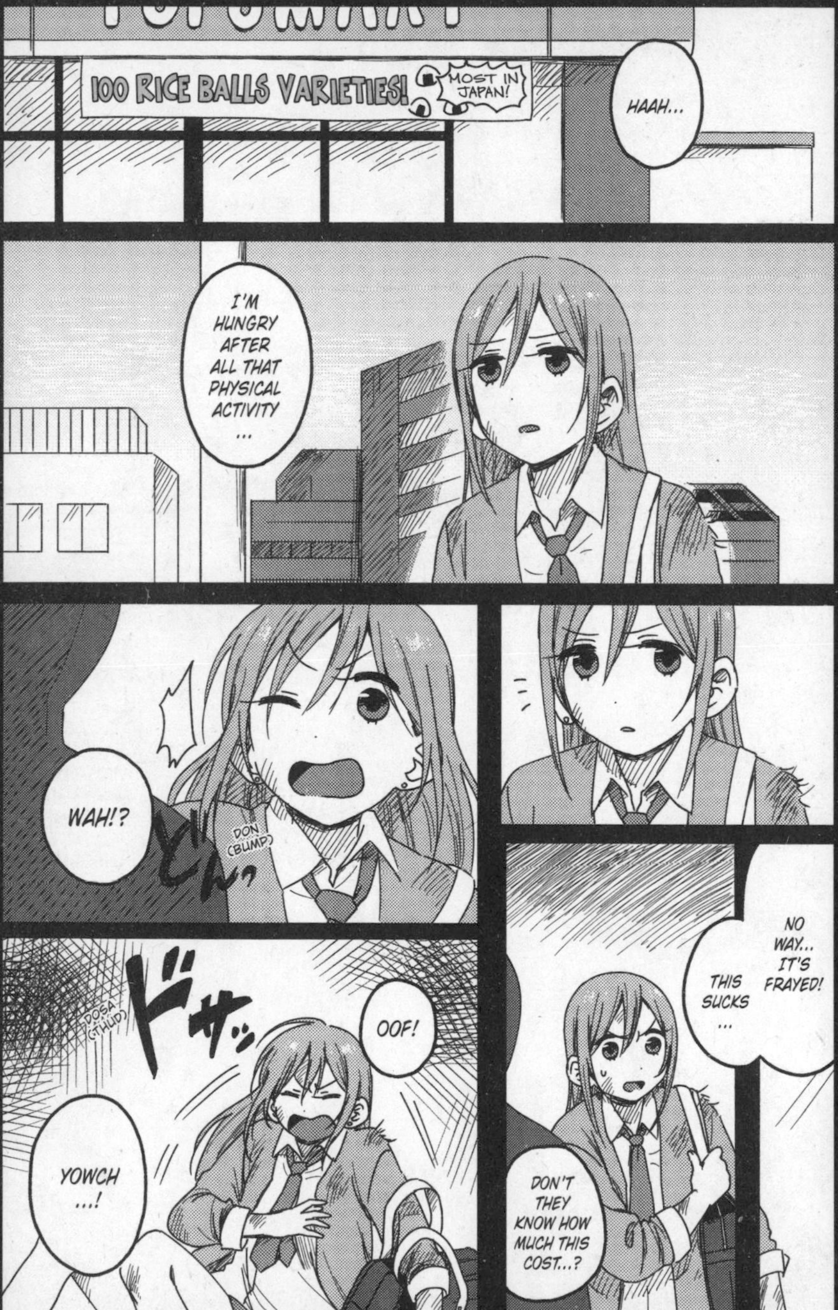
HAAH...
100 RICE BALLS VARIETIES!
MOST IN JAPAN!
I'M HUNGRY AFTER ALL THAT PHYSICAL ACTIVITY ...
WAH!?
DON (BUMP)
DOSA (THUD)
OOF!
YOWCH ...!
NO WAY... IT'S FRAYED!
THIS SUCKS ...
DON'T THEY KNOW HOW MUCH THIS COST...?

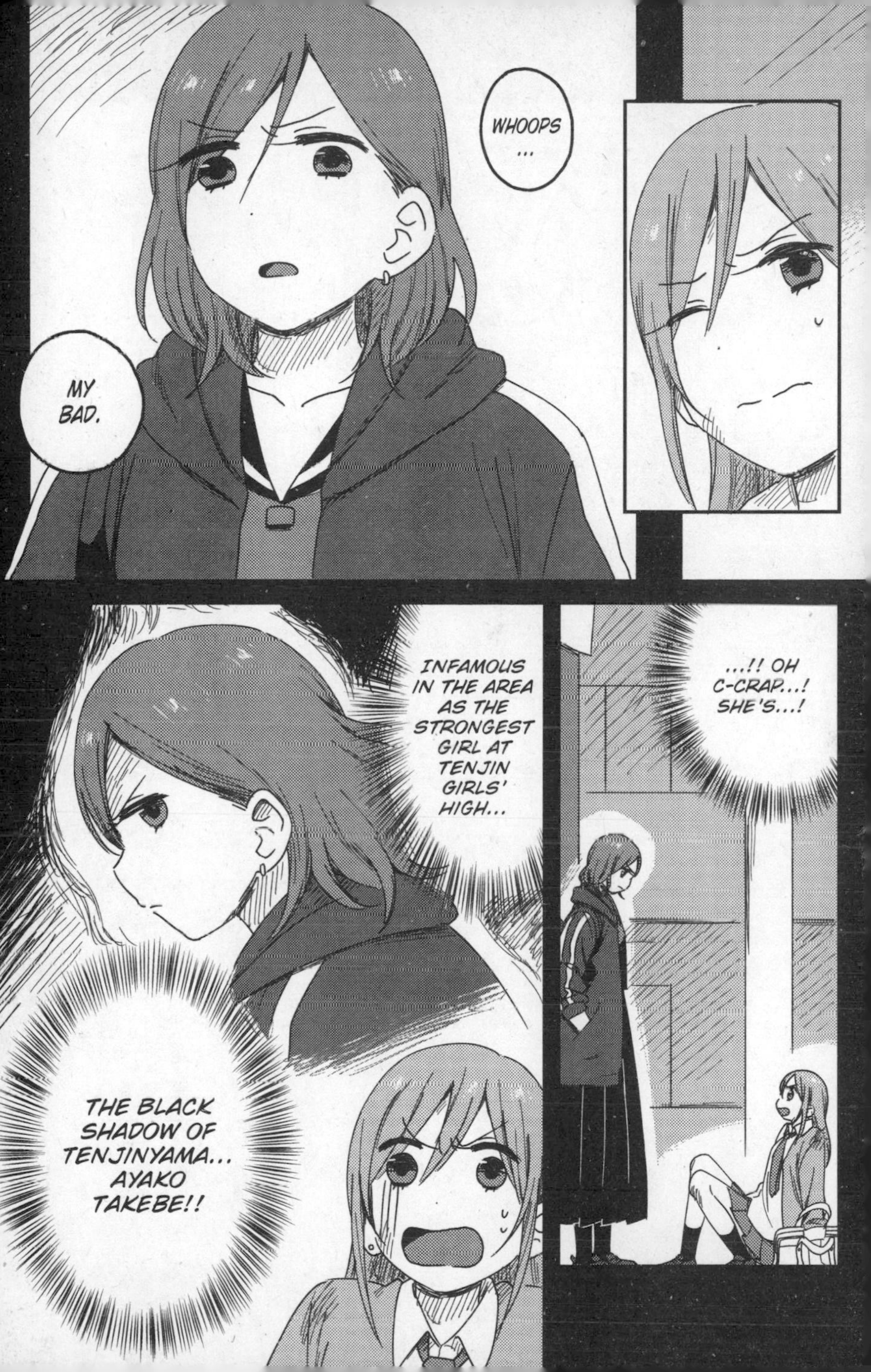
WHOOPS ...
MY BAD.
...!! OH C-CRAP...! SHE'S...!
INFAMOUS IN THE AREA AS THE STRONGEST GIRL AT TENJIN GIRLS' HIGH...
THE BLACK SHADOW OF TENJINYAMA... AYAKO TAKEBE!!

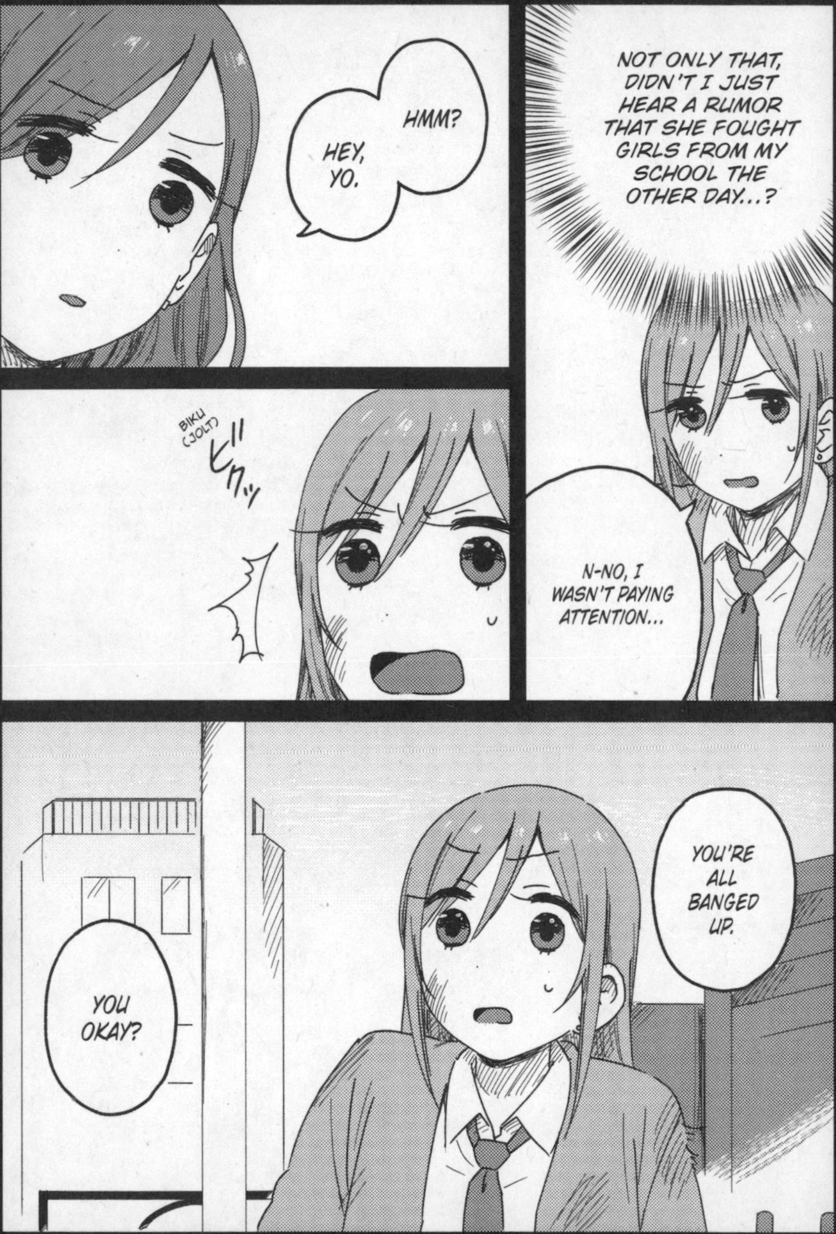
NOT ONLY THAT, DIDN'T I JUST HEAR A RUMOR THAT SHE FOUGHT GIRLS FROM MY SCHOOL THE OTHER DAY...?
N-NO, I WASN'T PAYING ATTENTION...
HMM?
HEY, YO.
BIKU (JOLT)
ビクッ
YOU'RE ALL BANGED UP.
YOU OKAY?

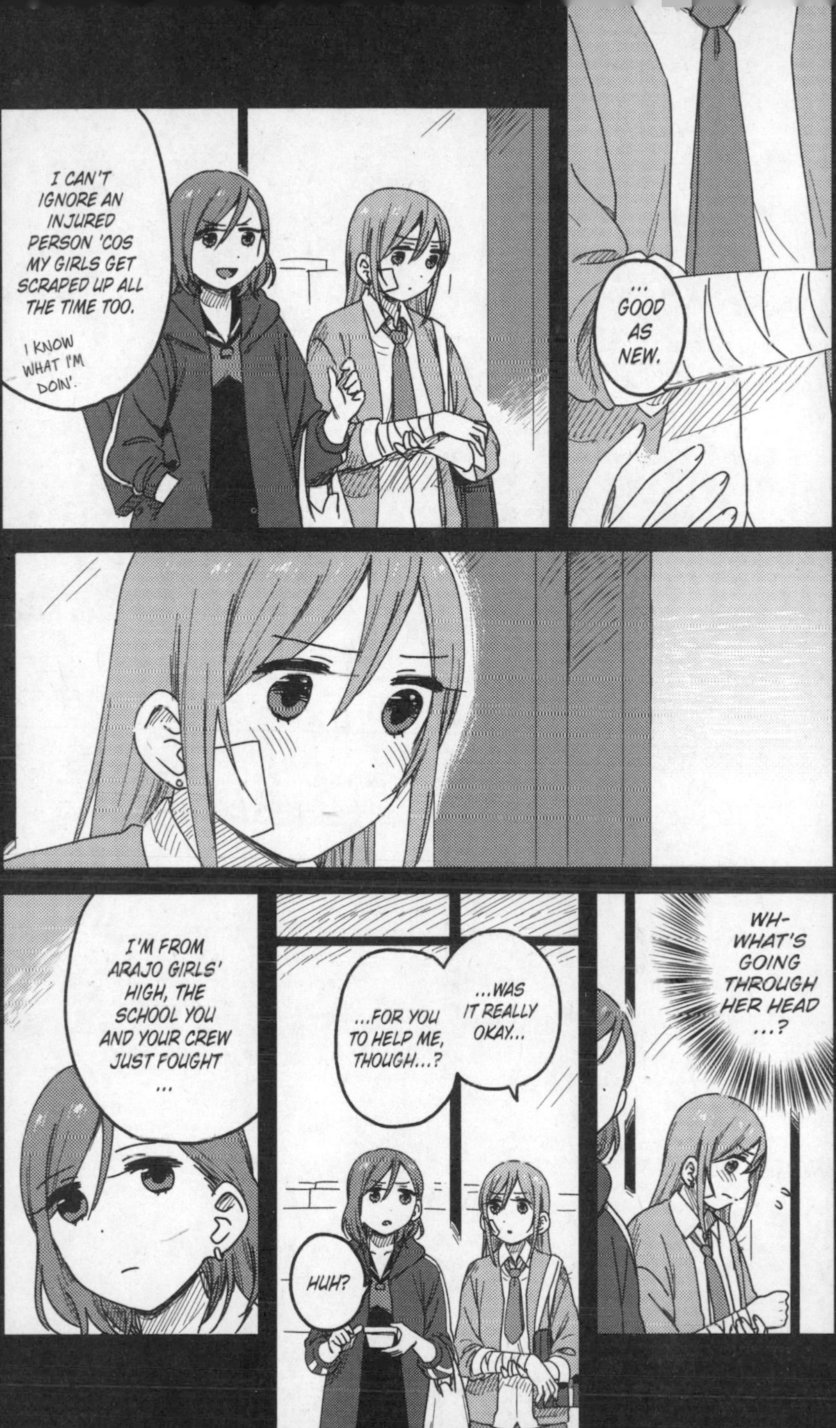
...GOOD AS NEW.
I CAN'T IGNORE AN INJURED PERSON 'COS MY GIRLS GET SCRAPED UP ALL THE TIME TOO.
I KNOW WHAT I'M DOIN'.
WH- WHAT'S GOING THROUGH HER HEAD...?
...WAS IT REALLY OKAY...
...FOR YOU TO HELP ME, THOUGH...?
HUH?
I'M FROM ARAJO GIRLS' HIGH, THE SCHOOL YOU AND YOUR CREW JUST FOUGHT...

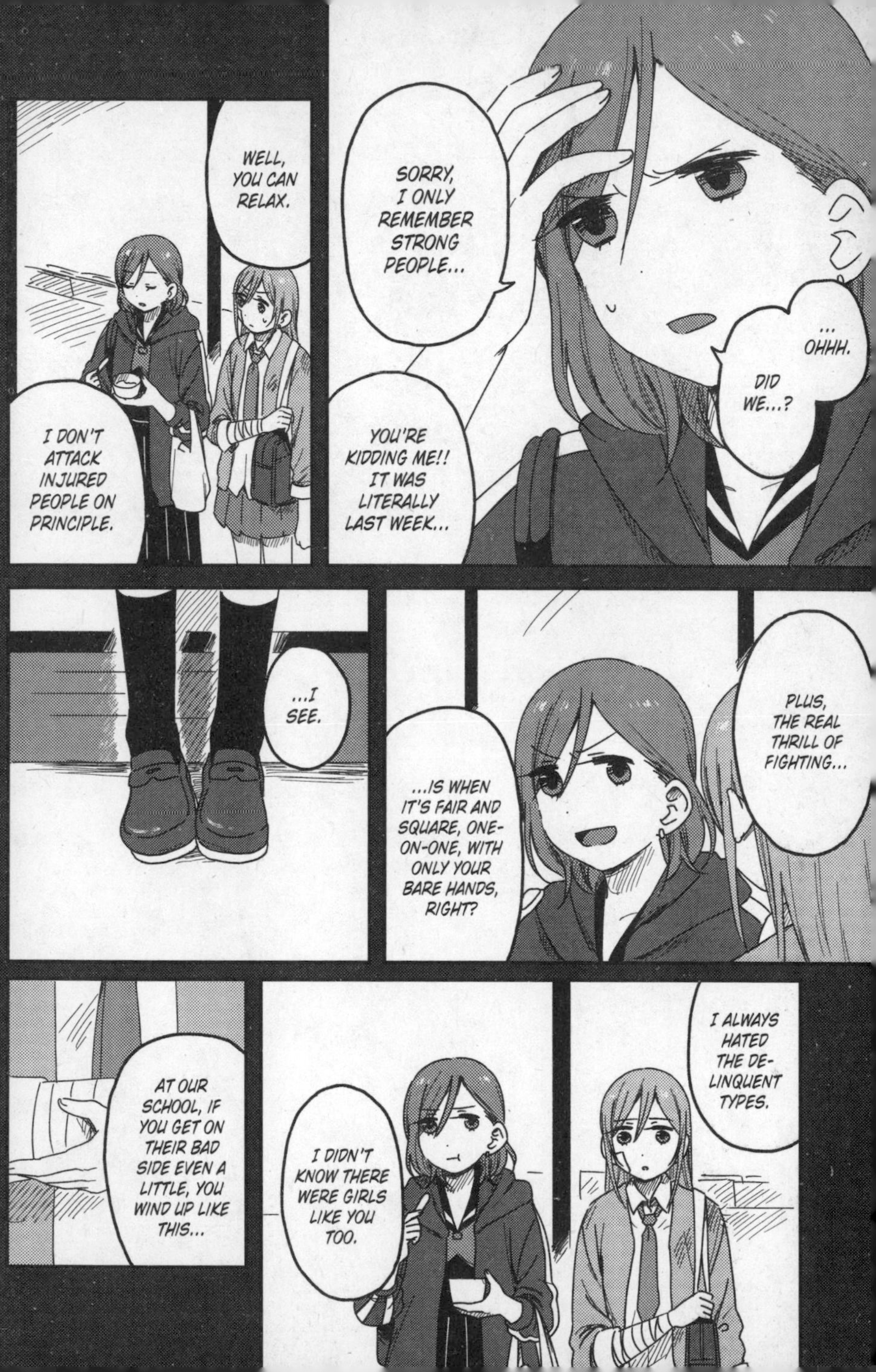
...OHHH.
DID WE...?
YOU'RE KIDDING ME!! IT WAS LITERALLY LAST WEEK...
SORRY, I ONLY REMEMBER STRONG PEOPLE...
WELL, YOU CAN RELAX.
I DON'T ATTACK INJURED PEOPLE ON PRINCIPLE.
PLUS, THE REAL THRILL OF FIGHTING...
...IS WHEN IT'S FAIR AND SQUARE, ONE-ON-ONE, WITH ONLY YOUR BARE HANDS, RIGHT?
...I SEE.
I ALWAYS HATED THE DE-LINQUENT TYPES.
I DIDN'T KNOW THERE WERE GIRLS LIKE YOU TOO.
AT OUR SCHOOL, IF YOU GET ON THEIR BAD SIDE EVEN A LITTLE, YOU WIND UP LIKE THIS...

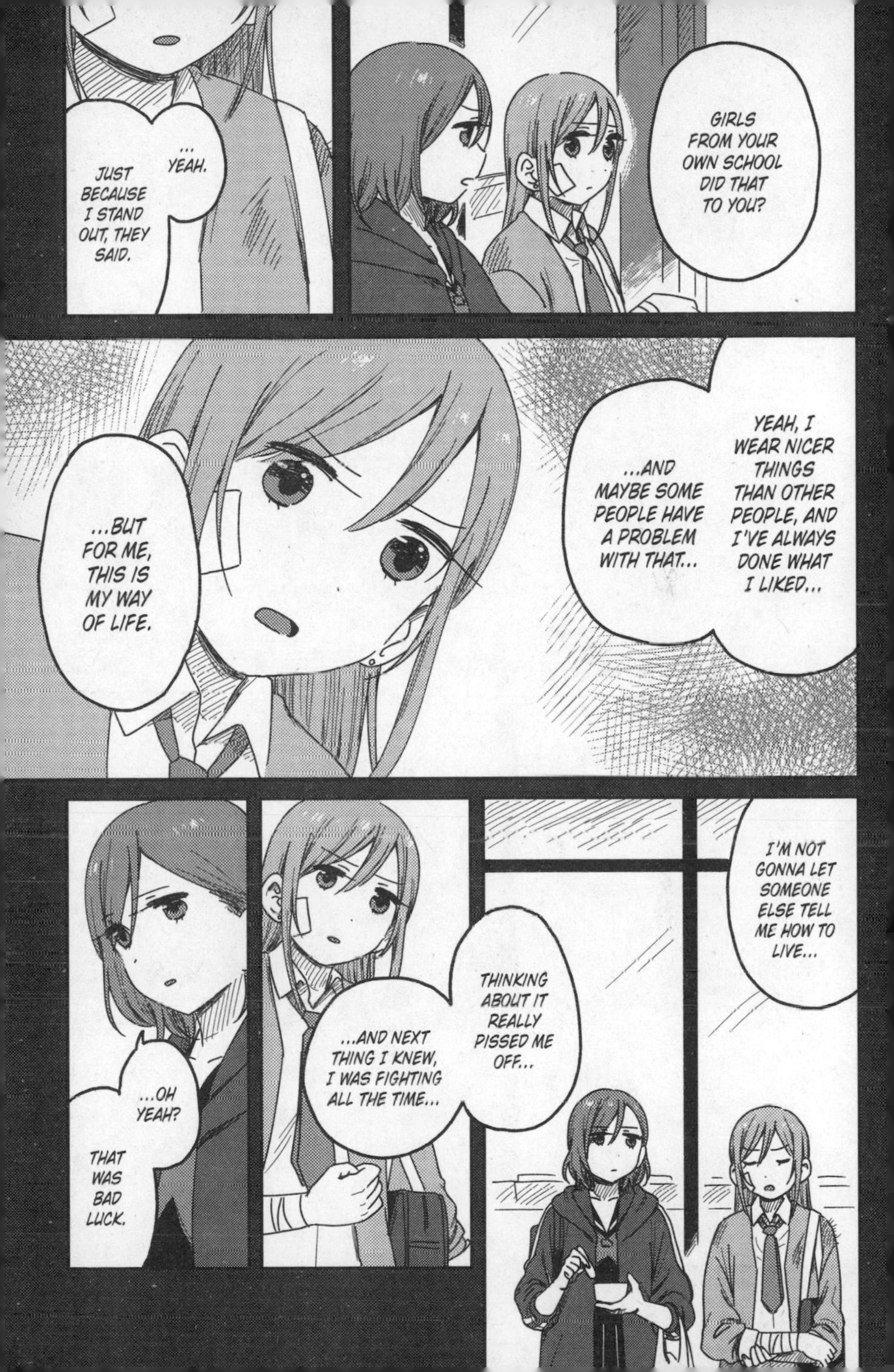
GIRLS FROM YOUR OWN SCHOOL DID THAT TO YOU?
...YEAH.
JUST BECAUSE I STAND OUT, THEY SAID.
YEAH, I WEAR NICER THINGS THAN OTHER PEOPLE, AND I'VE ALWAYS DONE WHAT I LIKED...
...AND MAYBE SOME PEOPLE HAVE A PROBLEM WITH THAT...
...BUT FOR ME, THIS IS MY WAY OF LIFE.
I'M NOT GONNA LET SOMEONE ELSE TELL ME HOW TO LIVE...
THINKING ABOUT IT REALLY PISSED ME OFF...
...AND NEXT THING I KNEW, I WAS FIGHTING ALL THE TIME...
...OH YEAH?
THAT WAS BAD LUCK.

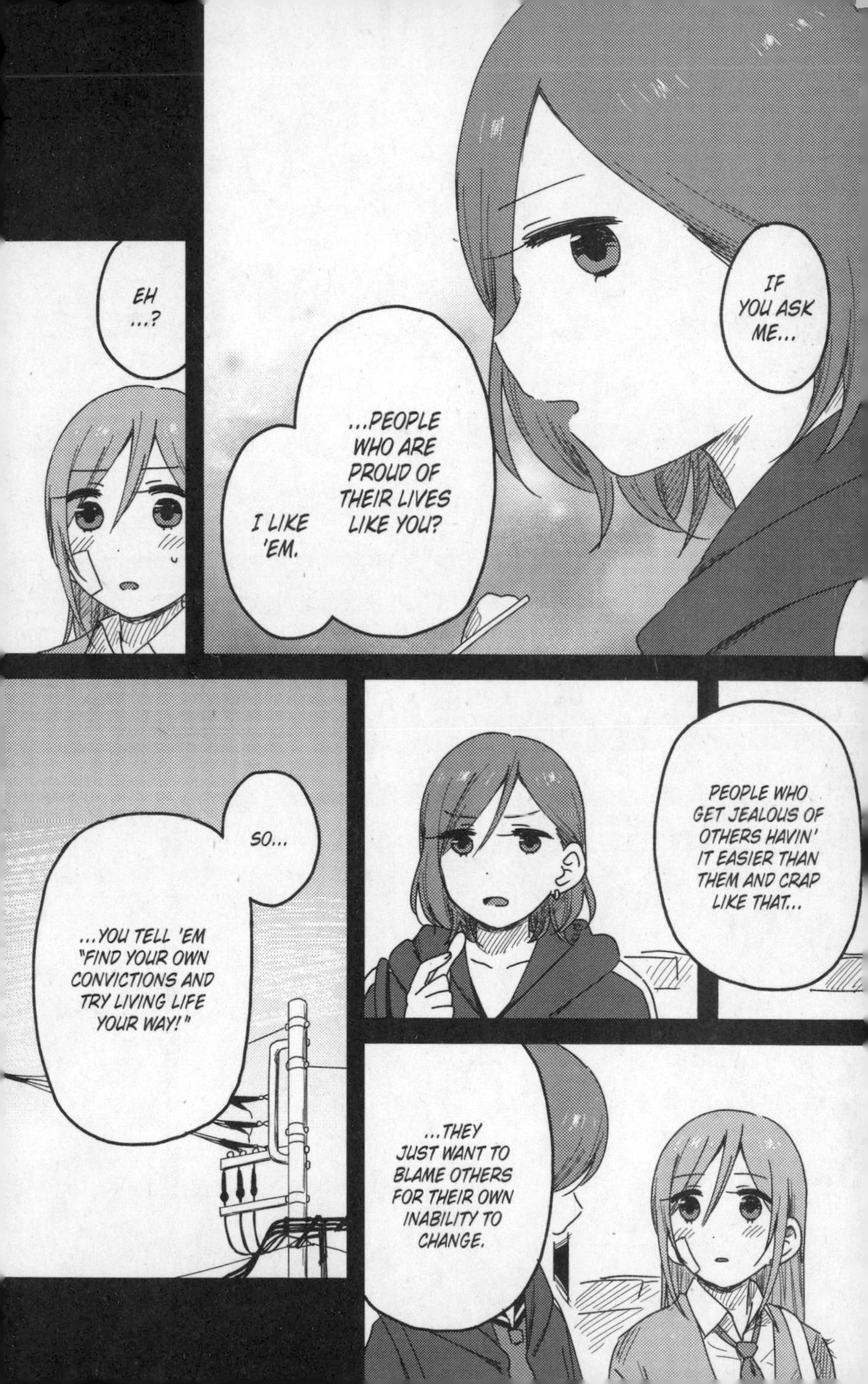
IF YOU ASK ME...
...PEOPLE WHO ARE PROUD OF THEIR LIVES LIKE YOU?
I LIKE 'EM.
EH ...?
PEOPLE WHO GET JEALOUS OF OTHERS HAVIN' IT EASIER THAN THEM AND CRAP LIKE THAT...
...THEY JUST WANT TO BLAME OTHERS FOR THEIR OWN INABILITY TO CHANGE.
SO...
...YOU TELL 'EM "FIND YOUR OWN CONVICTIONS AND TRY LIVING LIFE YOUR WAY!"

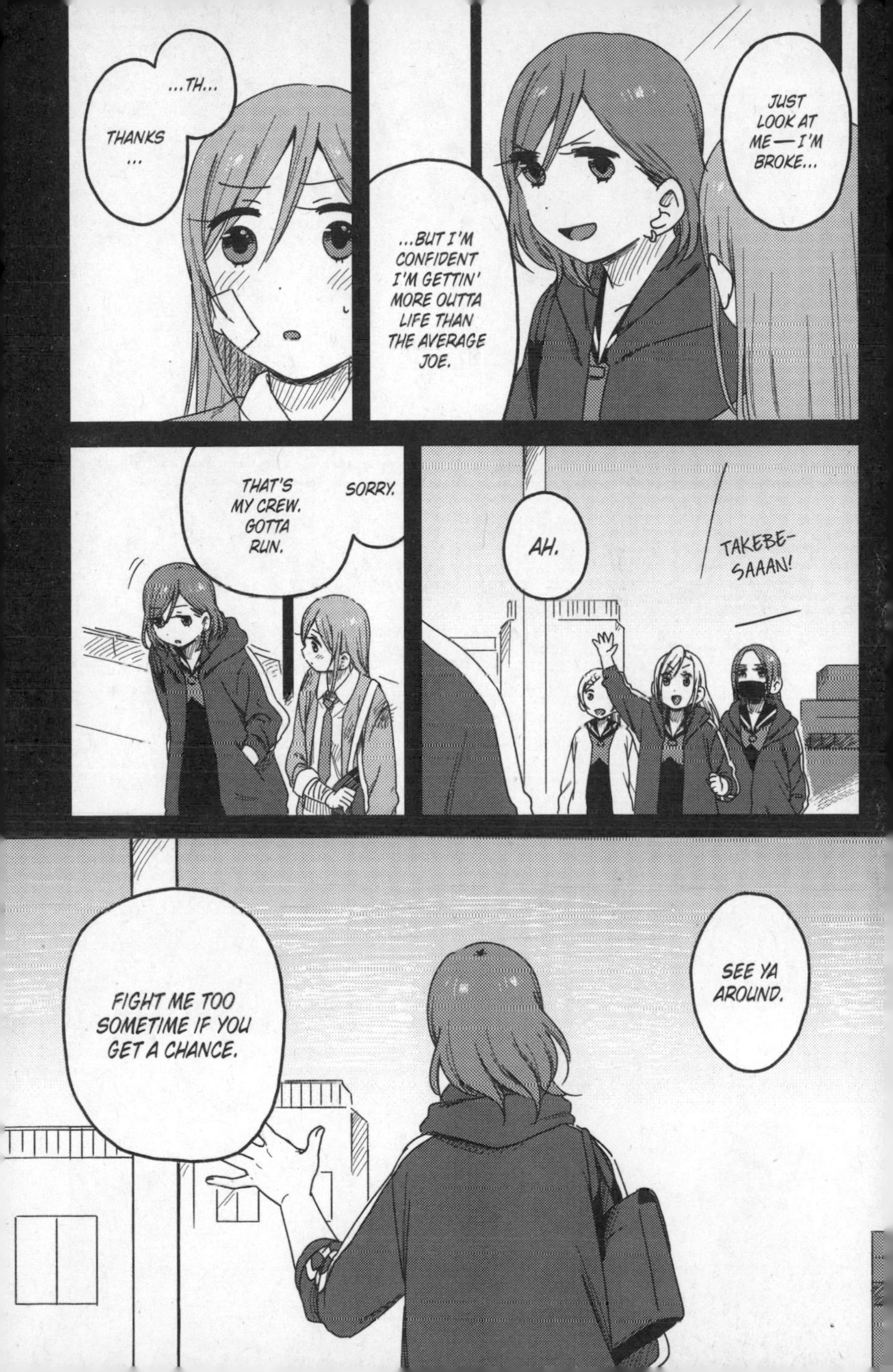
JUST LOOK AT ME—I'M BROKE...
...BUT I'M CONFIDENT I'M GETTIN' MORE OUTTA LIFE THAN THE AVERAGE JOE.
...TH...
THANKS ...
TAKEBE-SAAAN!
AH.
SORRY.
THAT'S MY CREW. GOTTA RUN.
SEE YA AROUND.
FIGHT ME TOO SOMETIME IF YOU GET A CHANCE.

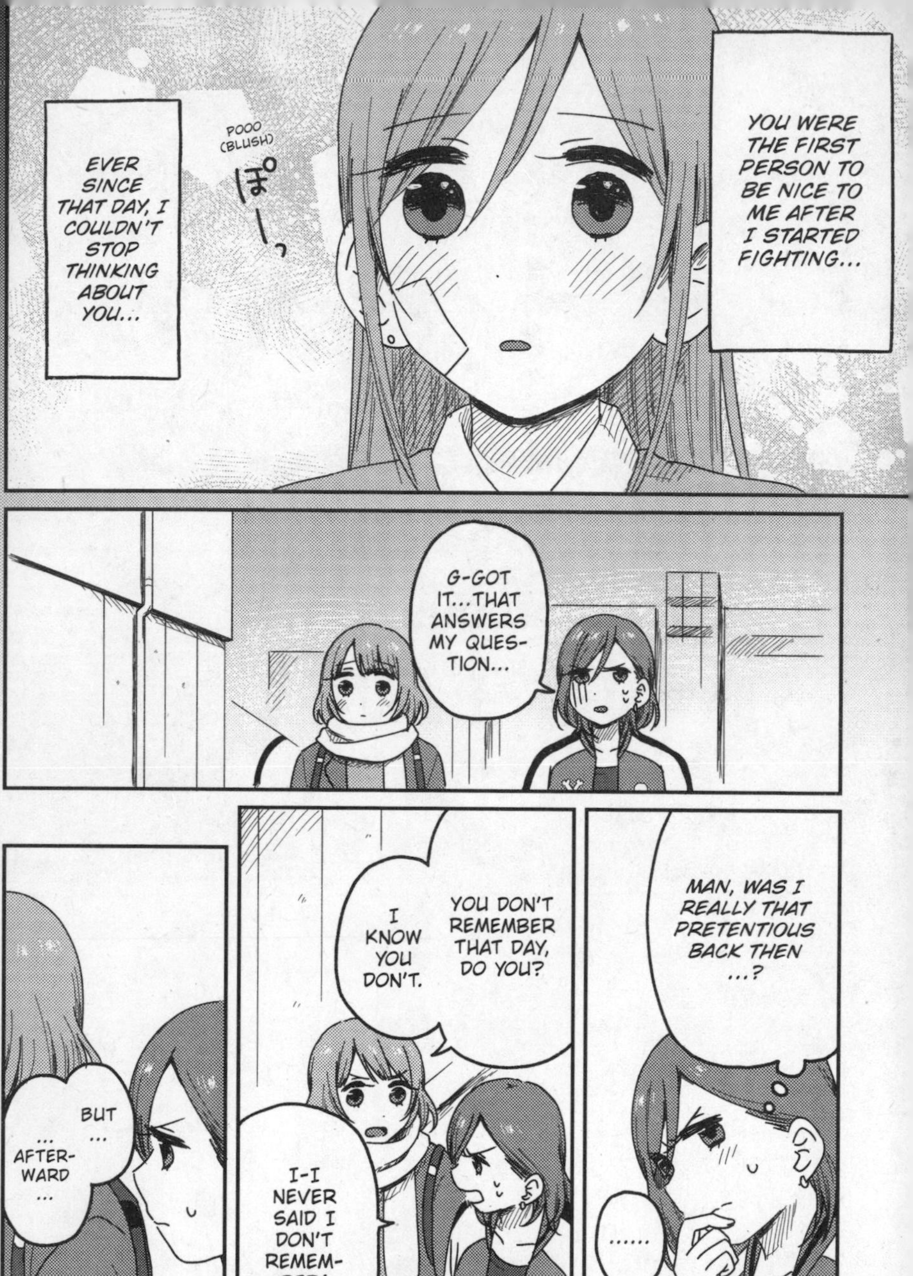
YOU WERE THE FIRST PERSON TO BE NICE TO ME AFTER I STARTED FIGHTING...
POOO (BLUSH)
ぽーっ
EVER SINCE THAT DAY, I COULDN'T STOP THINKING ABOUT YOU...
G-GOT IT...THAT ANSWERS MY QUES-TION...
MAN, WAS I REALLY THAT PRETENTIOUS BACK THEN ...?
......
YOU DON'T REMEMBER THAT DAY, DO YOU?
I KNOW YOU DON'T.
I-I NEVER SAID I DON'T REMEM-BER!
BUT ...
... AFTER-WARD ...

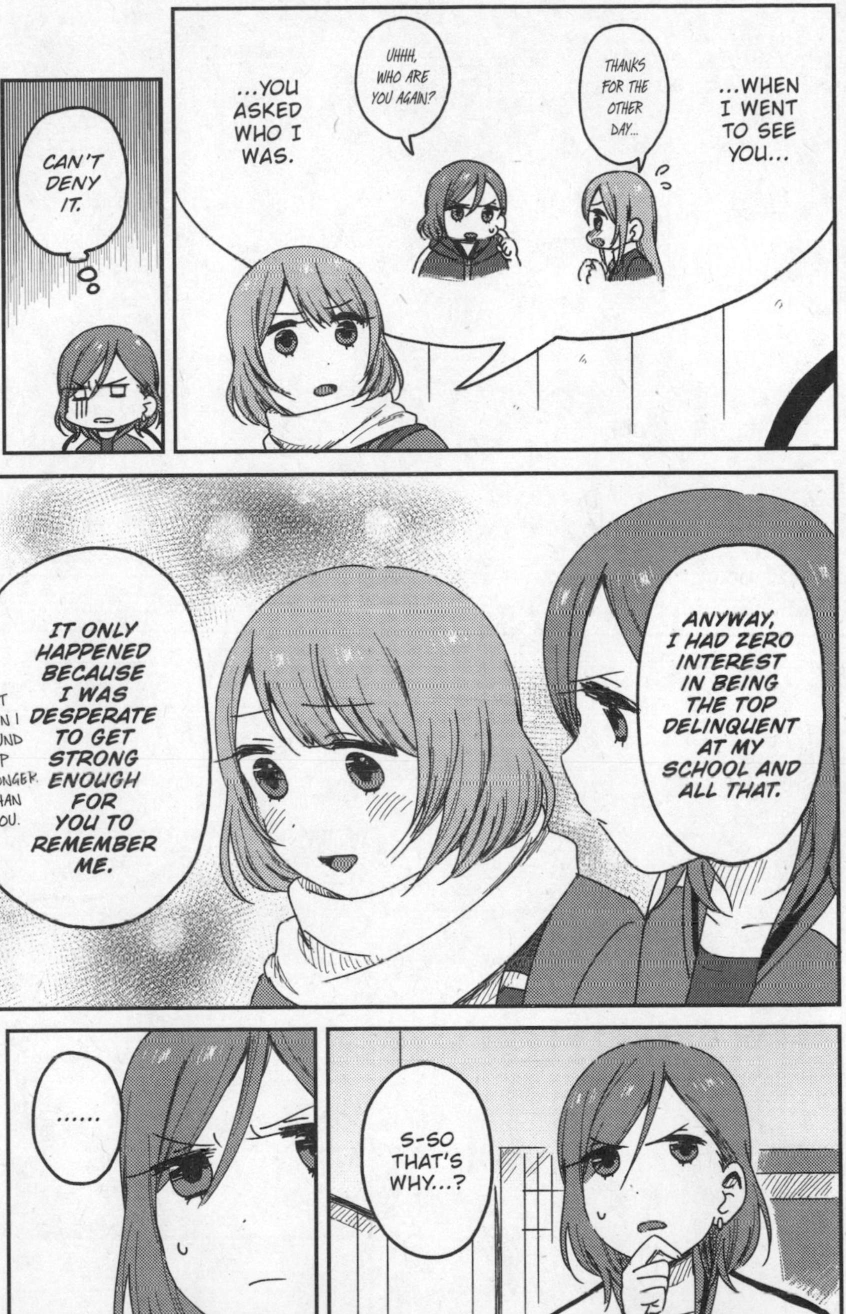
...WHEN I WENT TO SEE YOU...
THANKS FOR THE OTHER DAY...
UHHH, WHO ARE YOU AGAIN?
...YOU ASKED WHO I WAS.
CAN'T DENY IT.
ANYWAY, I HAD ZERO INTEREST IN BEING THE TOP DELINQUENT AT MY SCHOOL AND ALL THAT.
IT ONLY HAPPENED BECAUSE I WAS DESPERATE TO GET STRONG ENOUGH FOR YOU TO REMEMBER ME.
BUT THEN I WOUND UP STRONGER THAN YOU.
S-SO THAT'S WHY...?
......

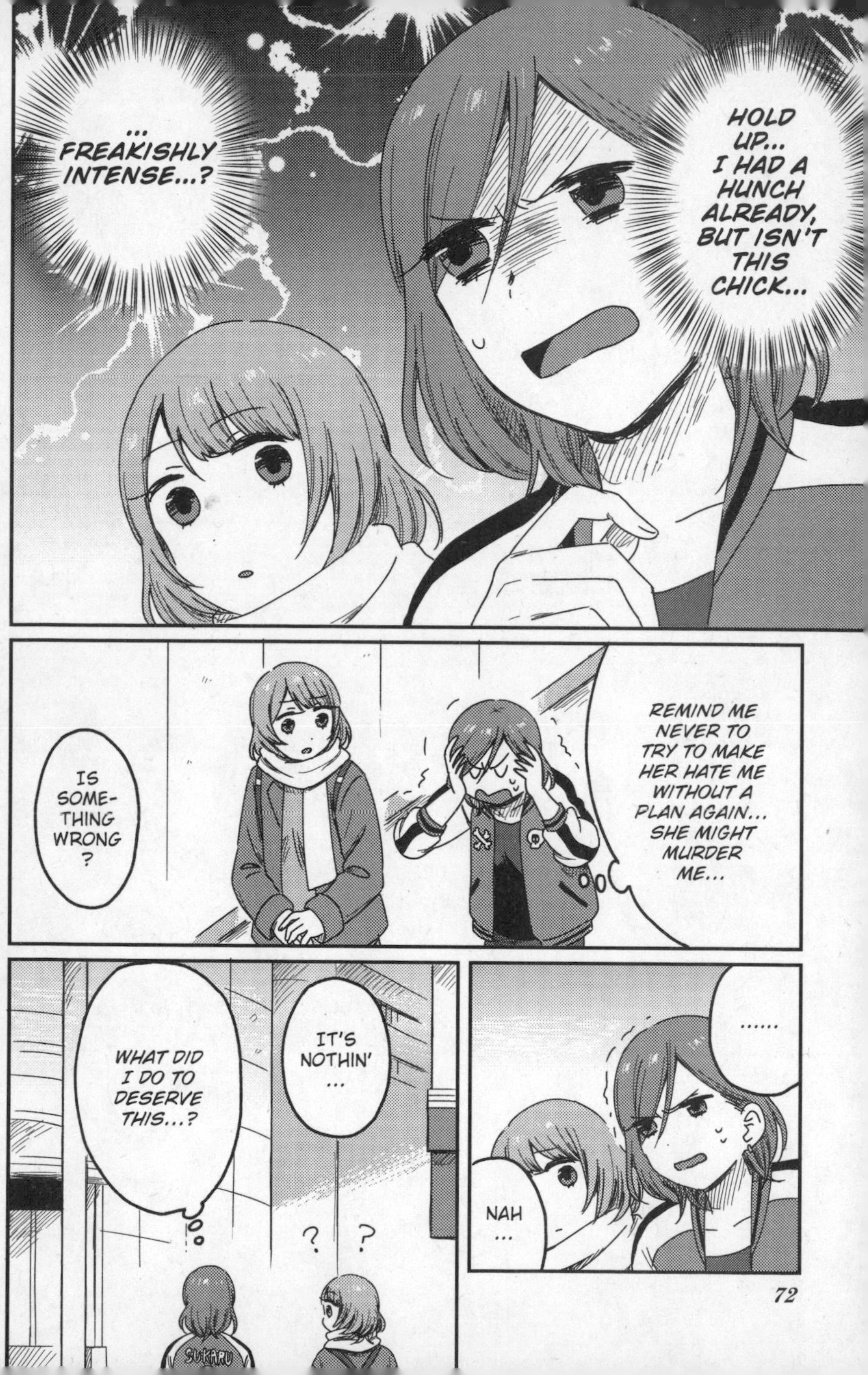
HOLD UP... I HAD A HUNCH ALREADY, BUT ISN'T THIS CHICK...
...FREAKISHLY INTENSE...?
REMIND ME NEVER TO TRY TO MAKE HER HATE ME WITHOUT A PLAN AGAIN... SHE MIGHT MURDER ME...
IS SOME-THING WRONG?
......
NAH...
IT'S NOTHIN'...
WHAT DID I DO TO DESERVE THIS...?
? ?

Catch These Hands!

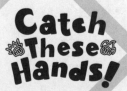

Catch These Hands!

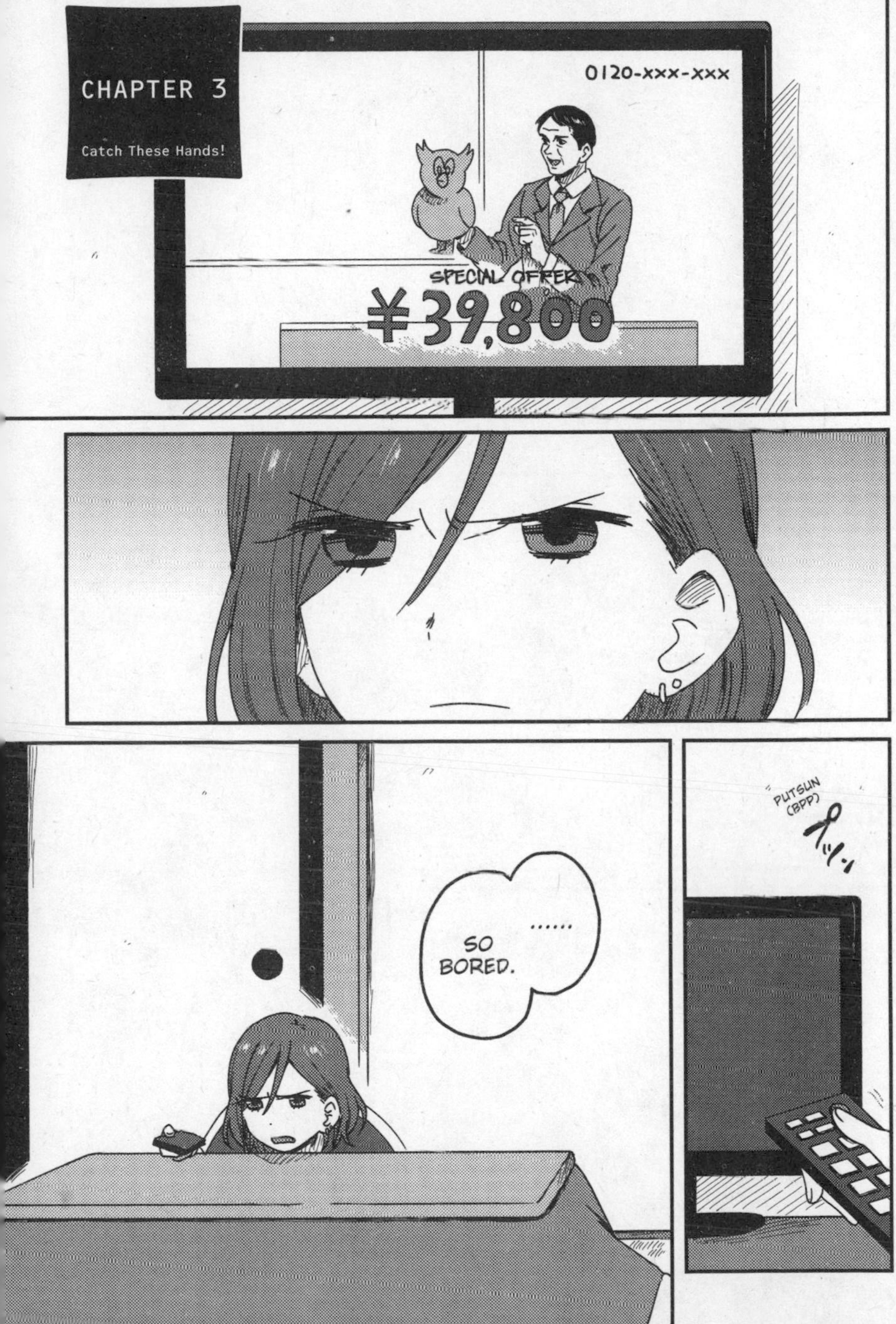
CHAPTER 3
Catch These Hands!
0120-xxx-xxx
SPECIAL OFFER
¥39,800
PUTSUN (BPP)
...... SO BORED.

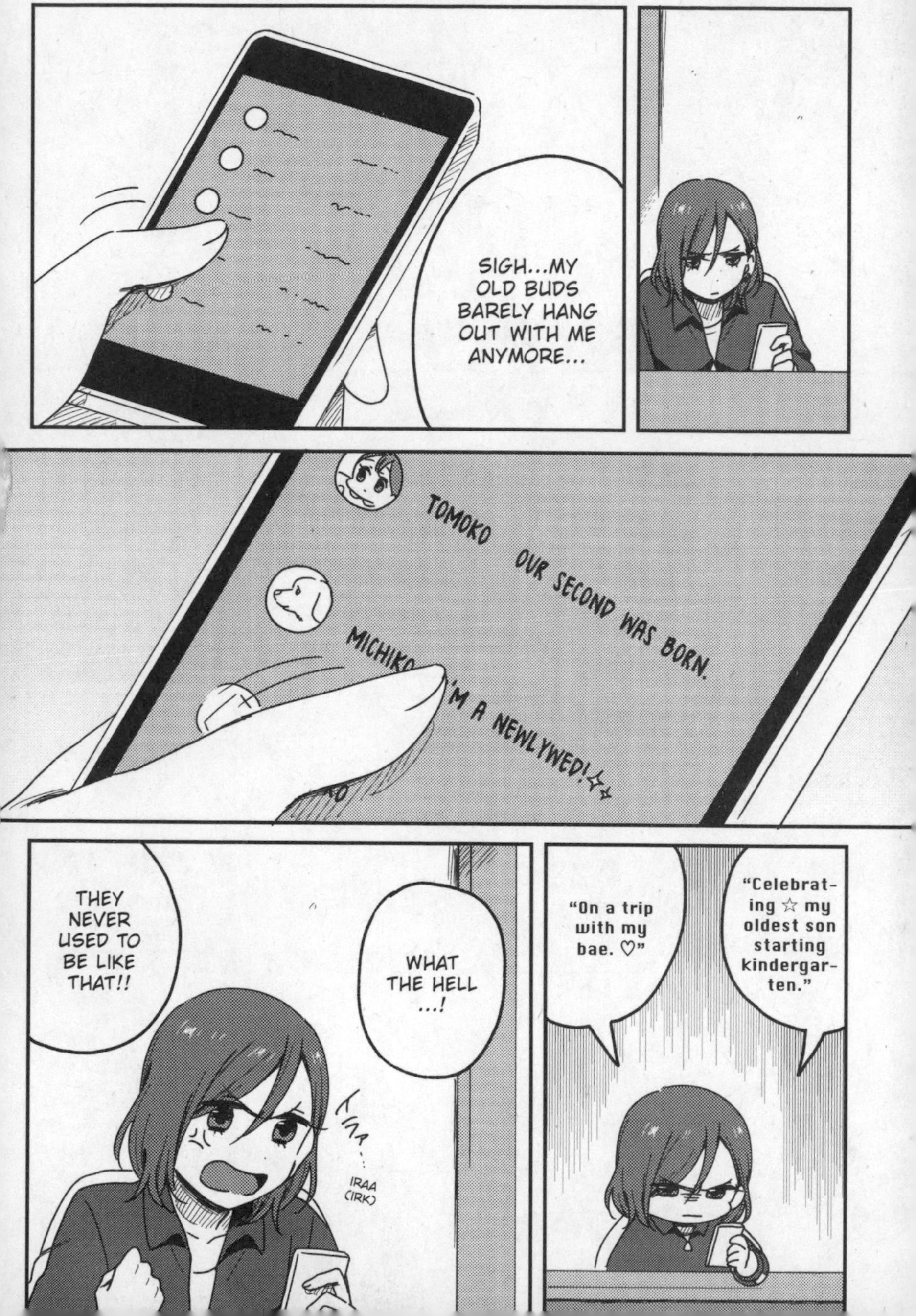
SIGH...MY OLD BUDS BARELY HANG OUT WITH ME ANYMORE...
TOMOKO
OUR SECOND WAS BORN.
MICHIKO
'M A NEWLYWED!☆☆
"Celebrat-ing ☆ my oldest son starting kindergar-ten."
"On a trip with my bae. ♡"
WHAT THE HELL ...!
IRAA (IRK)
THEY NEVER USED TO BE LIKE THAT!!

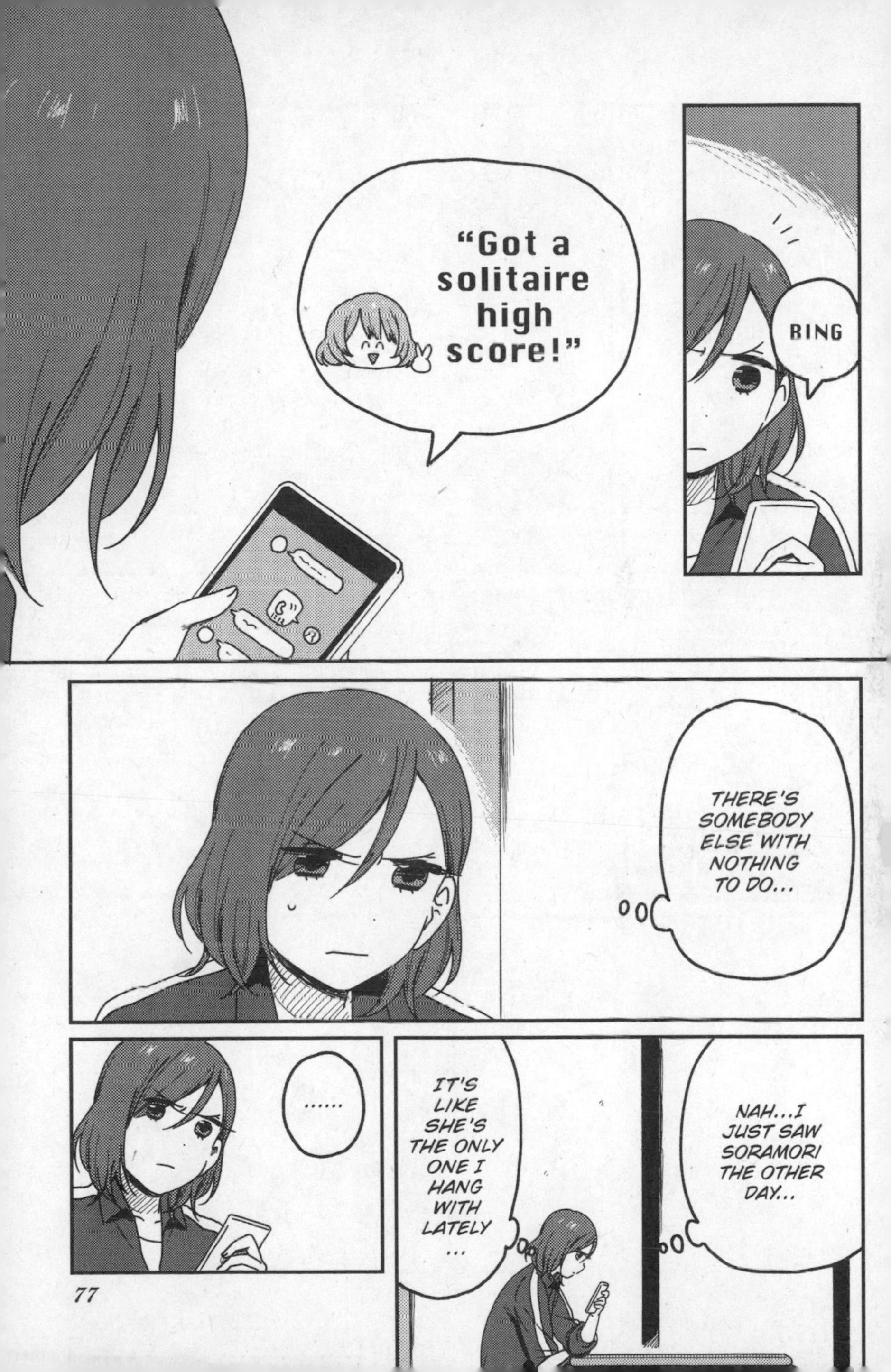
BING
"Got a solitaire high score!"
THERE'S SOMEBODY ELSE WITH NOTHING TO DO...
NAH...I JUST SAW SORAMORI THE OTHER DAY...
IT'S LIKE SHE'S THE ONLY ONE I HANG WITH LATELY...
......

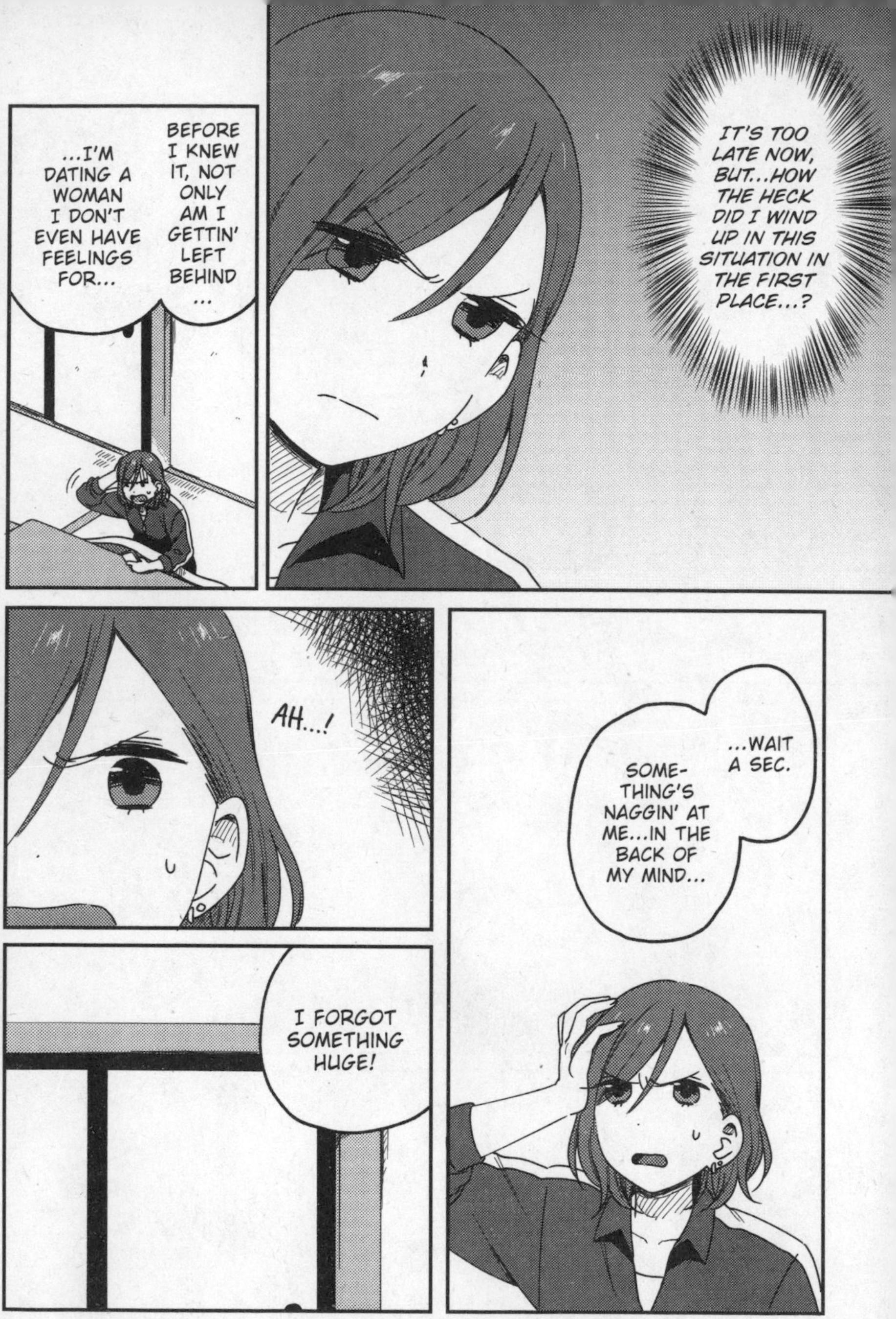
IT'S TOO LATE NOW, BUT...HOW THE HECK DID I WIND UP IN THIS SITUATION IN THE FIRST PLACE...?
BEFORE I KNEW IT, NOT ONLY AM I GETTIN' LEFT BEHIND...
...I'M DATING A WOMAN I DON'T EVEN HAVE FEELINGS FOR...
...WAIT A SEC.
SOME-THING'S NAGGIN' AT ME...IN THE BACK OF MY MIND...
AH...!
I FORGOT SOMETHING HUGE!

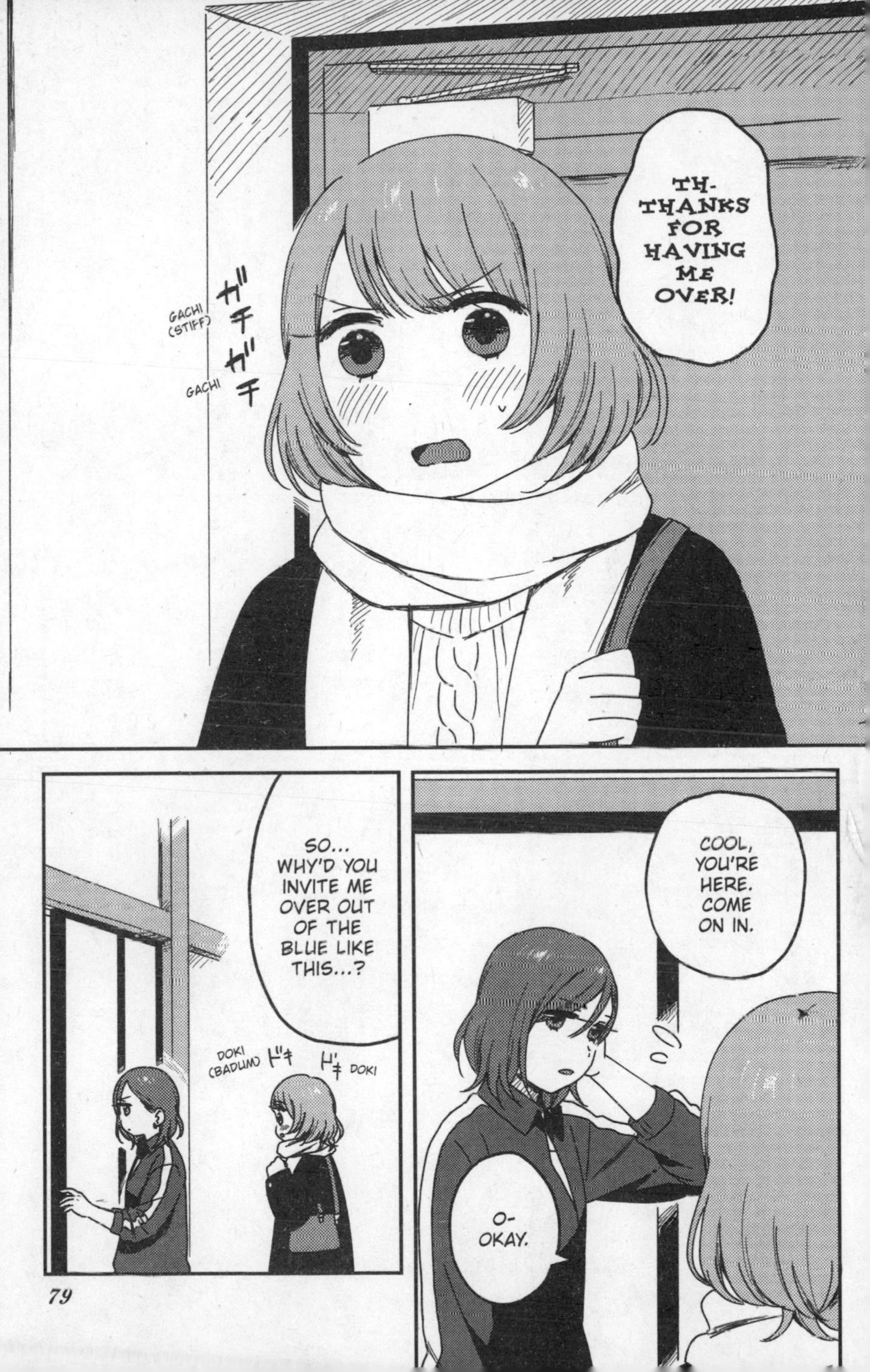
TH- THANKS FOR HAVING ME OVER!
ガチ GACHI (STIFF)
ガチ GACHI
COOL, YOU'RE HERE. COME ON IN.
O- OKAY.
SO... WHY'D YOU INVITE ME OVER OUT OF THE BLUE LIKE THIS...?
ドキ DOKI (BADUM)
ドキ DOKI

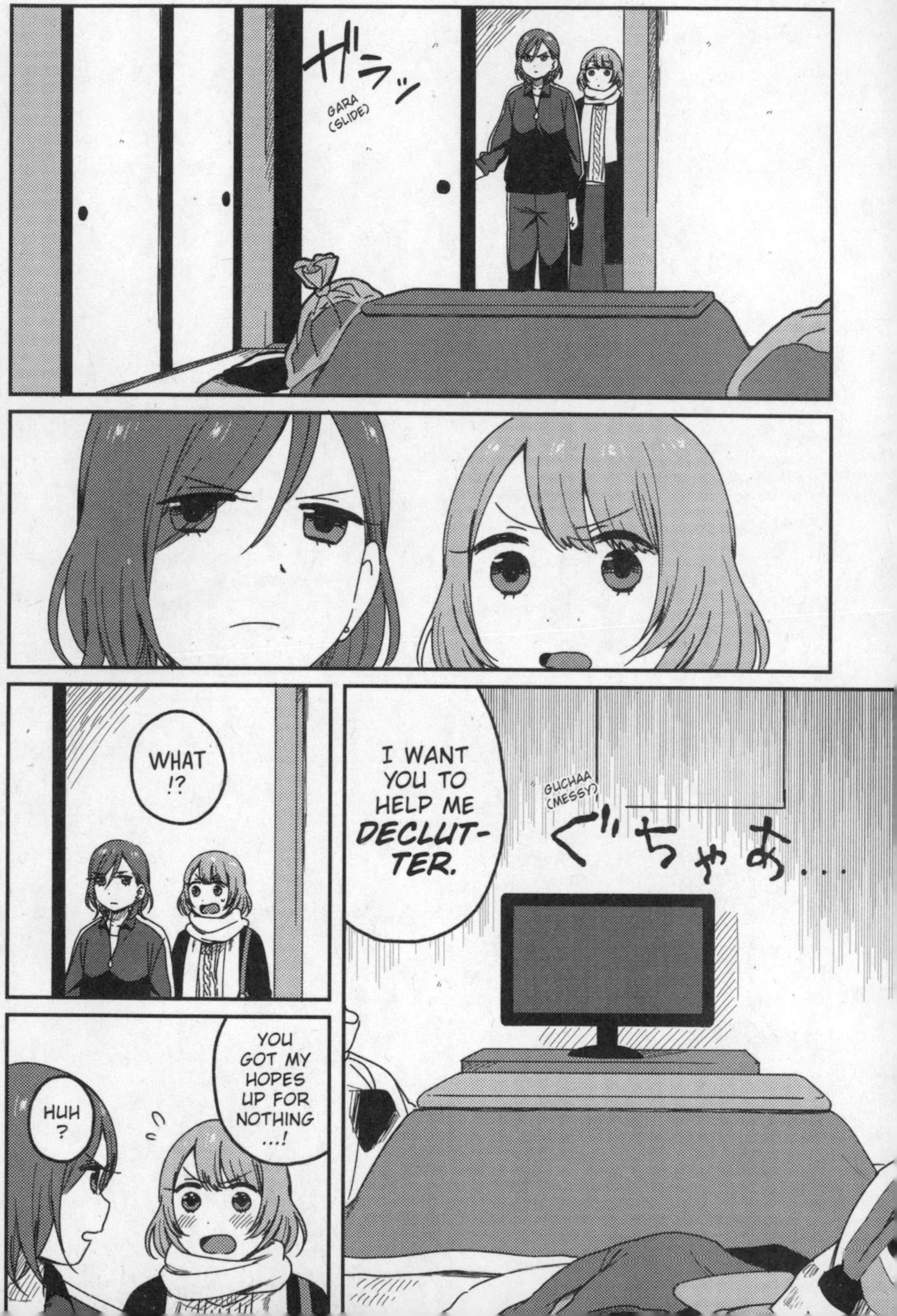
ガラッ
GARA (SLIDE)
I WANT YOU TO HELP ME DECLUTTER.
ぐちゃあ…
GUCHAA (MESSY)
WHAT!?
YOU GOT MY HOPES UP FOR NOTHING...!
HUH?

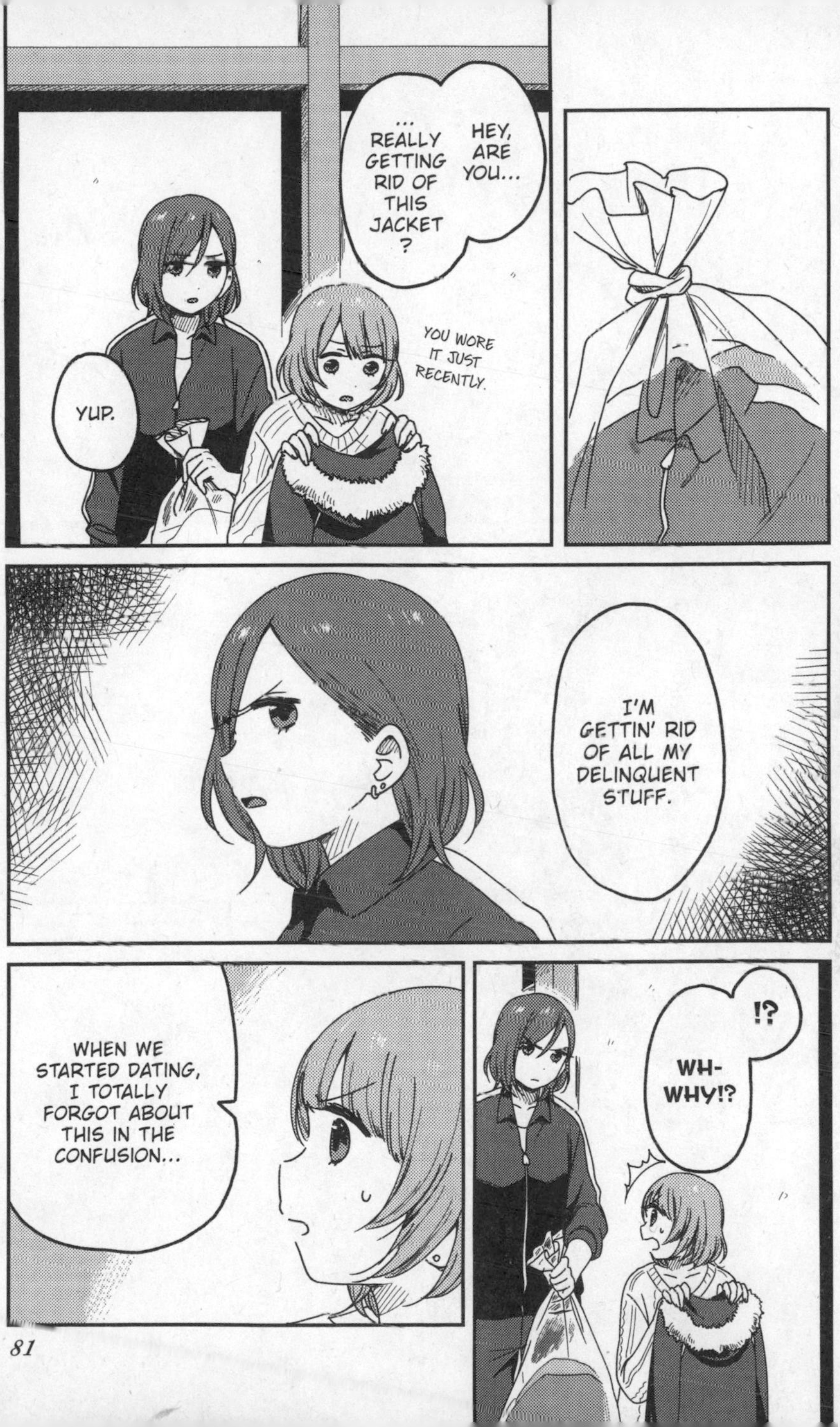
HEY, ARE YOU...
...REALLY GETTING RID OF THIS JACKET?
YOU WORE IT JUST RECENTLY.
YUP.
I'M GETTIN' RID OF ALL MY DELINQUENT STUFF.
!?
WH-WHY!?
WHEN WE STARTED DATING, I TOTALLY FORGOT ABOUT THIS IN THE CONFUSION...

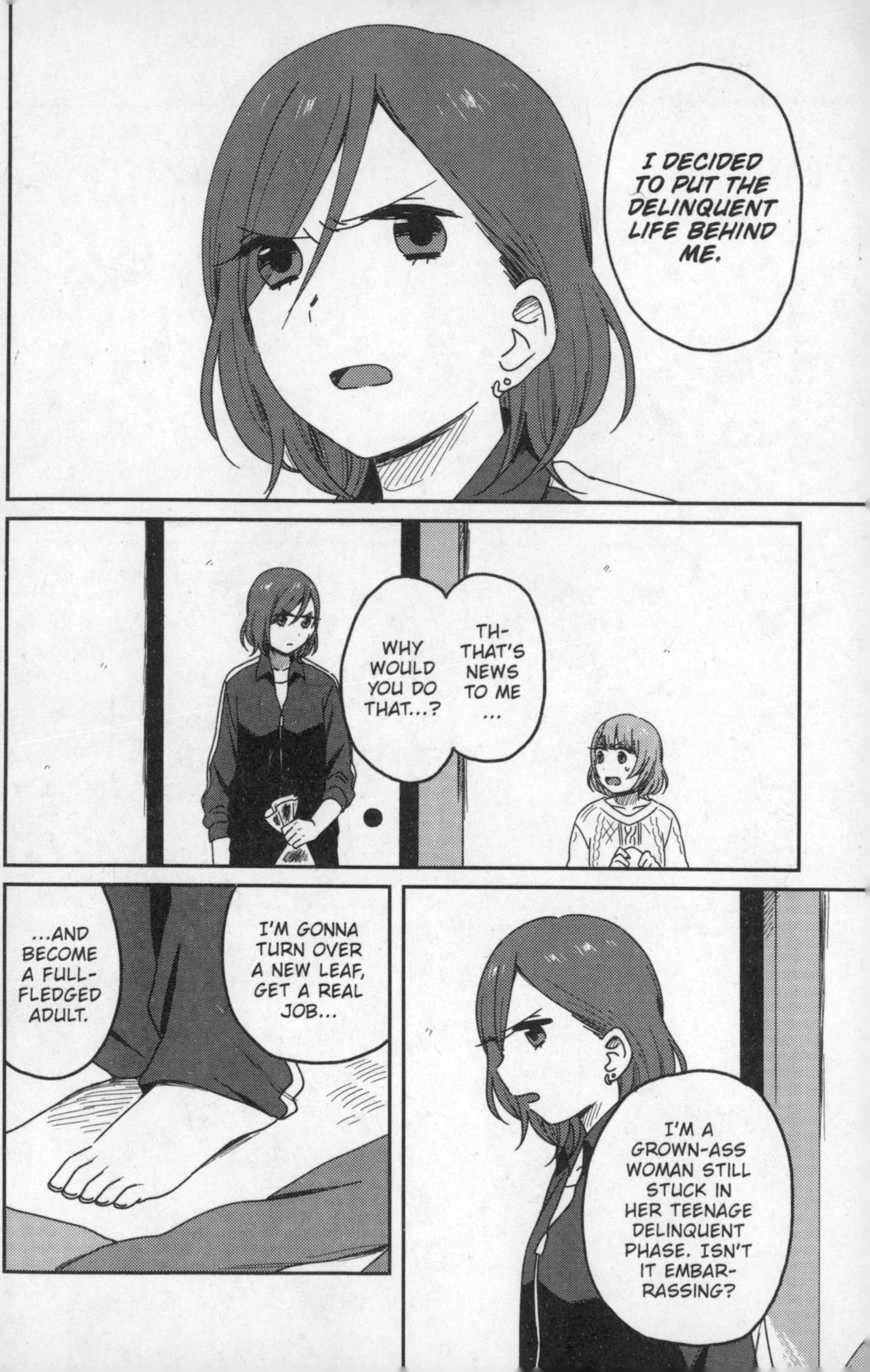
I DECIDED TO PUT THE DELINQUENT LIFE BEHIND ME.
TH-THAT'S NEWS TO ME...
WHY WOULD YOU DO THAT...?
I'M A GROWN-ASS WOMAN STILL STUCK IN HER TEENAGE DELINQUENT PHASE. ISN'T IT EMBARRASSING?
I'M GONNA TURN OVER A NEW LEAF, GET A REAL JOB...
...AND BECOME A FULL-FLEDGED ADULT.

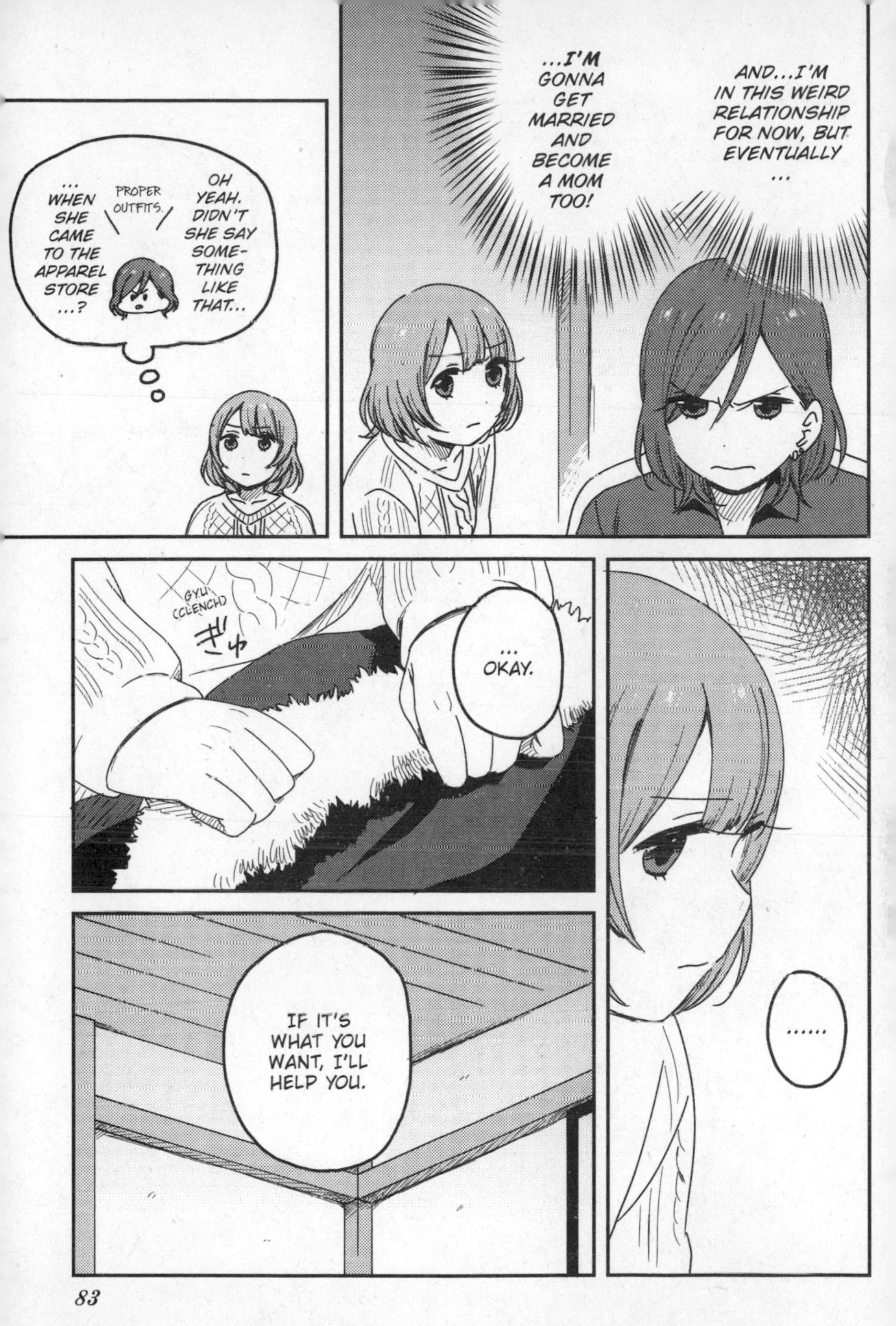
AND...I'M IN THIS WEIRD RELATIONSHIP FOR NOW, BUT EVENTUALLY ...
...I'M GONNA GET MARRIED AND BECOME A MOM TOO!
OH YEAH. DIDN'T SHE SAY SOMETHING LIKE THAT...
PROPER OUTFITS.
...WHEN SHE CAME TO THE APPAREL STORE ...?
......
GYU (CLENCH)
ぎゅ
...OKAY.
IF IT'S WHAT YOU WANT, I'LL HELP YOU.

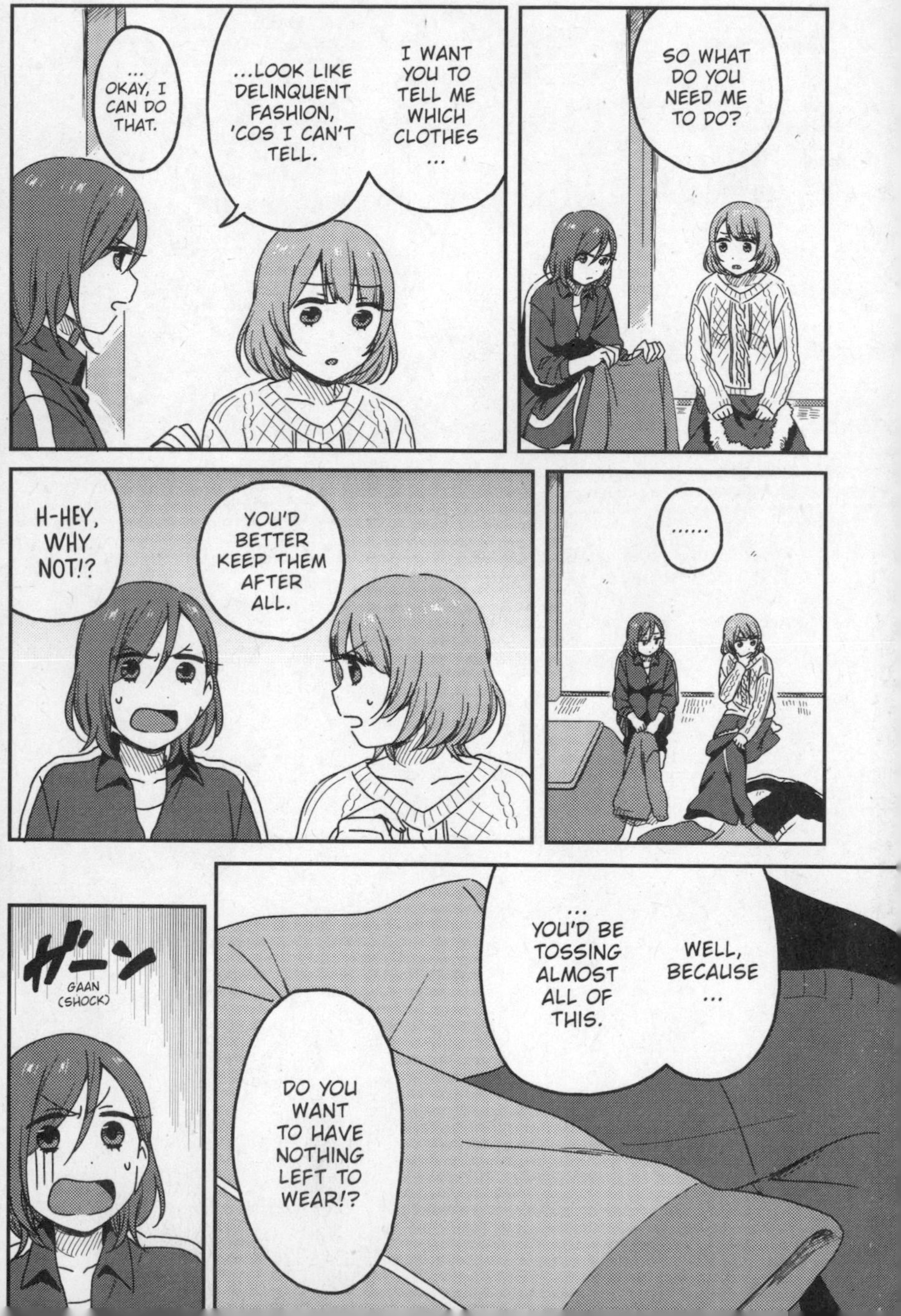
SO WHAT DO YOU NEED ME TO DO?
I WANT YOU TO TELL ME WHICH CLOTHES ...
...LOOK LIKE DELINQUENT FASHION, 'COS I CAN'T TELL.
... OKAY, I CAN DO THAT.
......
YOU'D BETTER KEEP THEM AFTER ALL.
H-HEY, WHY NOT!?
WELL, BECAUSE ...
... YOU'D BE TOSSING ALMOST ALL OF THIS.
DO YOU WANT TO HAVE NOTHING LEFT TO WEAR!?
ガーン
GAAN (SHOCK)

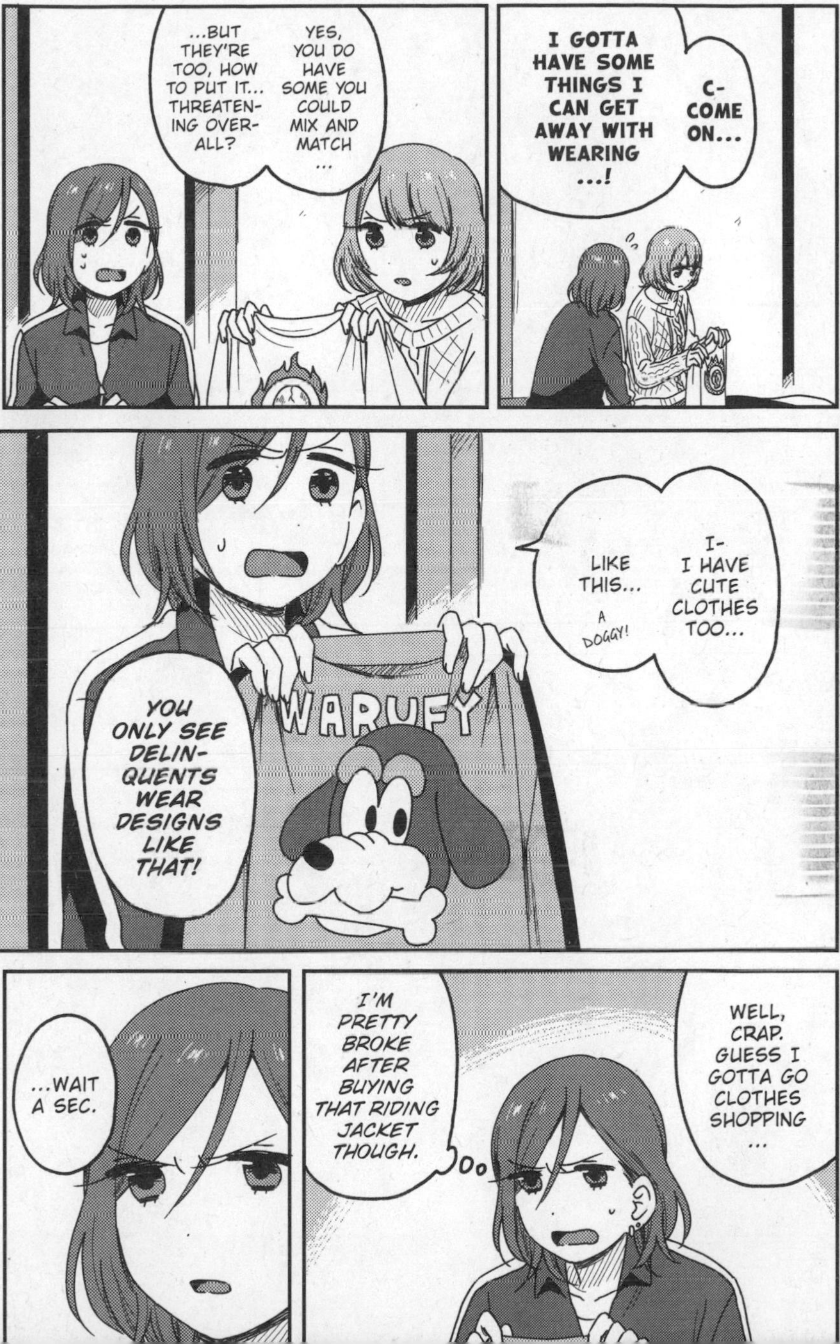
C-COME ON...
I GOTTA HAVE SOME THINGS I CAN GET AWAY WITH WEARING...!
YES, YOU DO HAVE SOME YOU COULD MIX AND MATCH...
...BUT THEY'RE TOO, HOW TO PUT IT... THREATENING OVERALL?
I- I HAVE CUTE CLOTHES TOO...
LIKE THIS...
A DOGGY!
WARUFY
YOU ONLY SEE DELINQUENTS WEAR DESIGNS LIKE THAT!
WELL, CRAP. GUESS I GOTTA GO CLOTHES SHOPPING...
I'M PRETTY BROKE AFTER BUYING THAT RIDING JACKET THOUGH.
...WAIT A SEC.

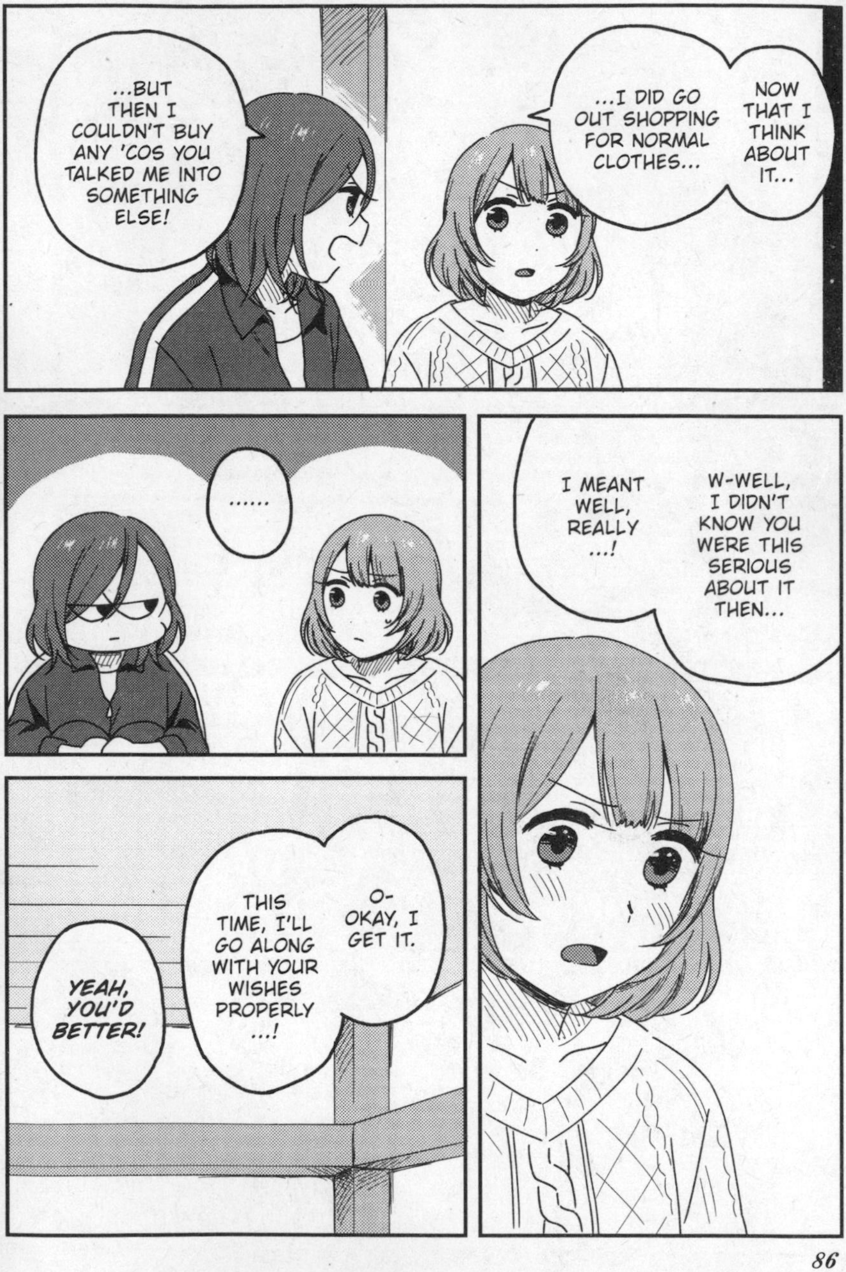
NOW THAT I THINK ABOUT IT...
...I DID GO OUT SHOPPING FOR NORMAL CLOTHES...
...BUT THEN I COULDN'T BUY ANY 'COS YOU TALKED ME INTO SOMETHING ELSE!
W-WELL, I DIDN'T KNOW YOU WERE THIS SERIOUS ABOUT IT THEN...
I MEANT WELL, REALLY ...!
......
O-OKAY, I GET IT.
THIS TIME, I'LL GO ALONG WITH YOUR WISHES PROPERLY ...!
YEAH, YOU'D BETTER!

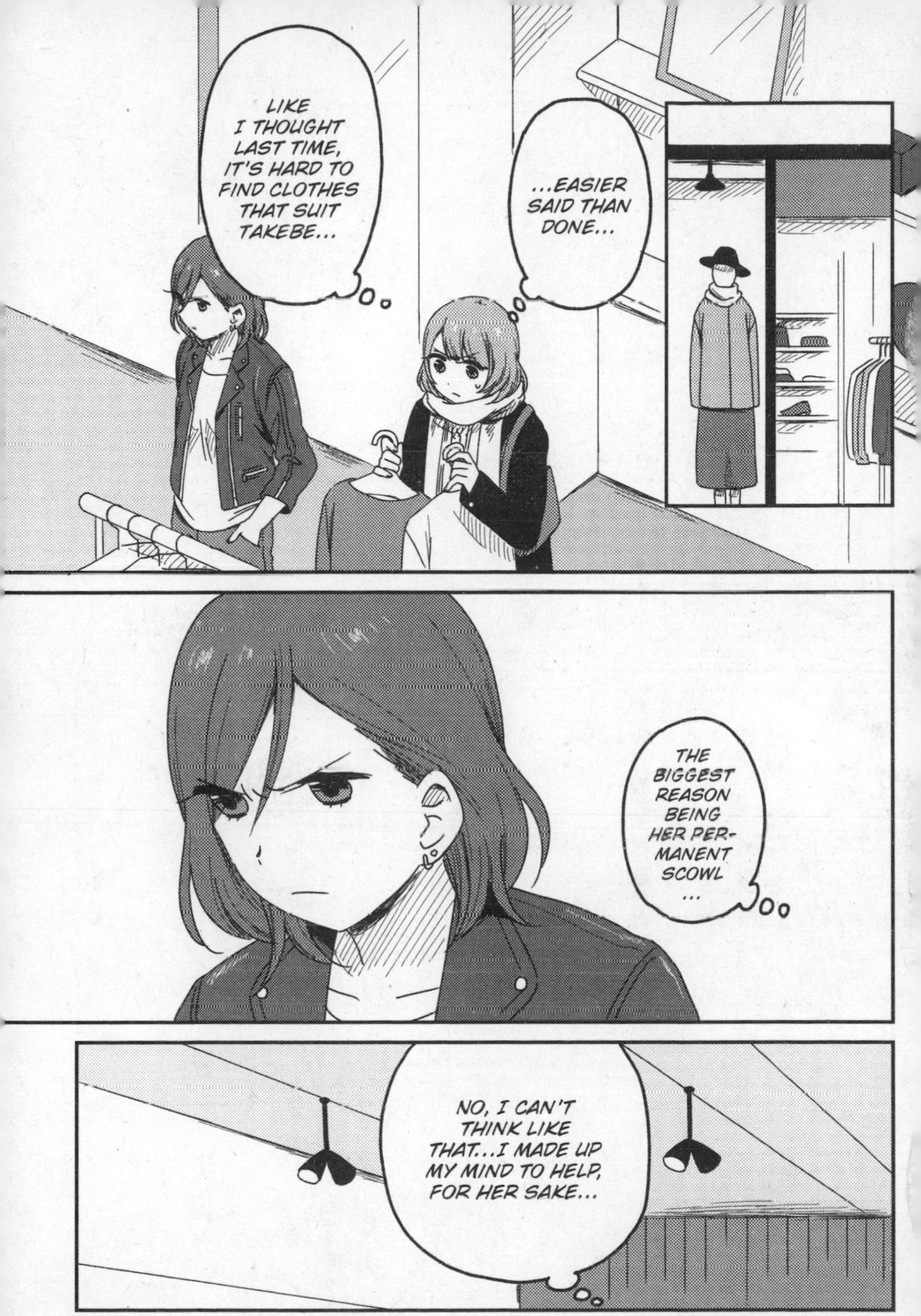
...EASIER SAID THAN DONE...
LIKE I THOUGHT LAST TIME, IT'S HARD TO FIND CLOTHES THAT SUIT TAKEBE...
THE BIGGEST REASON BEING HER PER-MANENT SCOWL ...
NO, I CAN'T THINK LIKE THAT...I MADE UP MY MIND TO HELP, FOR HER SAKE...

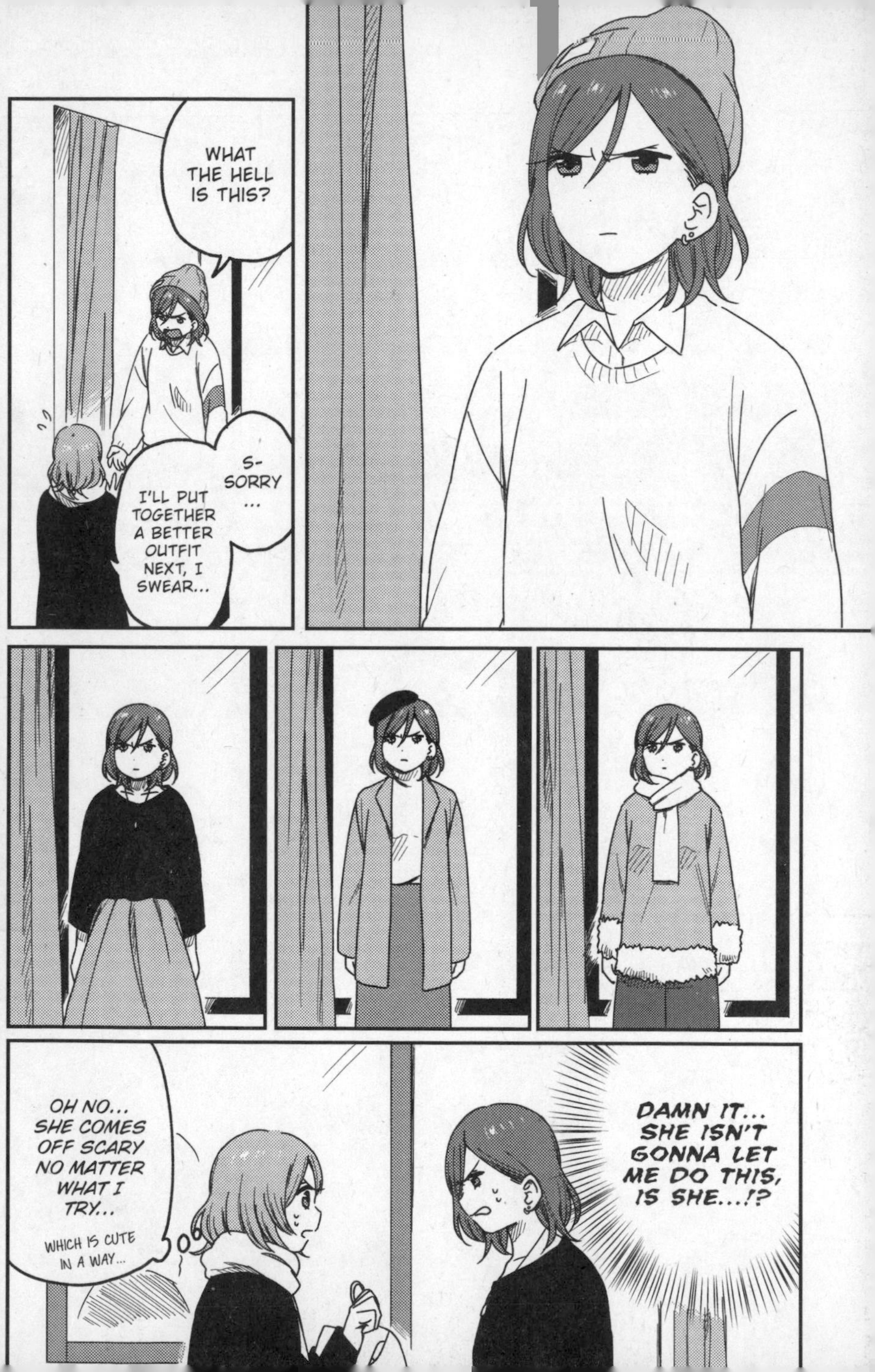
WHAT THE HELL IS THIS?
S-SORRY...
I'LL PUT TOGETHER A BETTER OUTFIT NEXT, I SWEAR...
DAMN IT... SHE ISN'T GONNA LET ME DO THIS, IS SHE...!?
OH NO... SHE COMES OFF SCARY NO MATTER WHAT I TRY...
WHICH IS CUTE IN A WAY...

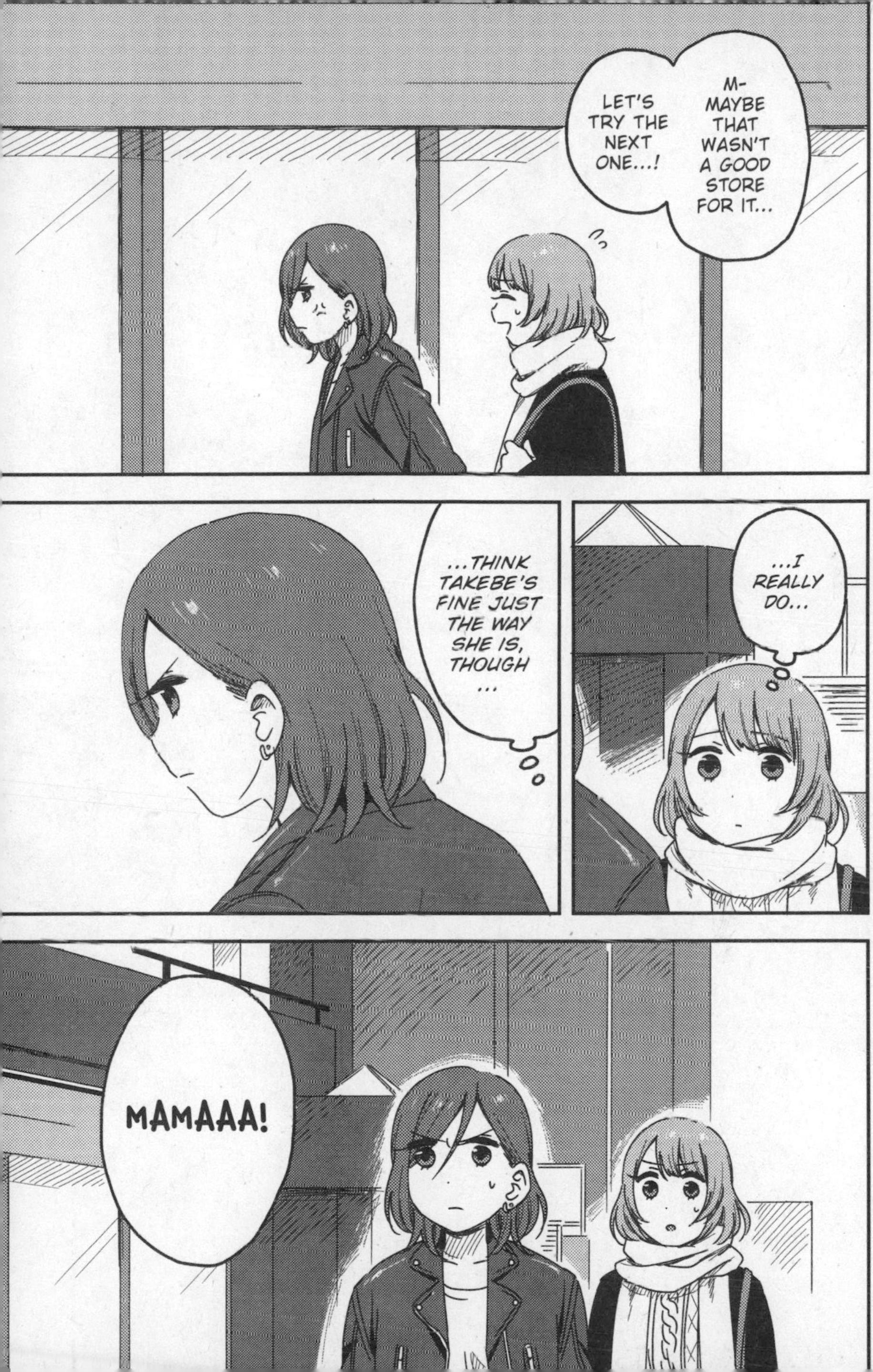
M-MAYBE THAT WASN'T A GOOD STORE FOR IT...
LET'S TRY THE NEXT ONE...!
...I REALLY DO...
...THINK TAKEBE'S FINE JUST THE WAY SHE IS, THOUGH ...
MAMAAA!

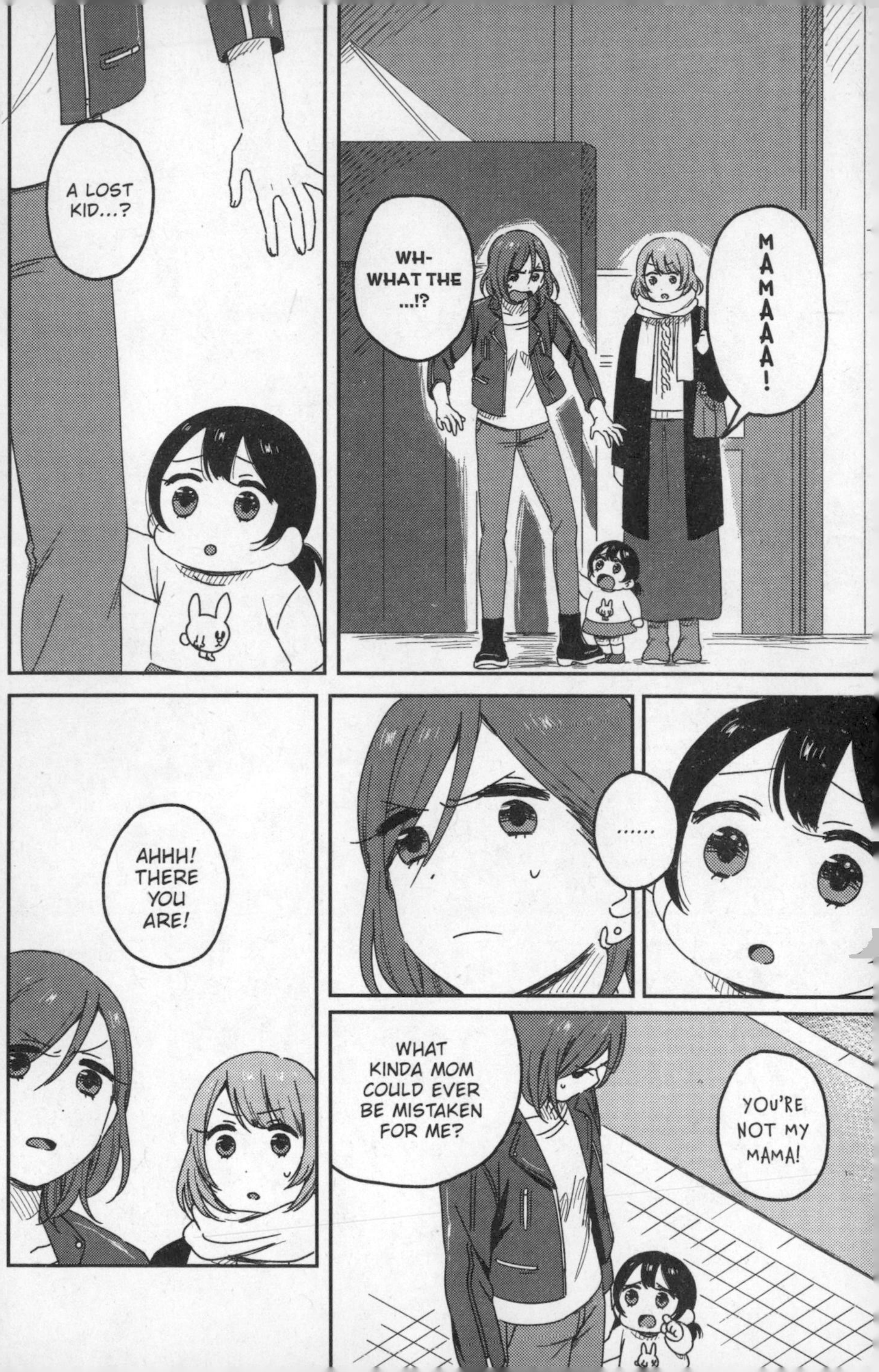
MAMAAA!
WH- WHAT THE ...!?
A LOST KID...?
......
YOU'RE NOT MY MAMA!
WHAT KINDA MOM COULD EVER BE MISTAKEN FOR ME?
AHHH! THERE YOU ARE!

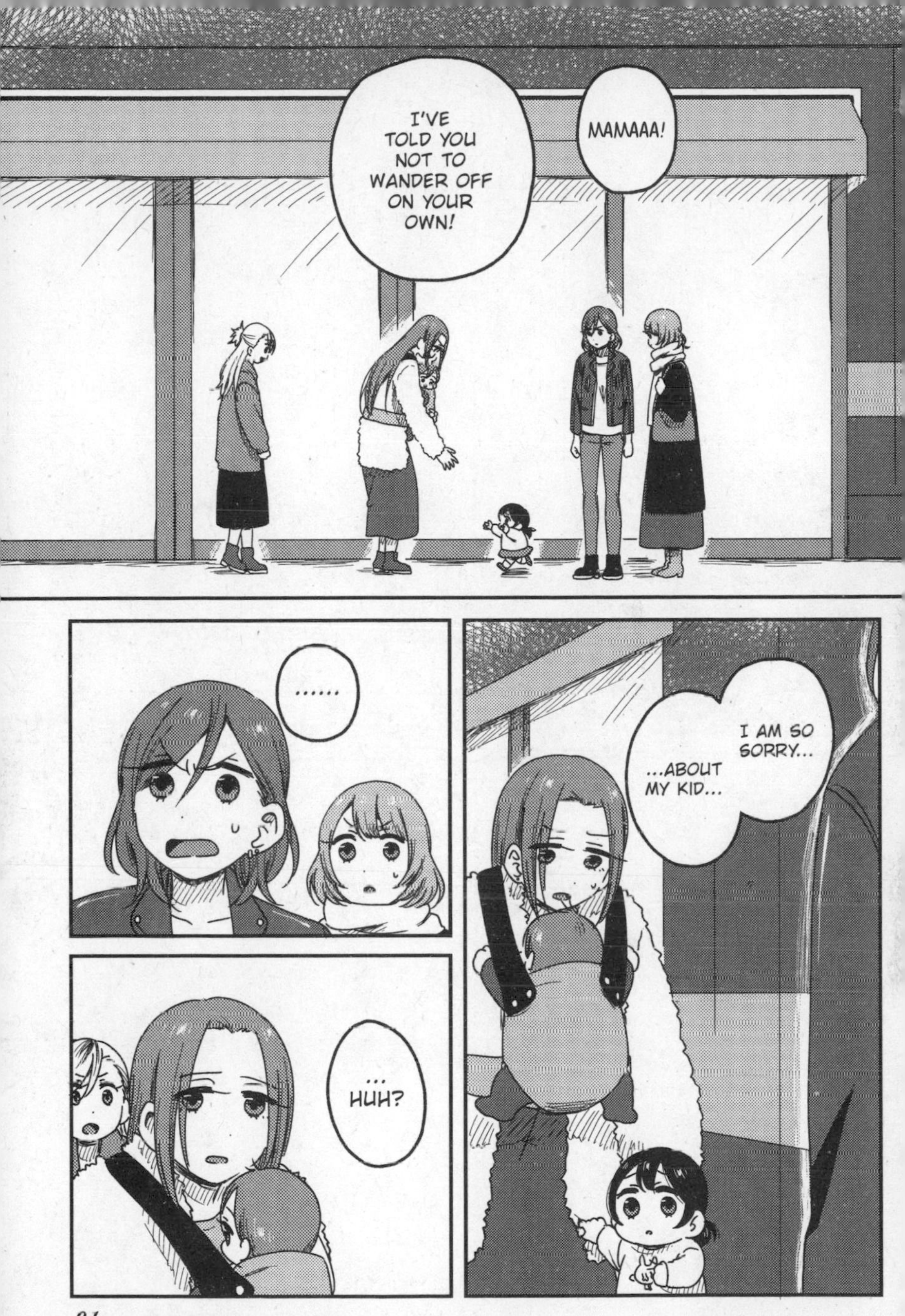
MAMAAA!
I'VE TOLD YOU NOT TO WANDER OFF ON YOUR OWN!
I AM SO SORRY...
...ABOUT MY KID...
......
... HUH?

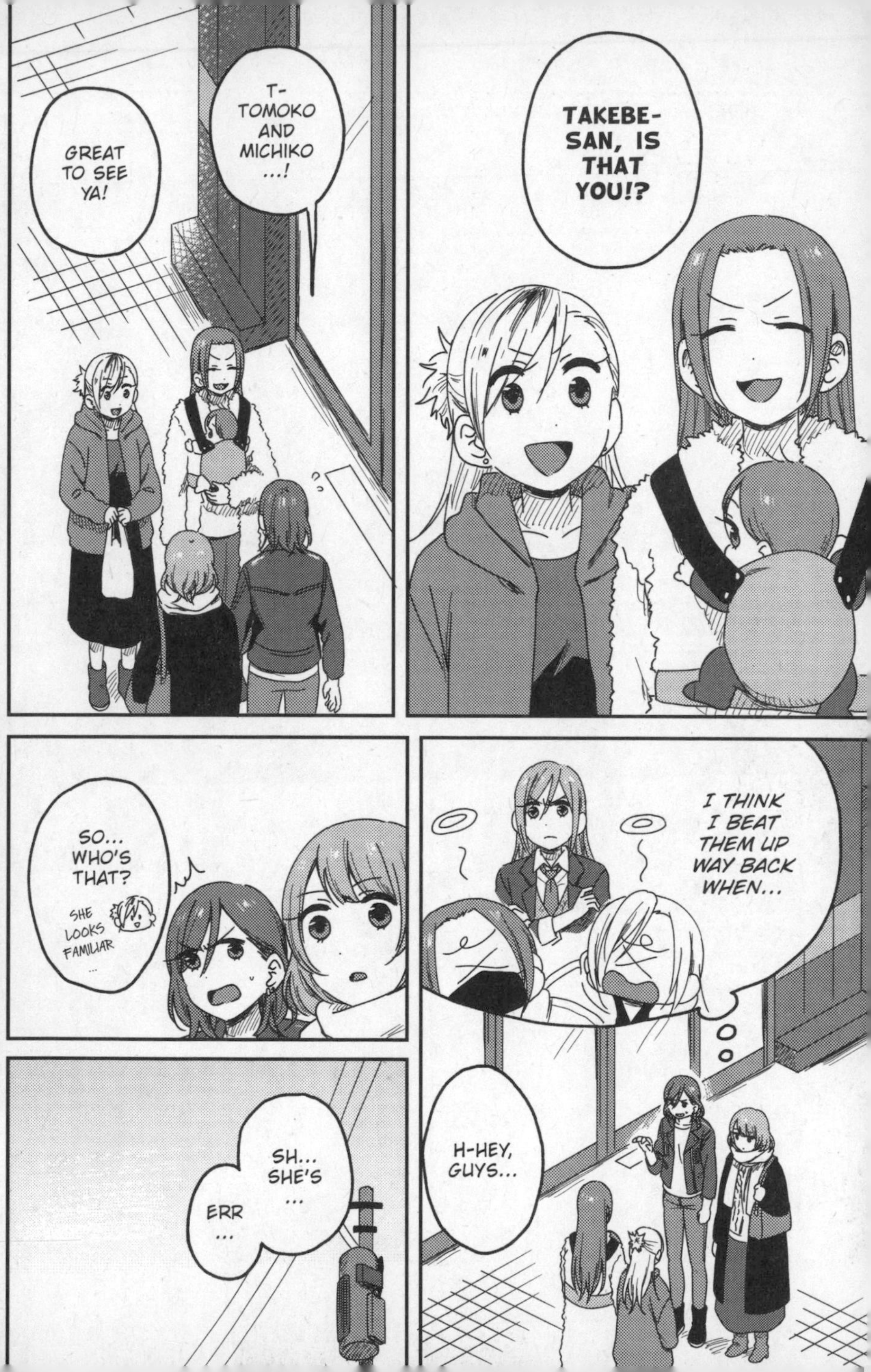
TAKEBE-SAN, IS THAT YOU!?
T-TOMOKO AND MICHIKO ...!
GREAT TO SEE YA!
I THINK I BEAT THEM UP WAY BACK WHEN...
SO... WHO'S THAT?
SHE LOOKS FAMILIAR ...
H-HEY, GUYS...
SH... SHE'S ...
ERR ...

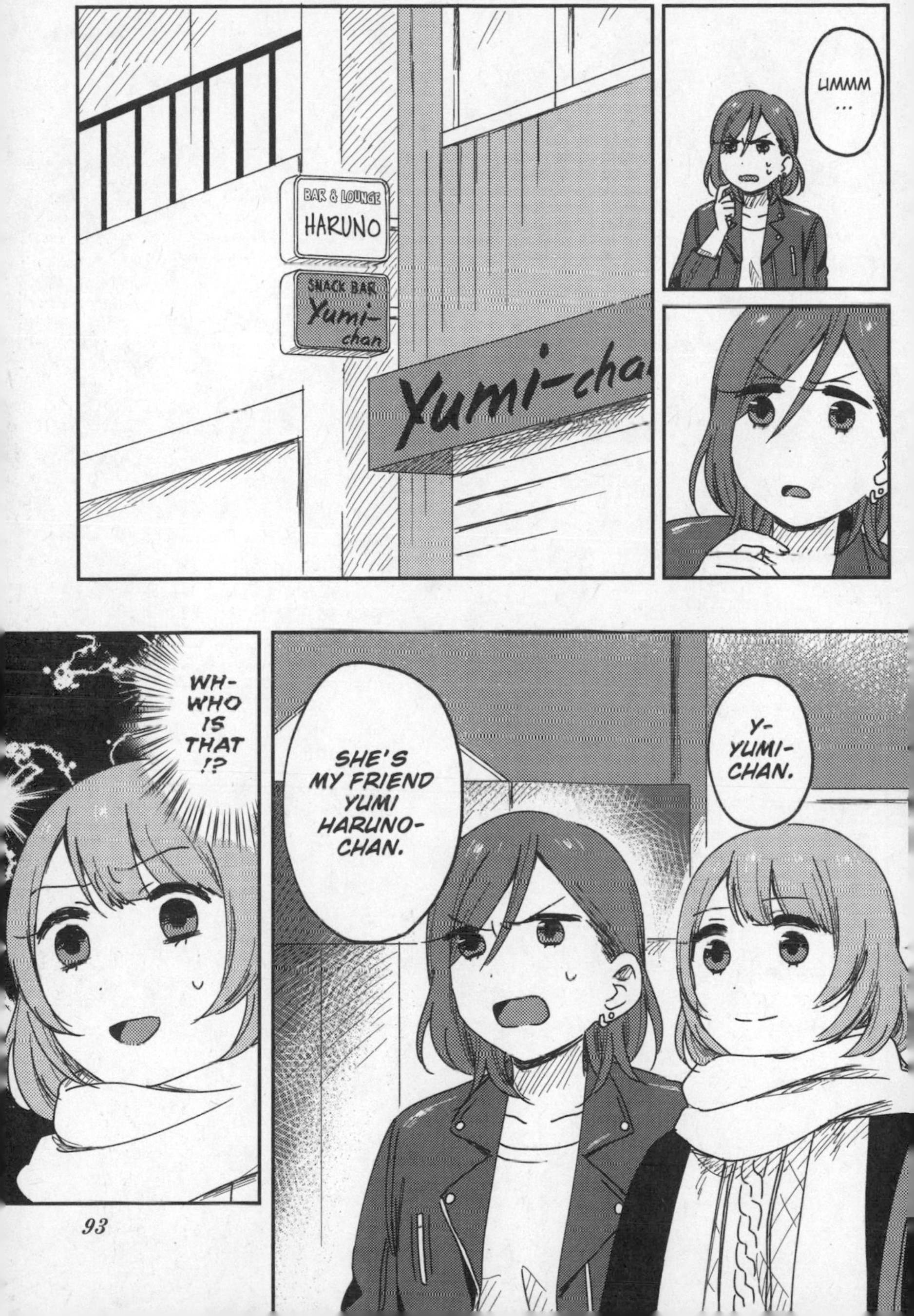
UMMM ...
BAR & LOUNGE
HARUNO
SNACK BAR
Yumi-chan
Yumi-cha
Y-YUMI-CHAN.
SHE'S MY FRIEND YUMI HARUNO-CHAN.
WH-WHO IS THAT!?

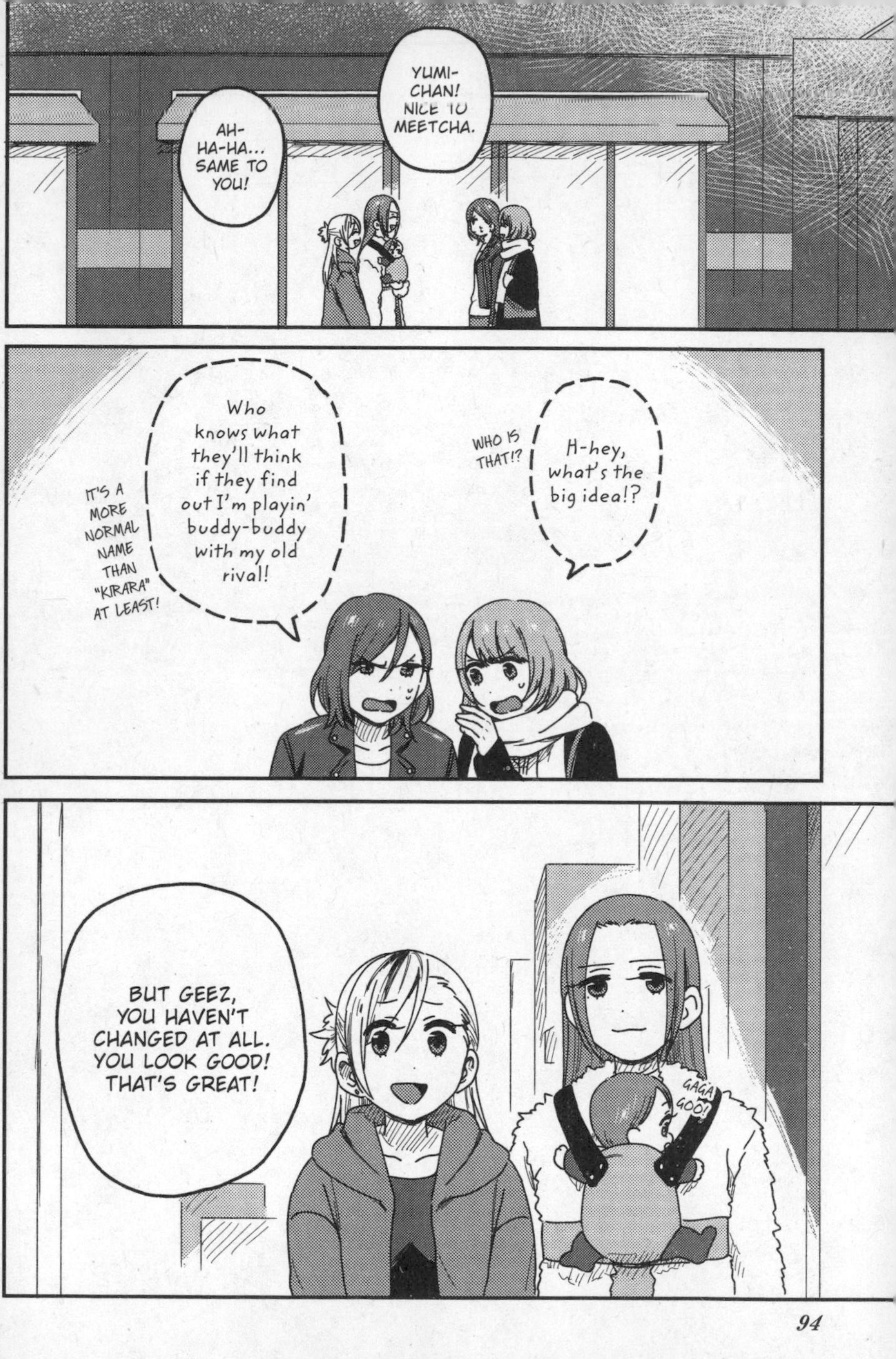
YUMI-CHAN! NICE TO MEETCHA.
AH-HA-HA... SAME TO YOU!
H-hey, what's the big idea!?
WHO IS THAT!?
Who knows what they'll think if they find out I'm playin' buddy-buddy with my old rival!
IT'S A MORE NORMAL NAME THAN "KIRARA" AT LEAST!
GAGA GOO!
BUT GEEZ, YOU HAVEN'T CHANGED AT ALL. YOU LOOK GOOD! THAT'S GREAT!

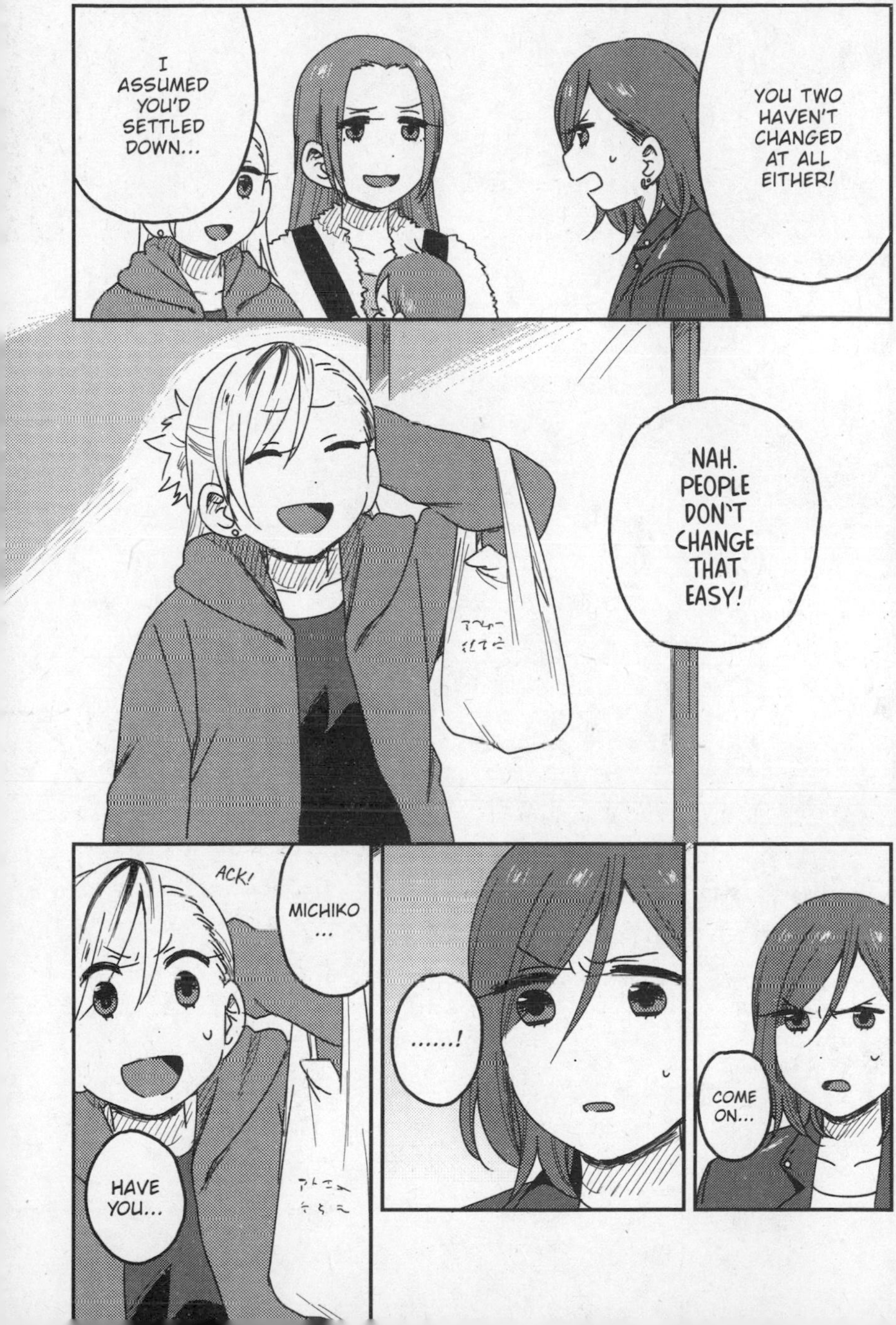
YOU TWO HAVEN'T CHANGED AT ALL EITHER!
I ASSUMED YOU'D SETTLED DOWN...
NAH. PEOPLE DON'T CHANGE THAT EASY!
COME ON...
......!
ACK!
MICHIKO ...
HAVE YOU...

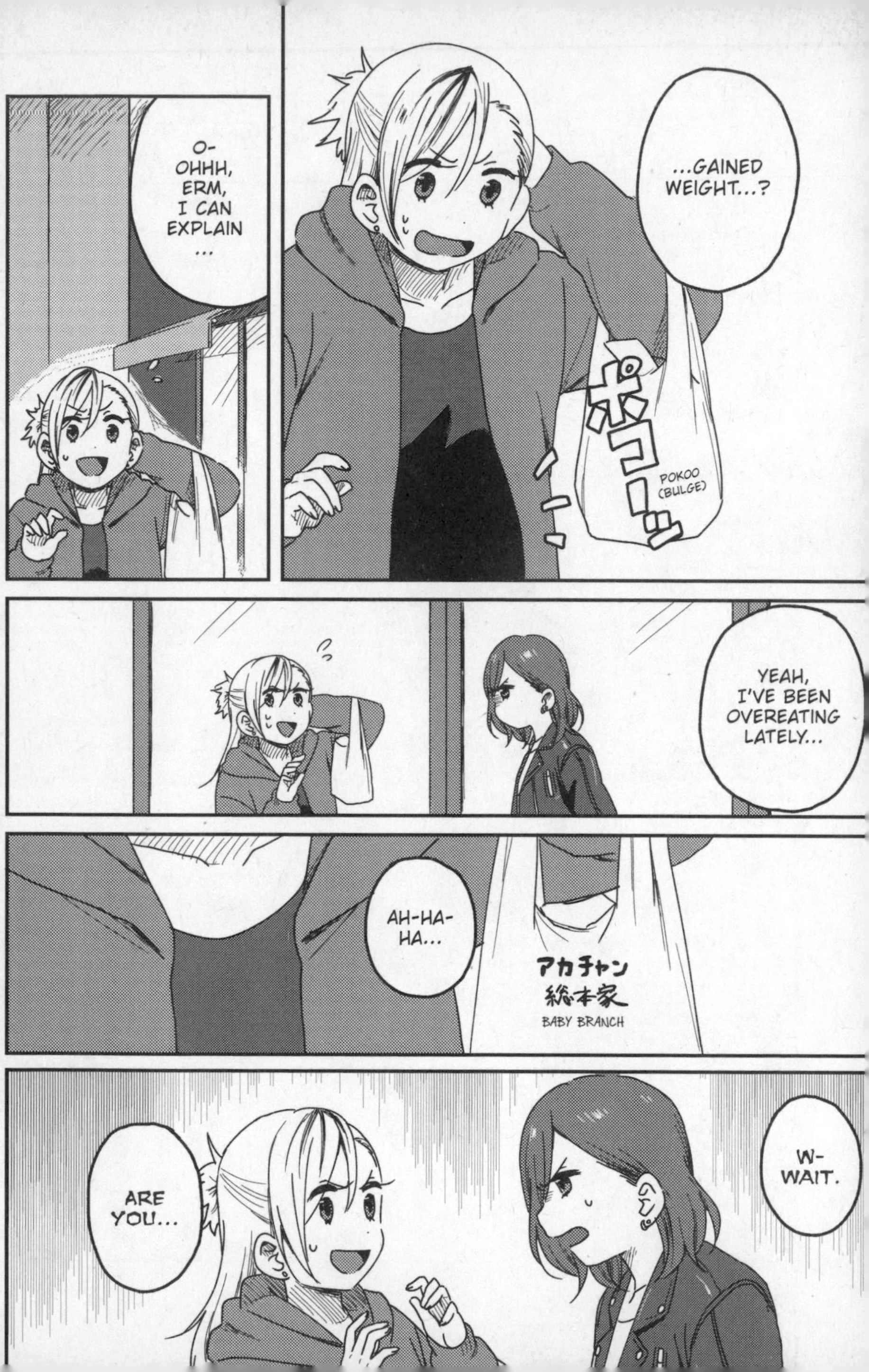
...GAINED WEIGHT...?
ポコーッ
POKOO (BULGE)
O-OHHH, ERM, I CAN EXPLAIN...
YEAH, I'VE BEEN OVEREATING LATELY...
アカチャン 総本家
BABY BRANCH
AH-HA-HA...
W-WAIT.
ARE YOU...

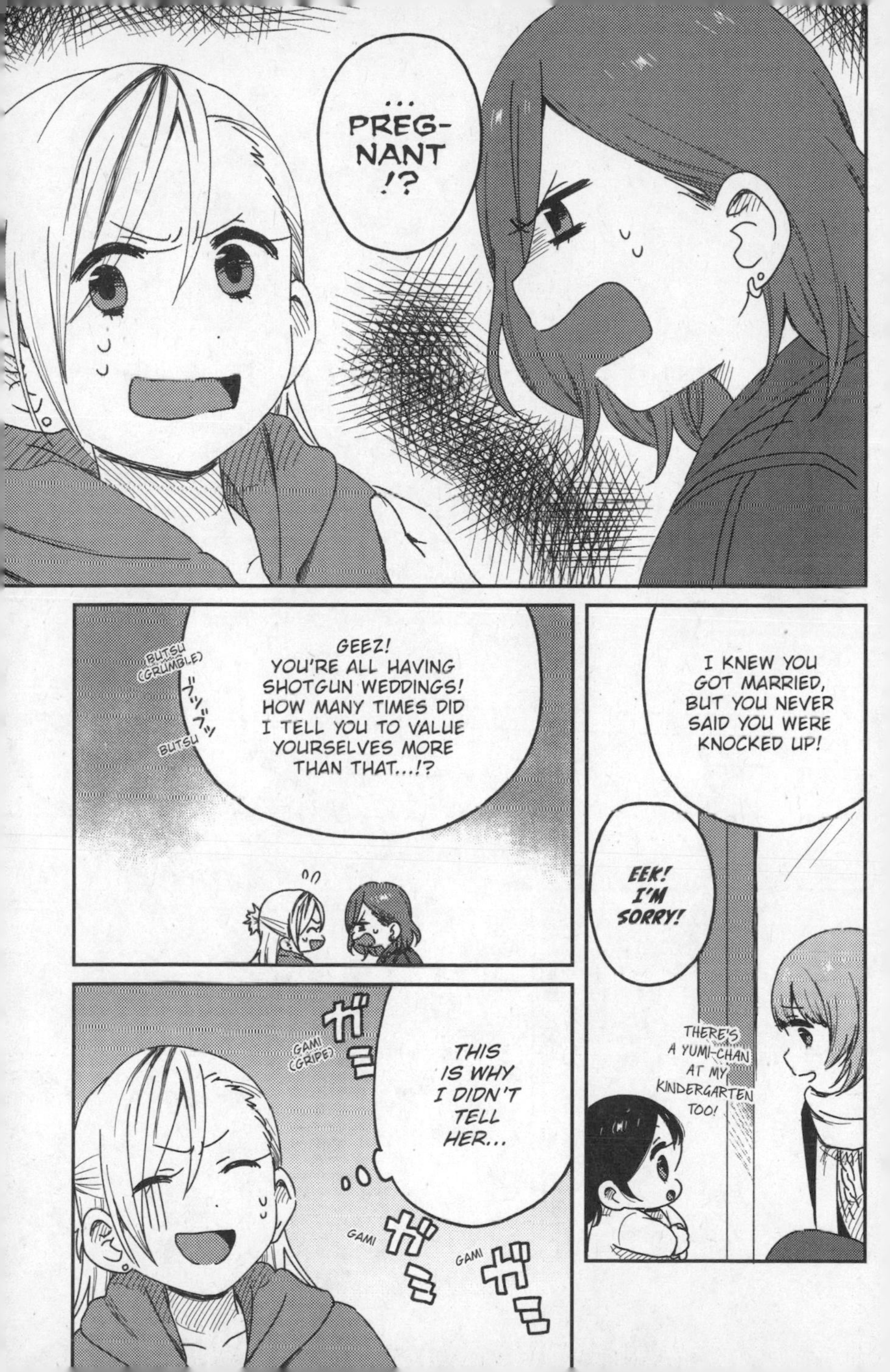
...PREG-NANT!?
I KNEW YOU GOT MARRIED, BUT YOU NEVER SAID YOU WERE KNOCKED UP!
EEK! I'M SORRY!
THERE'S A YUMI-CHAN AT MY KINDERGARTEN TOO!
GEEZ! YOU'RE ALL HAVING SHOTGUN WEDDINGS! HOW MANY TIMES DID I TELL YOU TO VALUE YOURSELVES MORE THAN THAT...!?
BUTSU (GRUMBLE)
ブツブツ
BUTSU
GAMI (GRIPE)
ガミ
THIS IS WHY I DIDN'T TELL HER...
GAMI
ガミ
GAMI
ガミ

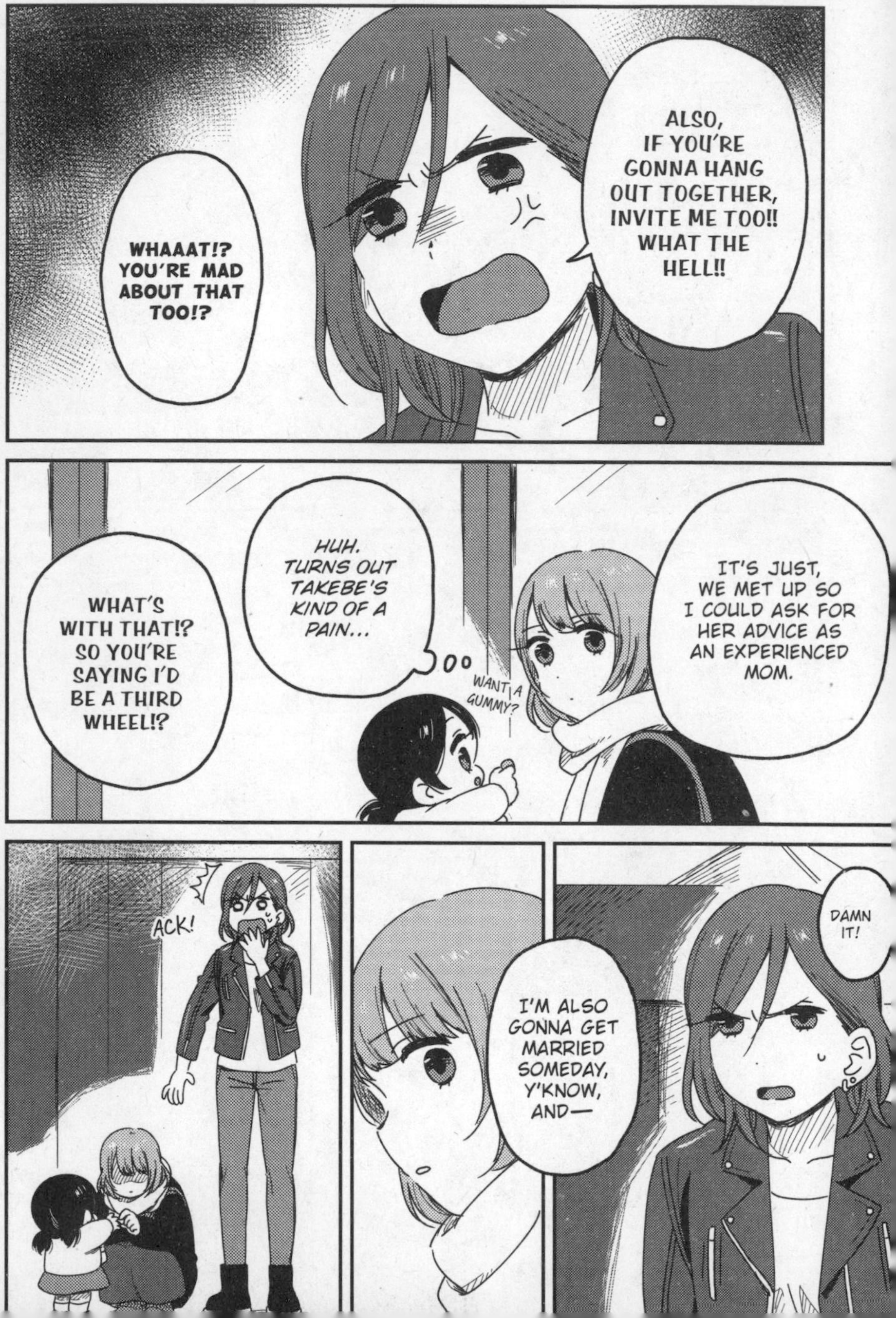
ALSO, IF YOU'RE GONNA HANG OUT TOGETHER, INVITE ME TOO!! WHAT THE HELL!!
WHAAAT!? YOU'RE MAD ABOUT THAT TOO!?
IT'S JUST, WE MET UP SO I COULD ASK FOR HER ADVICE AS AN EXPERIENCED MOM.
HUH. TURNS OUT TAKEBE'S KIND OF A PAIN...
WANT A GUMMY?
WHAT'S WITH THAT!? SO YOU'RE SAYING I'D BE A THIRD WHEEL!?
DAMN IT!
I'M ALSO GONNA GET MARRIED SOMEDAY, Y'KNOW, AND—
ACK!

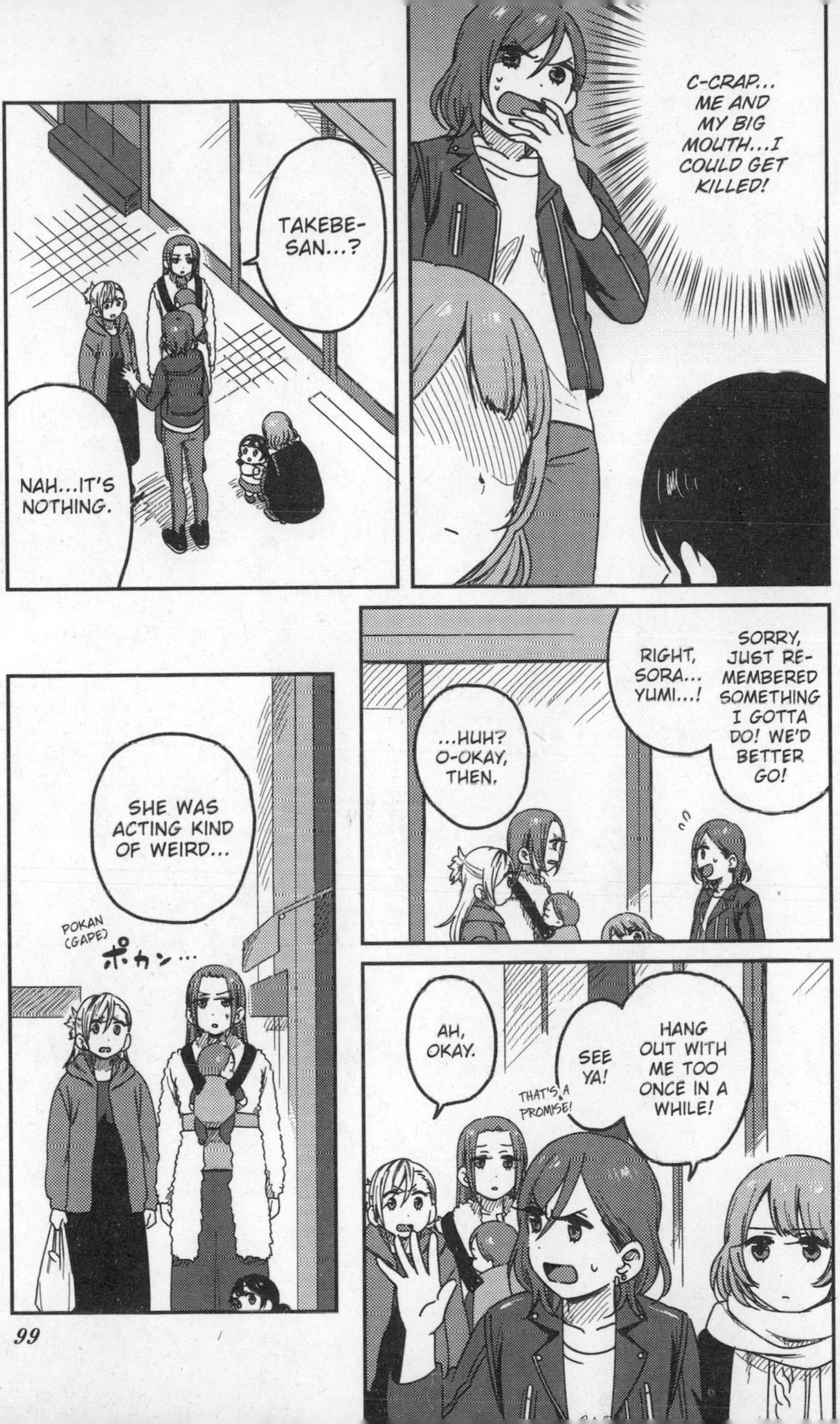
C-CRAP... ME AND MY BIG MOUTH...I COULD GET KILLED!
TAKEBE-SAN...?
NAH...IT'S NOTHING.
SORRY, JUST RE-MEMBERED SOMETHING I GOTTA DO! WE'D BETTER GO!
RIGHT, SORA... YUMI...!
...HUH? O-OKAY, THEN.
HANG OUT WITH ME TOO ONCE IN A WHILE!
SEE YA!
THAT'S A PROMISE!
AH, OKAY.
SHE WAS ACTING KIND OF WEIRD...
POKAN (GAPE)
ポカン…

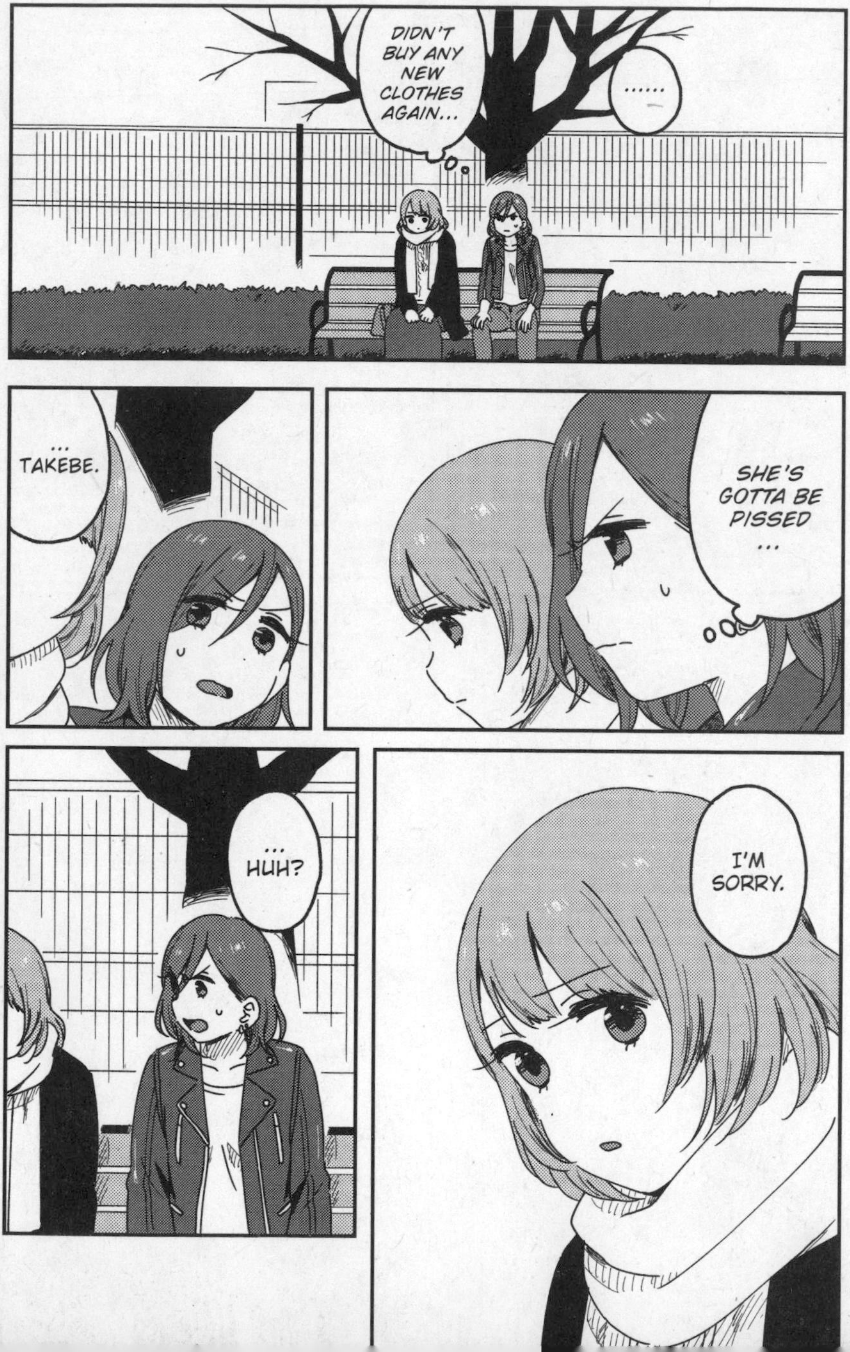
......
DIDN'T BUY ANY NEW CLOTHES AGAIN...
SHE'S GOTTA BE PISSED ...
... TAKEBE.
I'M SORRY.
... HUH?

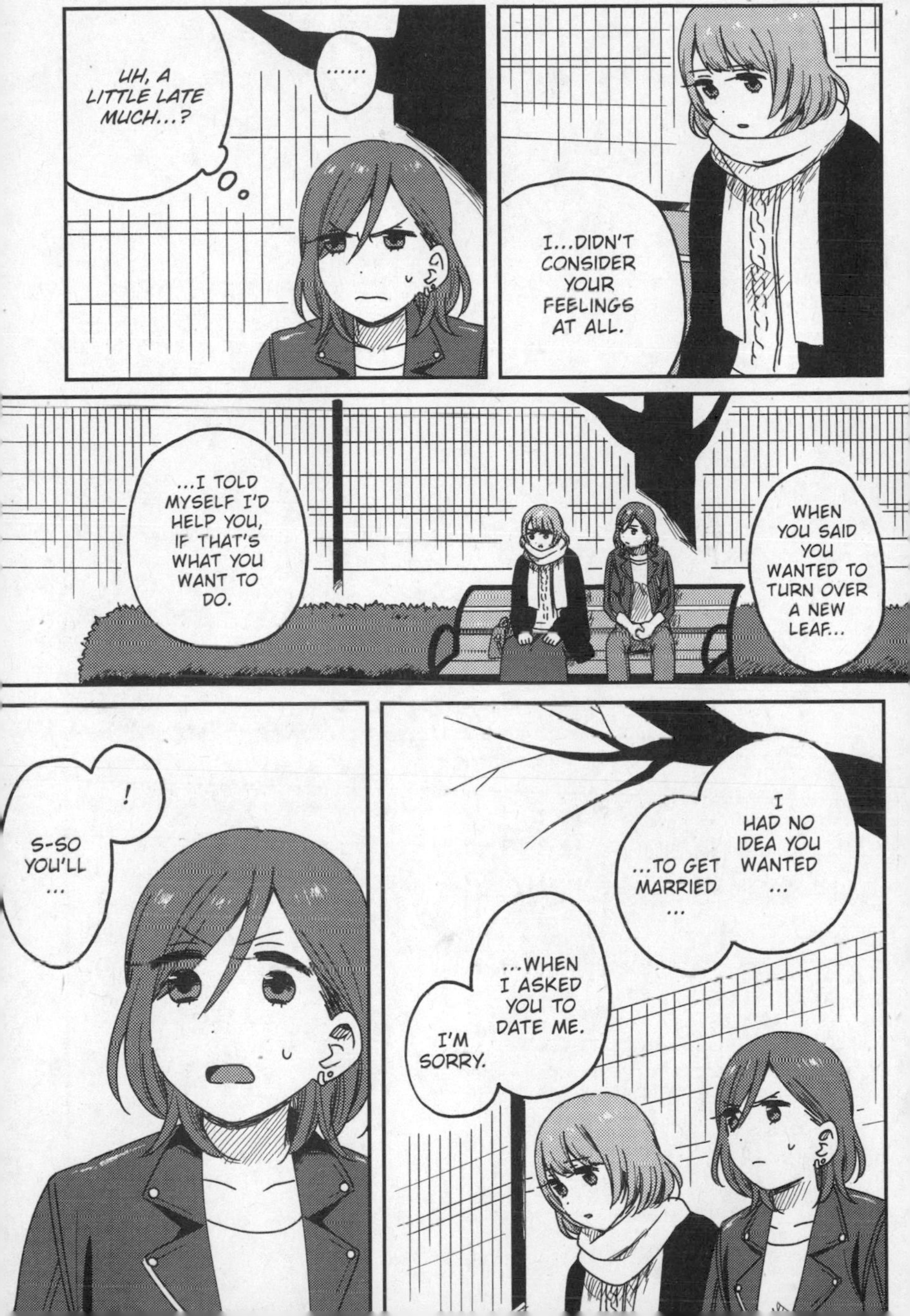
I...DIDN'T CONSIDER YOUR FEELINGS AT ALL.
......
UH, A LITTLE LATE MUCH...?
WHEN YOU SAID YOU WANTED TO TURN OVER A NEW LEAF...
...I TOLD MYSELF I'D HELP YOU, IF THAT'S WHAT YOU WANT TO DO.
I HAD NO IDEA YOU WANTED...
...TO GET MARRIED...
...WHEN I ASKED YOU TO DATE ME.
I'M SORRY.
!
S-SO YOU'LL ...

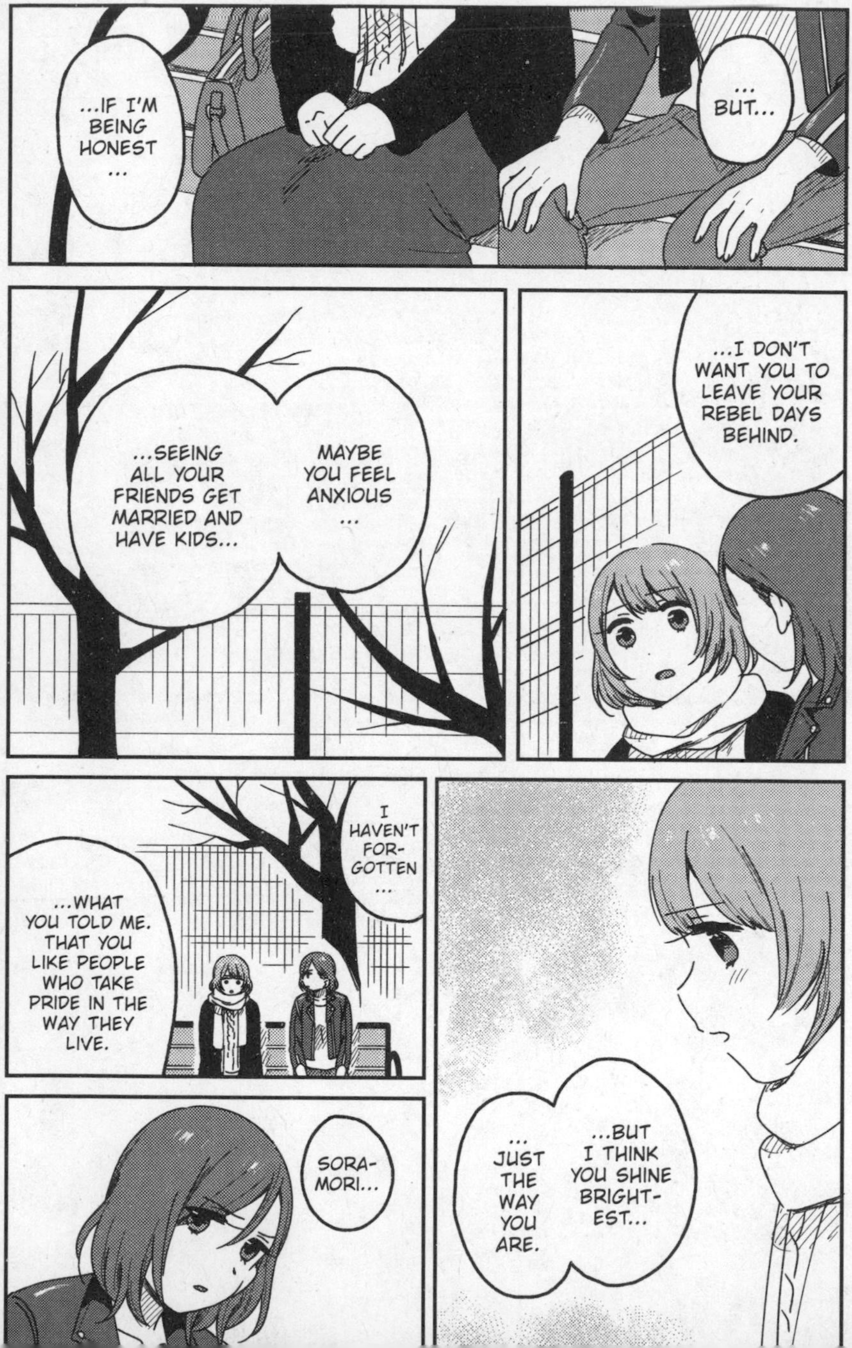

... BUT...
...IF I'M BEING HONEST ...
...I DON'T WANT YOU TO LEAVE YOUR REBEL DAYS BEHIND.
MAYBE YOU FEEL ANXIOUS ...
...SEEING ALL YOUR FRIENDS GET MARRIED AND HAVE KIDS...
...BUT I THINK YOU SHINE BRIGHT-EST...
... JUST THE WAY YOU ARE.
I HAVEN'T FOR-GOTTEN ...
...WHAT YOU TOLD ME. THAT YOU LIKE PEOPLE WHO TAKE PRIDE IN THE WAY THEY LIVE.
SORA-MORI...

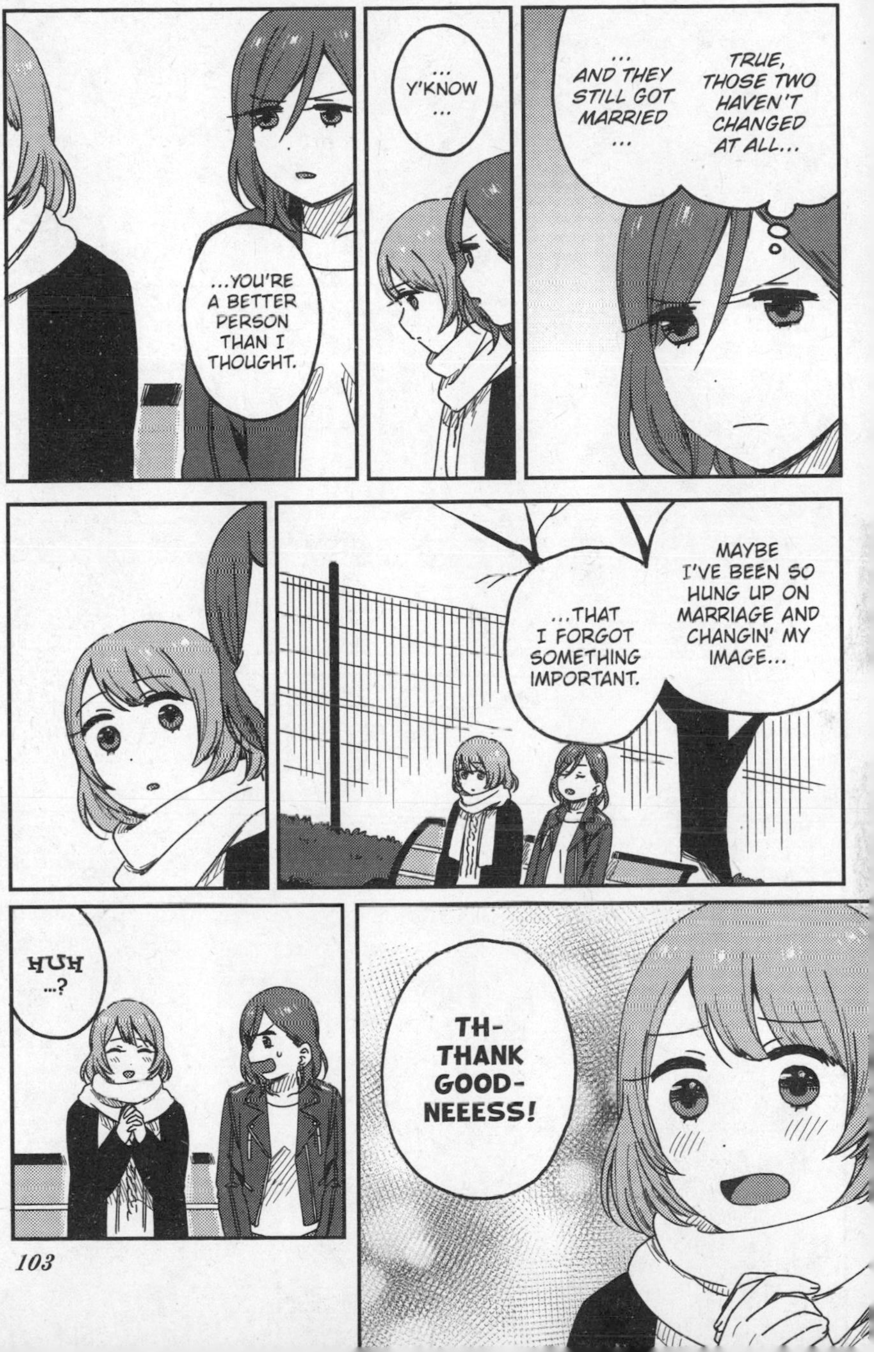
TRUE, THOSE TWO HAVEN'T CHANGED AT ALL...
... AND THEY STILL GOT MARRIED ...
... Y'KNOW ...
...YOU'RE A BETTER PERSON THAN I THOUGHT.
MAYBE I'VE BEEN SO HUNG UP ON MARRIAGE AND CHANGIN' MY IMAGE...
...THAT I FORGOT SOMETHING IMPORTANT.
TH-THANK GOOD-NEEESS!
HUH ...?

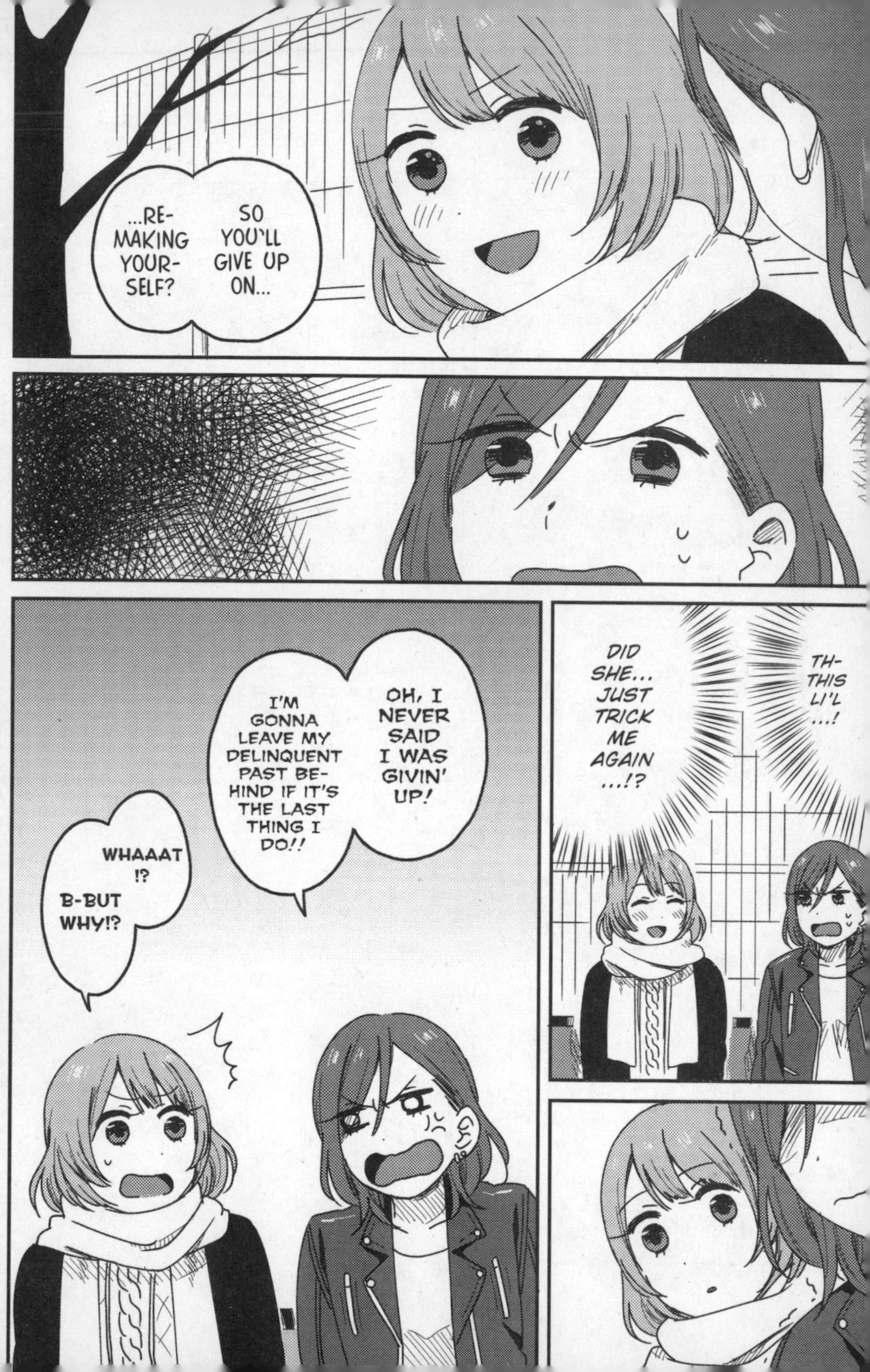
SO YOU'LL GIVE UP ON...
...RE-MAKING YOUR-SELF?
TH-THIS LI'L ...!
DID SHE... JUST TRICK ME AGAIN ...!?
OH, I NEVER SAID I WAS GIVIN' UP!
I'M GONNA LEAVE MY DELINQUENT PAST BE-HIND IF IT'S THE LAST THING I DO!!
WHAAAT!?
B-BUT WHY!?

Catch These Hands!

Catch These Hands!

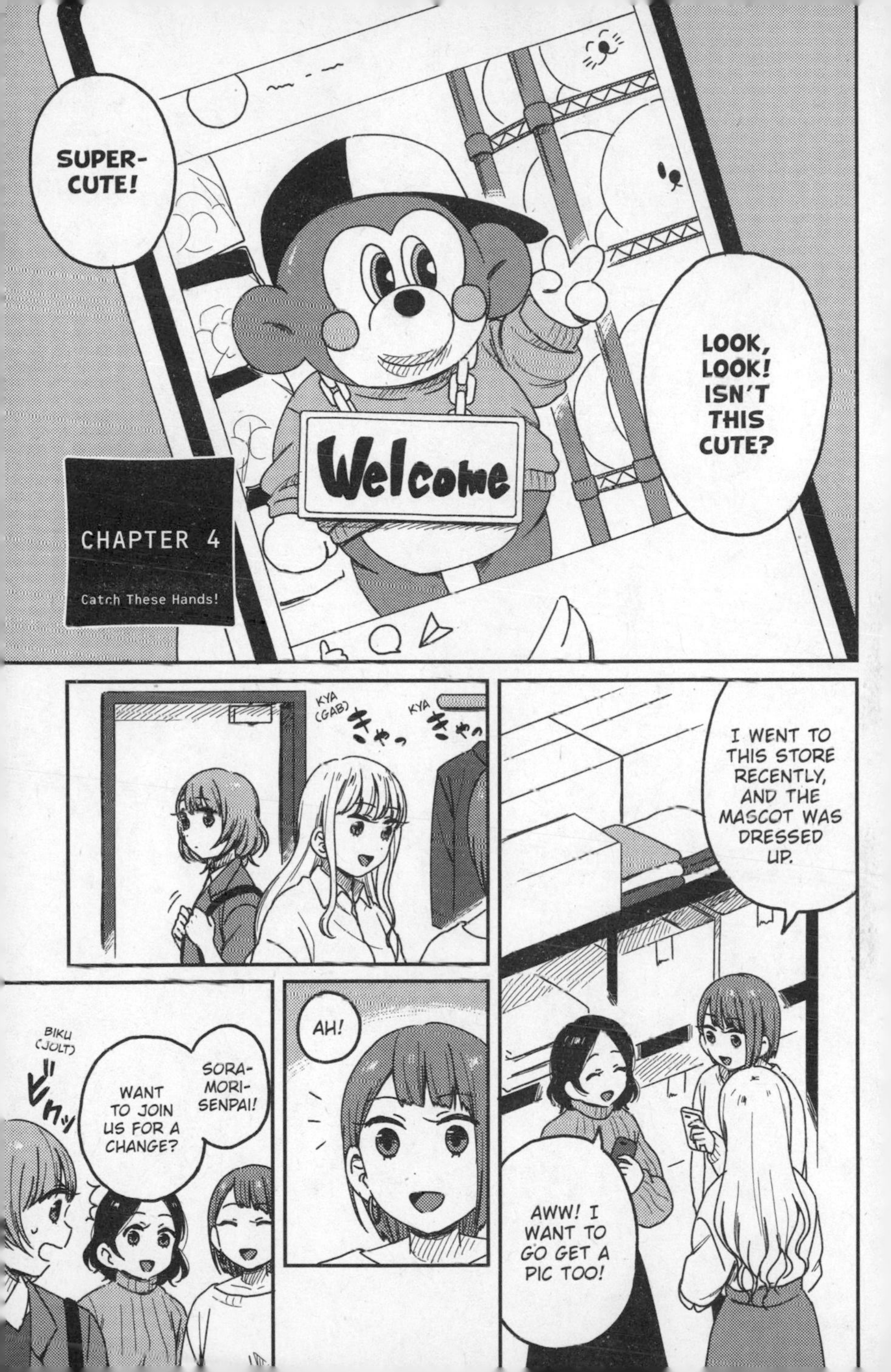
LOOK, LOOK! ISN'T THIS CUTE?
SUPER-CUTE!
Welcome
CHAPTER 4
Catch These Hands!
I WENT TO THIS STORE RECENTLY, AND THE MASCOT WAS DRESSED UP.
AWW! I WANT TO GO GET A PIC TOO!
KYA KYA (GAB)
きゃっ きゃっ
AH!
BIKU (JOLT)
ビクッ
SORA-MORI-SENPAI!
WANT TO JOIN US FOR A CHANGE?

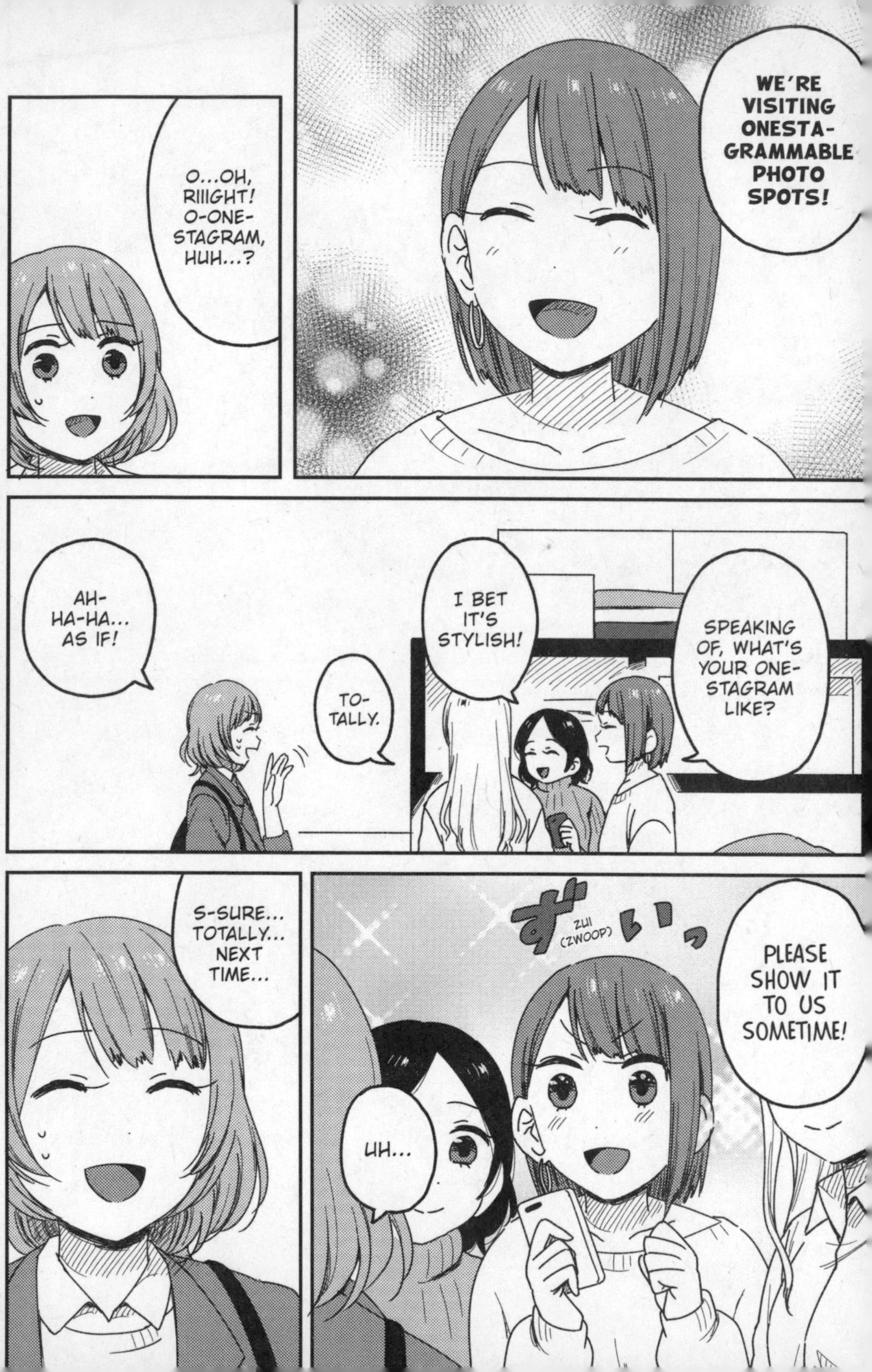
WE'RE VISITING ONESTA-GRAMMABLE PHOTO SPOTS!
O...OH, RIIIGHT! O-ONE-STAGRAM, HUH...?
SPEAKING OF, WHAT'S YOUR ONE-STAGRAM LIKE?
I BET IT'S STYLISH!
TO-TALLY.
AH-HA-HA... AS IF!
ZUI (ZWOOP)
PLEASE SHOW IT TO US SOMETIME!
UH...
S-SURE... TOTALLY... NEXT TIME...

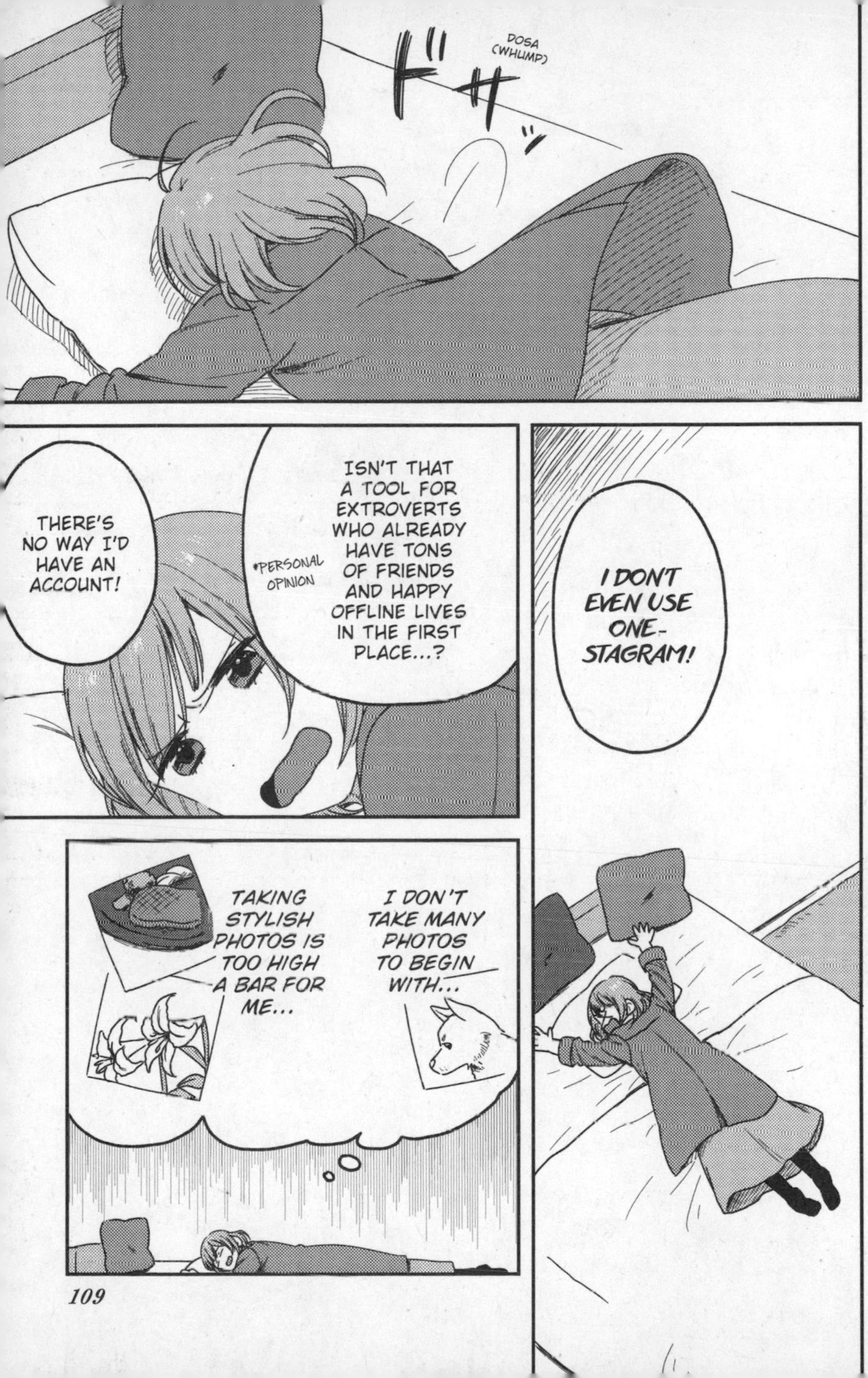
ドサッ
DOSA (WHUMP)
I DON'T EVEN USE ONE-STAGRAM!
ISN'T THAT A TOOL FOR EXTROVERTS WHO ALREADY HAVE TONS OF FRIENDS AND HAPPY OFFLINE LIVES IN THE FIRST PLACE...?
*PERSONAL OPINION
THERE'S NO WAY I'D HAVE AN ACCOUNT!
I DON'T TAKE MANY PHOTOS TO BEGIN WITH...
TAKING STYLISH PHOTOS IS TOO HIGH A BAR FOR ME...

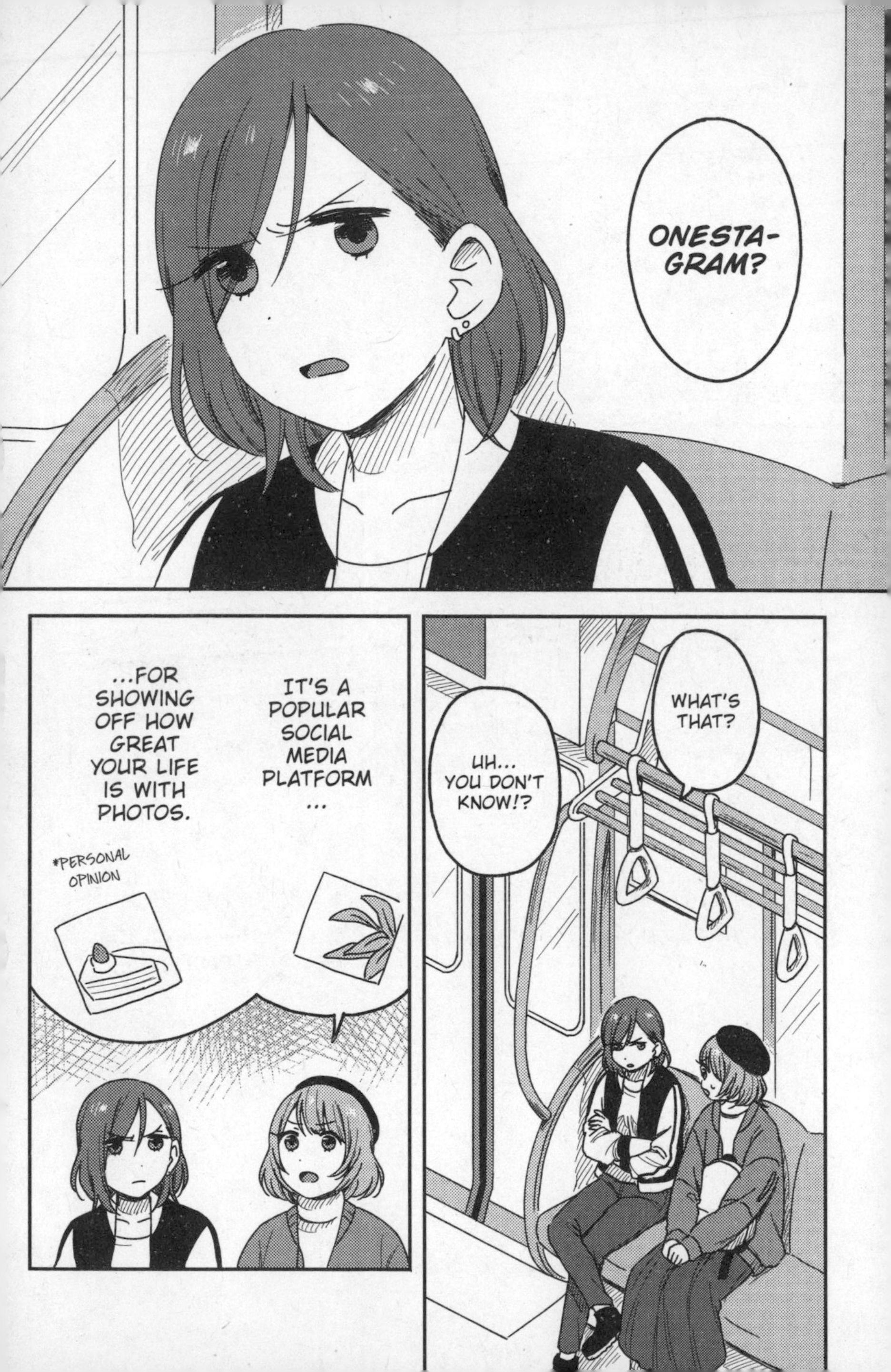
ONESTA-GRAM?
WHAT'S THAT?
UH... YOU DON'T KNOW!?
IT'S A POPULAR SOCIAL MEDIA PLATFORM ...
...FOR SHOWING OFF HOW GREAT YOUR LIFE IS WITH PHOTOS.
*PERSONAL OPINION

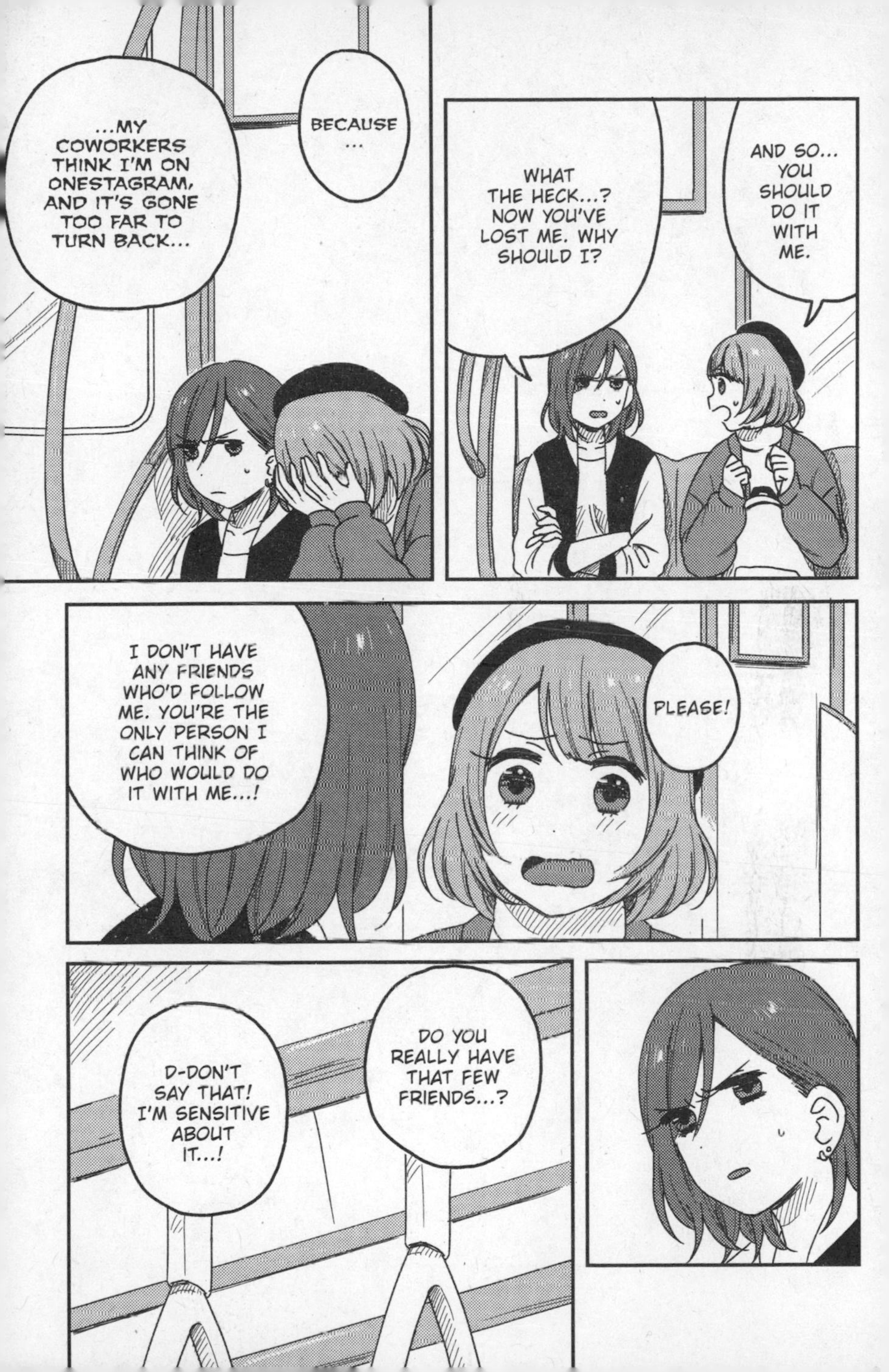
AND SO... YOU SHOULD DO IT WITH ME.
WHAT THE HECK...? NOW YOU'VE LOST ME. WHY SHOULD I?
BECAUSE ...
...MY COWORKERS THINK I'M ON ONESTAGRAM, AND IT'S GONE TOO FAR TO TURN BACK...
PLEASE!
I DON'T HAVE ANY FRIENDS WHO'D FOLLOW ME. YOU'RE THE ONLY PERSON I CAN THINK OF WHO WOULD DO IT WITH ME...!
DO YOU REALLY HAVE THAT FEW FRIENDS...?
D-DON'T SAY THAT! I'M SENSITIVE ABOUT IT...!

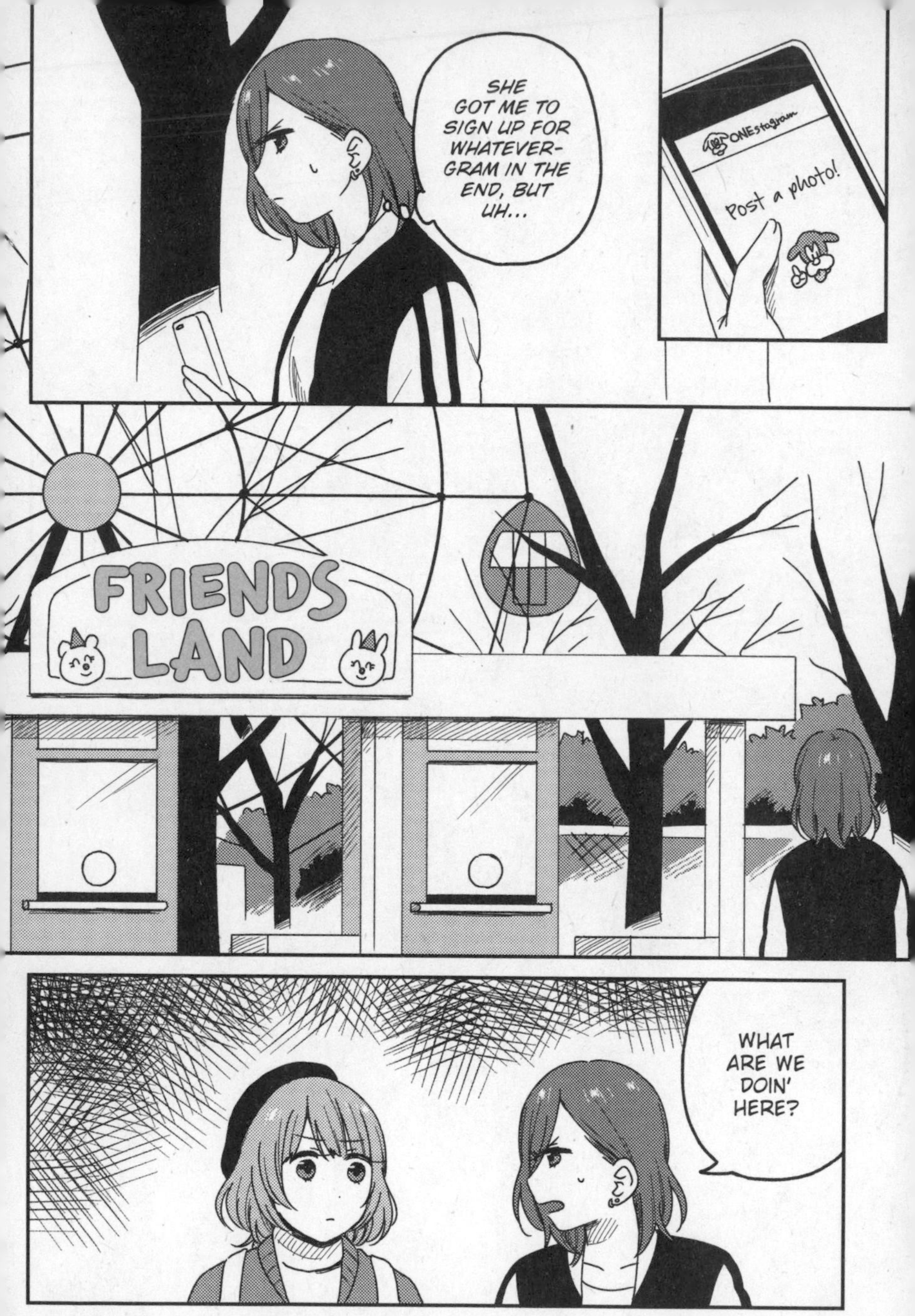
ONEstagram
Post a photo!
SHE GOT ME TO SIGN UP FOR WHATEVER-GRAM IN THE END, BUT UH...
FRIENDS LAND
WHAT ARE WE DOIN' HERE?

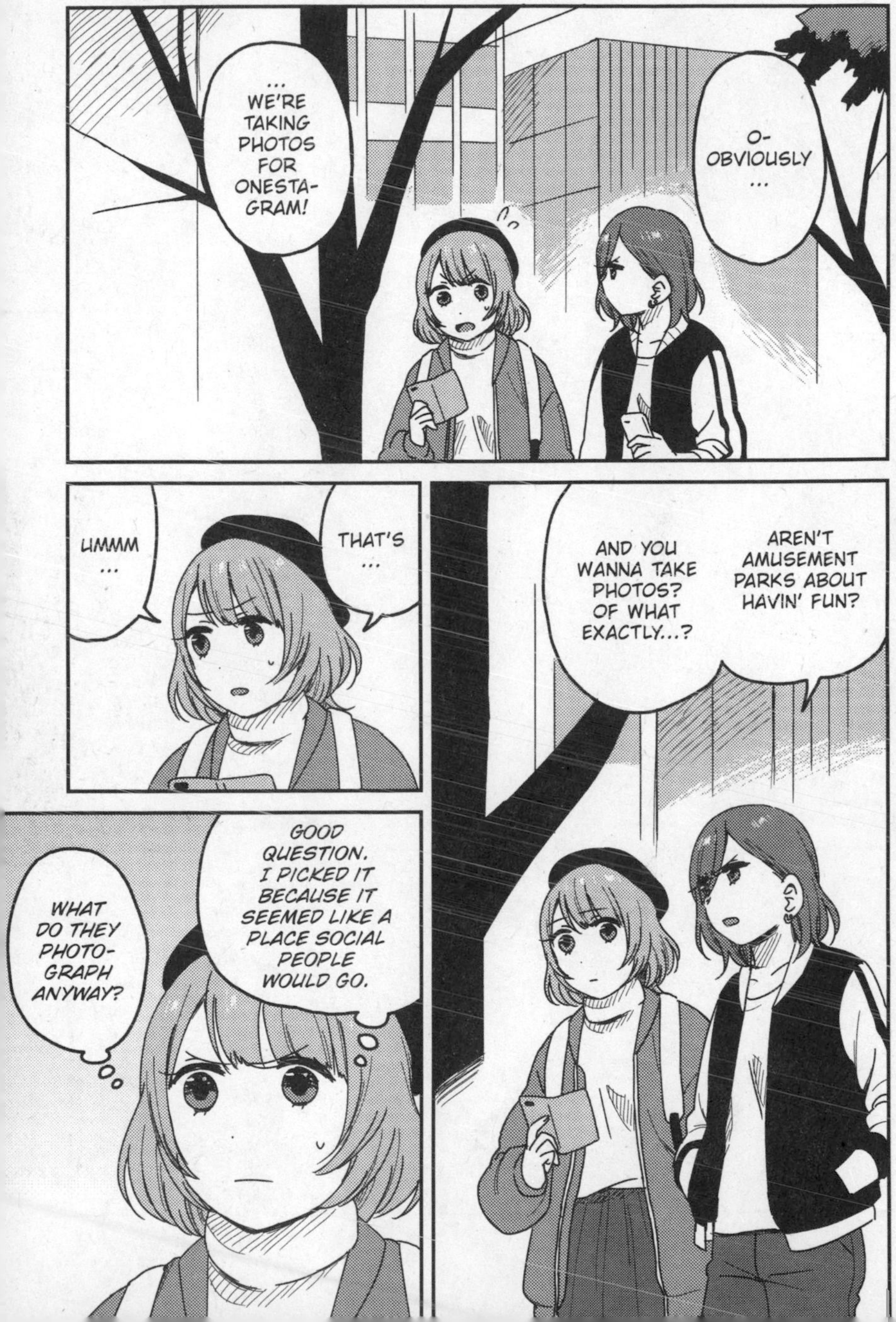
O-OBVIOUSLY...
...WE'RE TAKING PHOTOS FOR ONESTA-GRAM!
AREN'T AMUSEMENT PARKS ABOUT HAVIN' FUN?
AND YOU WANNA TAKE PHOTOS? OF WHAT EXACTLY...?
THAT'S...
UMMM...
GOOD QUESTION. I PICKED IT BECAUSE IT SEEMED LIKE A PLACE SOCIAL PEOPLE WOULD GO.
WHAT DO THEY PHOTO-GRAPH ANYWAY?

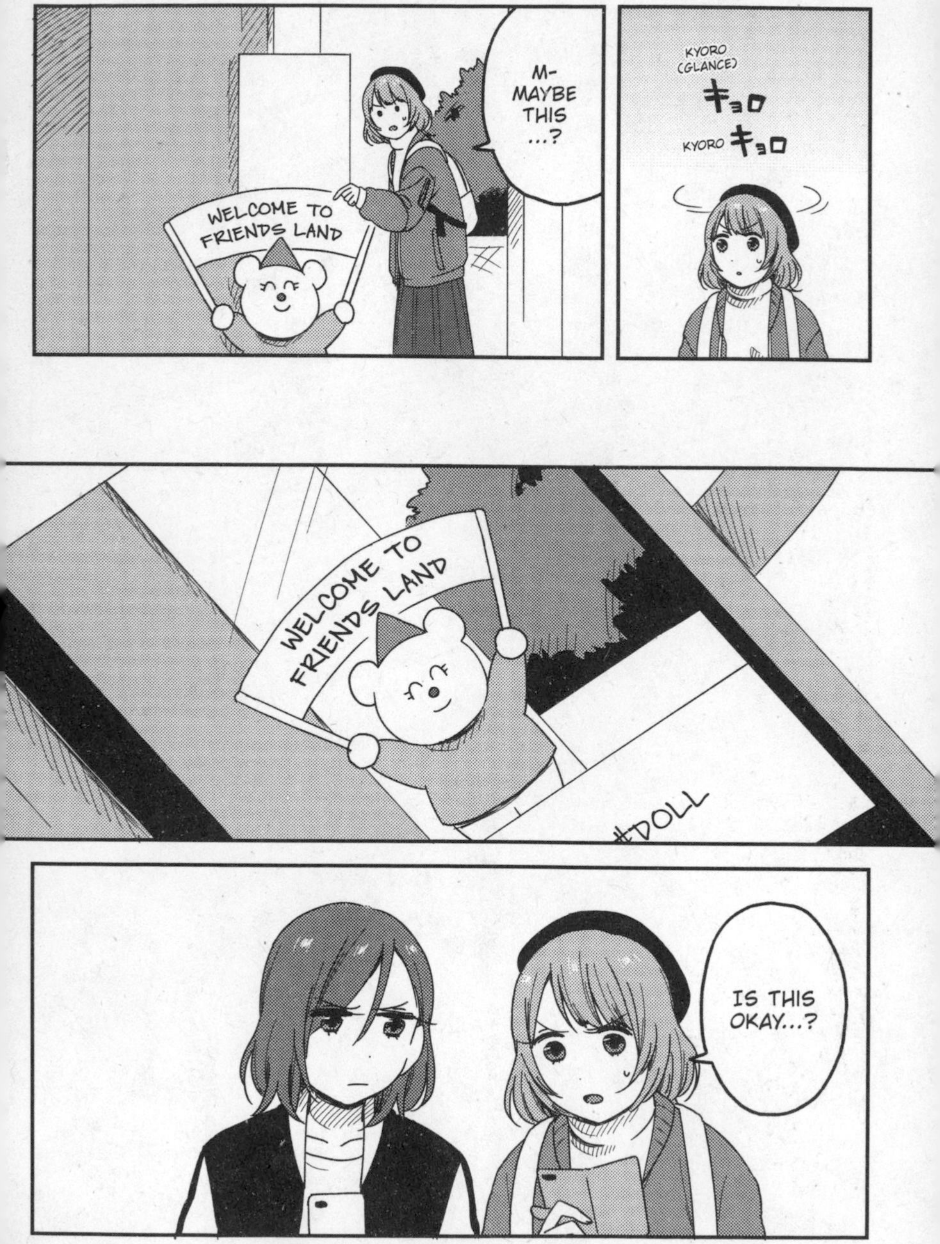
KYORO (GLANCE)
キョロ
KYORO
キョロ
M-MAYBE THIS ...?
WELCOME TO FRIENDS LAND
WELCOME TO FRIENDS LAND
#DOLL
IS THIS OKAY...?

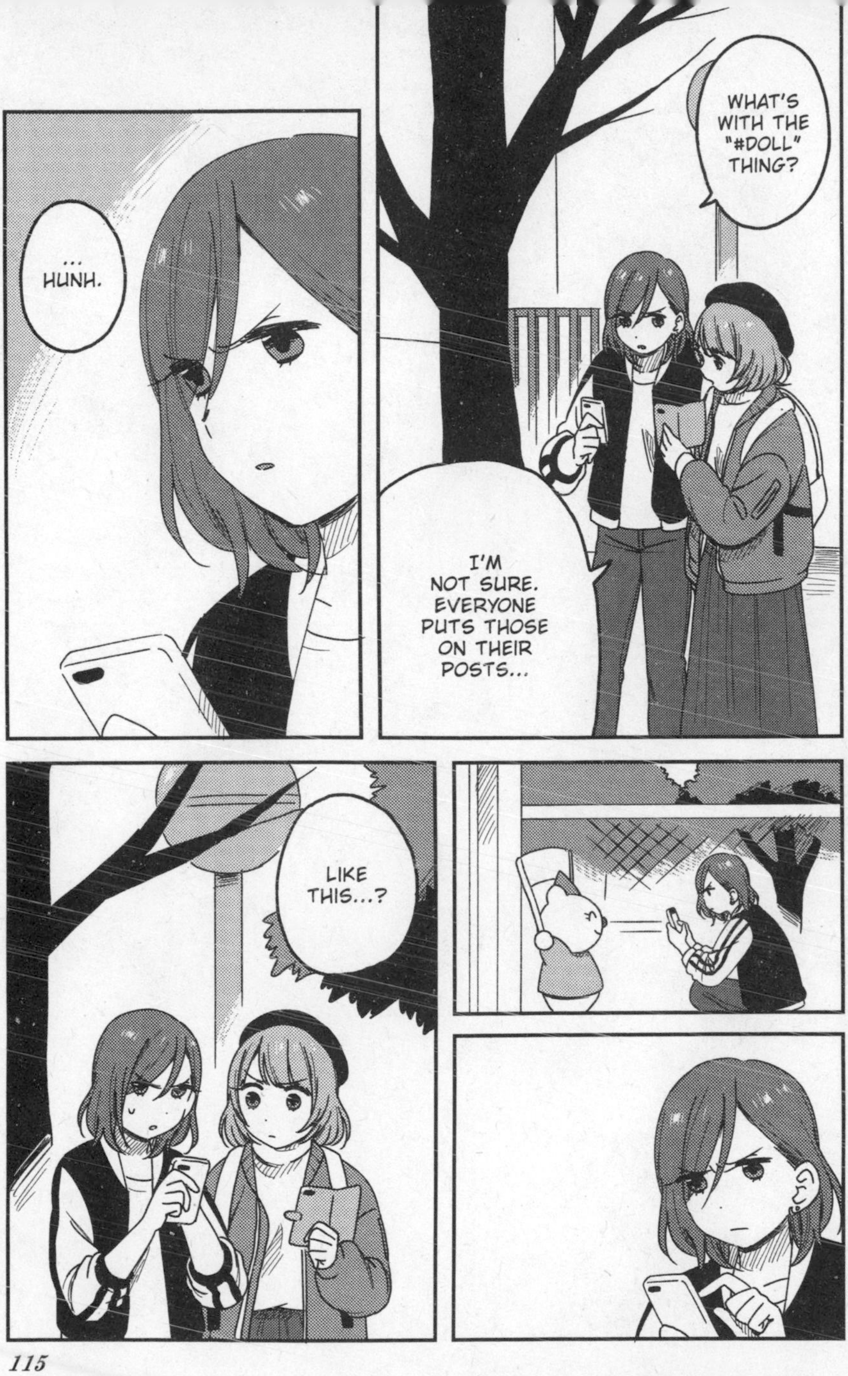
WHAT'S WITH THE "#DOLL" THING?
I'M NOT SURE. EVERYONE PUTS THOSE ON THEIR POSTS...
... HUNH.
LIKE THIS...?

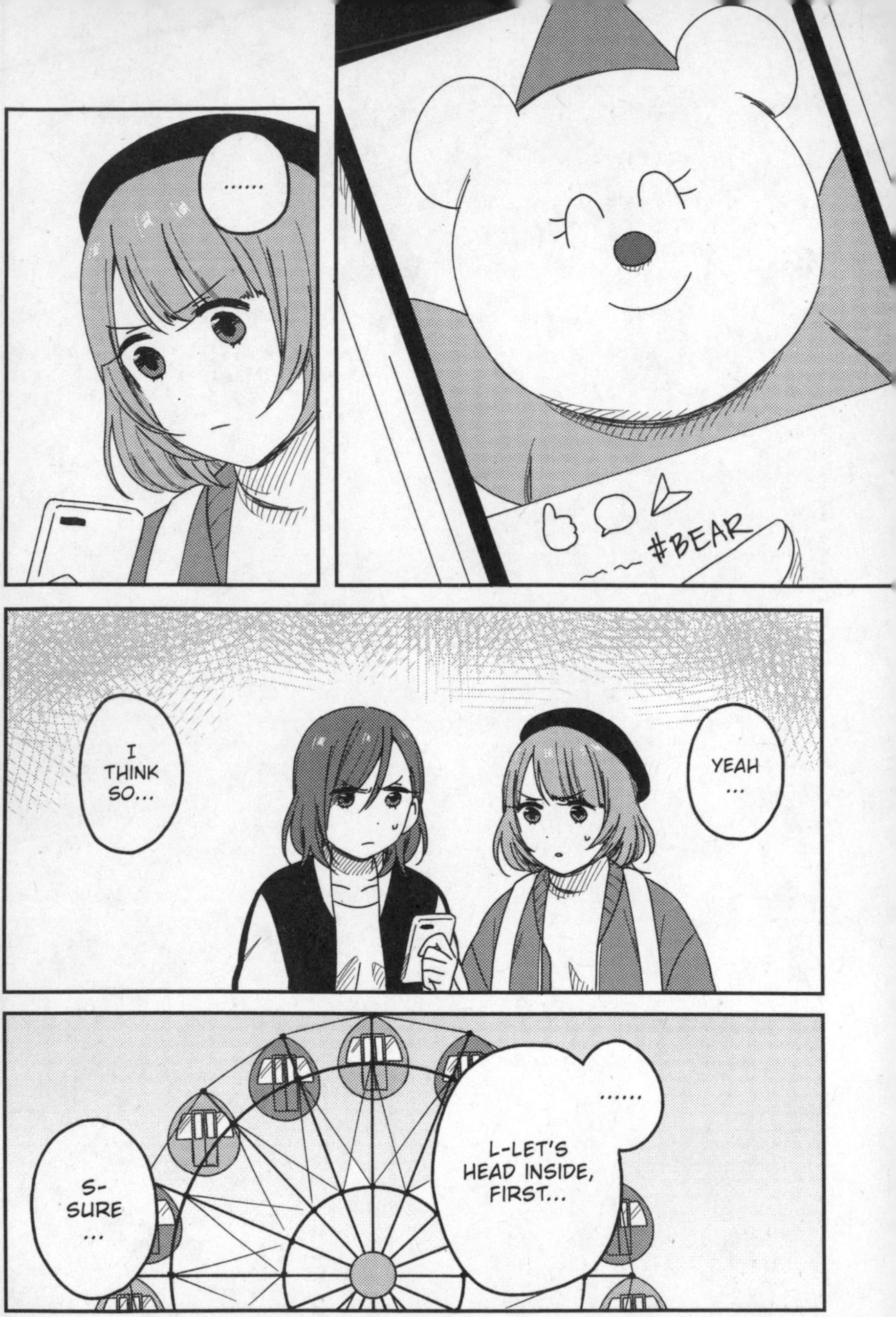
#BEAR
......
YEAH ...
I THINK SO...
......
L-LET'S HEAD INSIDE, FIRST...
S-SURE ...

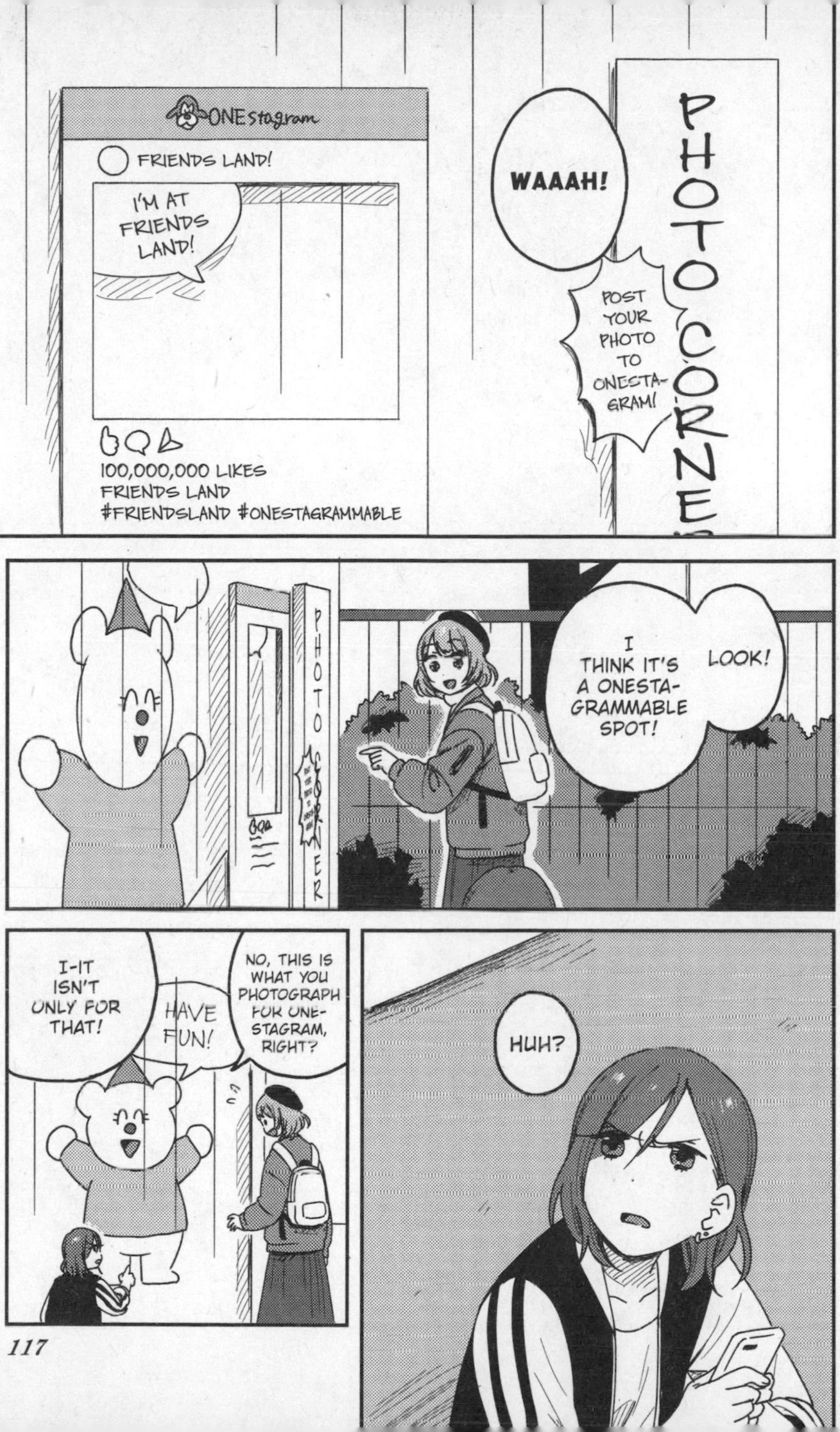
WAAAH!
PHOTO CORNER
POST YOUR PHOTO TO ONESTAGRAM!
ONEstagram
FRIENDS LAND!
I'M AT FRIENDS LAND!
100,000,000 LIKES
FRIENDS LAND
#FRIENDSLAND #ONESTAGRAMMABLE
LOOK!
I THINK IT'S A ONESTAGRAMMABLE SPOT!
PHOTO CORNER
HUH?
NO, THIS IS WHAT YOU PHOTOGRAPH FOR ONESTAGRAM, RIGHT?
HAVE FUN!
I-IT ISN'T ONLY FOR THAT!

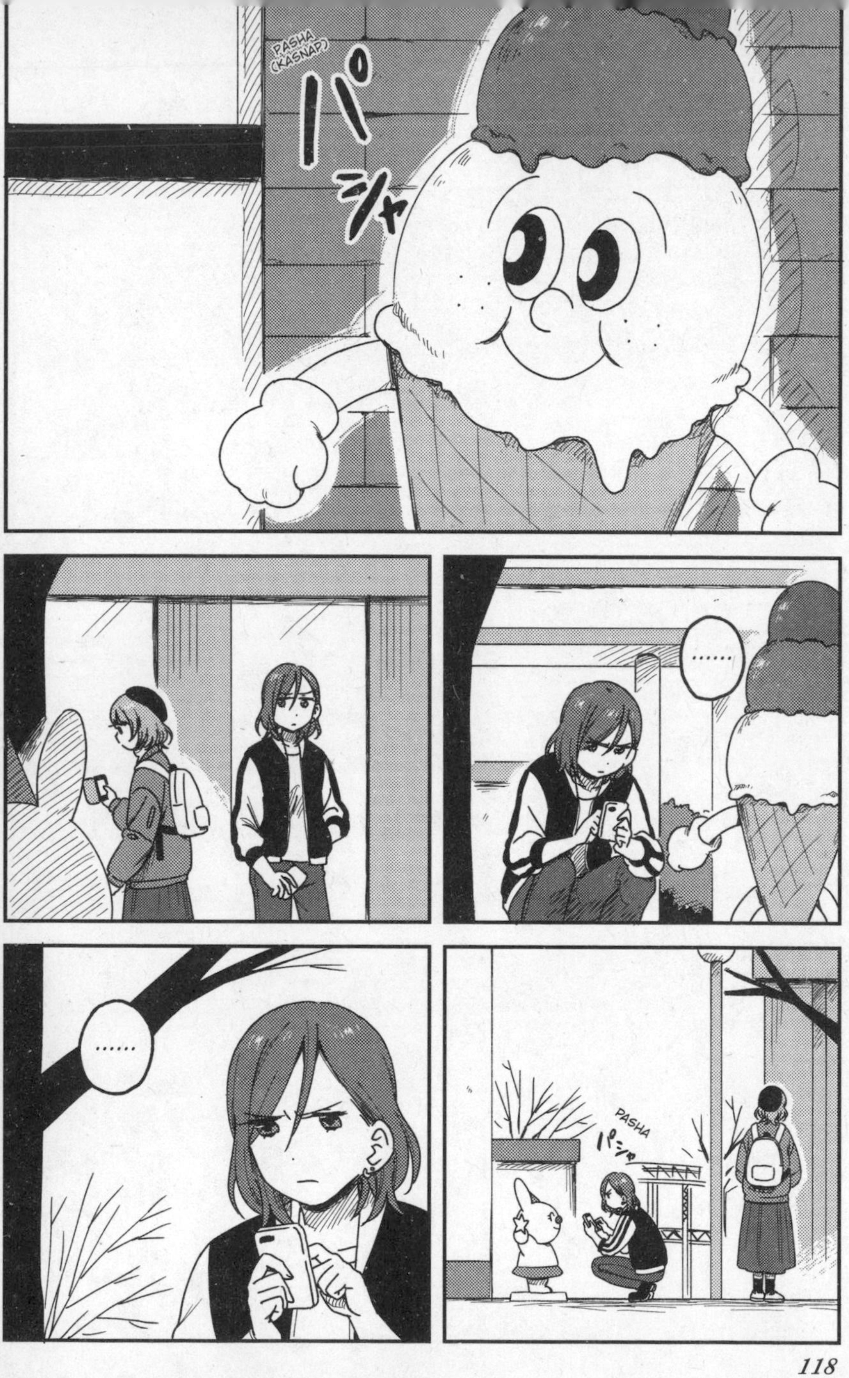
PASHA (KASNAP)
パシャ
......
PASHA
パシャ
......

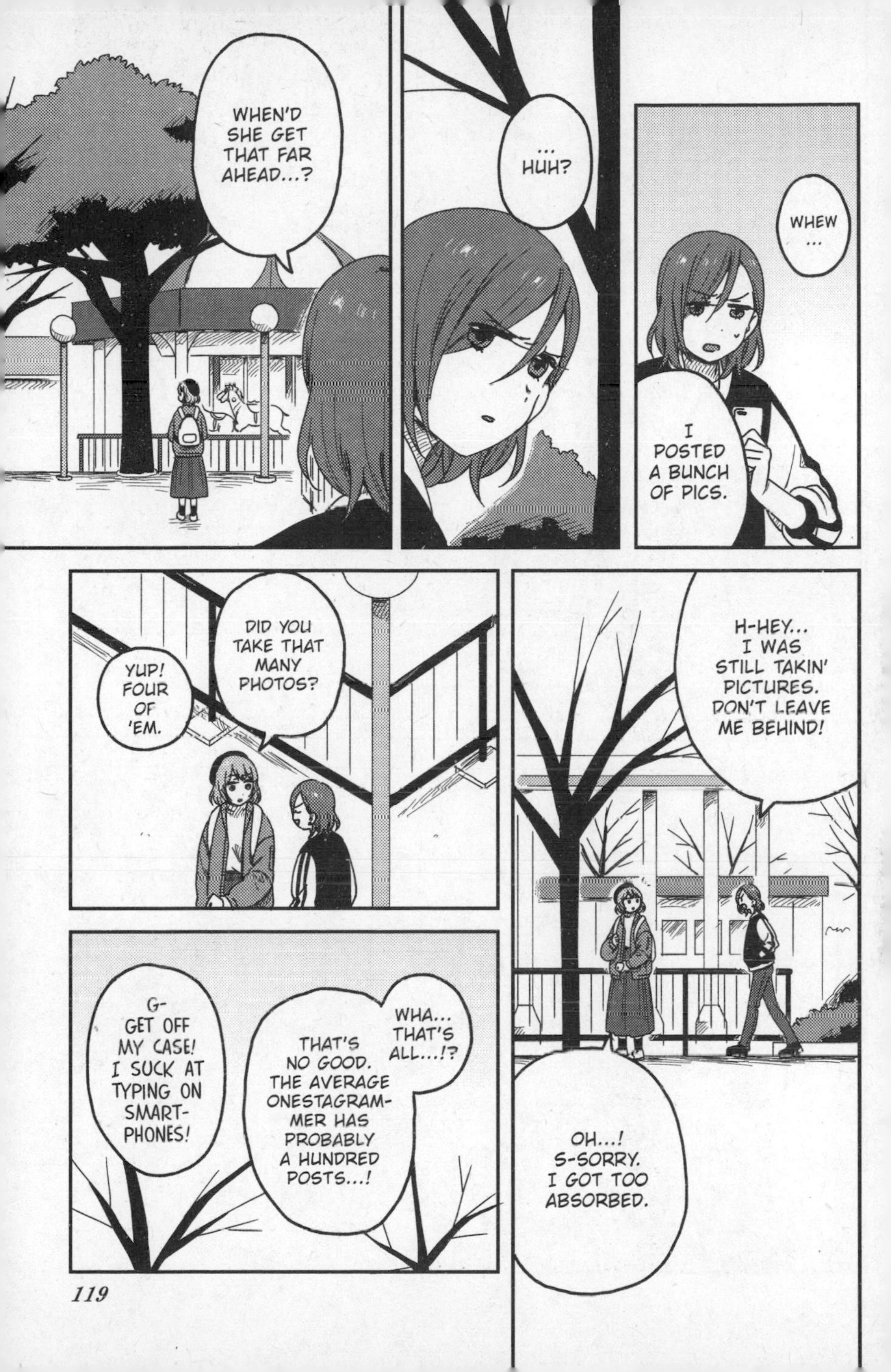
WHEW...
I POSTED A BUNCH OF PICS.
... HUH?
WHEN'D SHE GET THAT FAR AHEAD...?
H-HEY... I WAS STILL TAKIN' PICTURES. DON'T LEAVE ME BEHIND!
OH...! S-SORRY. I GOT TOO ABSORBED.
DID YOU TAKE THAT MANY PHOTOS?
YUP! FOUR OF 'EM.
WHA... THAT'S ALL...!?
THAT'S NO GOOD. THE AVERAGE ONESTAGRAMMER HAS PROBABLY A HUNDRED POSTS...!
G-GET OFF MY CASE! I SUCK AT TYPING ON SMARTPHONES!

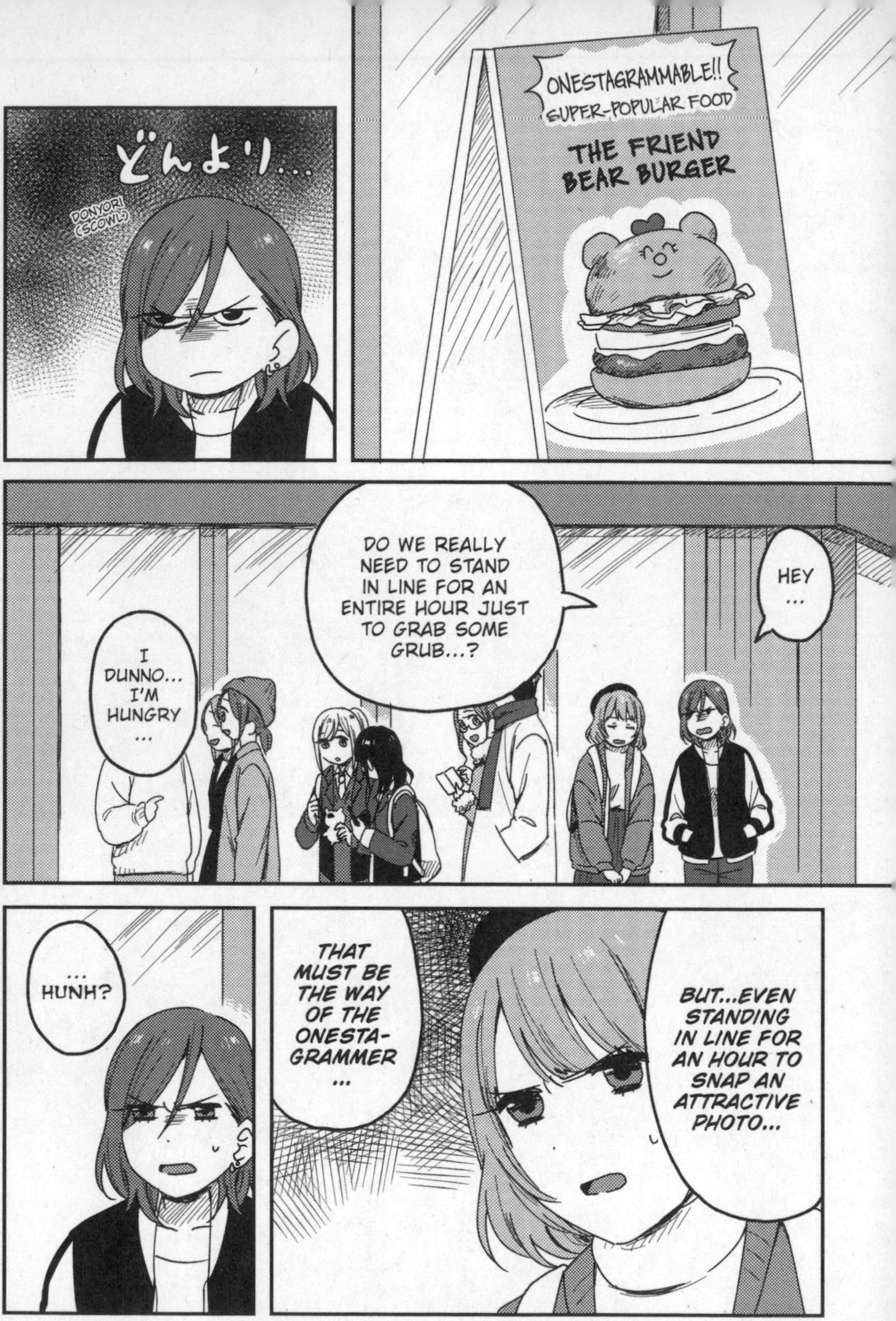
ONESTAGRAMMABLE!!
SUPER-POPULAR FOOD
THE FRIEND BEAR BURGER
どんより…
DONYORI (SCOWL)
HEY ...
DO WE REALLY NEED TO STAND IN LINE FOR AN ENTIRE HOUR JUST TO GRAB SOME GRUB...?
I DUNNO... I'M HUNGRY ...
BUT...EVEN STANDING IN LINE FOR AN HOUR TO SNAP AN ATTRACTIVE PHOTO...
THAT MUST BE THE WAY OF THE ONESTA-GRAMMER ...
... HUNH?

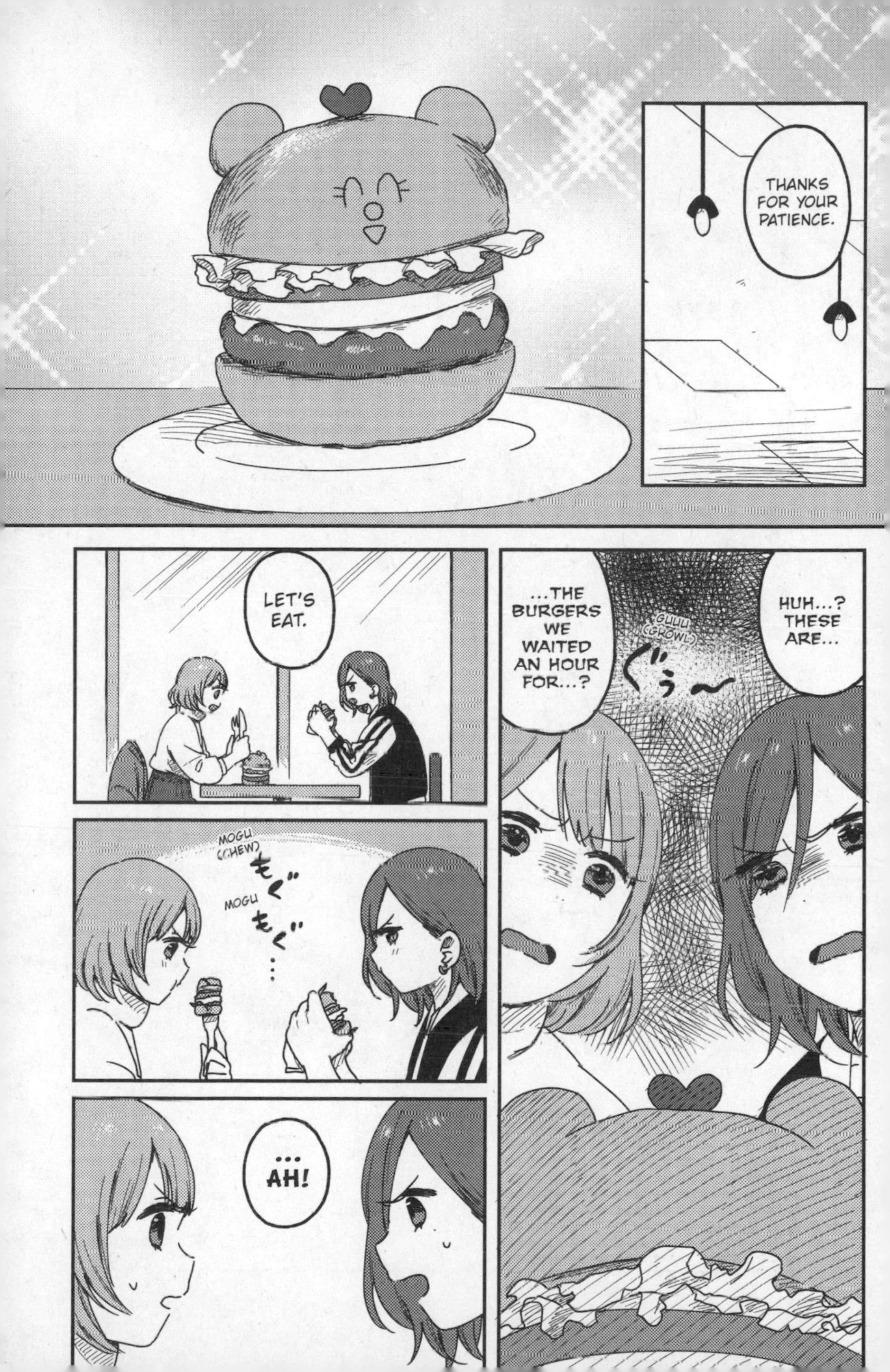
THANKS FOR YOUR PATIENCE.
HUH...? THESE ARE...
GUUU (GROWL)
ぐぅ〜
...THE BURGERS WE WAITED AN HOUR FOR...?
LET'S EAT.
MOGU (CHEW)
もぐ
MOGU
もぐ...
...AH!

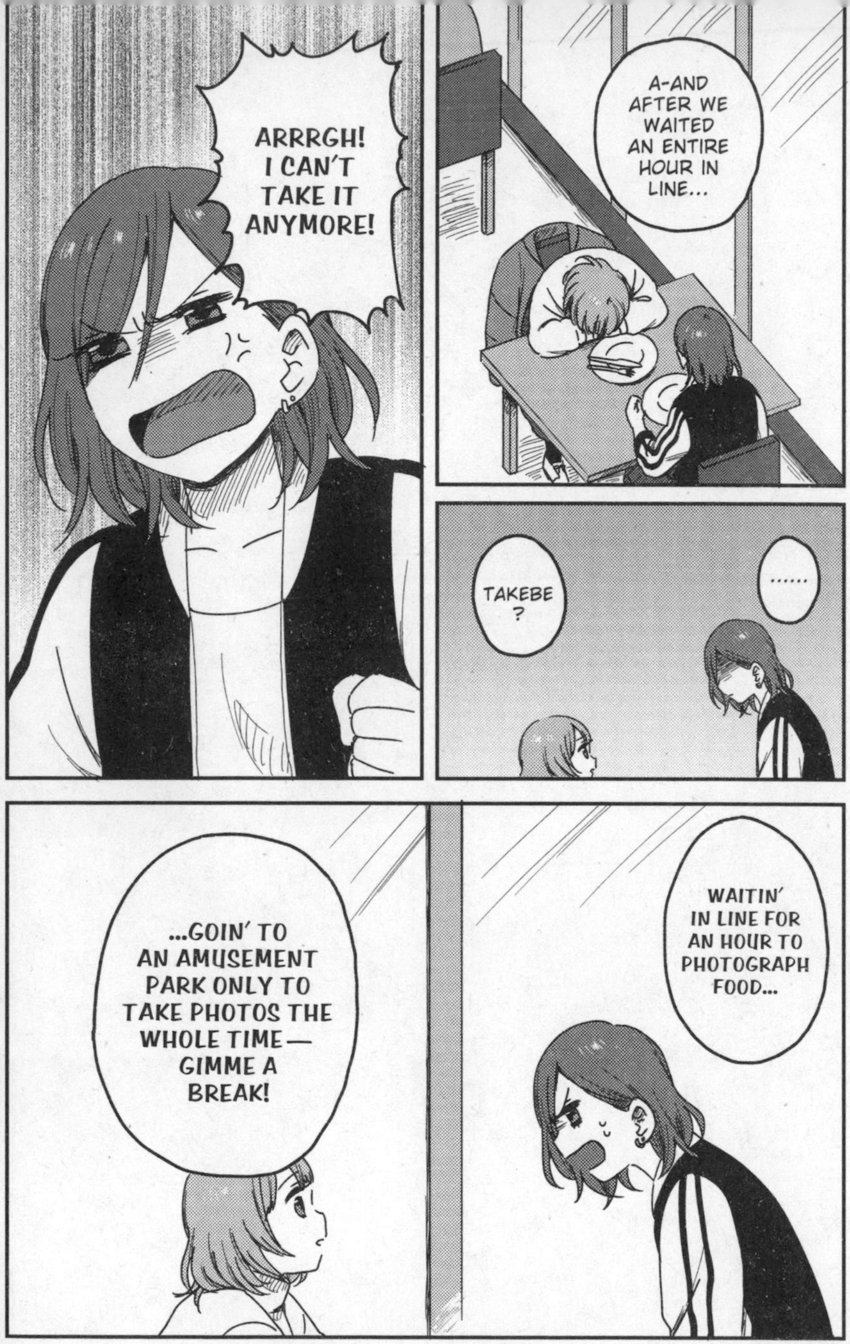
A-AND AFTER WE WAITED AN ENTIRE HOUR IN LINE...
......
TAKEBE ?
ARRRGH! I CAN'T TAKE IT ANYMORE!
WAITIN' IN LINE FOR AN HOUR TO PHOTOGRAPH FOOD...
...GOIN' TO AN AMUSEMENT PARK ONLY TO TAKE PHOTOS THE WHOLE TIME— GIMME A BREAK!

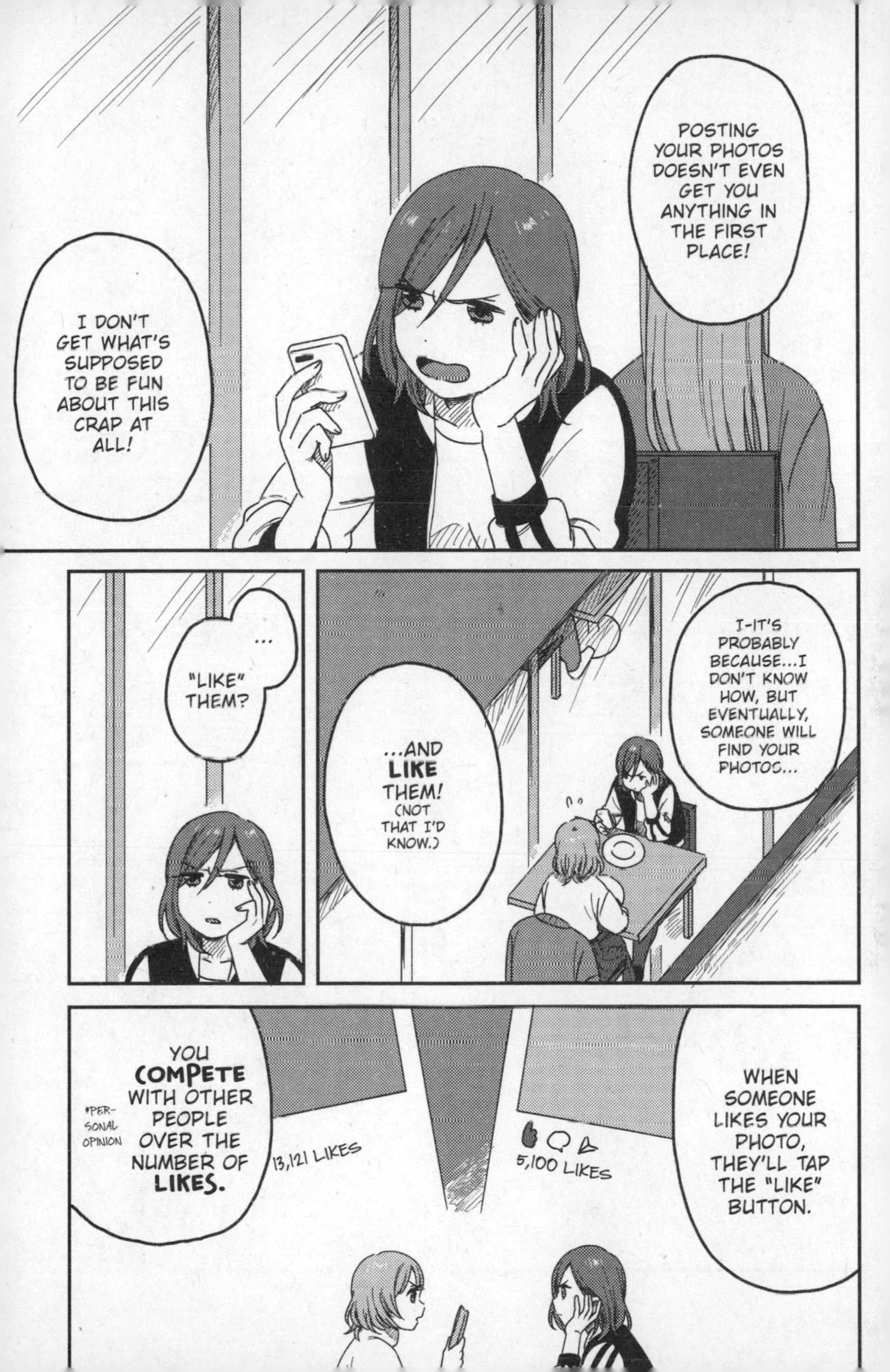
POSTING YOUR PHOTOS DOESN'T EVEN GET YOU ANYTHING IN THE FIRST PLACE!
I DON'T GET WHAT'S SUPPOSED TO BE FUN ABOUT THIS CRAP AT ALL!
I-IT'S PROBABLY BECAUSE...I DON'T KNOW HOW, BUT EVENTUALLY, SOMEONE WILL FIND YOUR PHOTOS...
...AND LIKE THEM! (NOT THAT I'D KNOW.)
... "LIKE" THEM?
WHEN SOMEONE LIKES YOUR PHOTO, THEY'LL TAP THE "LIKE" BUTTON.
5,100 LIKES
13,121 LIKES
YOU COMPETE WITH OTHER PEOPLE OVER THE NUMBER OF LIKES.
*PERSONAL OPINION

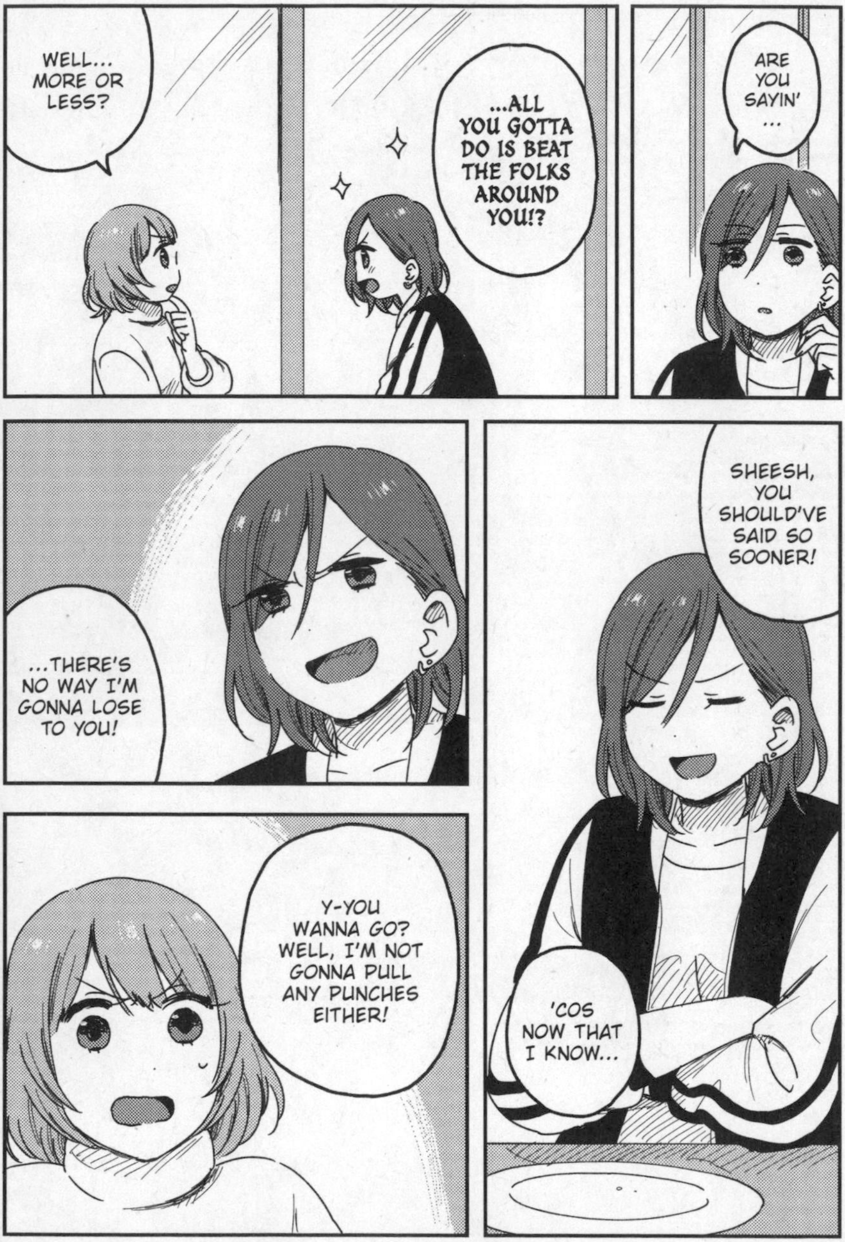

ARE YOU SAYIN' ...
...ALL YOU GOTTA DO IS BEAT THE FOLKS AROUND YOU!?
WELL... MORE OR LESS?
SHEESH, YOU SHOULD'VE SAID SO SOONER!
'COS NOW THAT I KNOW...
...THERE'S NO WAY I'M GONNA LOSE TO YOU!
Y-YOU WANNA GO? WELL, I'M NOT GONNA PULL ANY PUNCHES EITHER!

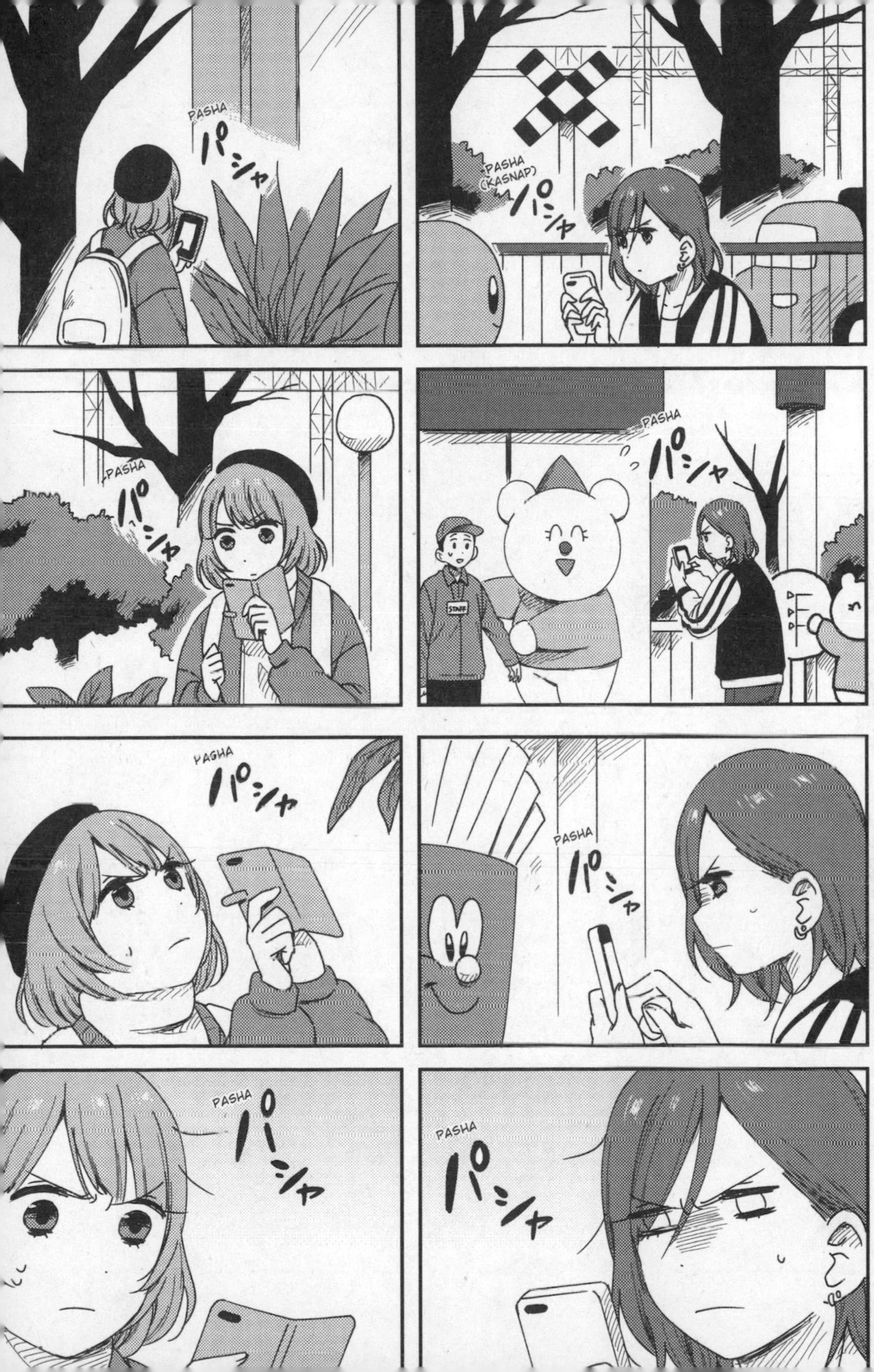
PASHA (KASNAP)
パシャ
PASHA
パシャ
PASHA
パシャ
STAFF
PASHA
パシャ
PASHA
パシャ
PASHA
パシャ
PASHA
パシャ
PASHA
パシャ

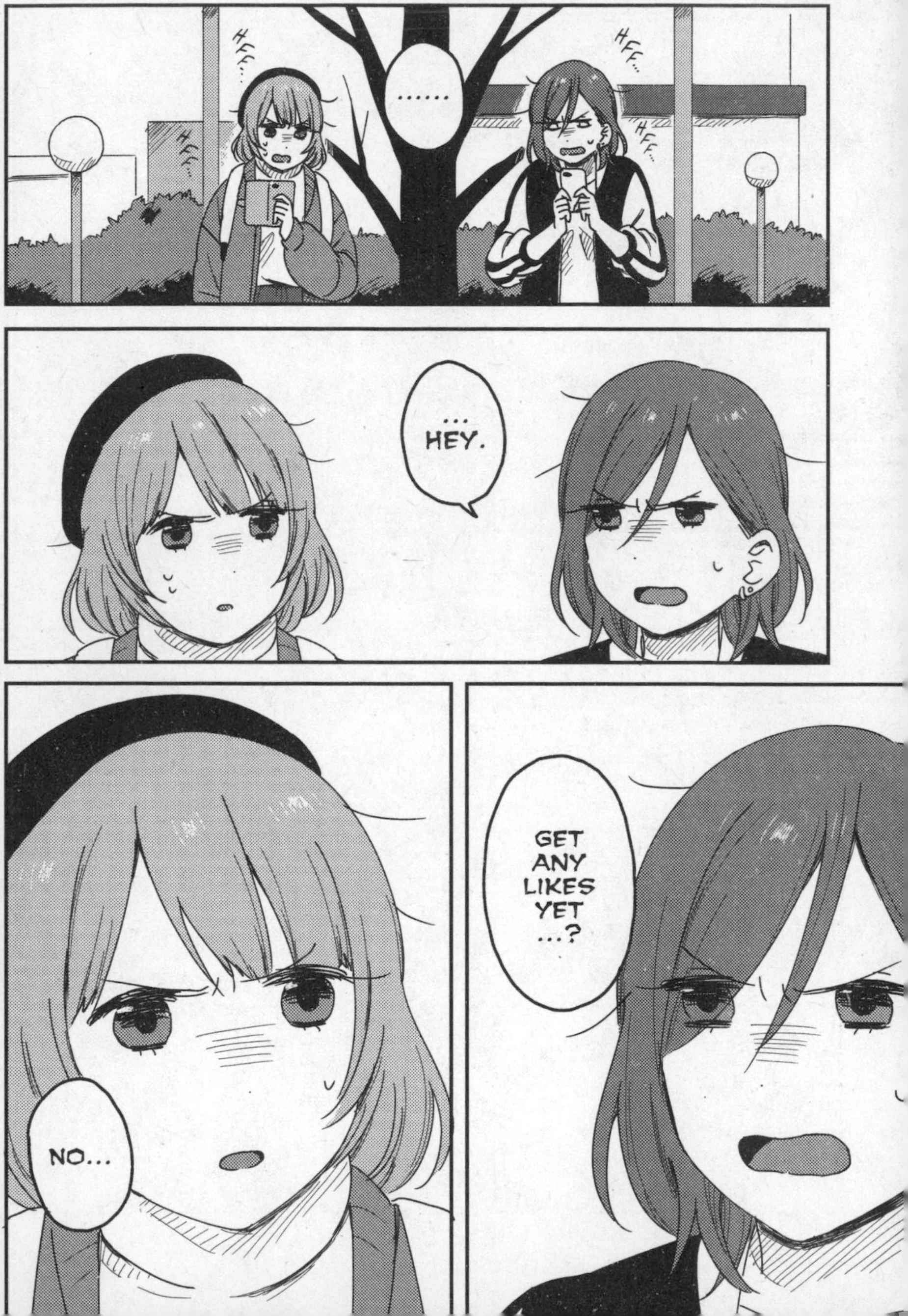
HFF...
HFF...
......
HFF...
HFF...
... HEY.
GET ANY LIKES YET ...?
NO...

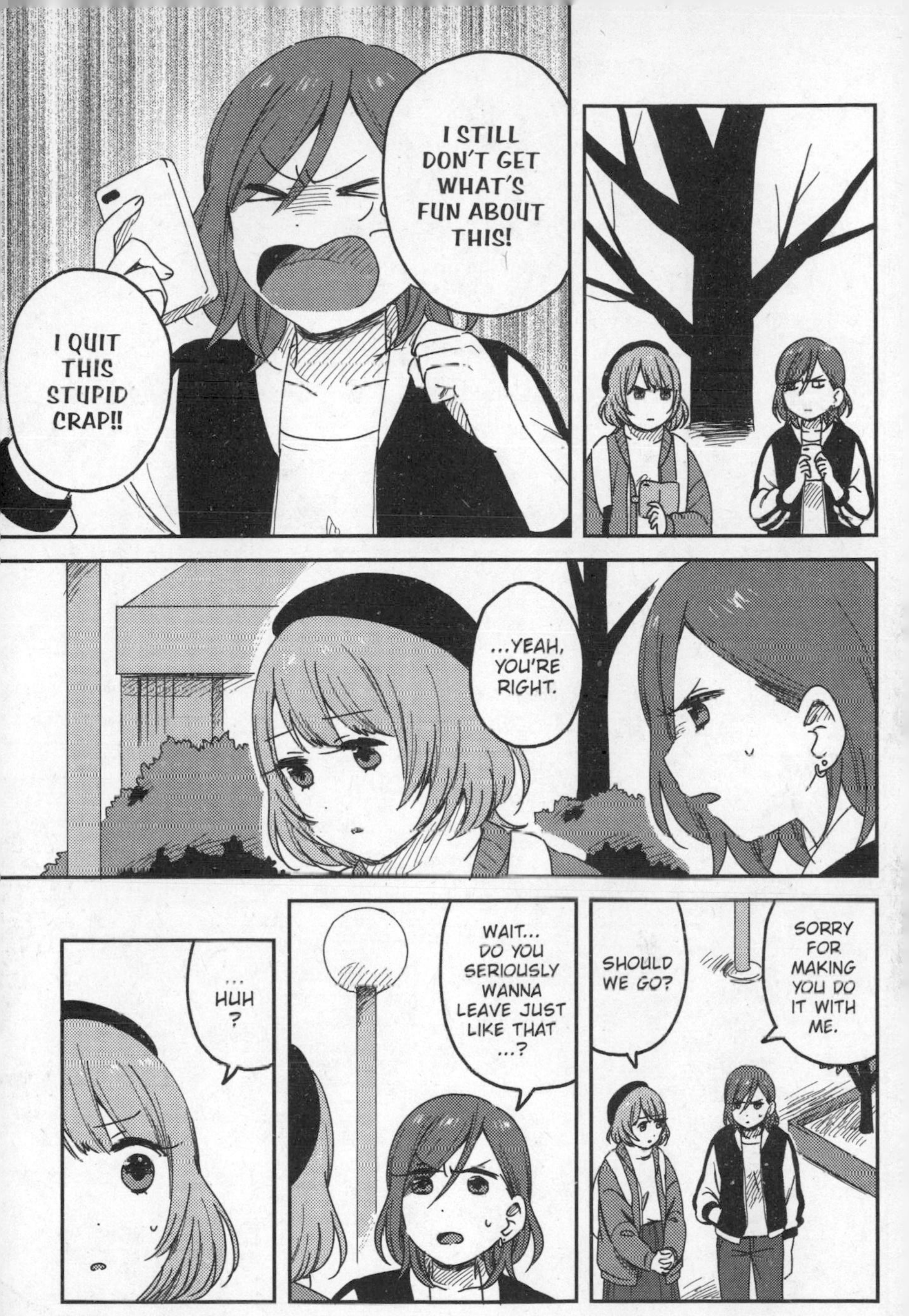
I STILL DON'T GET WHAT'S FUN ABOUT THIS!
I QUIT THIS STUPID CRAP!!
...YEAH, YOU'RE RIGHT.
SORRY FOR MAKING YOU DO IT WITH ME.
SHOULD WE GO?
WAIT... DO YOU SERIOUSLY WANNA LEAVE JUST LIKE THAT ...?
... HUH ?

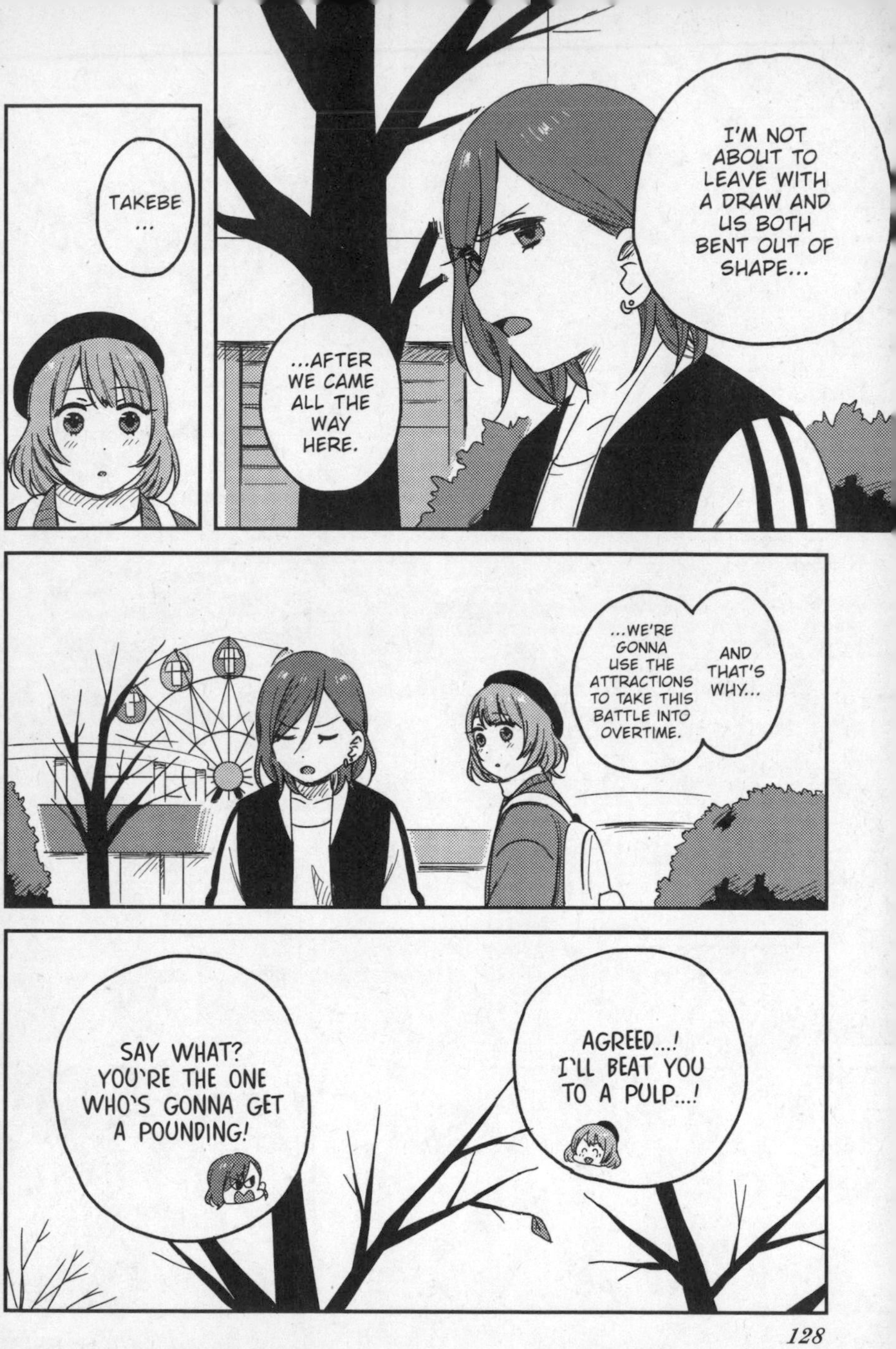
I'M NOT ABOUT TO LEAVE WITH A DRAW AND US BOTH BENT OUT OF SHAPE...
...AFTER WE CAME ALL THE WAY HERE.
TAKEBE ...
AND THAT'S WHY...
...WE'RE GONNA USE THE ATTRACTIONS TO TAKE THIS BATTLE INTO OVERTIME.
AGREED...! I'LL BEAT YOU TO A PULP...!
SAY WHAT? YOU'RE THE ONE WHO'S GONNA GET A POUNDING!

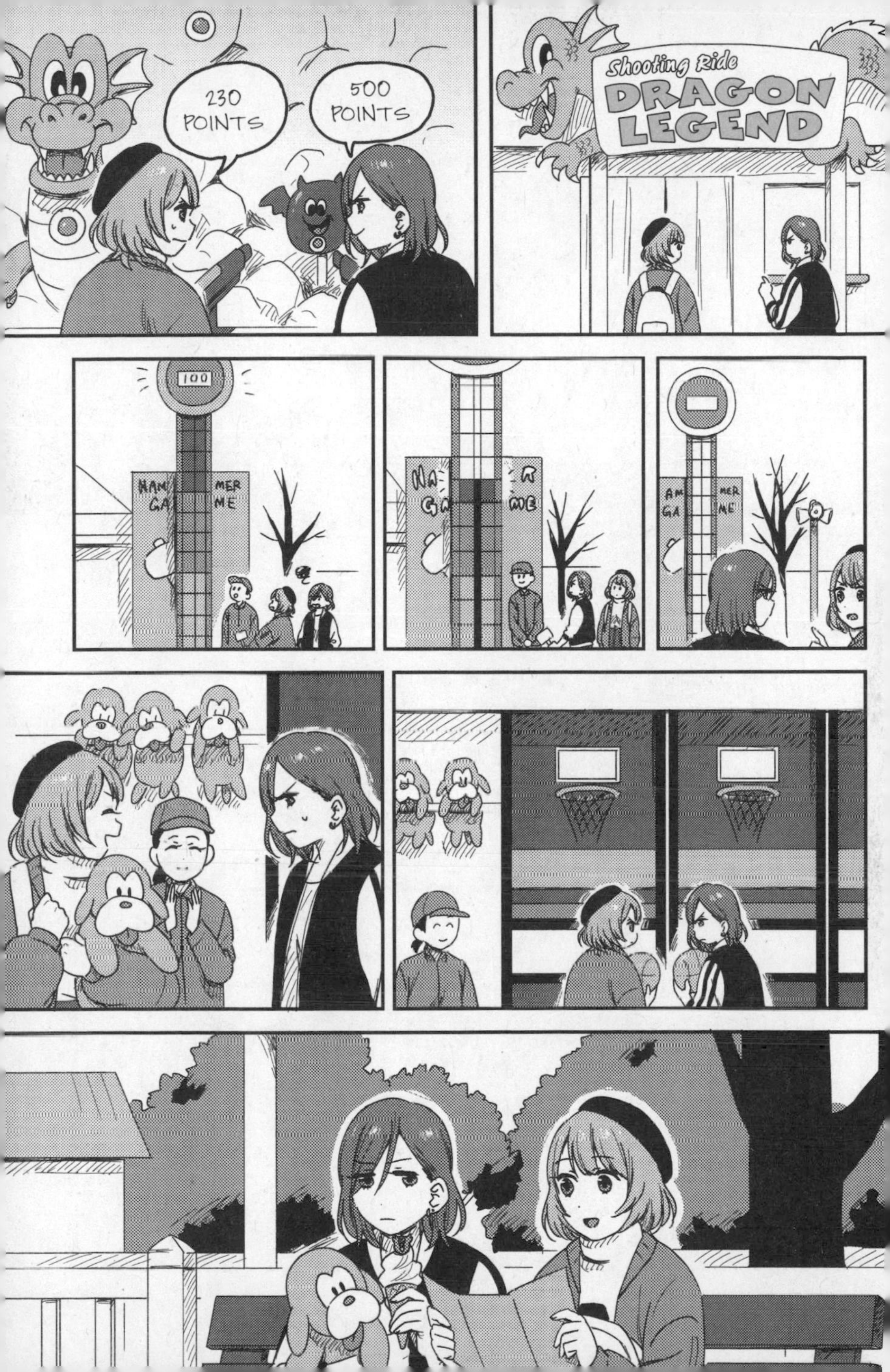
Shooting Ride
DRAGON LEGEND
500 POINTS
230 POINTS
100

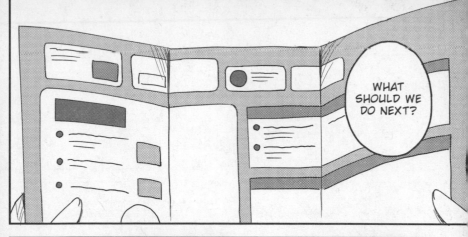

WHAT SHOULD WE DO NEXT?

LET'S SEE...

DOESN'T THIS TOTALLY FEEL LIKE A DATE...?

HUH ...?

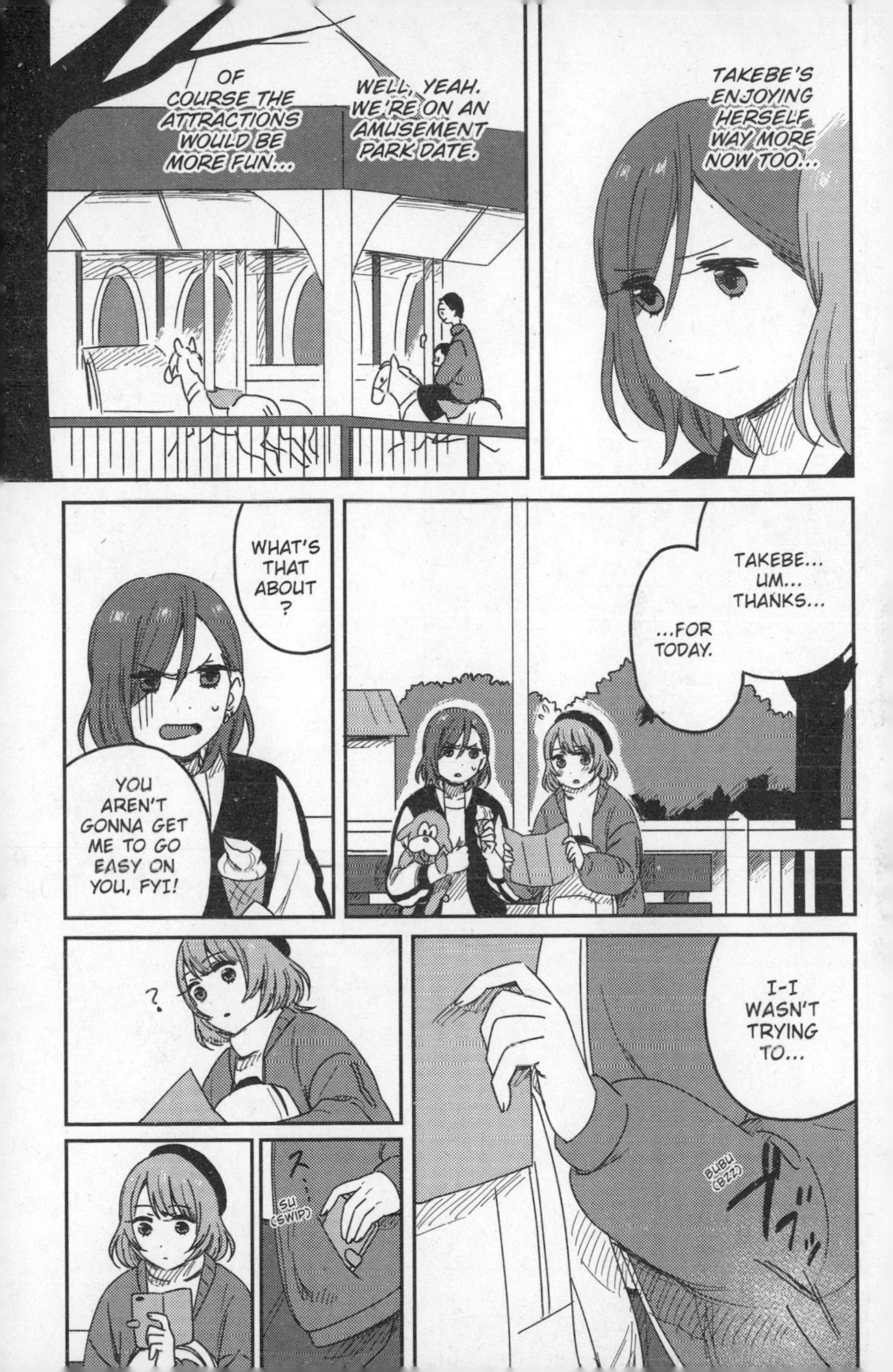
TAKEBE'S ENJOYING HERSELF WAY MORE NOW TOO...
WELL, YEAH. WE'RE ON AN AMUSEMENT PARK DATE.
OF COURSE THE ATTRACTIONS WOULD BE MORE FUN...
TAKEBE... UM... THANKS...
...FOR TODAY.
WHAT'S THAT ABOUT?
YOU AREN'T GONNA GET ME TO GO EASY ON YOU, FYI!
I-I WASN'T TRYING TO...
BUBU (BZZ)
?
SU (SWIP)

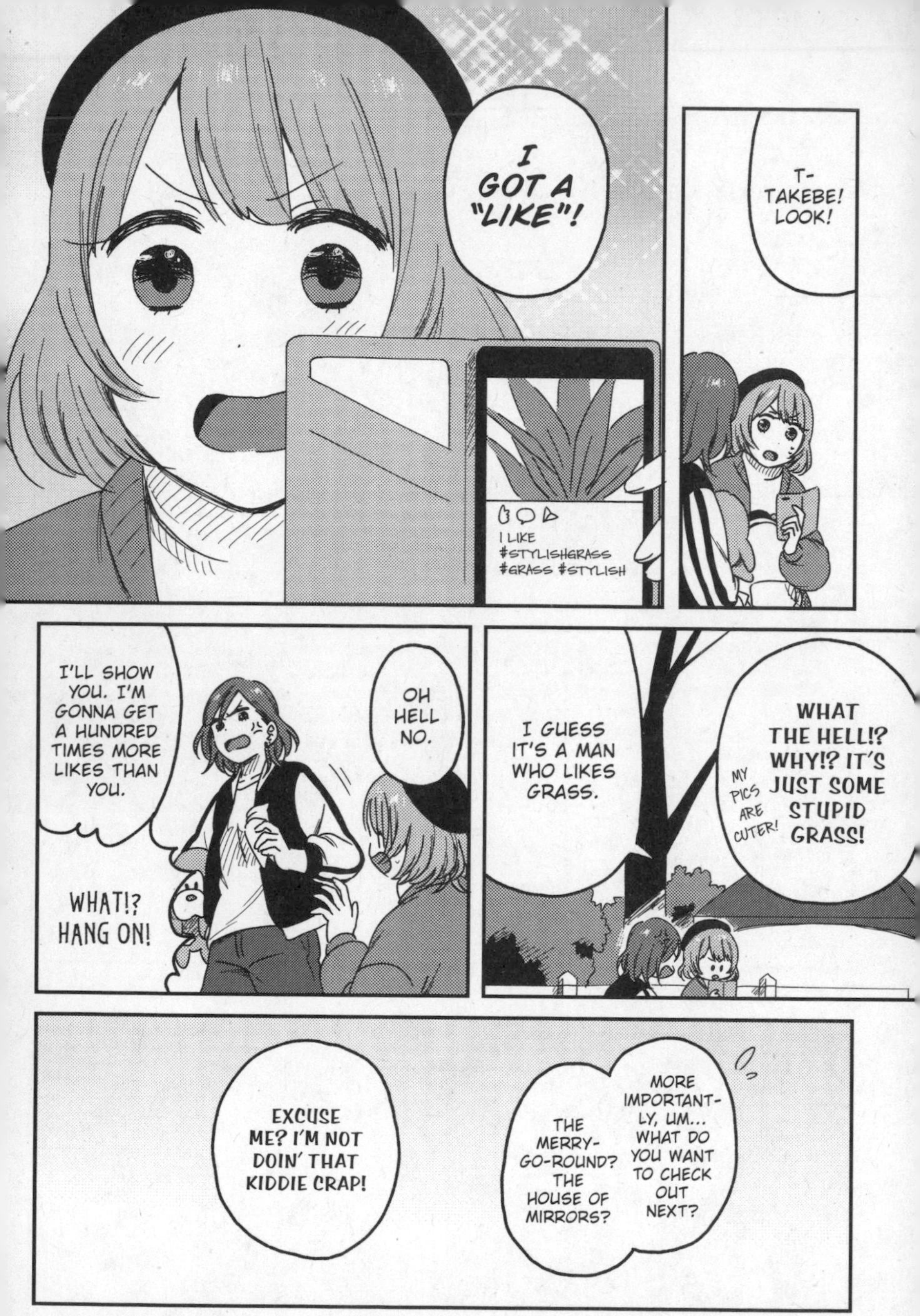
T-TAKEBE! LOOK!
I GOT A "LIKE"!
I LIKE #STYLISHGRASS #GRASS #STYLISH
WHAT THE HELL!? WHY!? IT'S JUST SOME STUPID GRASS!
MY PICS ARE CUTER!
I GUESS IT'S A MAN WHO LIKES GRASS.
OH HELL NO.
I'LL SHOW YOU. I'M GONNA GET A HUNDRED TIMES MORE LIKES THAN YOU.
WHAT!? HANG ON!
MORE IMPORTANTLY, UM... WHAT DO YOU WANT TO CHECK OUT NEXT?
THE MERRY-GO-ROUND? THE HOUSE OF MIRRORS?
EXCUSE ME? I'M NOT DOIN' THAT KIDDIE CRAP!

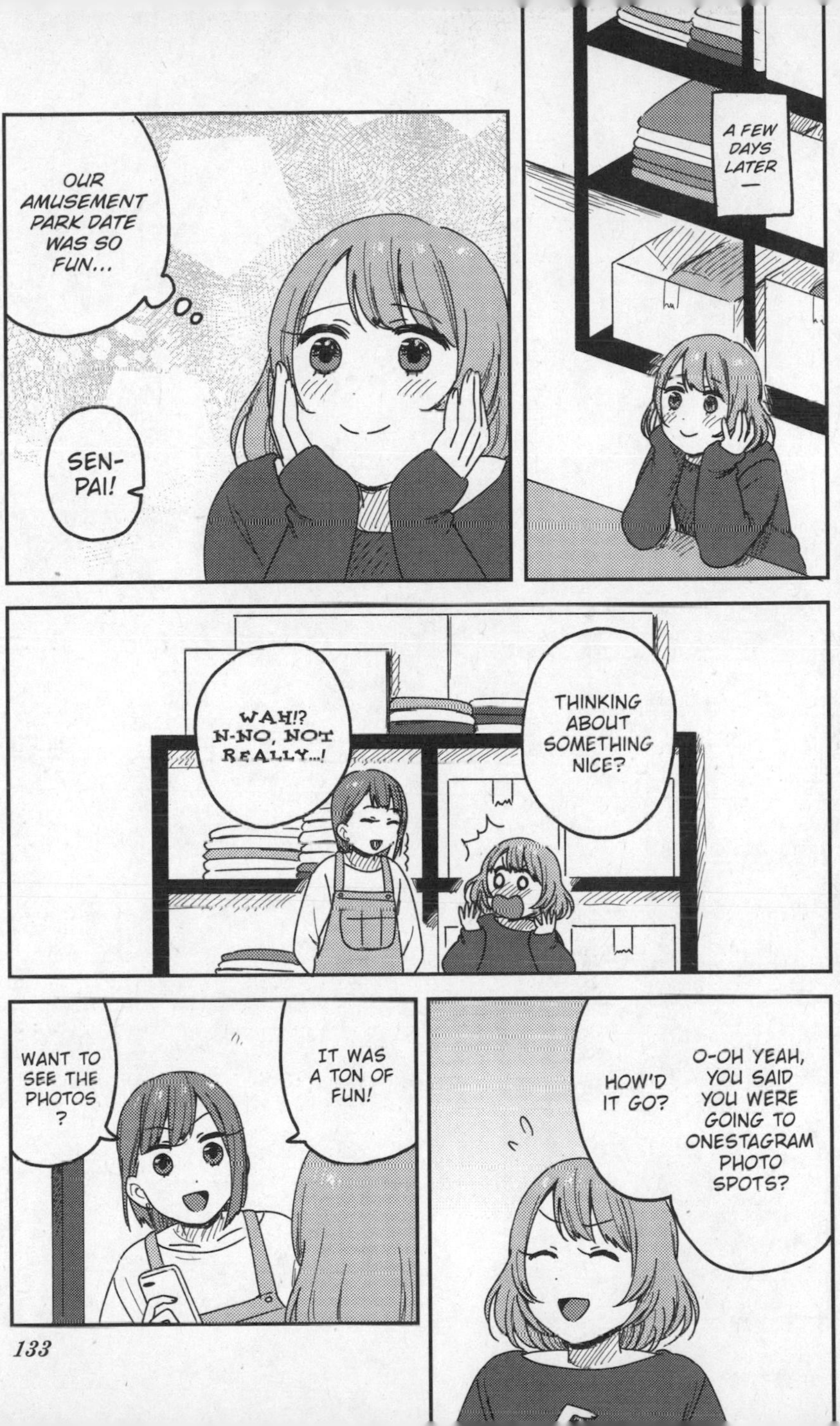
A FEW DAYS LATER —
OUR AMUSEMENT PARK DATE WAS SO FUN...
SEN-PAI!
THINKING ABOUT SOMETHING NICE?
WAH!? N-NO, NOT REALLY...!
O-OH YEAH, YOU SAID YOU WERE GOING TO ONESTAGRAM PHOTO SPOTS?
HOW'D IT GO?
IT WAS A TON OF FUN!
WANT TO SEE THE PHOTOS?

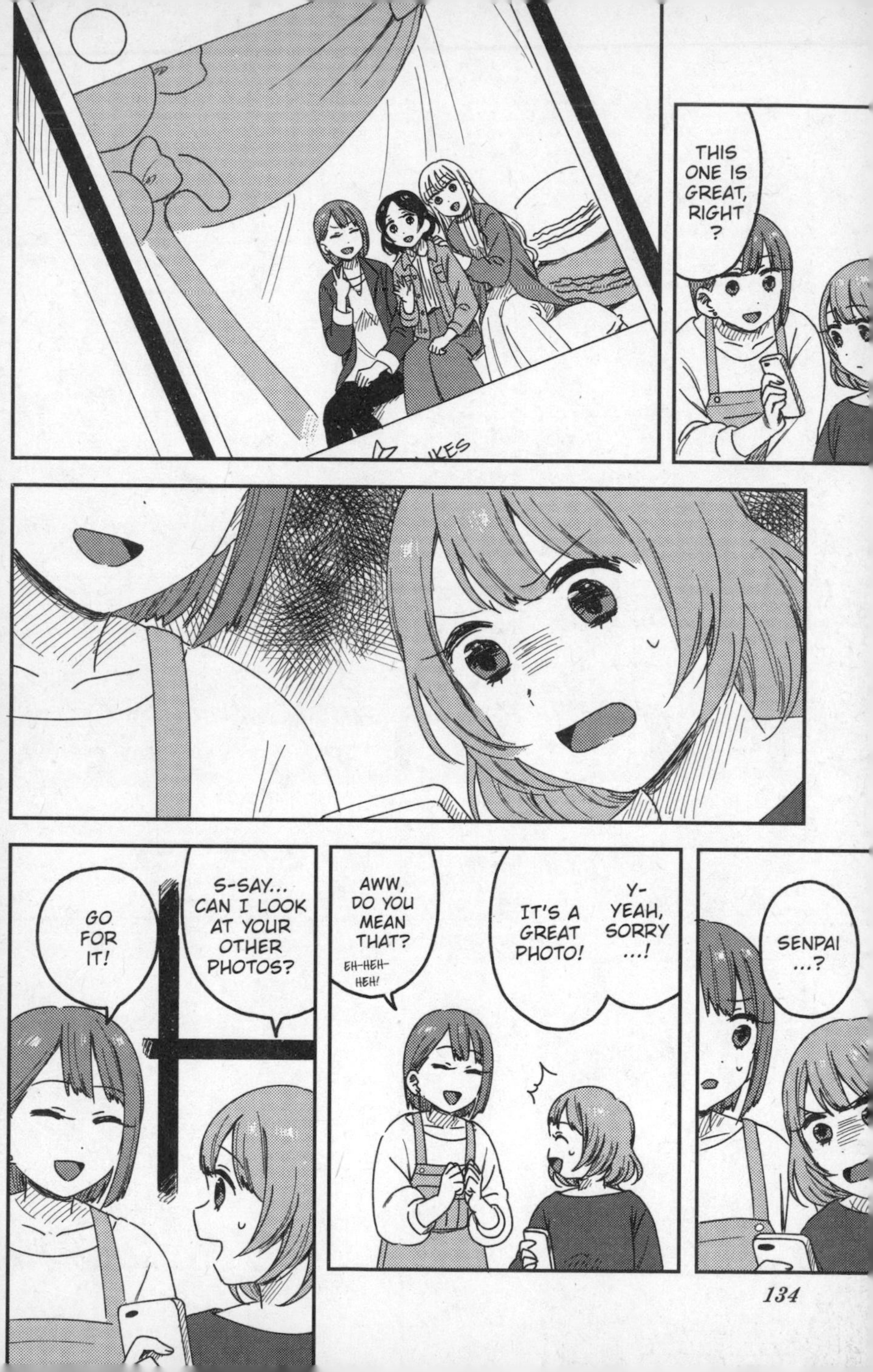
THIS ONE IS GREAT, RIGHT?
SENPAI ...?
Y-YEAH, SORRY ...!
IT'S A GREAT PHOTO!
AWW, DO YOU MEAN THAT?
EH-HEH-HEH!
S-SAY... CAN I LOOK AT YOUR OTHER PHOTOS?
GO FOR IT!

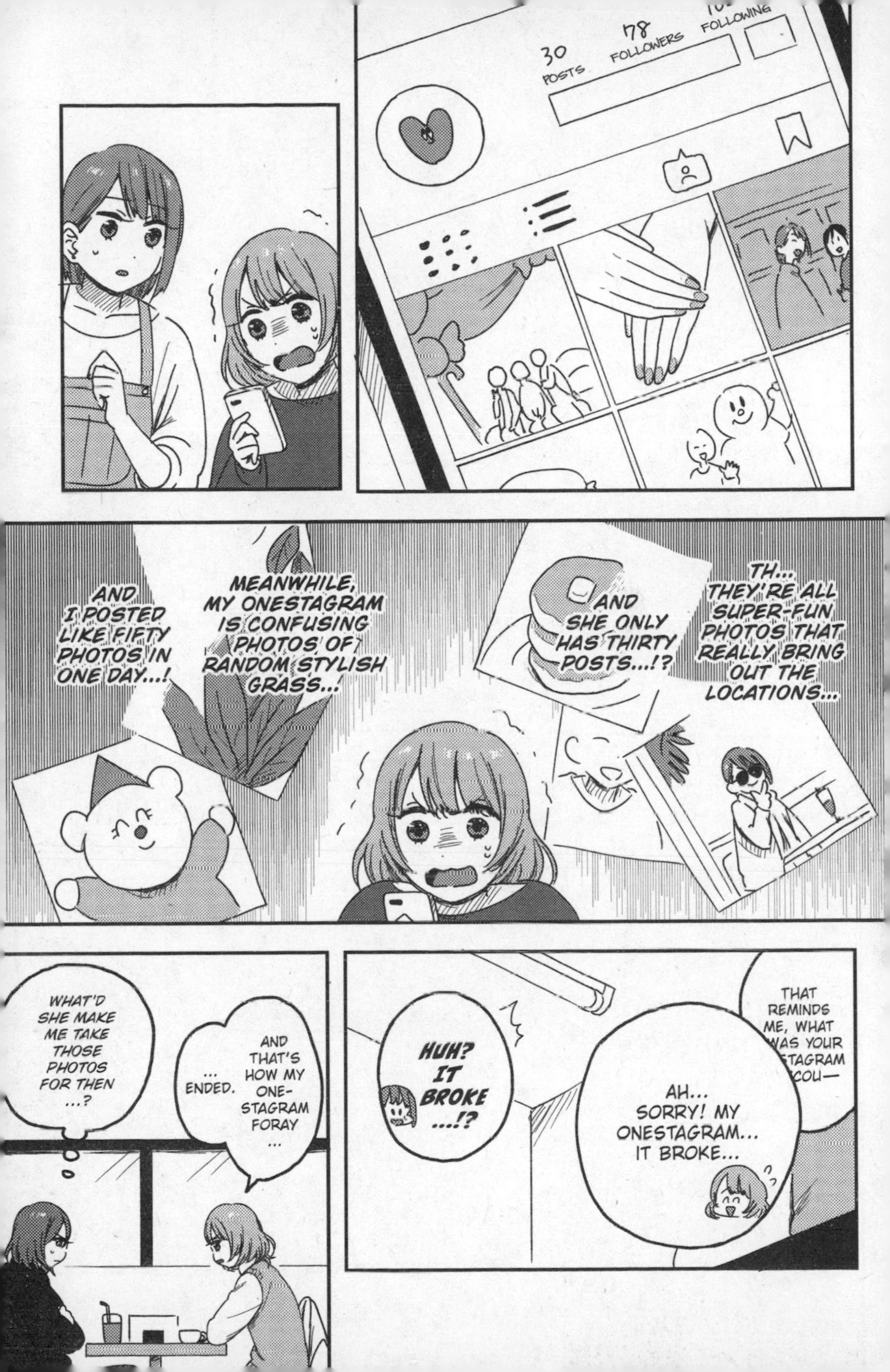
30 POSTS
178 FOLLOWERS
FOLLOWING
TH... THEY'RE ALL SUPER-FUN PHOTOS THAT REALLY BRING OUT THE LOCATIONS...
AND SHE ONLY HAS THIRTY POSTS...!?
MEANWHILE, MY ONESTAGRAM IS CONFUSING PHOTOS OF RANDOM STYLISH GRASS...
AND I POSTED LIKE FIFTY PHOTOS IN ONE DAY...!
THAT REMINDS ME, WHAT WAS YOUR STAGRAM COU—
AH... SORRY! MY ONESTAGRAM... IT BROKE...
HUH? IT BROKE ....!?
AND THAT'S HOW MY ONE-STAGRAM FORAY ... ... ENDED.
WHAT'D SHE MAKE ME TAKE THOSE PHOTOS FOR THEN ...?

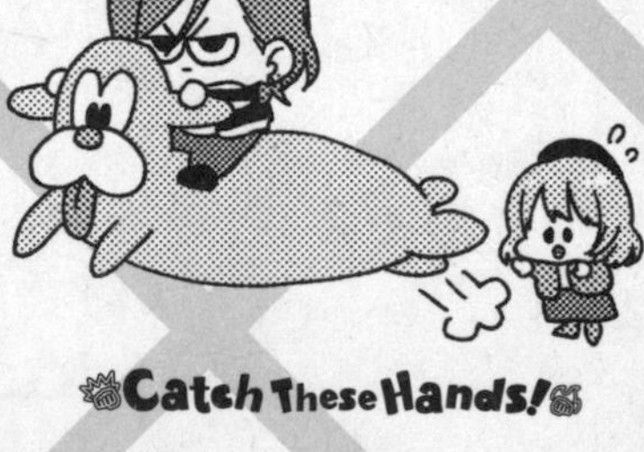

Catch These Hands!

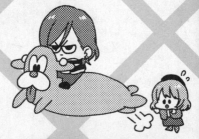

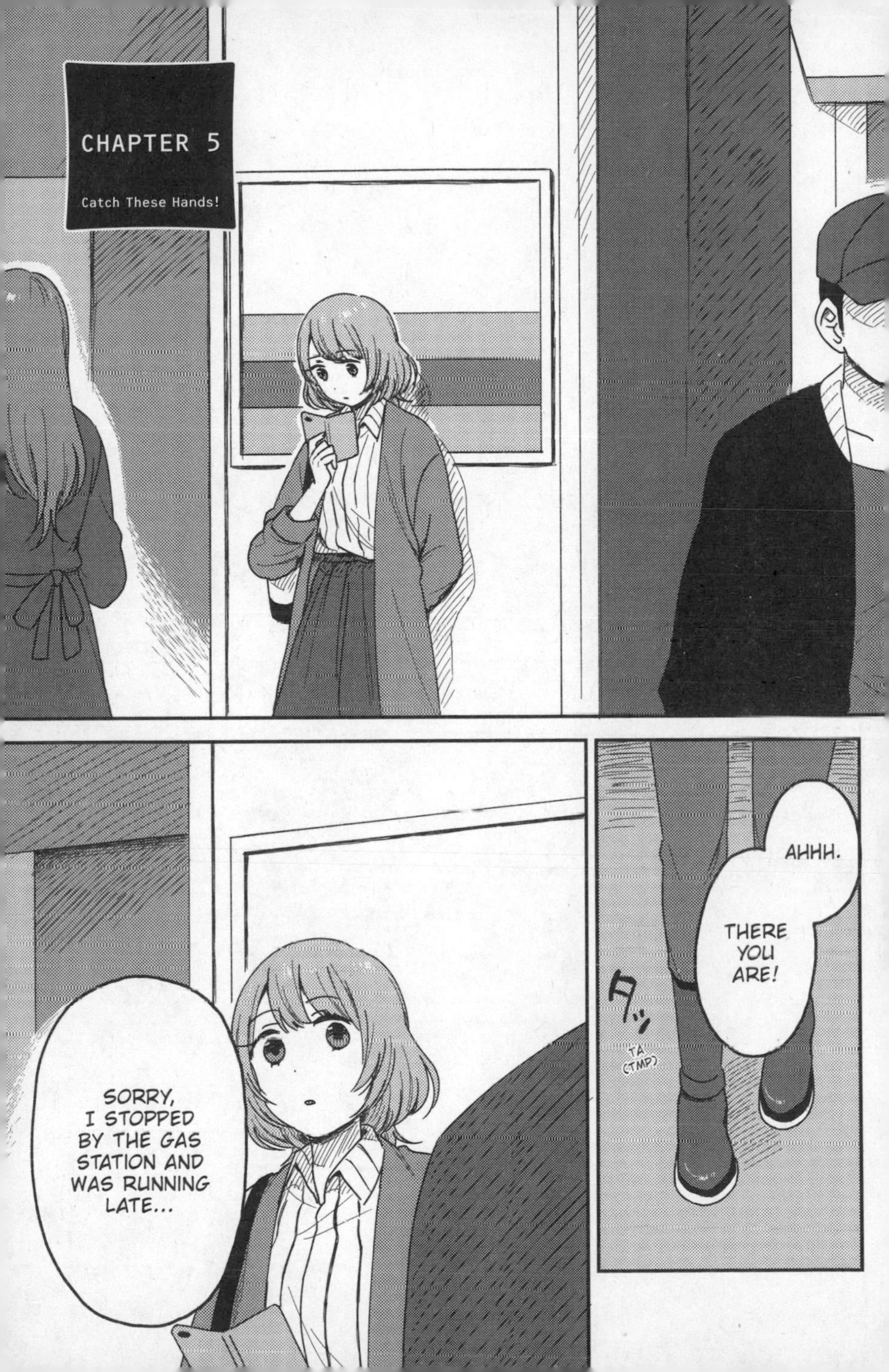
CHAPTER 5
Catch These Hands!
AHHH.
THERE YOU ARE!
タッ
TA (TMP)
SORRY, I STOPPED BY THE GAS STATION AND WAS RUNNING LATE...

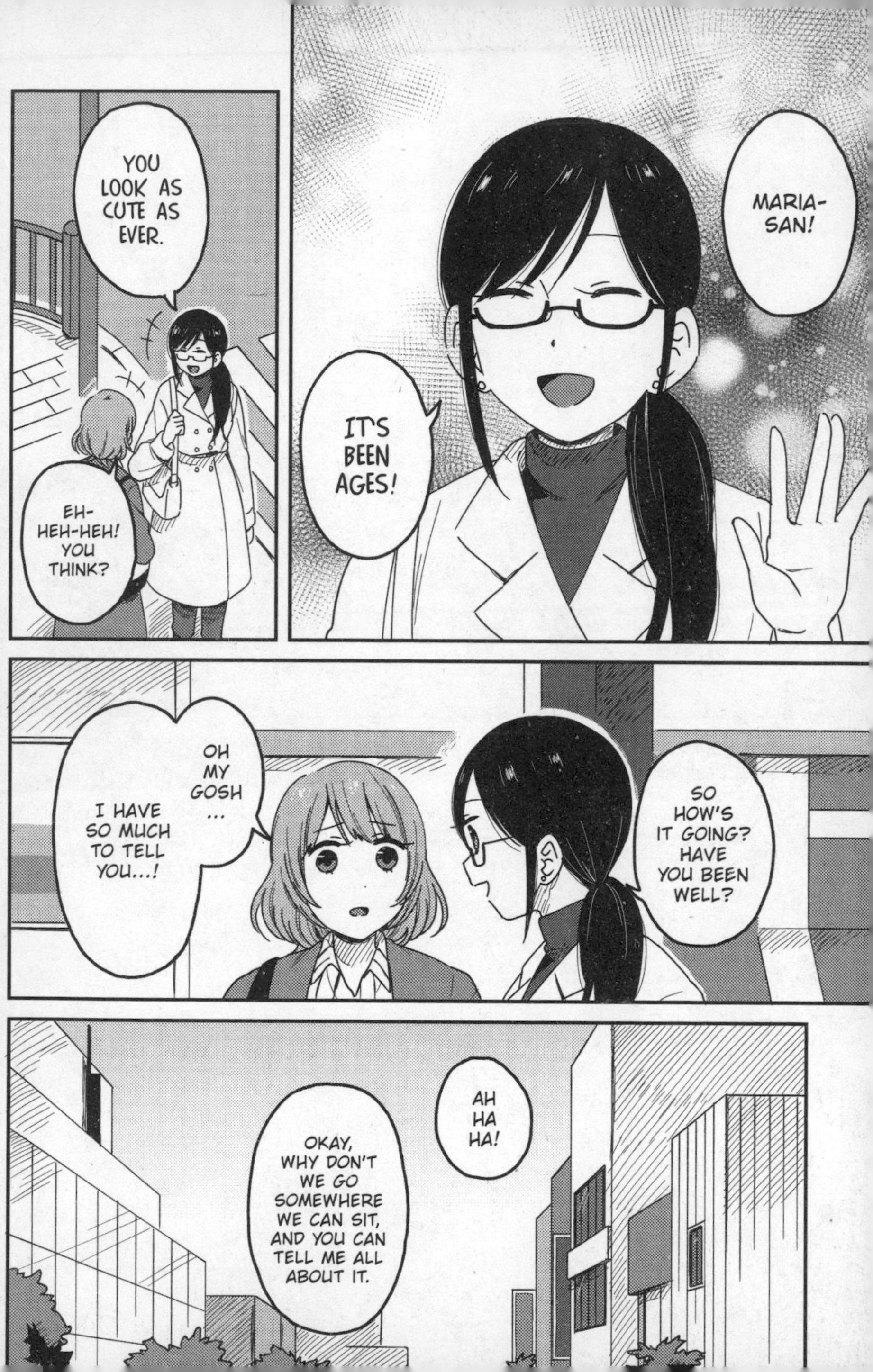
MARIA-SAN!
IT'S BEEN AGES!
YOU LOOK AS CUTE AS EVER.
EH-HEH-HEH! YOU THINK?
SO HOW'S IT GOING? HAVE YOU BEEN WELL?
OH MY GOSH ...
I HAVE SO MUCH TO TELL YOU...!
AH HA HA!
OKAY, WHY DON'T WE GO SOMEWHERE WE CAN SIT, AND YOU CAN TELL ME ALL ABOUT IT.

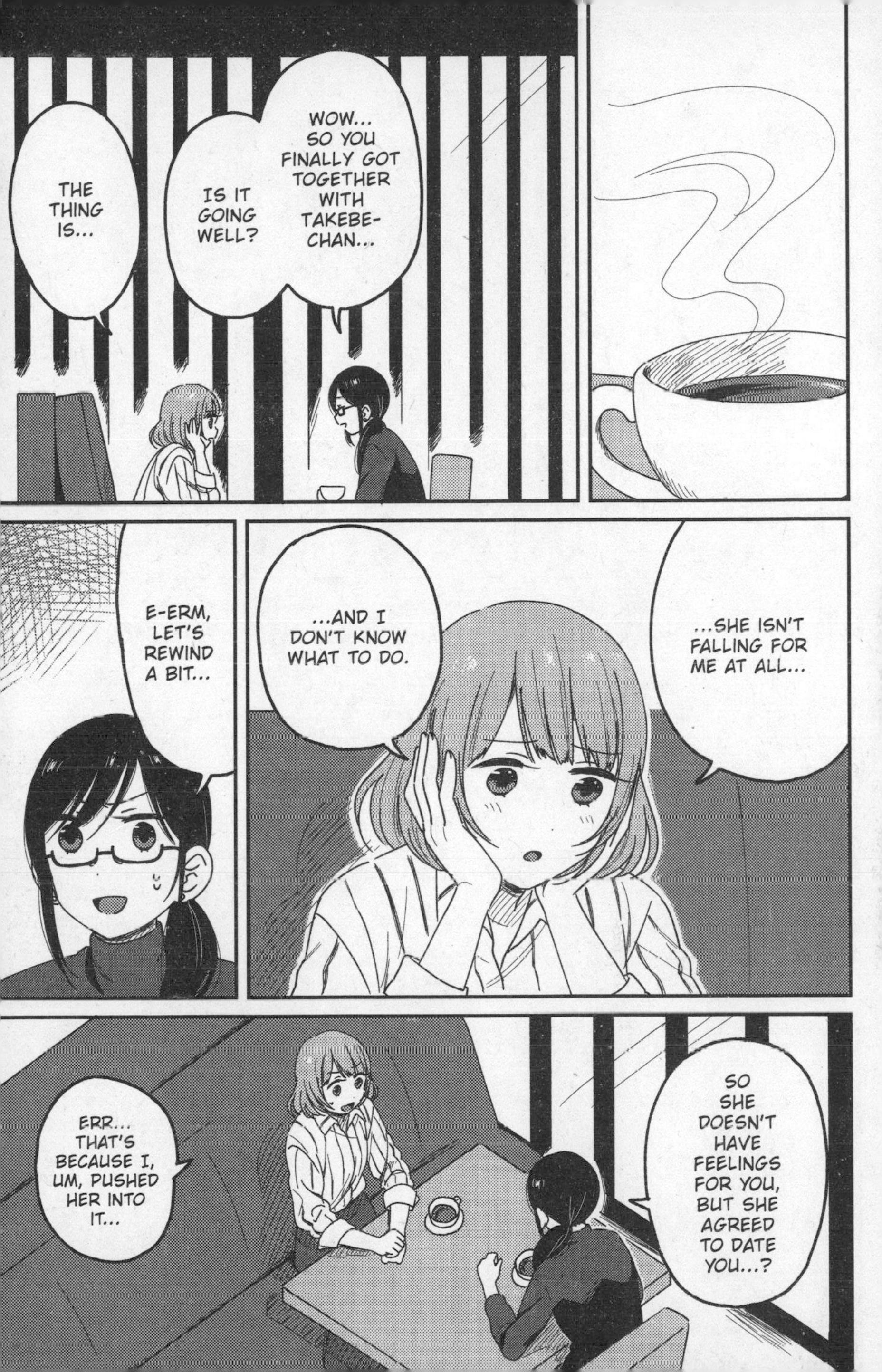
WOW... SO YOU FINALLY GOT TOGETHER WITH TAKEBE-CHAN...
IS IT GOING WELL?
THE THING IS...
...SHE ISN'T FALLING FOR ME AT ALL...
...AND I DON'T KNOW WHAT TO DO.
E-ERM, LET'S REWIND A BIT...
SO SHE DOESN'T HAVE FEELINGS FOR YOU, BUT SHE AGREED TO DATE YOU...?
ERR... THAT'S BECAUSE I, UM, PUSHED HER INTO IT...

DIDN'T YOU ALWAYS SAY TAKEBE-CHAN WAS THE STRAIGHT-ARROW, TAKE-CHARGE TYPE...?
COULD IT BE...A PERSON-ALITY CHANGE?
HUH ...?
N-NO, I THINK SHE HASN'T CHANGED MUCH...
I MEAN, I GUESS SHE'S LESS OF A STRAIGHT ARROW THAN SHE IS WOBBLY NOW...
WHAT I DID TODAY? I STARED AT THE CEILING ALL DAY.
NOW
I ENJOY EVERY DAY!
THE PAST
...LIKE SHE'S GOTTEN A LITTLE UNRELIABLE ...
UHHH... ARE YOU SURE SHE'S A GOOD CHOICE?

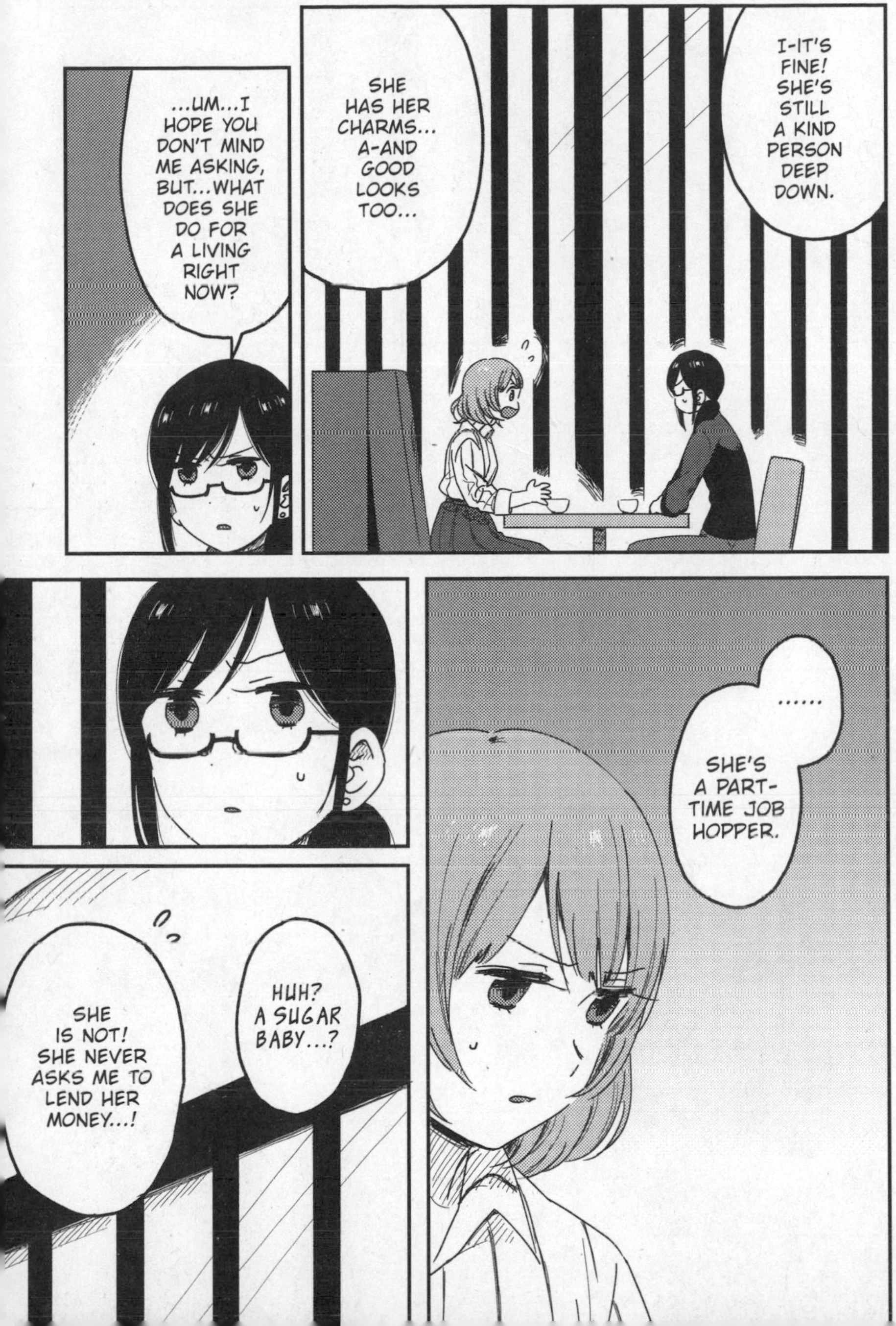
I-IT'S FINE! SHE'S STILL A KIND PERSON DEEP DOWN.
SHE HAS HER CHARMS... A-AND GOOD LOOKS TOO...
...UM...I HOPE YOU DON'T MIND ME ASKING, BUT...WHAT DOES SHE DO FOR A LIVING RIGHT NOW?
......
SHE'S A PART-TIME JOB HOPPER.
HUH? A SUGAR BABY...?
SHE IS NOT! SHE NEVER ASKS ME TO LEND HER MONEY...!

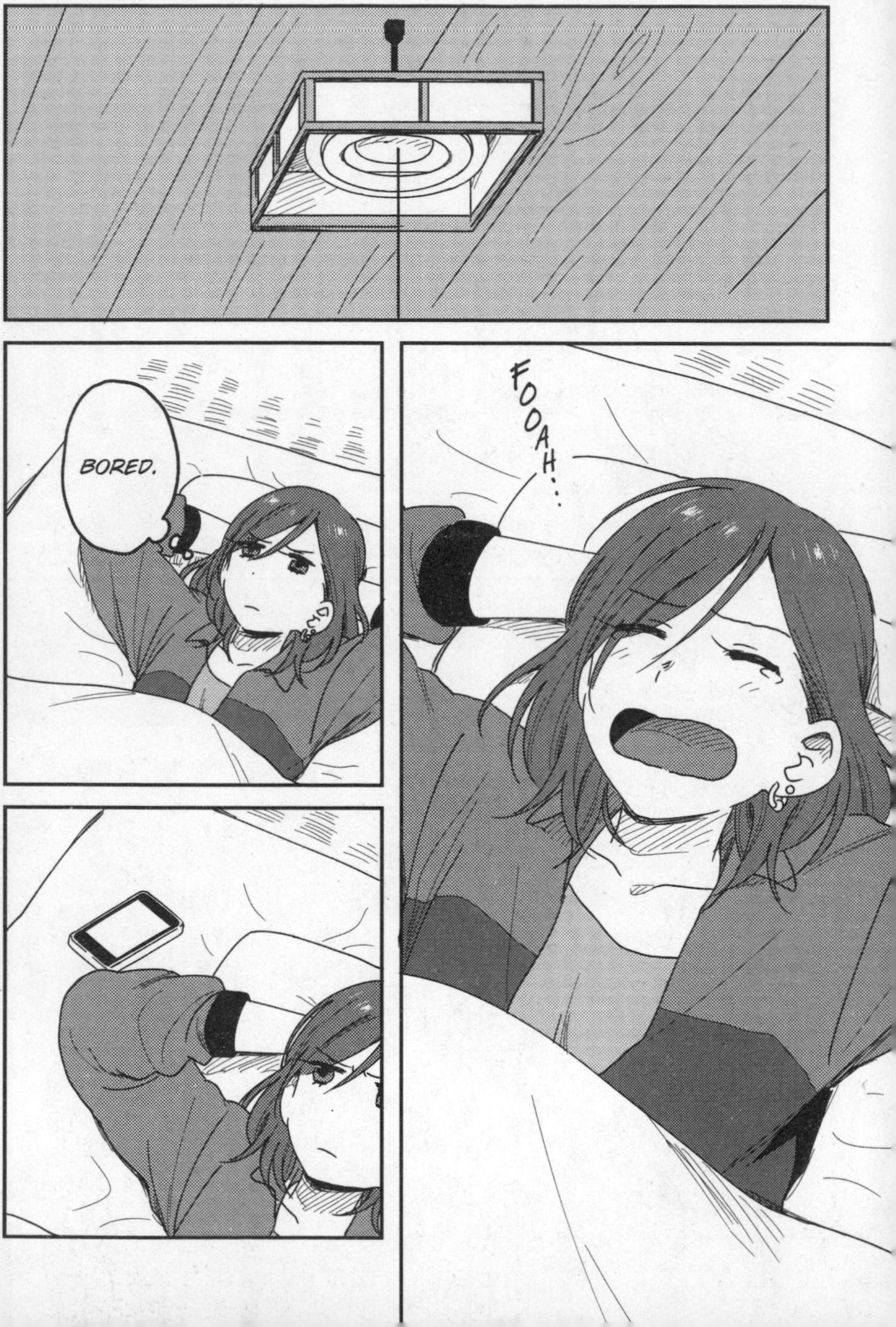
FOOAH...
BORED.

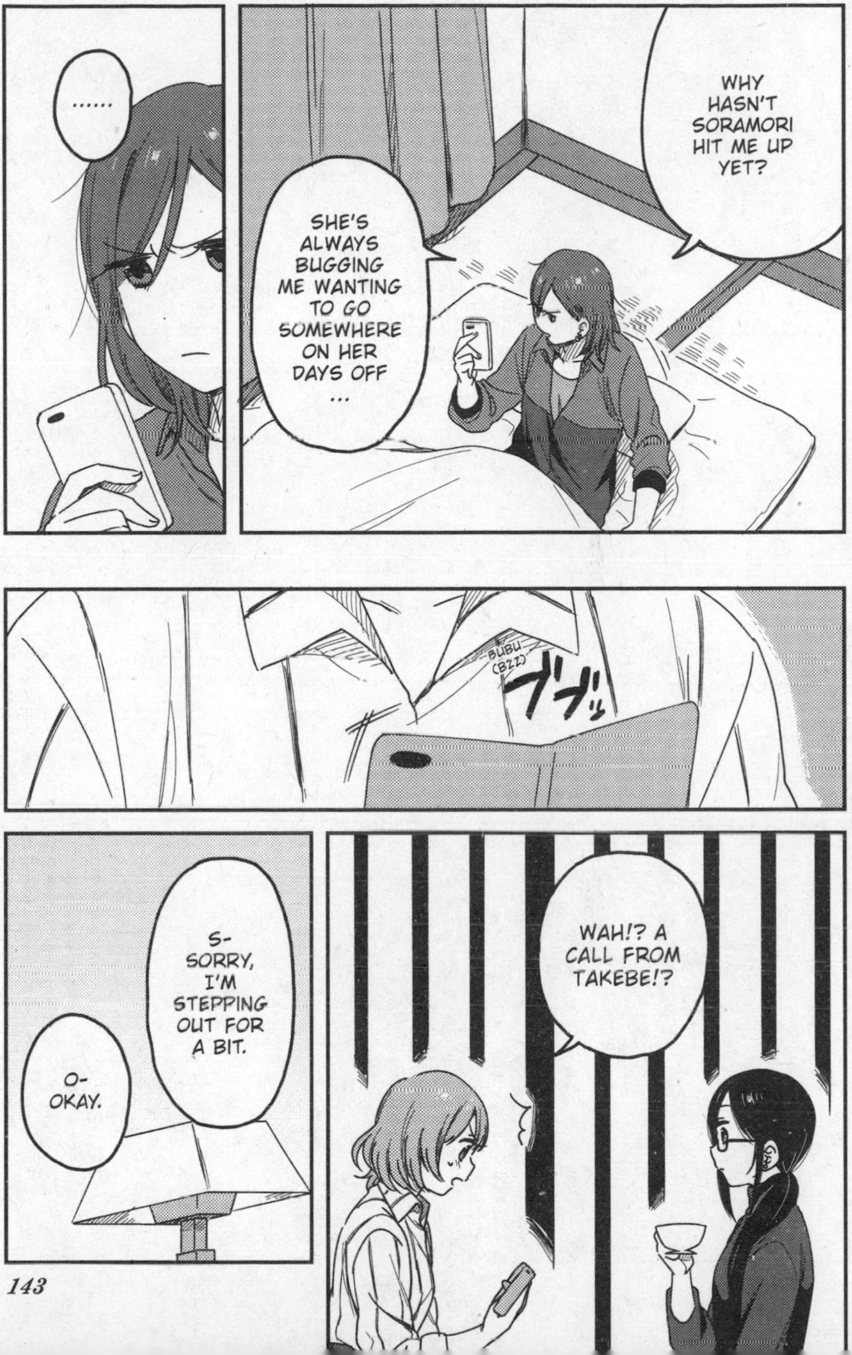
WHY HASN'T SORAMORI HIT ME UP YET?
SHE'S ALWAYS BUGGING ME WANTING TO GO SOMEWHERE ON HER DAYS OFF ...
......
BUBU (BZZ)
ブブッ
WAH!? A CALL FROM TAKEBE!?
S-SORRY, I'M STEPPING OUT FOR A BIT.
O-OKAY.

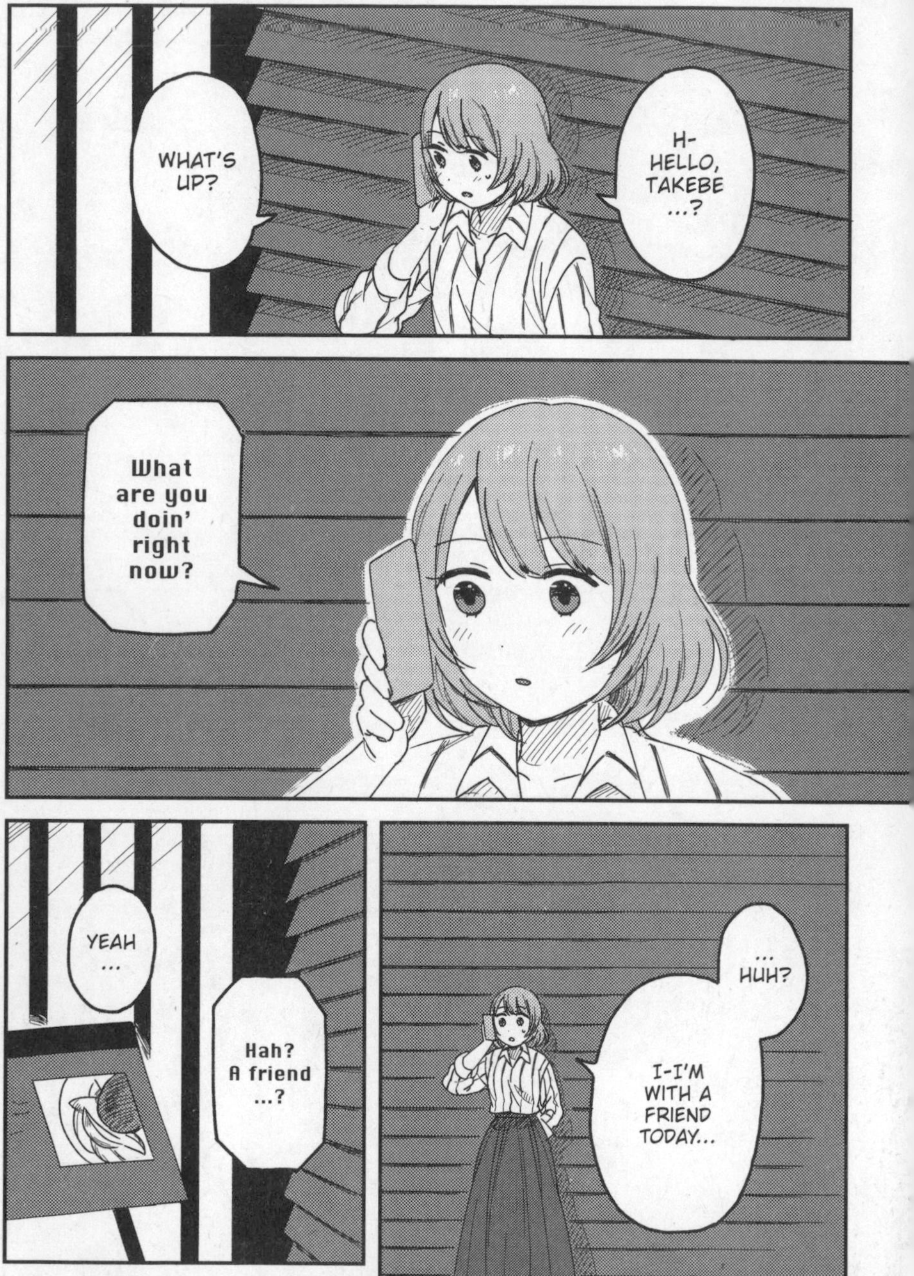
H-HELLO, TAKEBE ...?
WHAT'S UP?
What are you doin' right now?
... HUH?
I-I'M WITH A FRIEND TODAY...
Hah? A friend ...?
YEAH ...

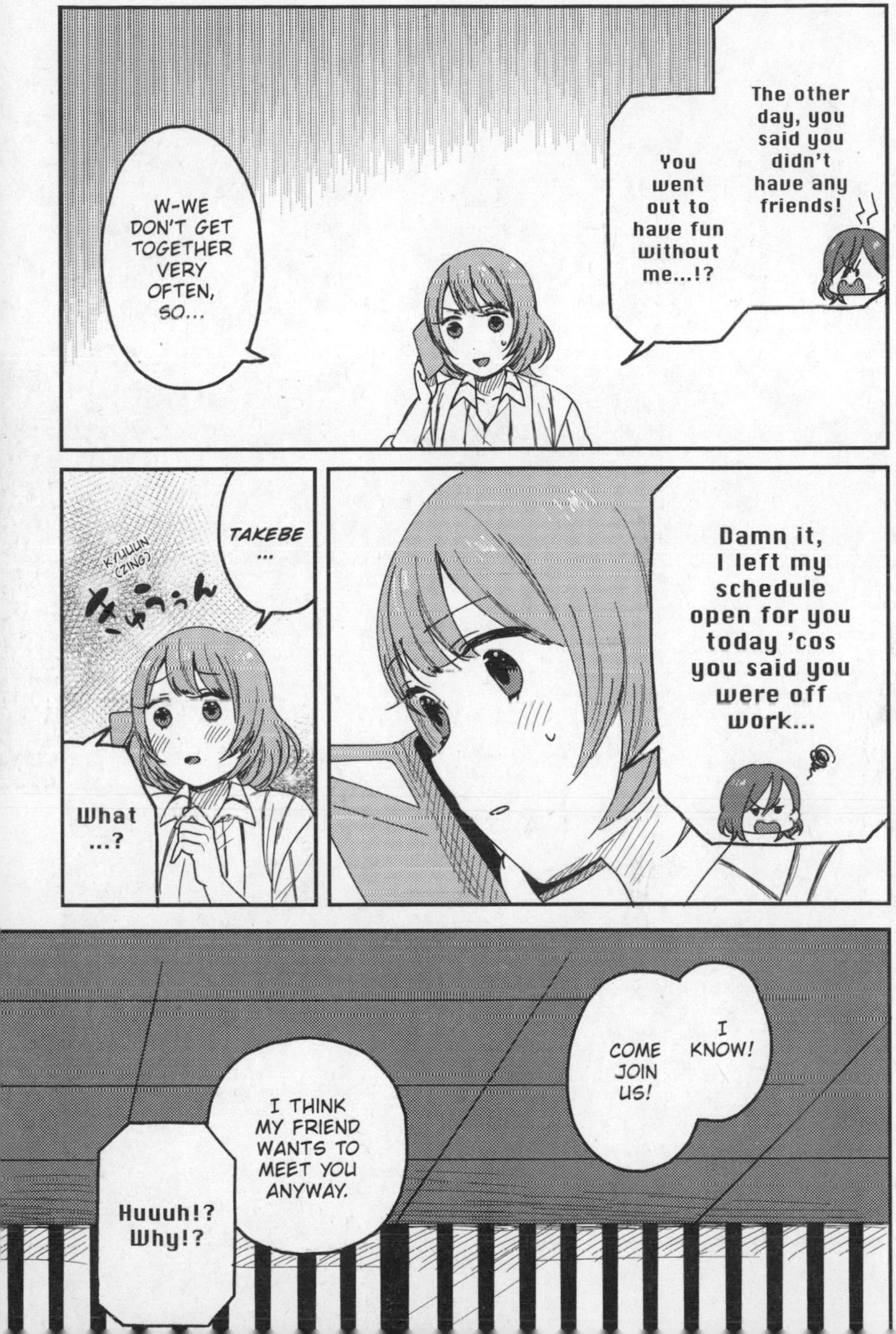
The other day, you said you didn't have any friends!
You went out to have fun without me...!?
W-WE DON'T GET TOGETHER VERY OFTEN, SO...
Damn it, I left my schedule open for you today 'cos you said you were off work...
TAKEBE ...
KYUUUN (ZING)
きゅううん
What ...?
I KNOW!
COME JOIN US!
I THINK MY FRIEND WANTS TO MEET YOU ANYWAY.
Huuuh!? Why!?

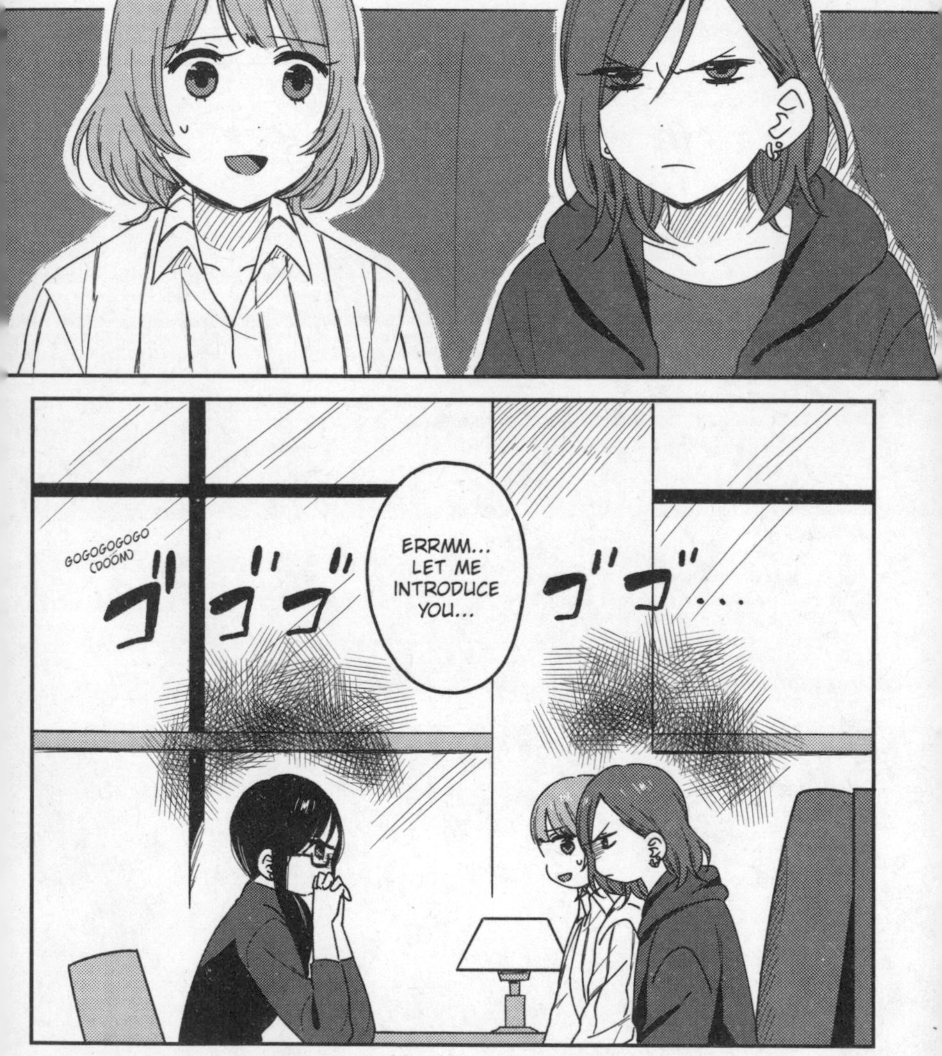
GIRO (GLARE)
ギロ…
ERRMM... LET ME INTRODUCE YOU...
ゴゴゴ
ゴゴ…
GOGOGOGOGO (DOOM)

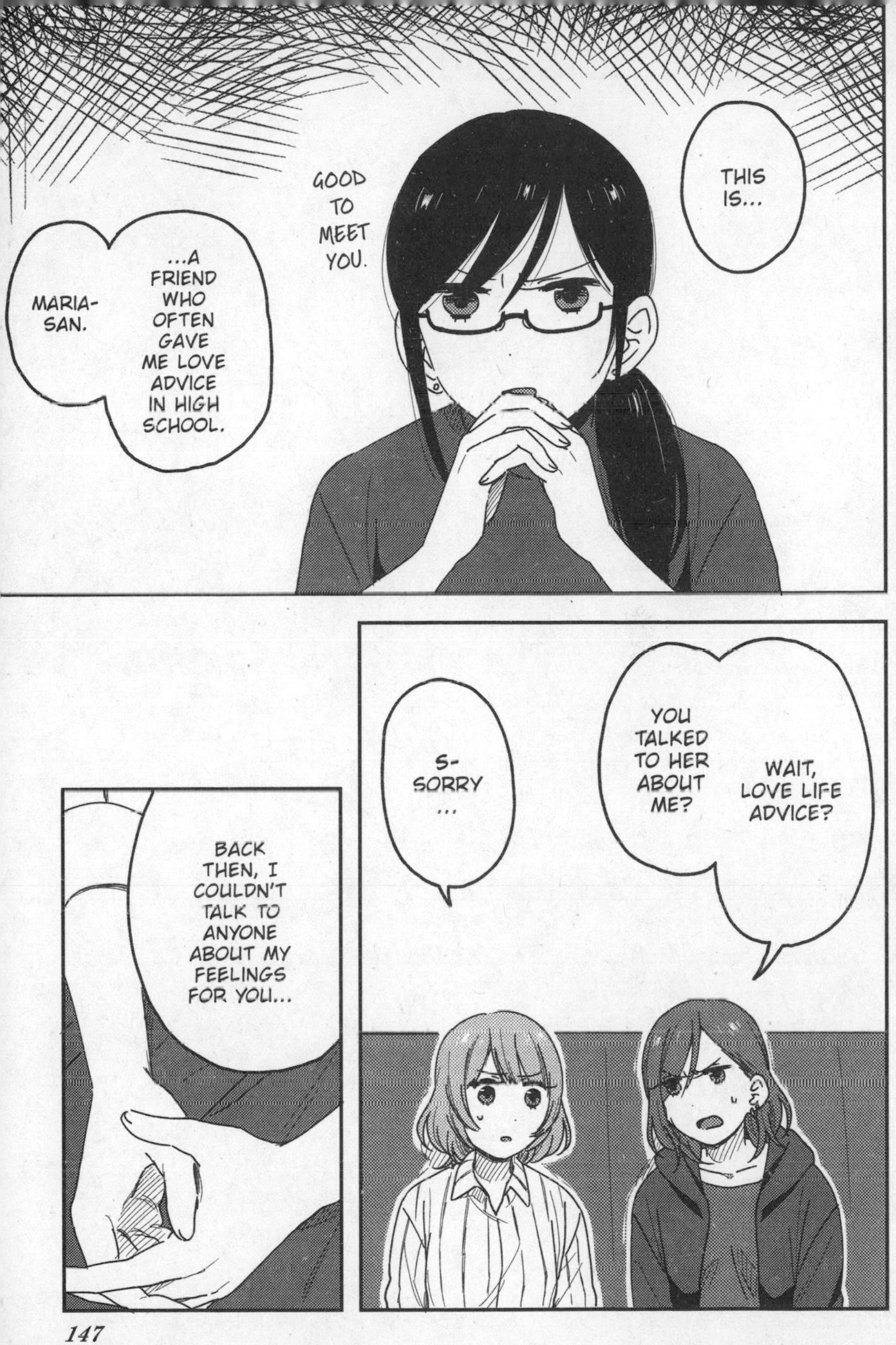
THIS IS...
GOOD TO MEET YOU.
MARIA-SAN.
...A FRIEND WHO OFTEN GAVE ME LOVE ADVICE IN HIGH SCHOOL.
WAIT, LOVE LIFE ADVICE?
YOU TALKED TO HER ABOUT ME?
S-SORRY...
BACK THEN, I COULDN'T TALK TO ANYONE ABOUT MY FEELINGS FOR YOU...

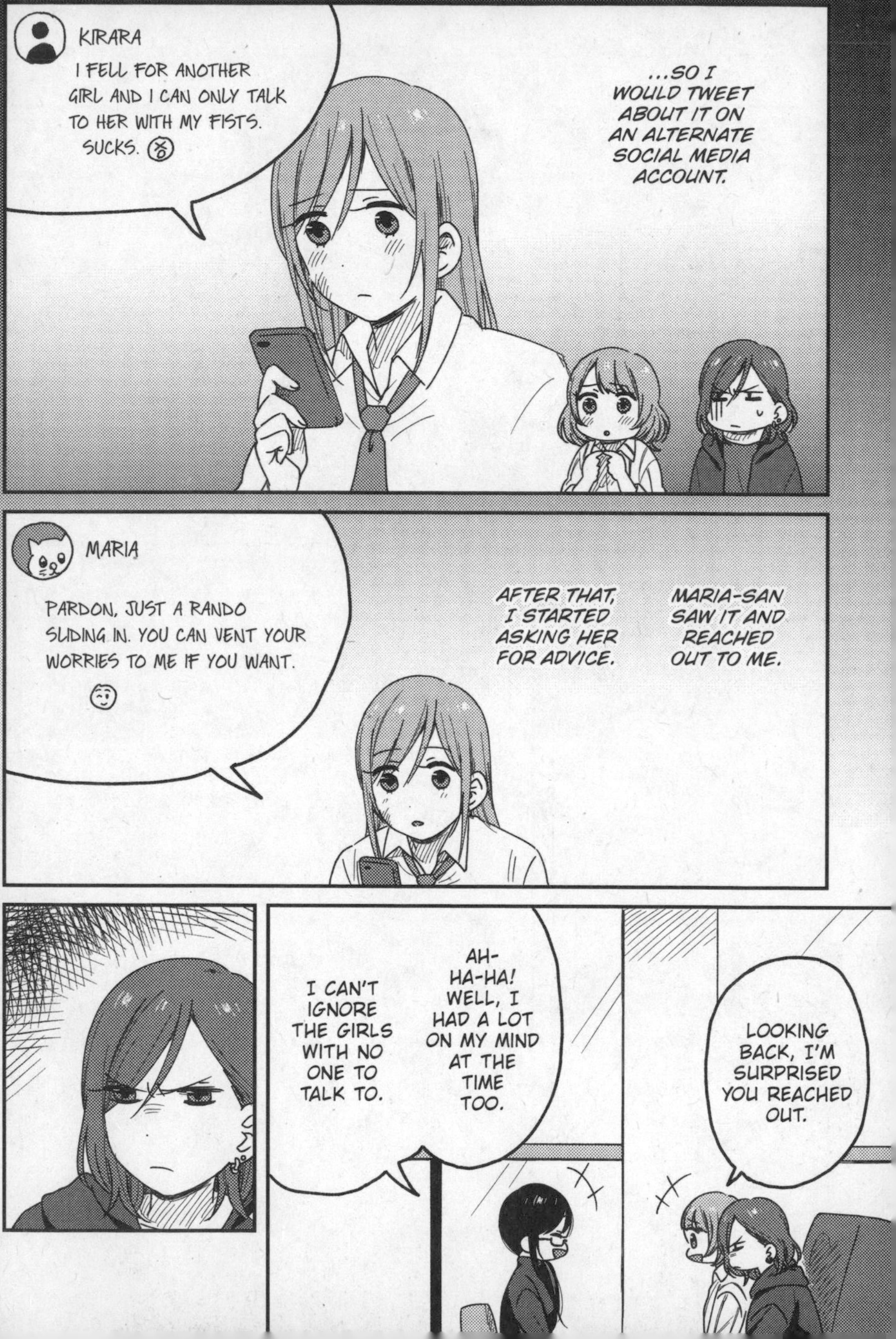
...SO I WOULD TWEET ABOUT IT ON AN ALTERNATE SOCIAL MEDIA ACCOUNT.
KIRARA
I FELL FOR ANOTHER GIRL AND I CAN ONLY TALK TO HER WITH MY FISTS. SUCKS.
MARIA-SAN SAW IT AND REACHED OUT TO ME.
AFTER THAT, I STARTED ASKING HER FOR ADVICE.
MARIA
PARDON, JUST A RANDO SLIDING IN. YOU CAN VENT YOUR WORRIES TO ME IF YOU WANT.
LOOKING BACK, I'M SURPRISED YOU REACHED OUT.
AH-HA-HA! WELL, I HAD A LOT ON MY MIND AT THE TIME TOO.
I CAN'T IGNORE THE GIRLS WITH NO ONE TO TALK TO.

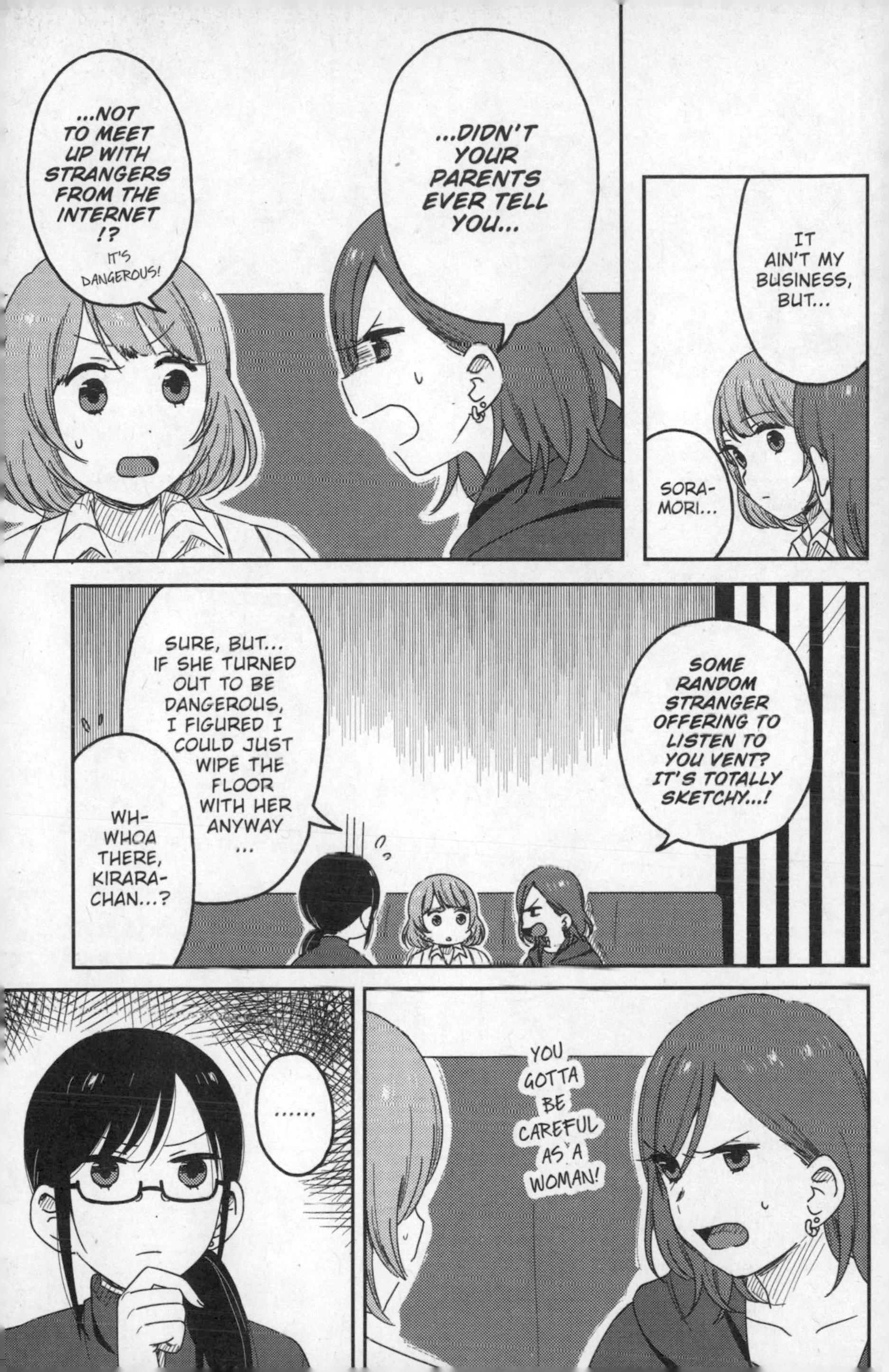
IT AIN'T MY BUSINESS, BUT...
SORA-MORI...
...DIDN'T YOUR PARENTS EVER TELL YOU...
...NOT TO MEET UP WITH STRANGERS FROM THE INTERNET!?
IT'S DANGEROUS!
SOME RANDOM STRANGER OFFERING TO LISTEN TO YOU VENT? IT'S TOTALLY SKETCHY...!
SURE, BUT... IF SHE TURNED OUT TO BE DANGEROUS, I FIGURED I COULD JUST WIPE THE FLOOR WITH HER ANYWAY...
WH-WHOA THERE, KIRARA-CHAN...?
YOU GOTTA BE CAREFUL AS A WOMAN!
......

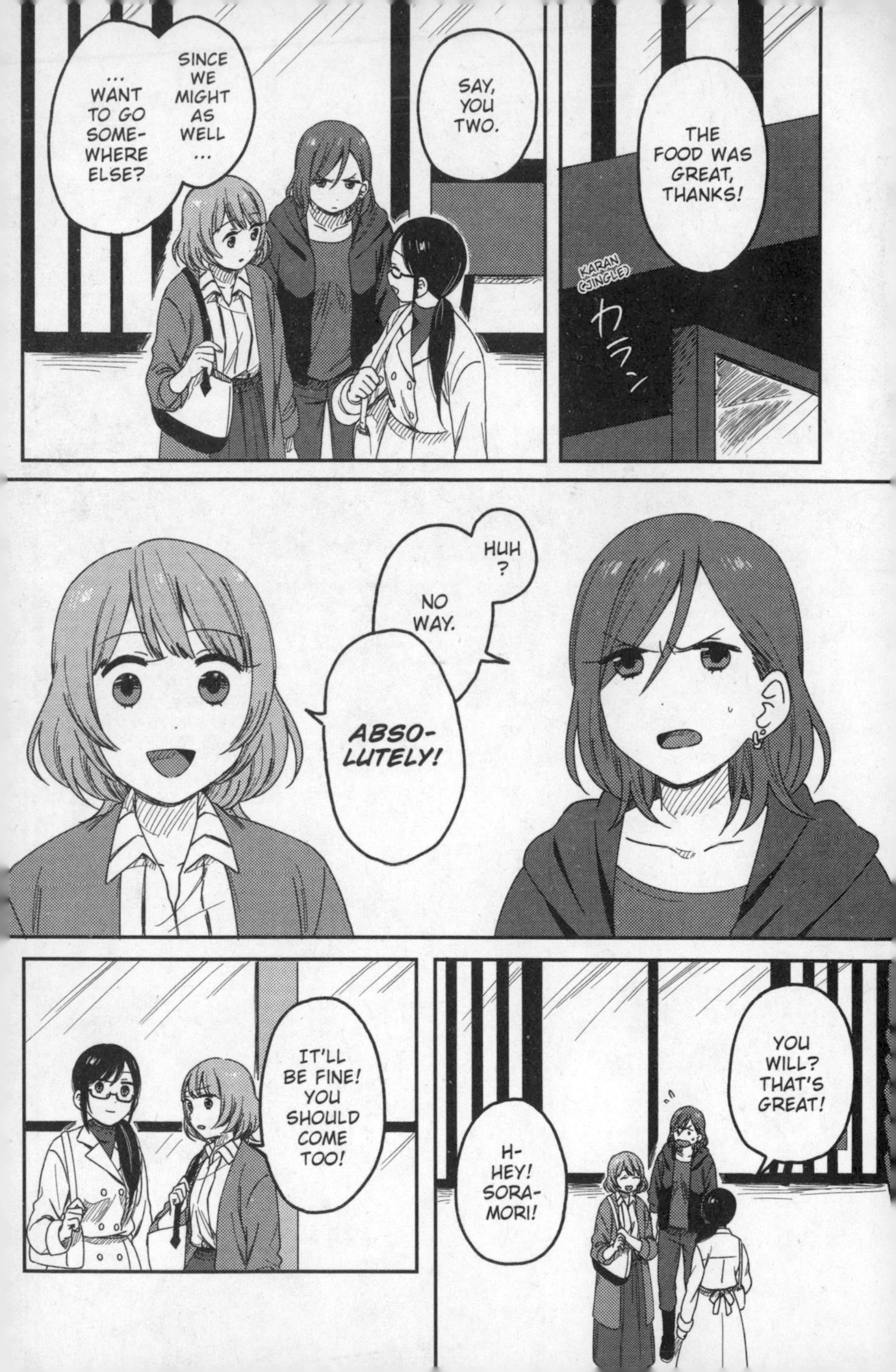
THE FOOD WAS GREAT, THANKS!
KARAN (JINGLE)
カラン
SAY, YOU TWO.
SINCE WE MIGHT AS WELL ...
... WANT TO GO SOME-WHERE ELSE?
HUH?
NO WAY.
ABSO-LUTELY!
YOU WILL? THAT'S GREAT!
H-HEY! SORA-MORI!
IT'LL BE FINE! YOU SHOULD COME TOO!

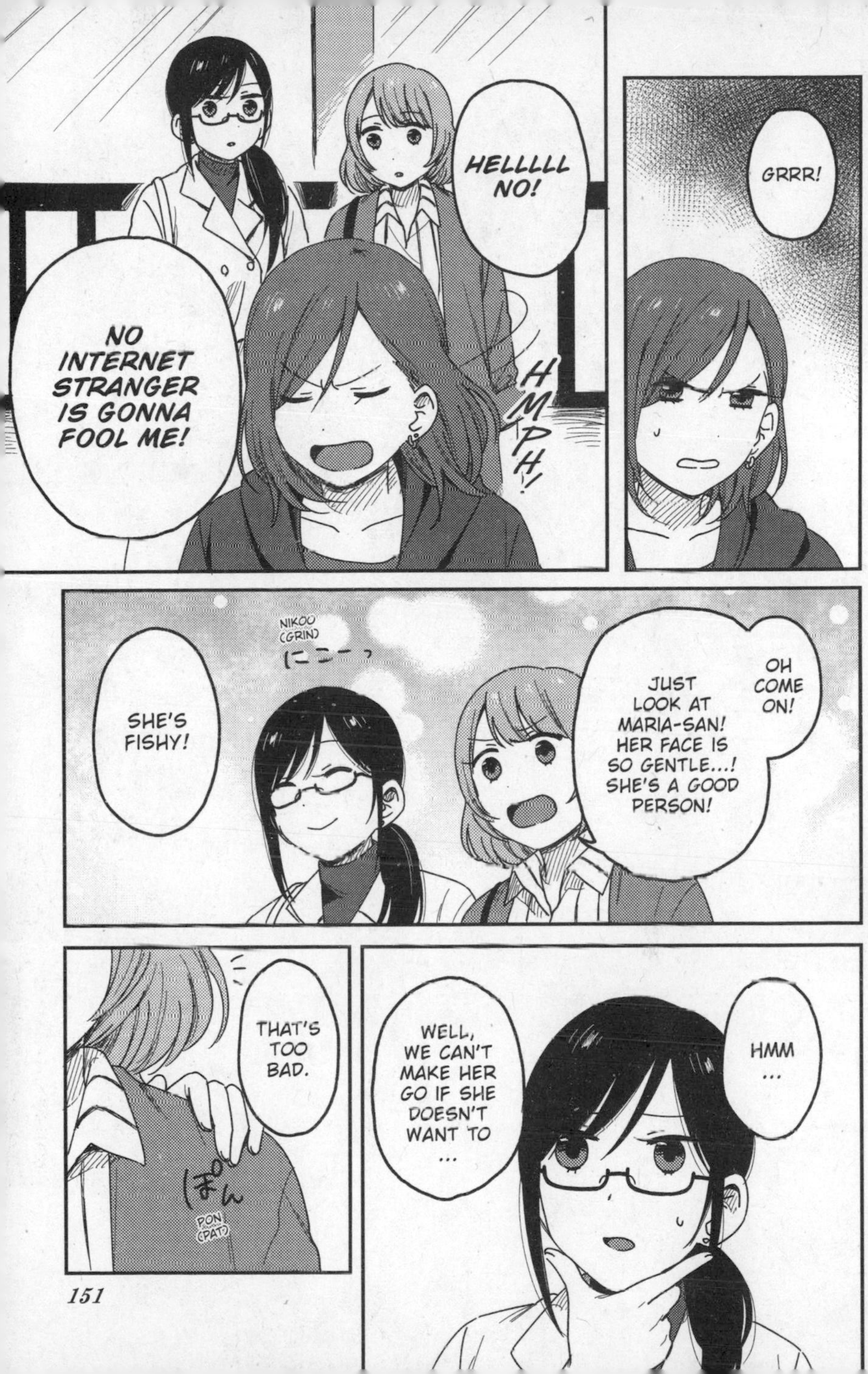
GRRR!
HELLLLL NO!
NO INTERNET STRANGER IS GONNA FOOL ME!
HMPH!
OH COME ON!
JUST LOOK AT MARIA-SAN! HER FACE IS SO GENTLE...! SHE'S A GOOD PERSON!
NIKOO (GRIN)
SHE'S FISHY!
HMM ...
WELL, WE CAN'T MAKE HER GO IF SHE DOESN'T WANT TO ...
THAT'S TOO BAD.
ぽん
PON (PAT)

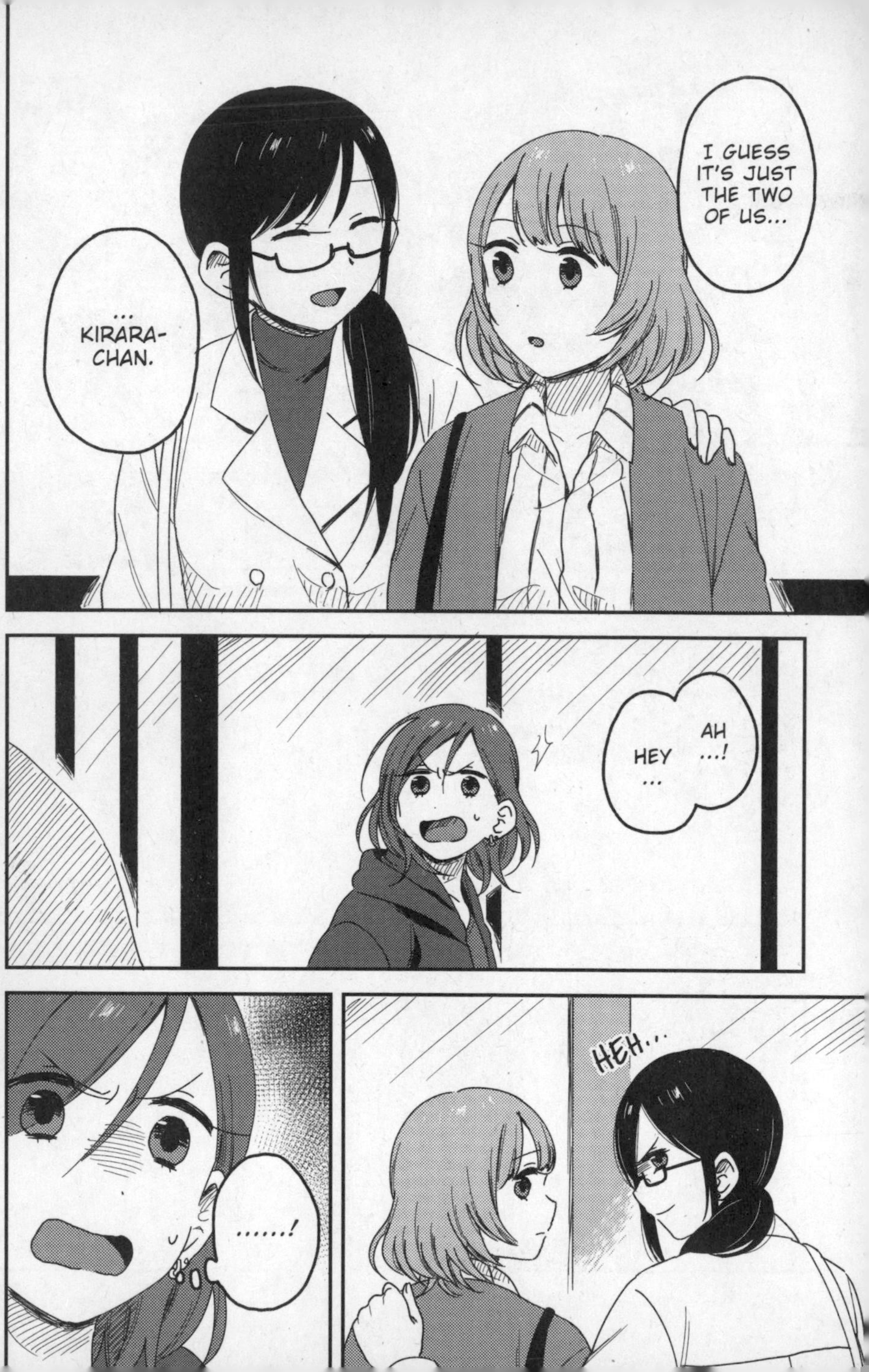
I GUESS IT'S JUST THE TWO OF US...
... KIRARA-CHAN.
AH ...! HEY ...
HEH...
......!

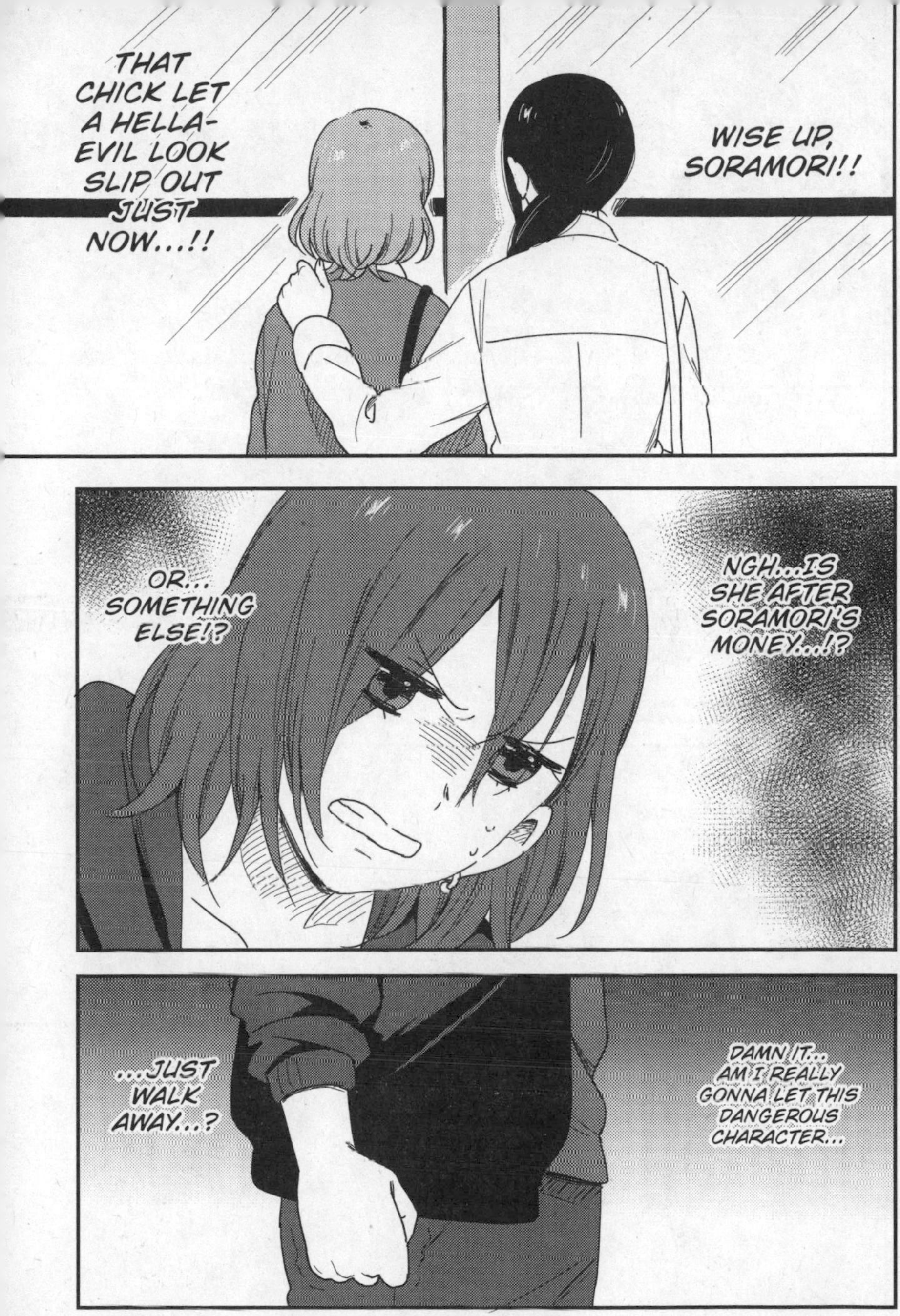
WISE UP, SORAMORI!!
THAT CHICK LET A HELLA-EVIL LOOK SLIP OUT JUST NOW...!!
NGH...IS SHE AFTER SORAMORI'S MONEY...!?
OR... SOMETHING ELSE!?
DAMN IT... AM I REALLY GONNA LET THIS DANGEROUS CHARACTER...
...JUST WALK AWAY...?

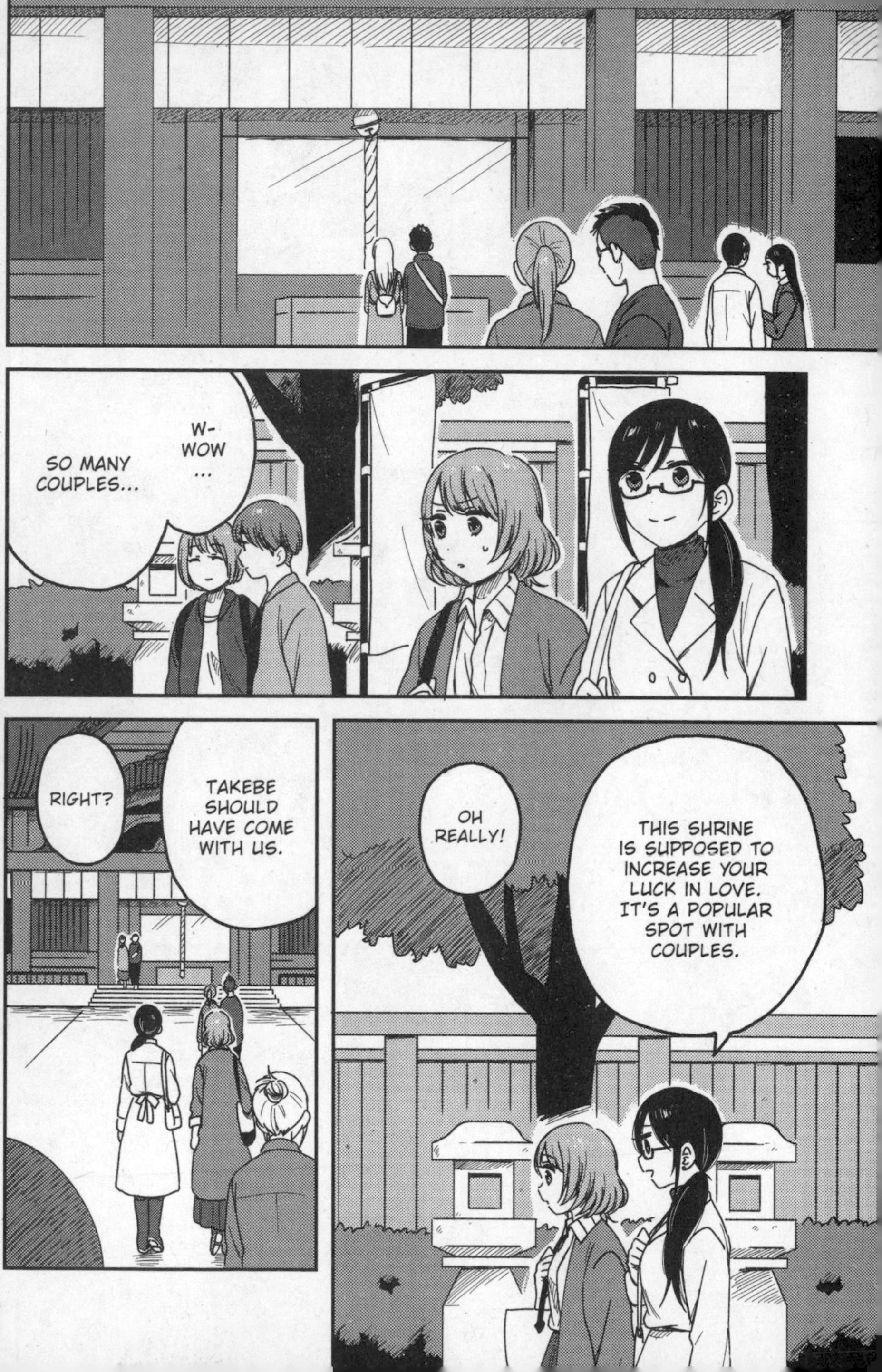
W-WOW...
SO MANY COUPLES...
THIS SHRINE IS SUPPOSED TO INCREASE YOUR LUCK IN LOVE. IT'S A POPULAR SPOT WITH COUPLES.
OH REALLY!
TAKEBE SHOULD HAVE COME WITH US.
RIGHT?

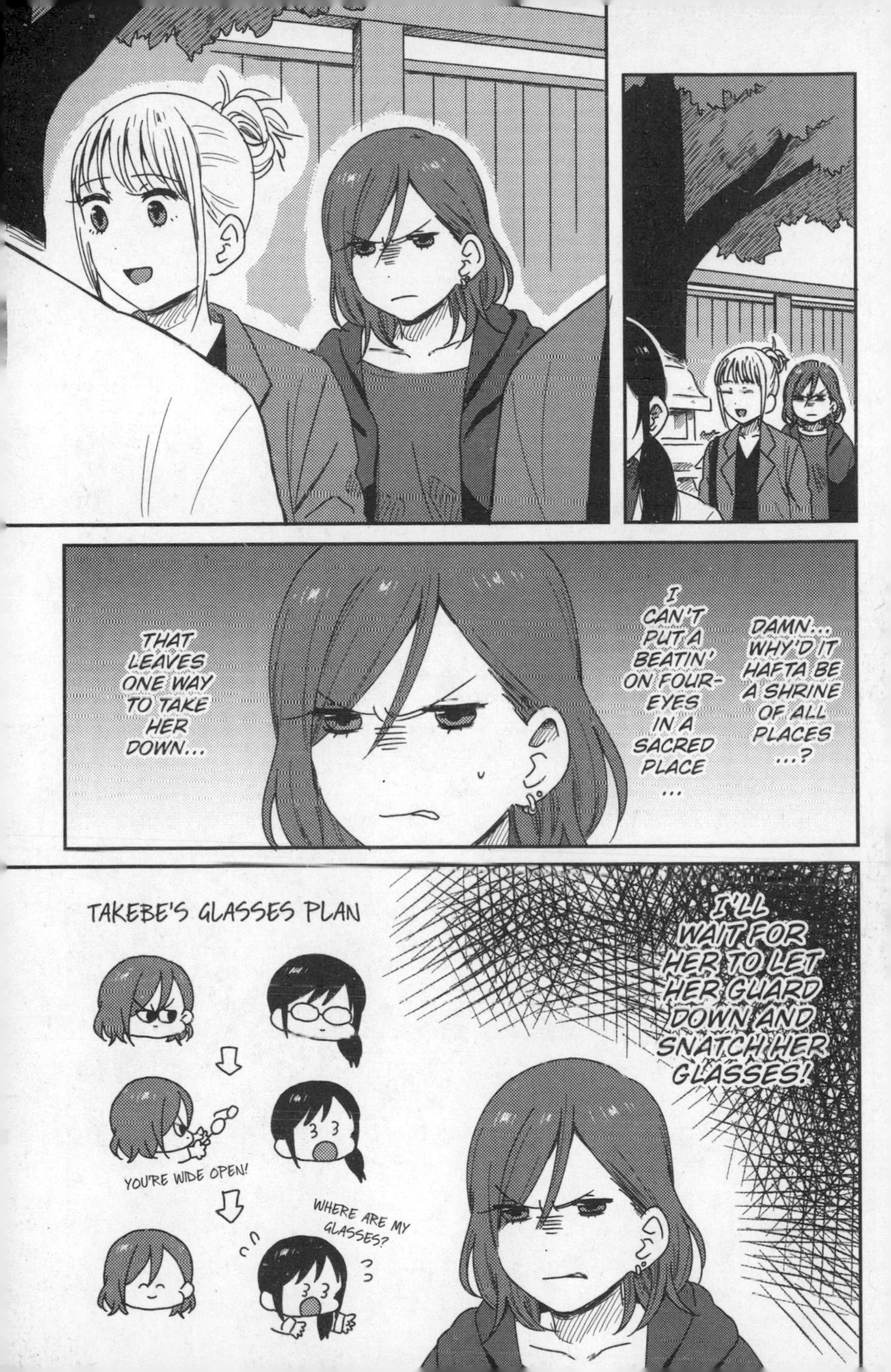
DAMN... WHY'D IT HAFTA BE A SHRINE OF ALL PLACES ...?
I CAN'T PUT A BEATIN' ON FOUR-EYES IN A SACRED PLACE ...
THAT LEAVES ONE WAY TO TAKE HER DOWN...
I'LL WAIT FOR HER TO LET HER GUARD DOWN AND SNATCH HER GLASSES!
TAKEBE'S GLASSES PLAN
YOU'RE WIDE OPEN!
WHERE ARE MY GLASSES?

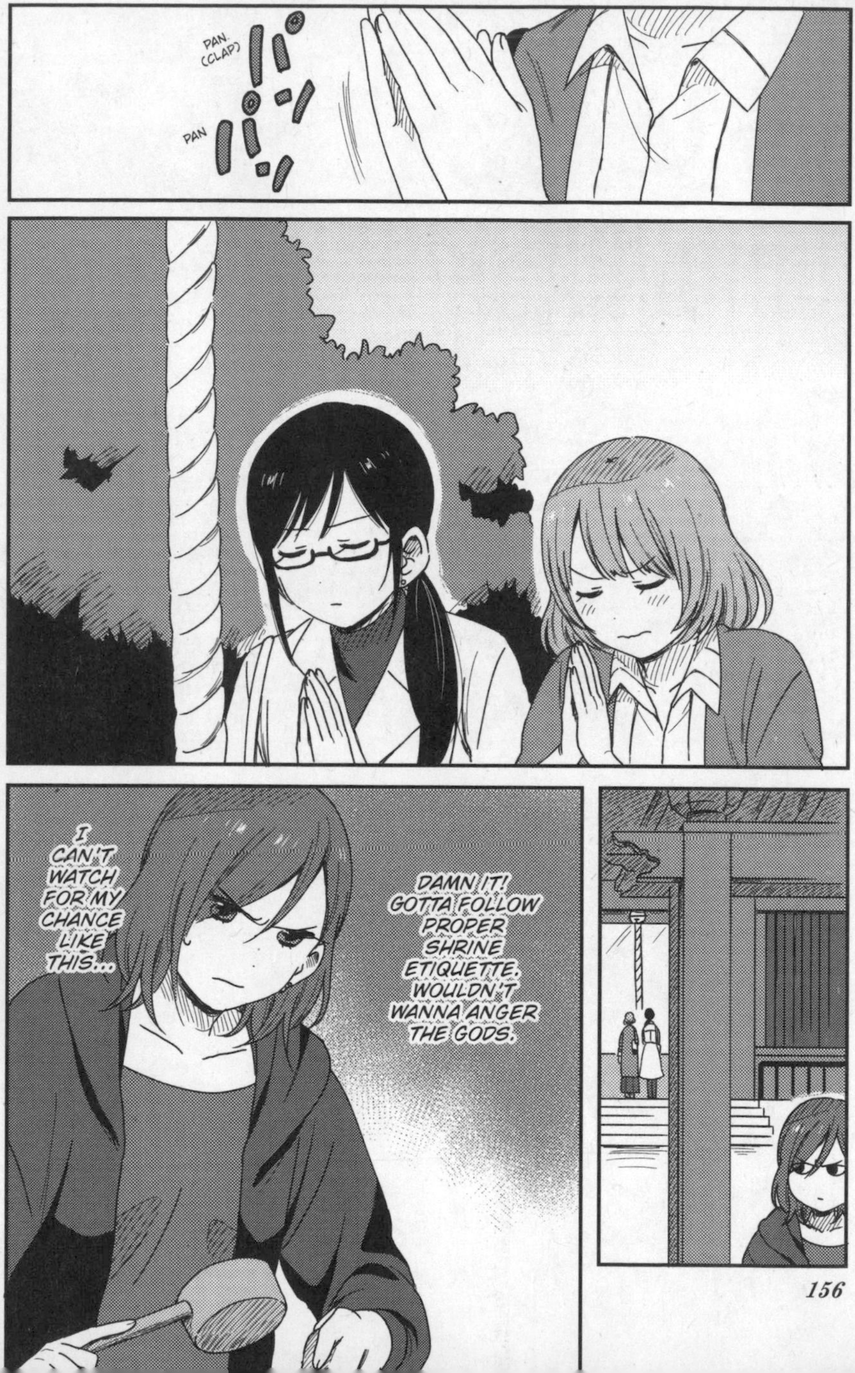
PAN (CLAP)
PAN
DAMN IT! GOTTA FOLLOW PROPER SHRINE ETIQUETTE. WOULDN'T WANNA ANGER THE GODS.
I CAN'T WATCH FOR MY CHANCE LIKE THIS...

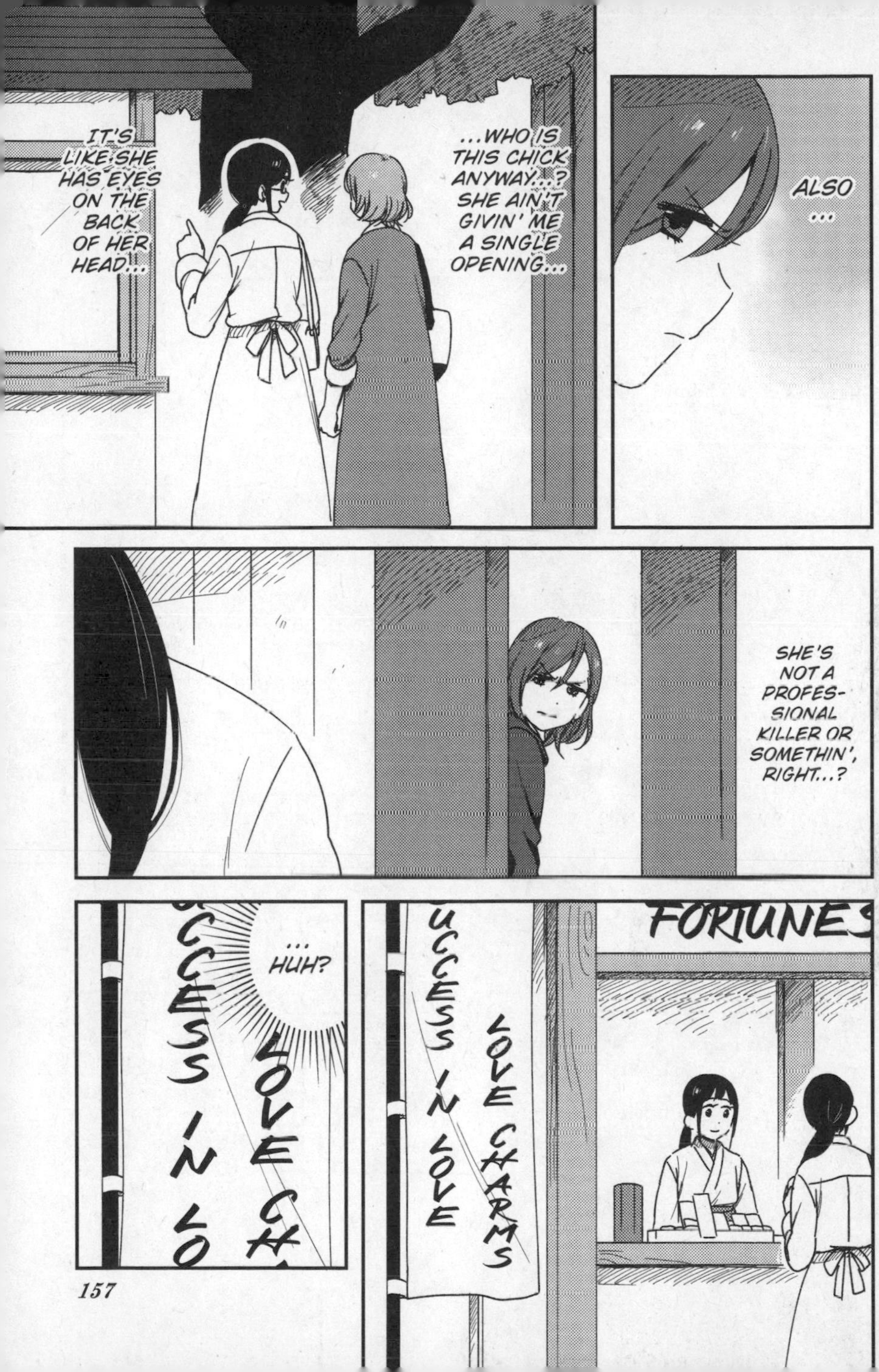
ALSO...
...WHO IS THIS CHICK ANYWAY...? SHE AIN'T GIVIN' ME A SINGLE OPENING...
IT'S LIKE SHE HAS EYES ON THE BACK OF HER HEAD...
SHE'S NOT A PROFESSIONAL KILLER OR SOMETHIN', RIGHT...?
FORTUNES
UCCESS IN LOVE
LOVE CHARMS
...HUH?
CCESS IN LO
LOVE CH

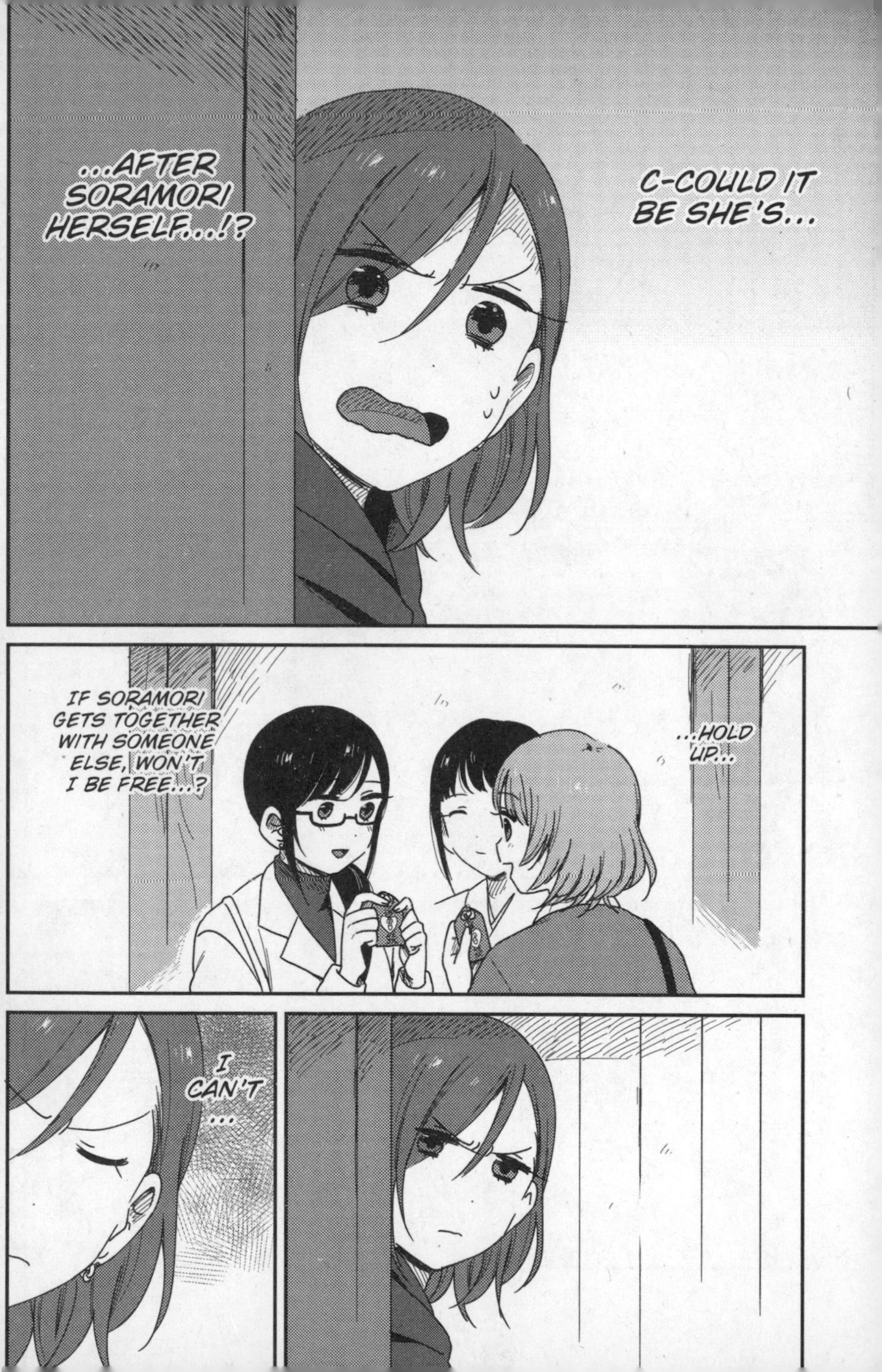
C-COULD IT BE SHE'S...
...AFTER SORAMORI HERSELF...!?
...HOLD UP...
IF SORAMORI GETS TOGETHER WITH SOMEONE ELSE, WON'T I BE FREE...?
I CAN'T ...

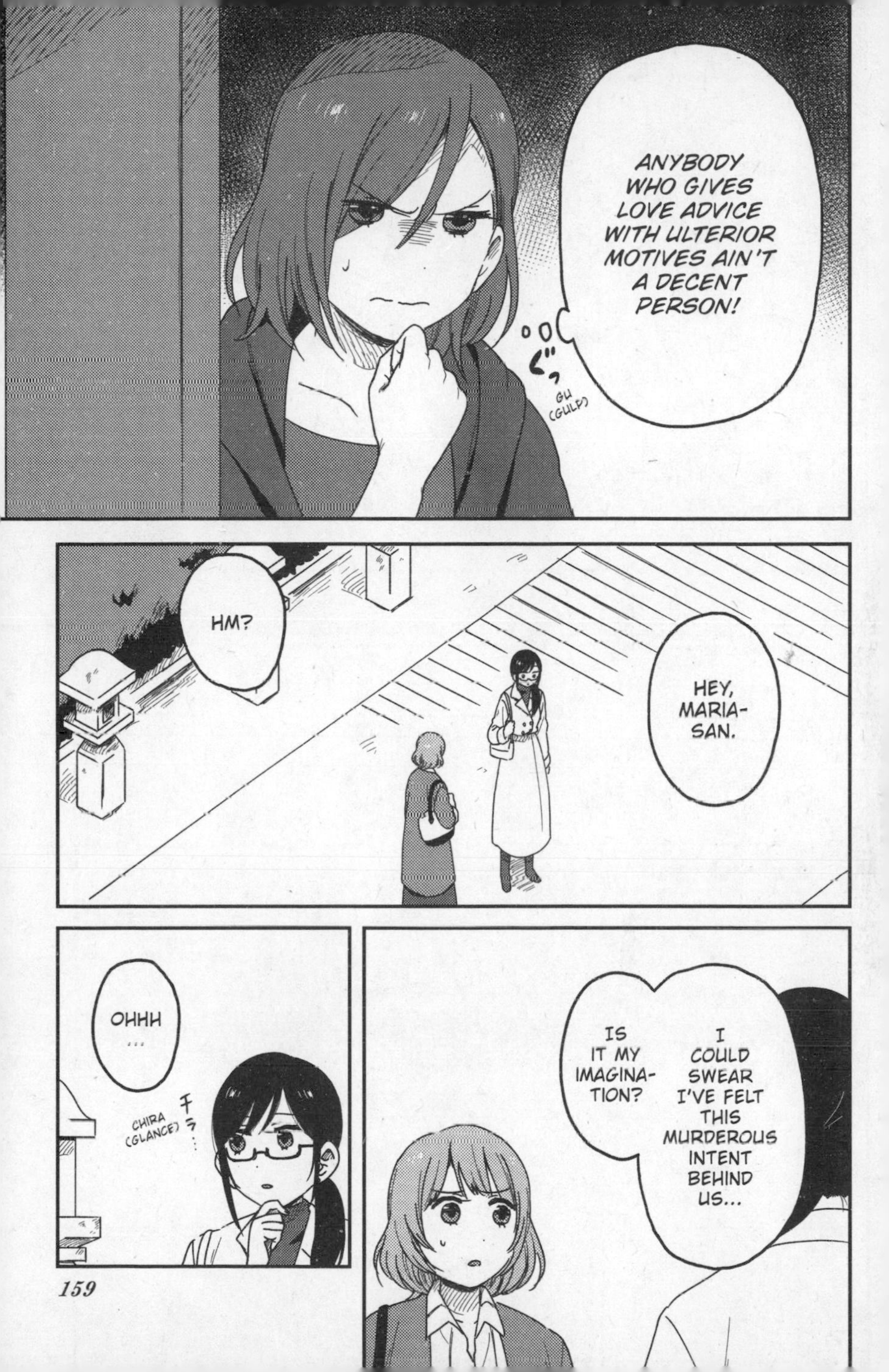
ANYBODY WHO GIVES LOVE ADVICE WITH ULTERIOR MOTIVES AIN'T A DECENT PERSON!
GU (GULP)
HEY, MARIA-SAN.
HM?
IS IT MY IMAGINATION? I COULD SWEAR I'VE FELT THIS MURDEROUS INTENT BEHIND US...
OHHH ...
CHIRA (GLANCE)

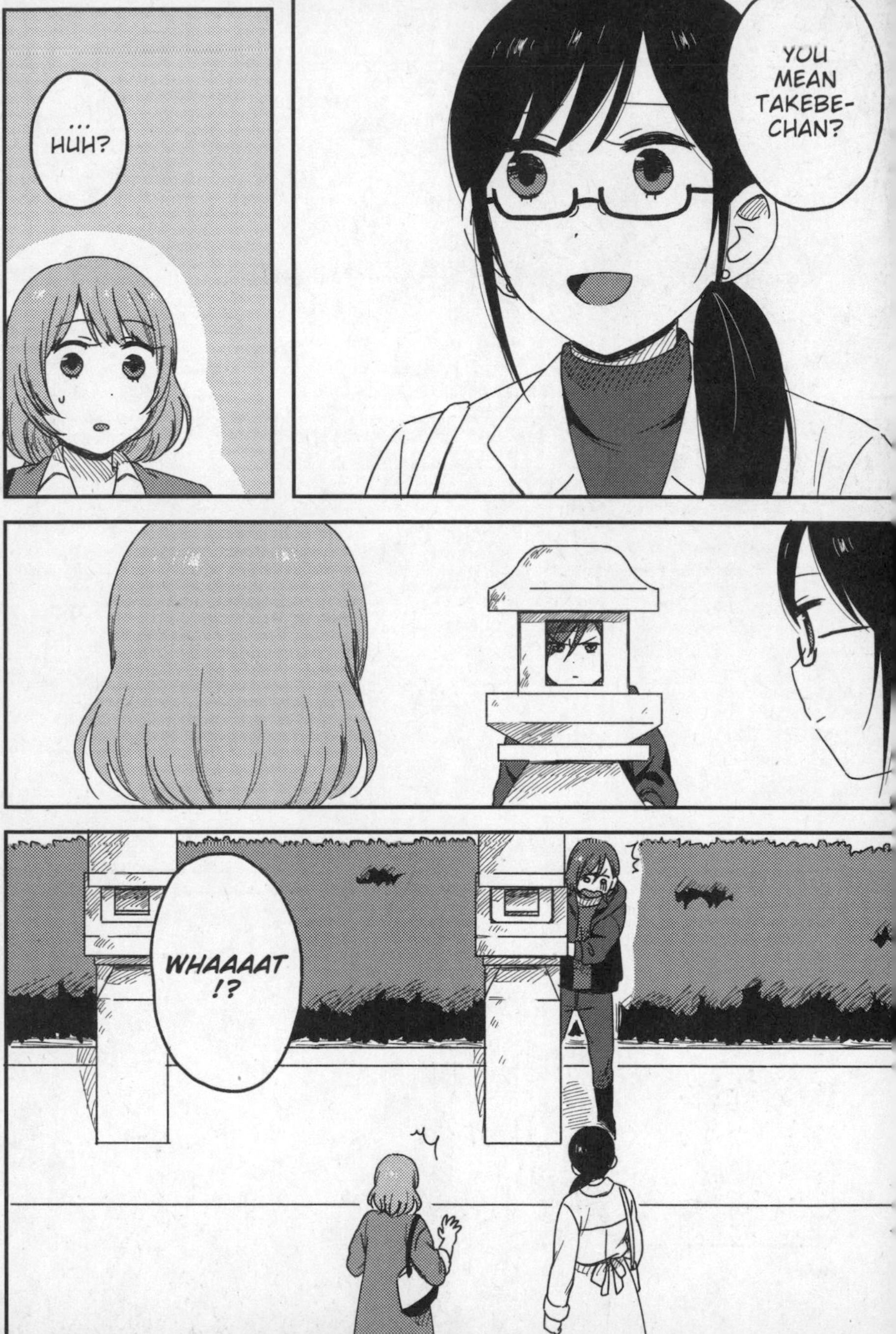
YOU MEAN TAKEBE-CHAN?
... HUH?
WHAAAAT!?

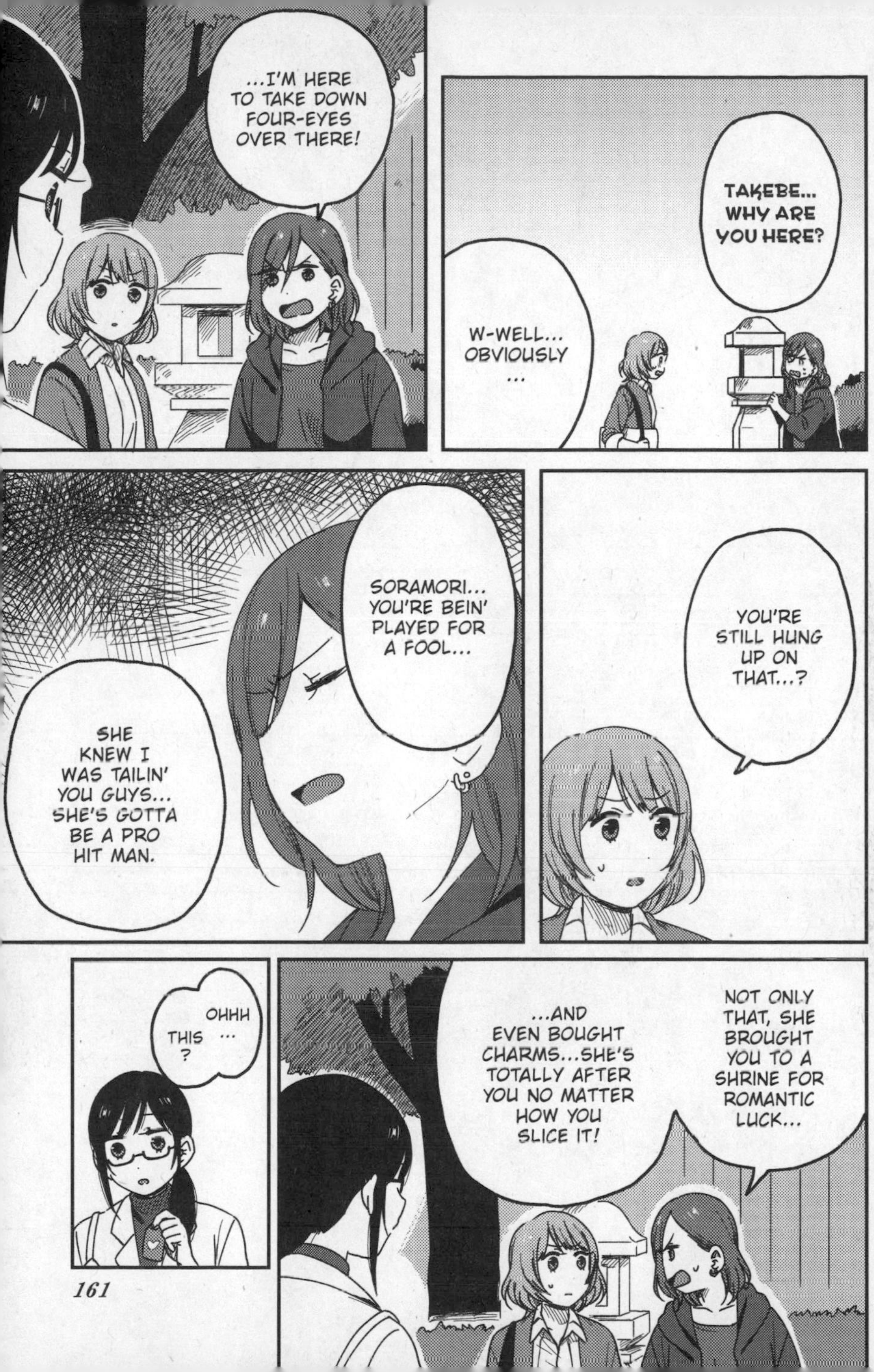
TAKEBE... WHY ARE YOU HERE?
W-WELL... OBVIOUSLY...
...I'M HERE TO TAKE DOWN FOUR-EYES OVER THERE!
YOU'RE STILL HUNG UP ON THAT...?
SORAMORI... YOU'RE BEIN' PLAYED FOR A FOOL...
SHE KNEW I WAS TAILIN' YOU GUYS... SHE'S GOTTA BE A PRO HIT MAN.
NOT ONLY THAT, SHE BROUGHT YOU TO A SHRINE FOR ROMANTIC LUCK...
...AND EVEN BOUGHT CHARMS...SHE'S TOTALLY AFTER YOU NO MATTER HOW YOU SLICE IT!
OHHH... THIS?

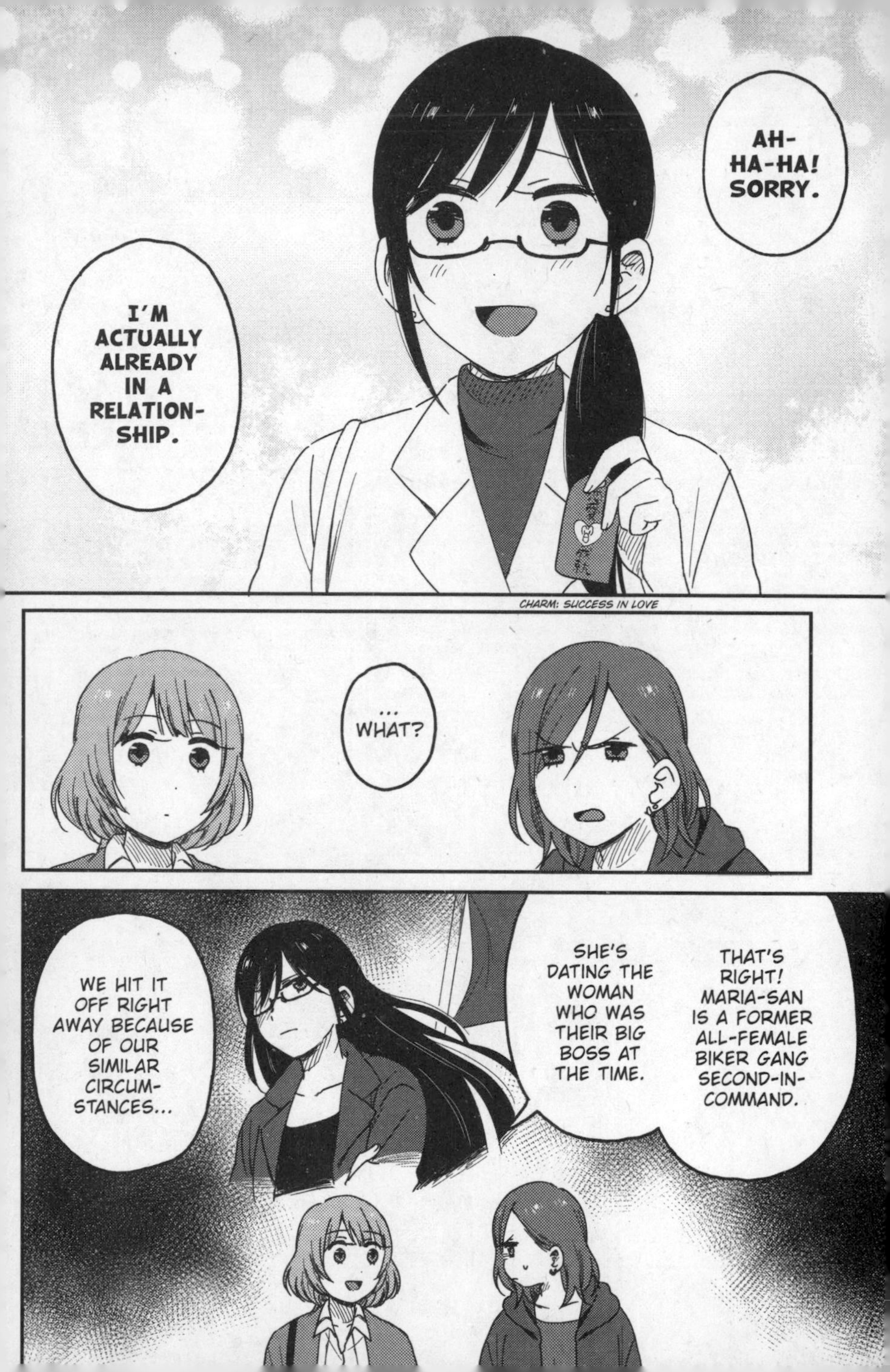
AH-HA-HA! SORRY.
I'M ACTUALLY ALREADY IN A RELATION-SHIP.
CHARM: SUCCESS IN LOVE
... WHAT?
THAT'S RIGHT! MARIA-SAN IS A FORMER ALL-FEMALE BIKER GANG SECOND-IN-COMMAND.
SHE'S DATING THE WOMAN WHO WAS THEIR BIG BOSS AT THE TIME.
WE HIT IT OFF RIGHT AWAY BECAUSE OF OUR SIMILAR CIRCUM-STANCES...

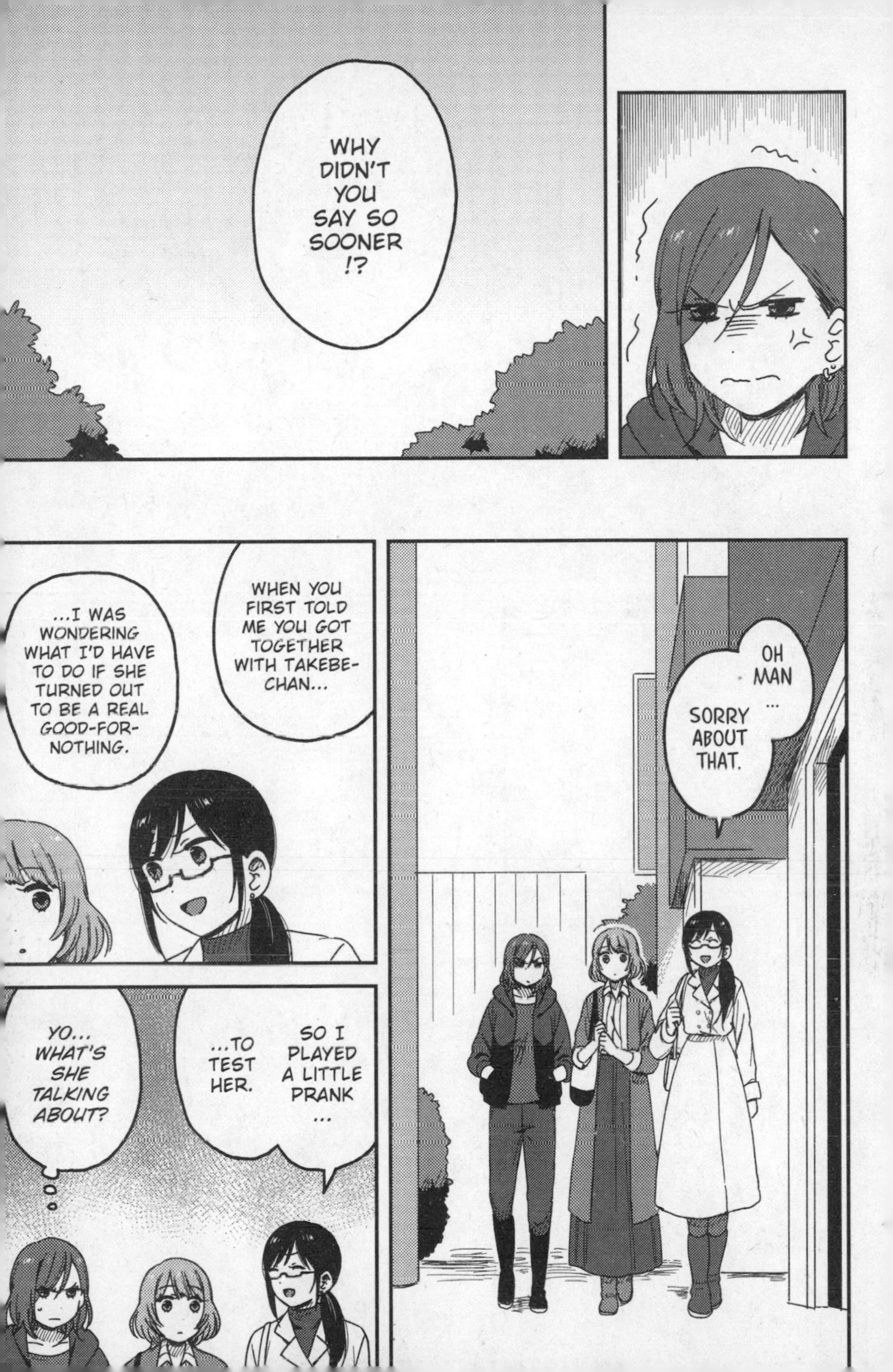
WHY DIDN'T YOU SAY SO SOONER!?
OH MAN...
SORRY ABOUT THAT.
WHEN YOU FIRST TOLD ME YOU GOT TOGETHER WITH TAKEBE-CHAN...
...I WAS WONDERING WHAT I'D HAVE TO DO IF SHE TURNED OUT TO BE A REAL GOOD-FOR-NOTHING.
SO I PLAYED A LITTLE PRANK...
...TO TEST HER.
YO... WHAT'S SHE TALKING ABOUT?

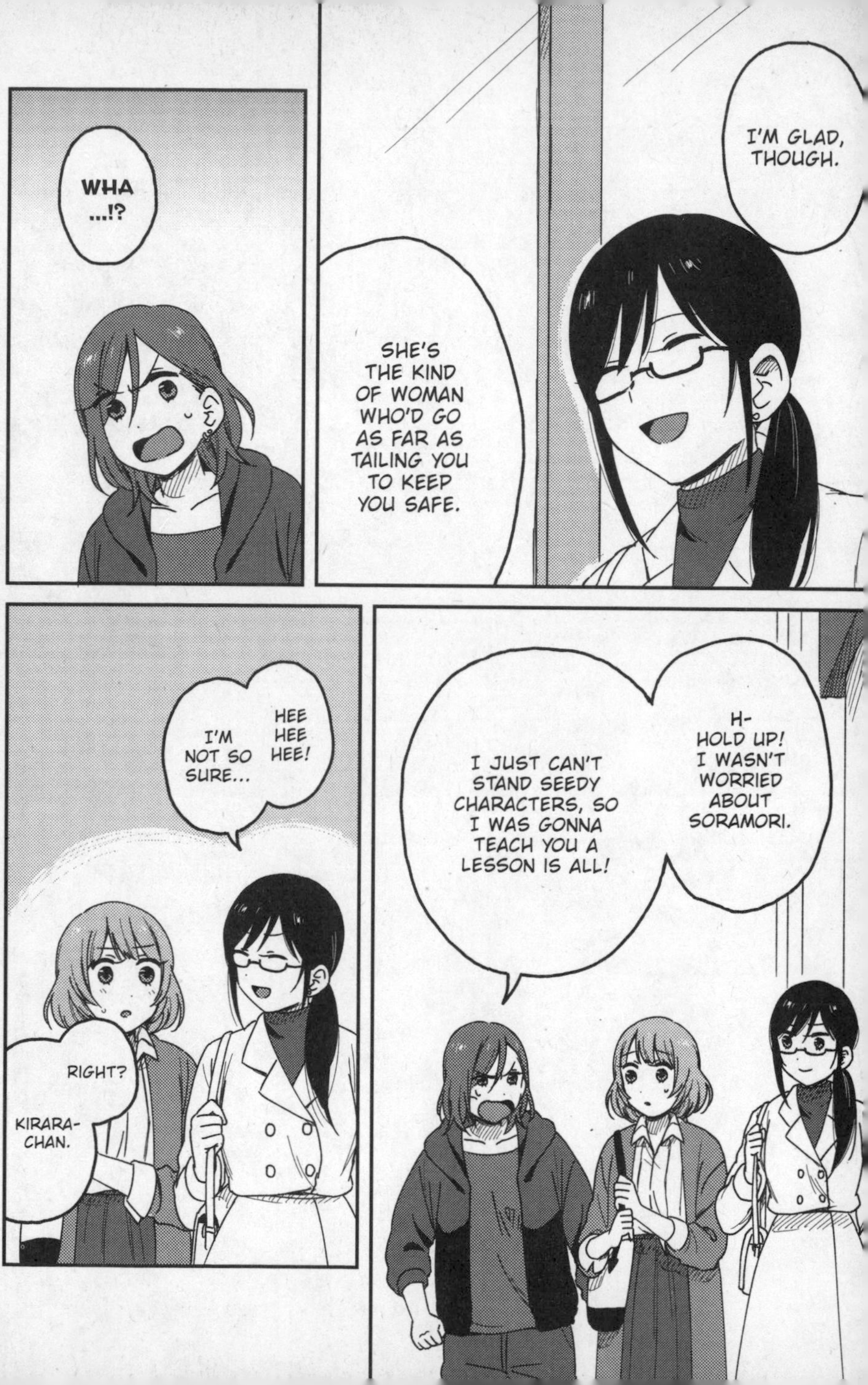
I'M GLAD, THOUGH.
SHE'S THE KIND OF WOMAN WHO'D GO AS FAR AS TAILING YOU TO KEEP YOU SAFE.
WHA ...!?
H- HOLD UP! I WASN'T WORRIED ABOUT SORAMORI.
I JUST CAN'T STAND SEEDY CHARACTERS, SO I WAS GONNA TEACH YOU A LESSON IS ALL!
HEE HEE HEE!
I'M NOT SO SURE...
RIGHT?
KIRARA-CHAN.

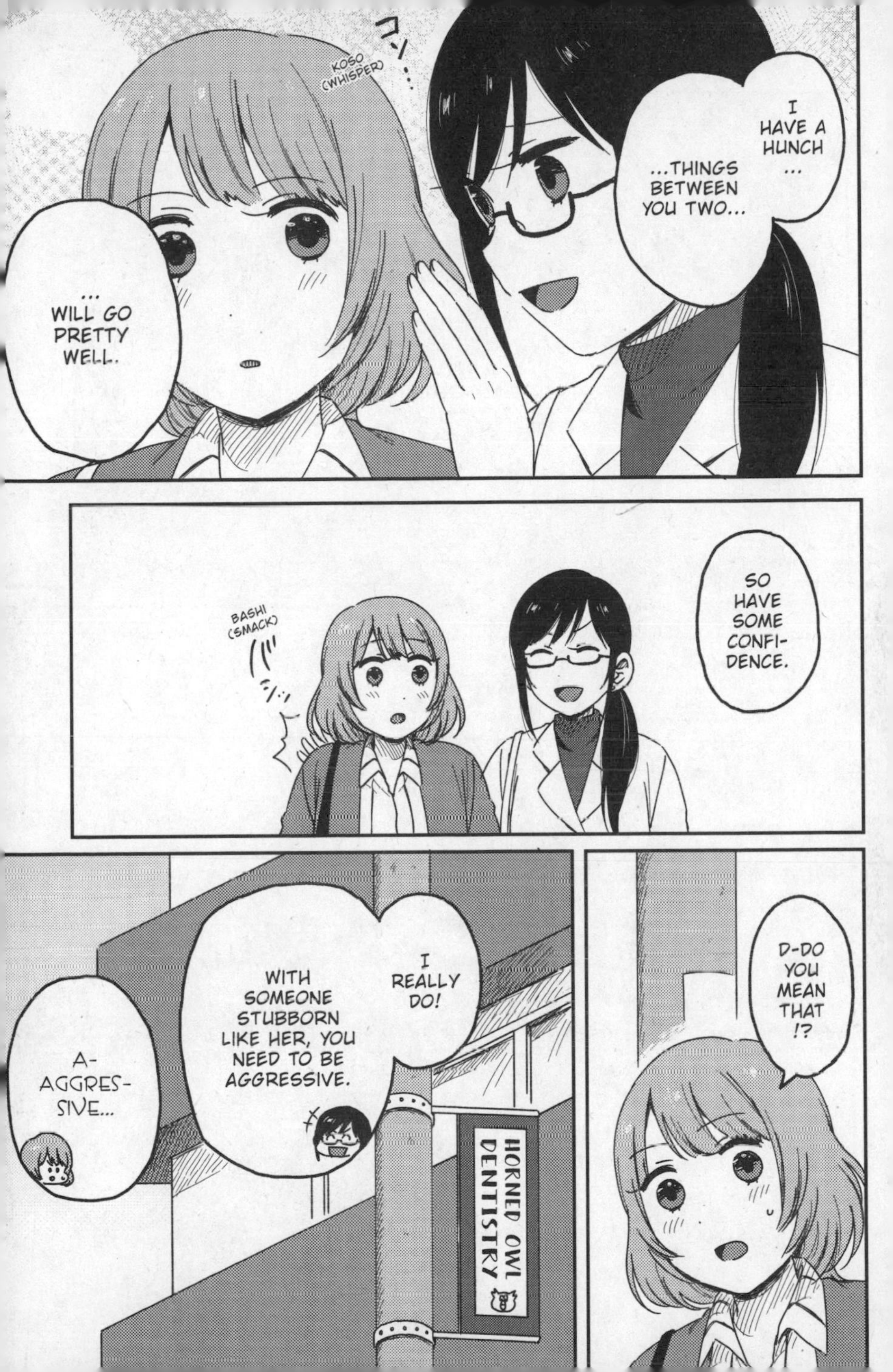
I HAVE A HUNCH ...
...THINGS BETWEEN YOU TWO...
KOSO (WHISPER)
... WILL GO PRETTY WELL.
SO HAVE SOME CONFI-DENCE.
BASHI (SMACK)
D-DO YOU MEAN THAT !?
I REALLY DO!
WITH SOMEONE STUBBORN LIKE HER, YOU NEED TO BE AGGRESSIVE.
HORNED OWL DENTISTRY
A-AGGRES-SIVE...

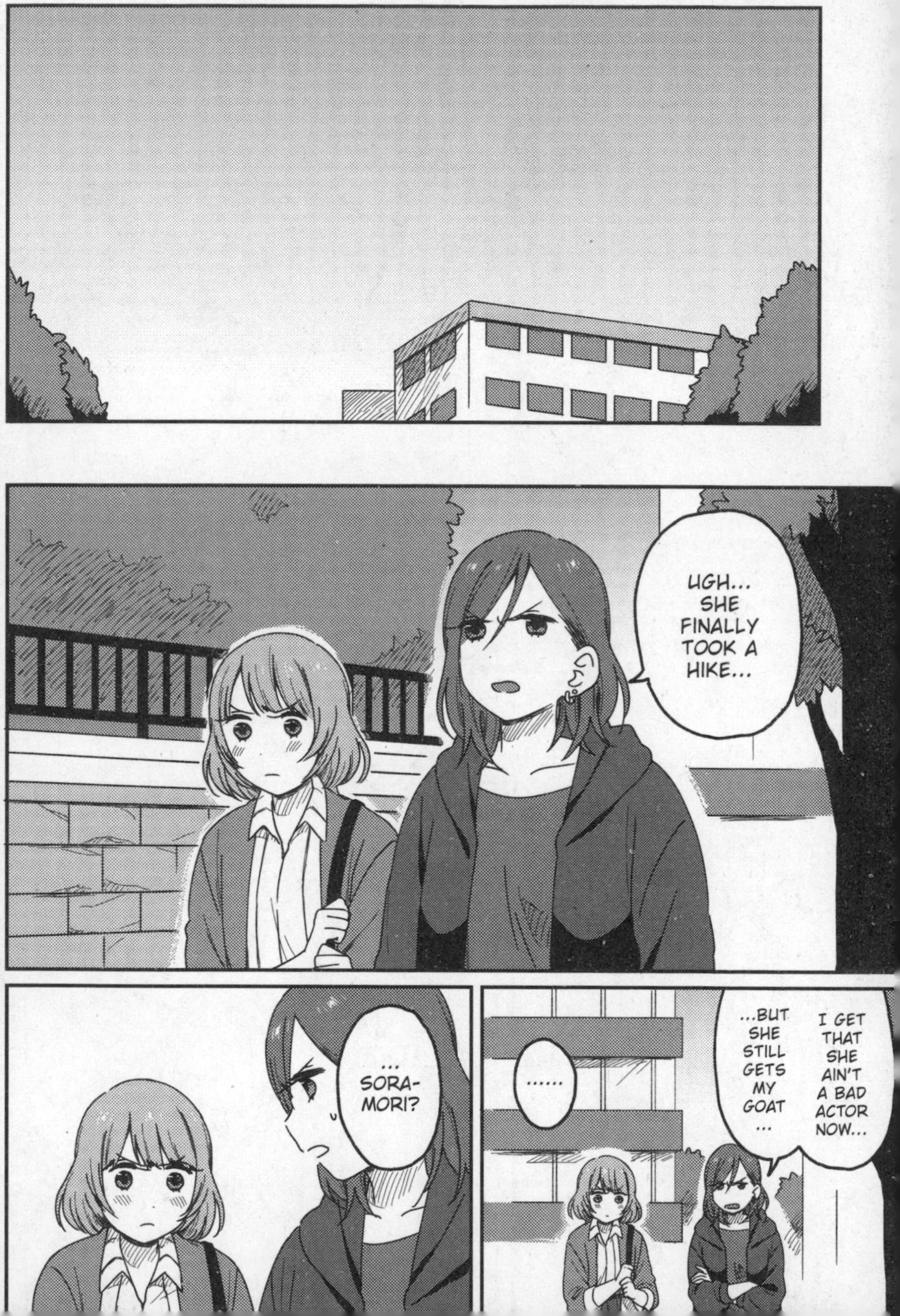
UGH... SHE FINALLY TOOK A HIKE...
I GET THAT SHE AIN'T A BAD ACTOR NOW...
...BUT SHE STILL GETS MY GOAT...
......
...SORA-MORI?

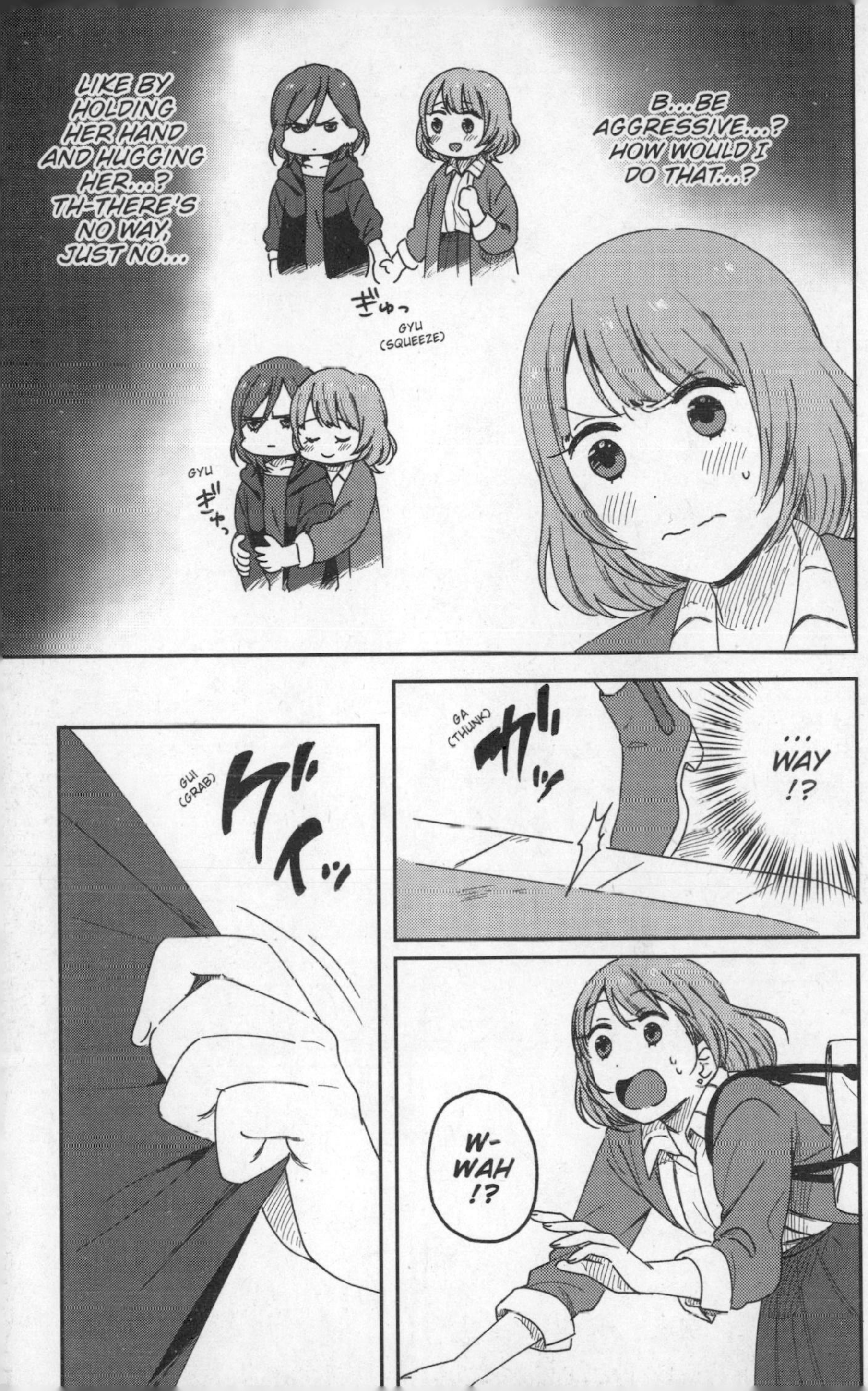

B...BE AGGRESSIVE...? HOW WOULD I DO THAT...?
LIKE BY HOLDING HER HAND AND HUGGING HER...? TH-THERE'S NO WAY, JUST NO...
ぎゅっ
GYU (SQUEEZE)
GYU
ぎゅっ
GA (THUNK)
ガッ
...WAY!?
W-WAH!?
GUI (GRAB)
グイッ

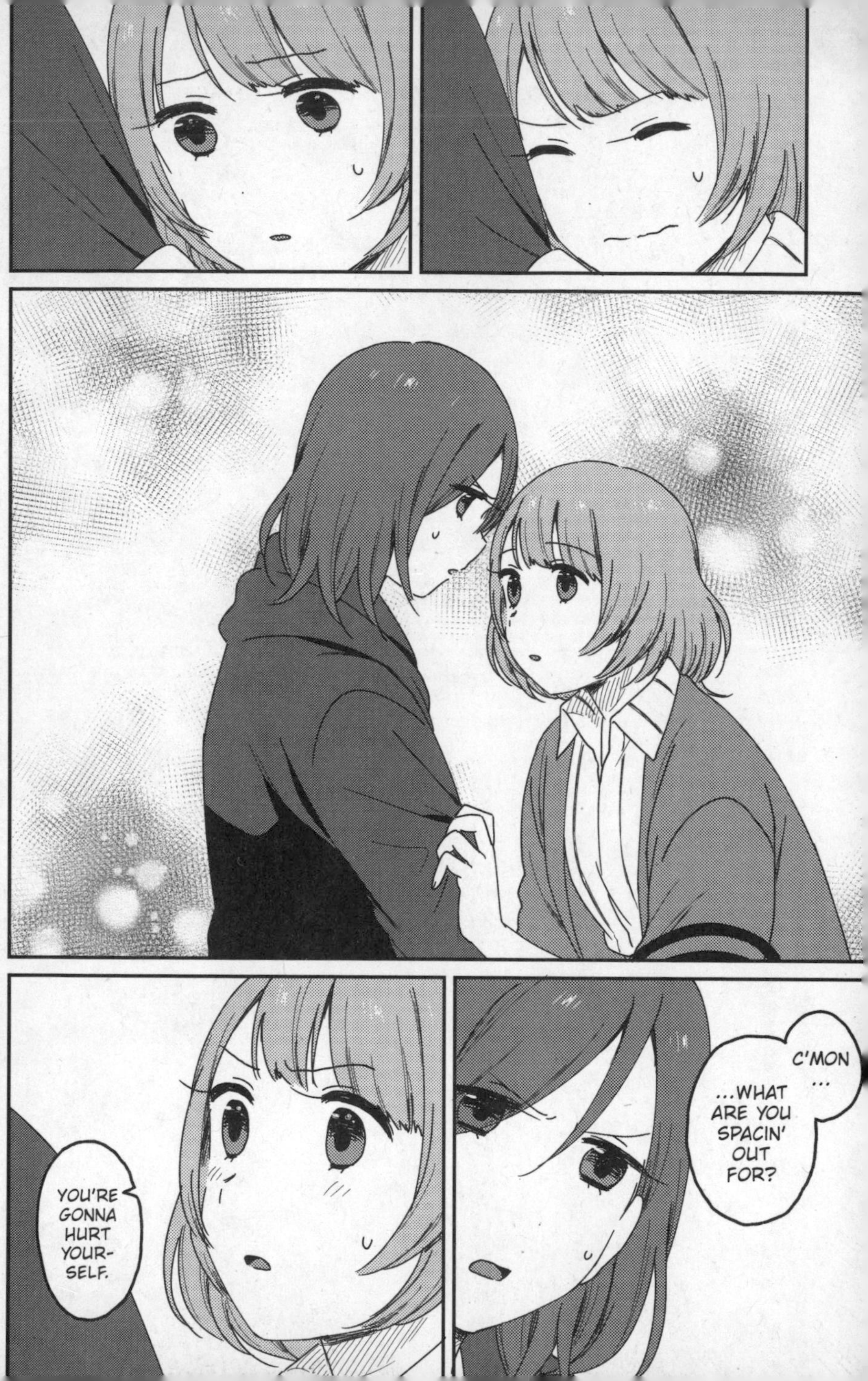
C'MON ...
...WHAT ARE YOU SPACIN' OUT FOR?
YOU'RE GONNA HURT YOUR-SELF.

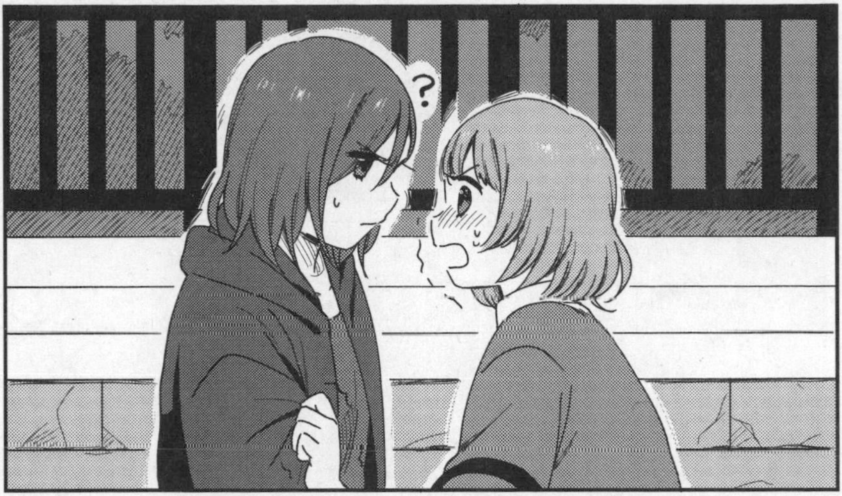
?

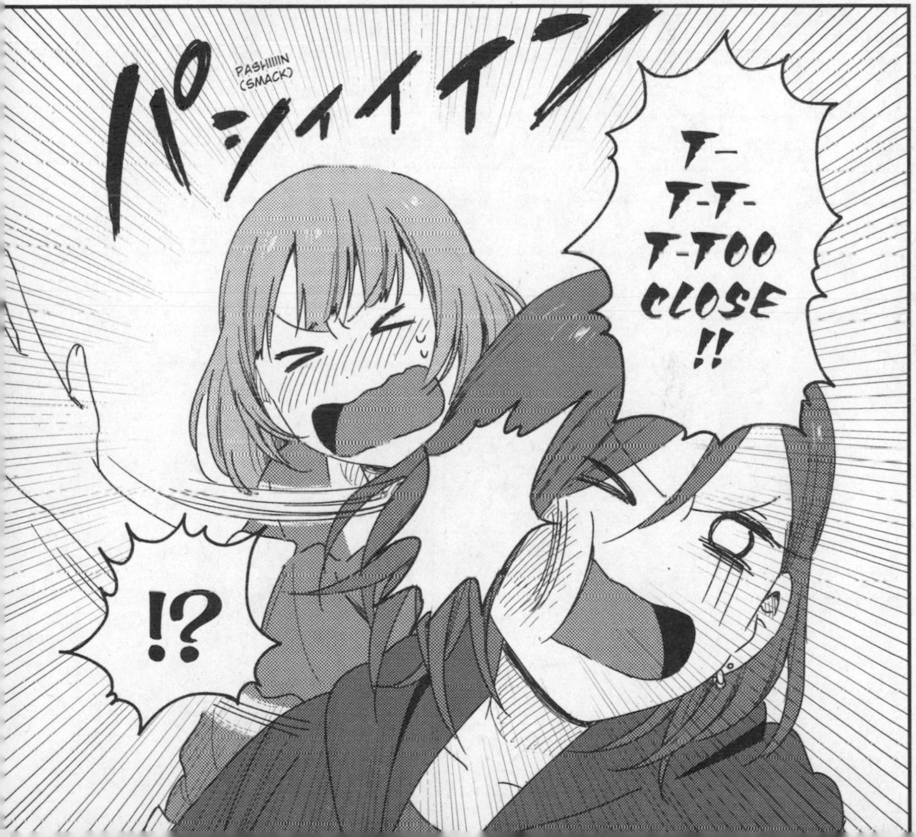
T— T-T-T-TOO CLOSE!!
パシィイイン
PASHIIIIN (SMACK)
!?

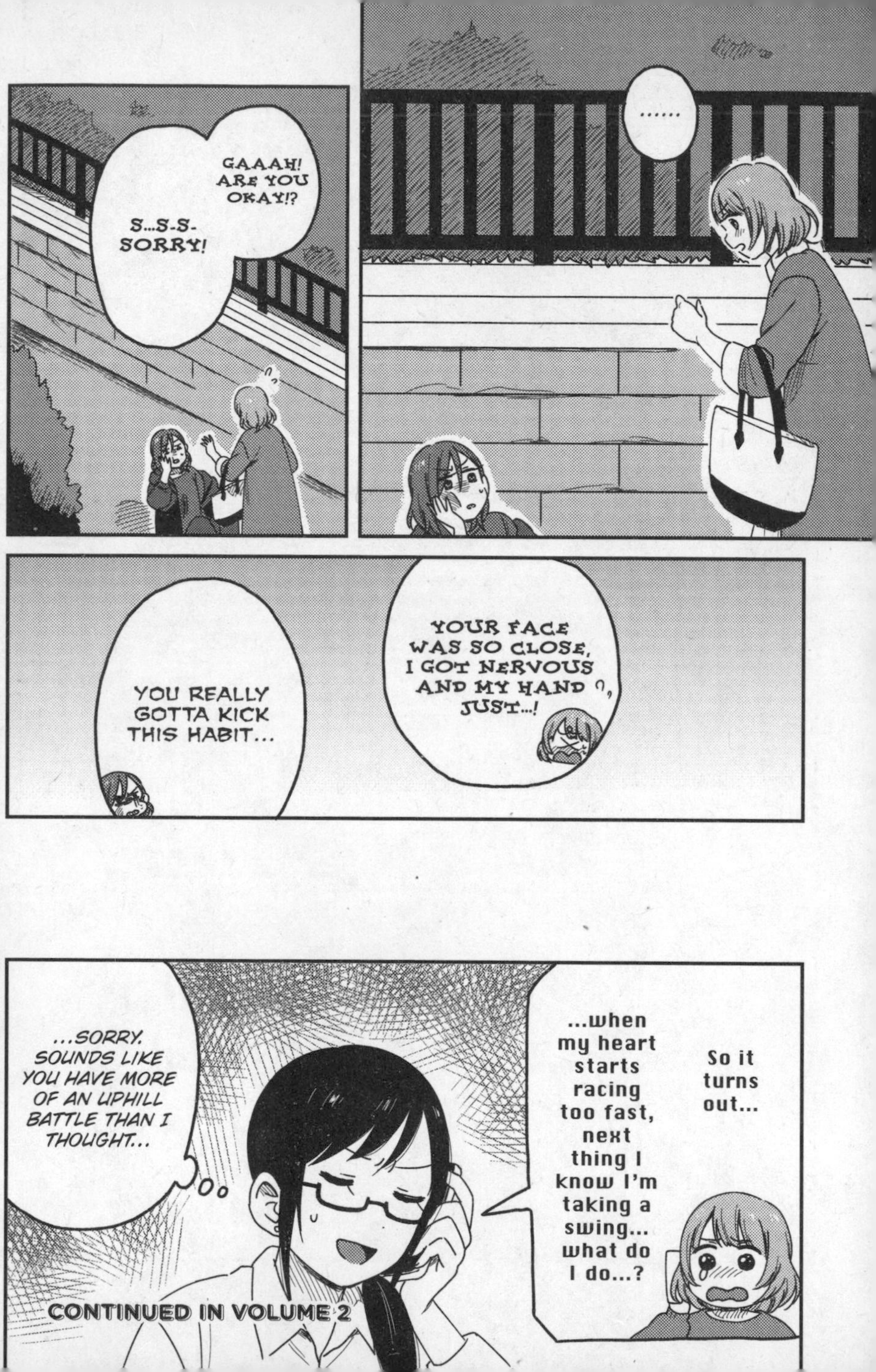
......
GAAAH! ARE YOU OKAY!?
S...S-S-SORRY!
YOUR FACE WAS SO CLOSE, I GOT NERVOUS AND MY HAND JUST...!
YOU REALLY GOTTA KICK THIS HABIT...
So it turns out...
...when my heart starts racing too fast, next thing I know I'm taking a swing... what do I do...?
...SORRY. SOUNDS LIKE YOU HAVE MORE OF AN UPHILL BATTLE THAN I THOUGHT...
CONTINUED IN VOLUME 2

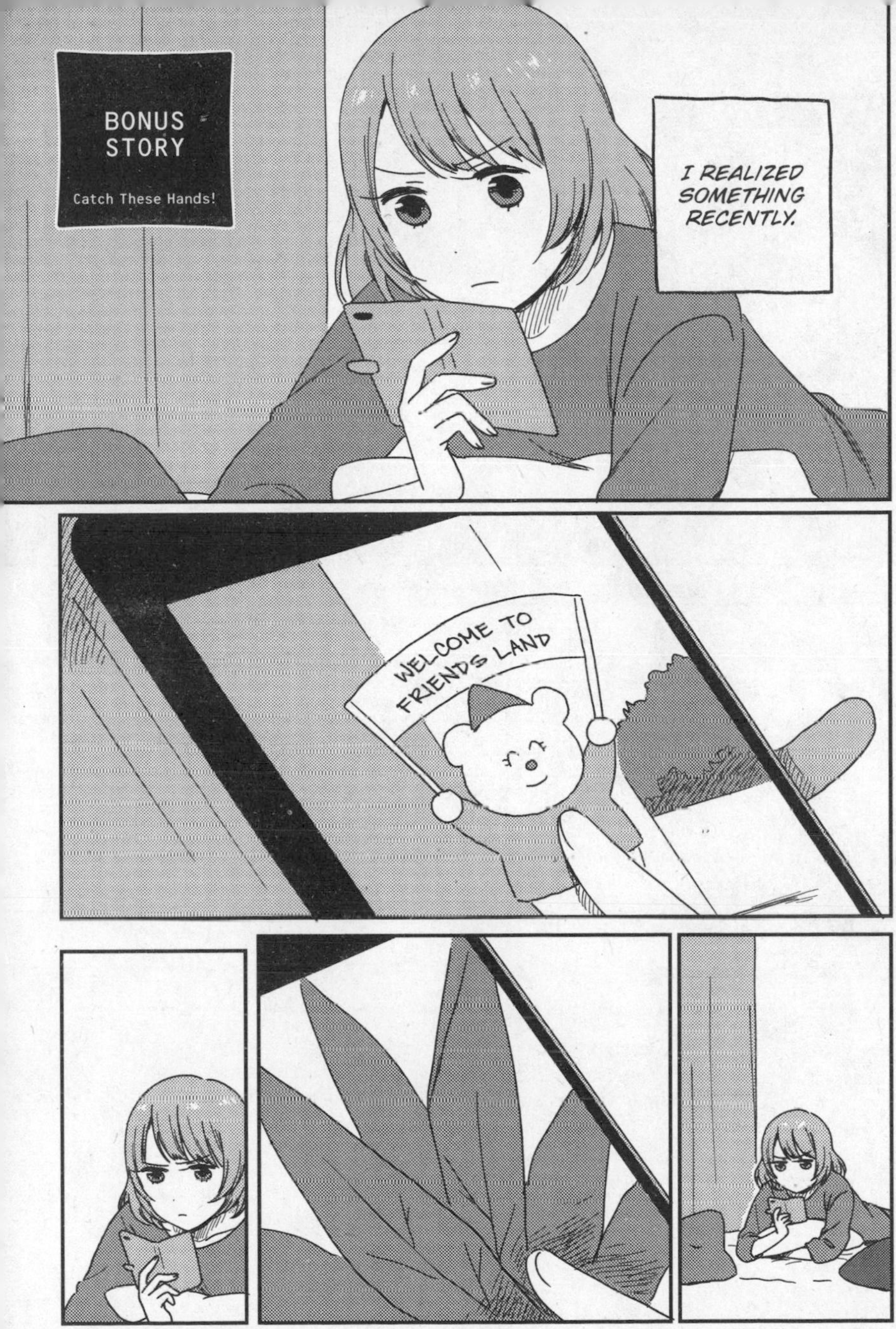
I REALIZED SOMETHING RECENTLY.
BONUS STORY
Catch These Hands!
WELCOME TO FRIENDS LAND

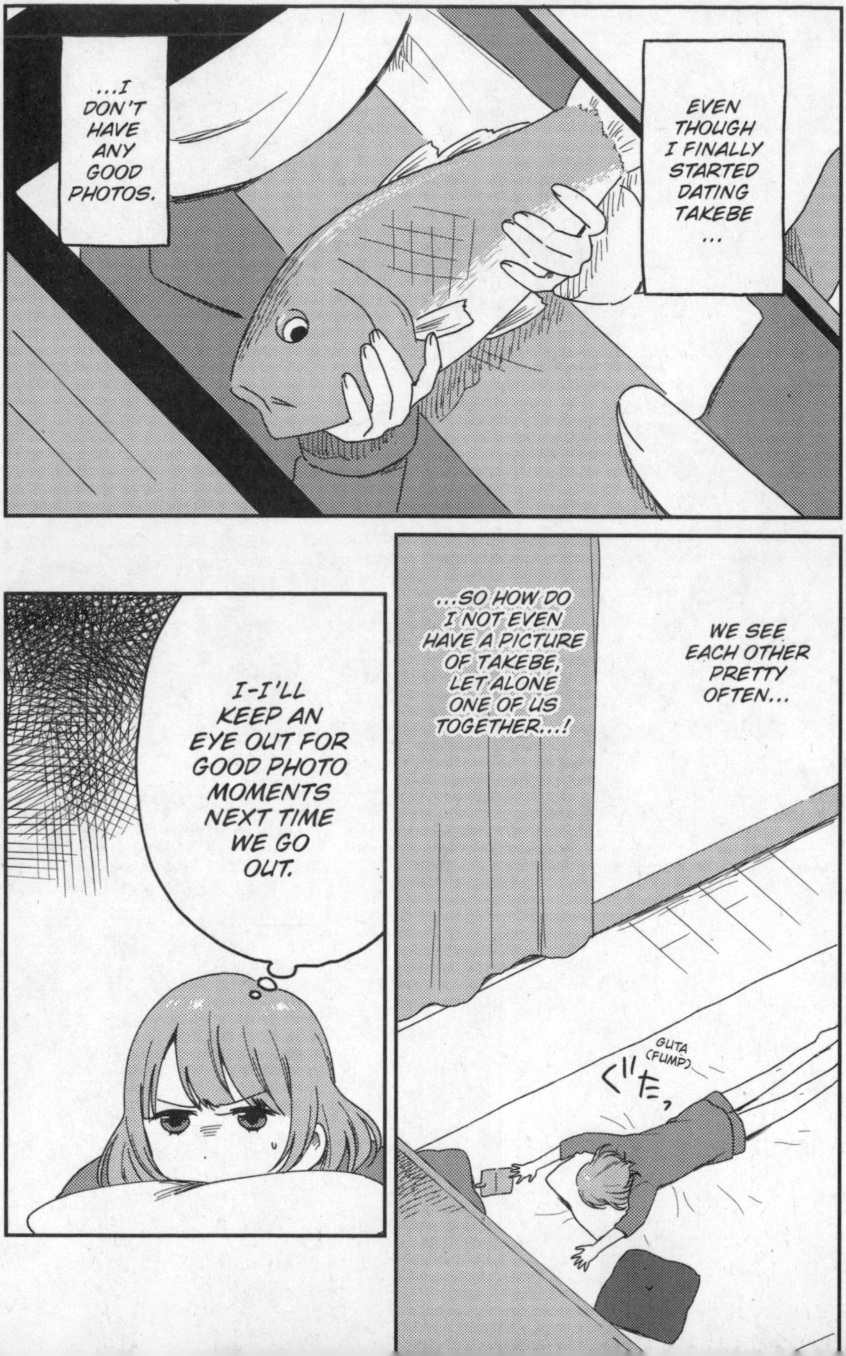
EVEN THOUGH I FINALLY STARTED DATING TAKEBE ...
...I DON'T HAVE ANY GOOD PHOTOS.
WE SEE EACH OTHER PRETTY OFTEN...
...SO HOW DO I NOT EVEN HAVE A PICTURE OF TAKEBE, LET ALONE ONE OF US TOGETHER...!
GUTA (FUMP)
I-I'LL KEEP AN EYE OUT FOR GOOD PHOTO MOMENTS NEXT TIME WE GO OUT.

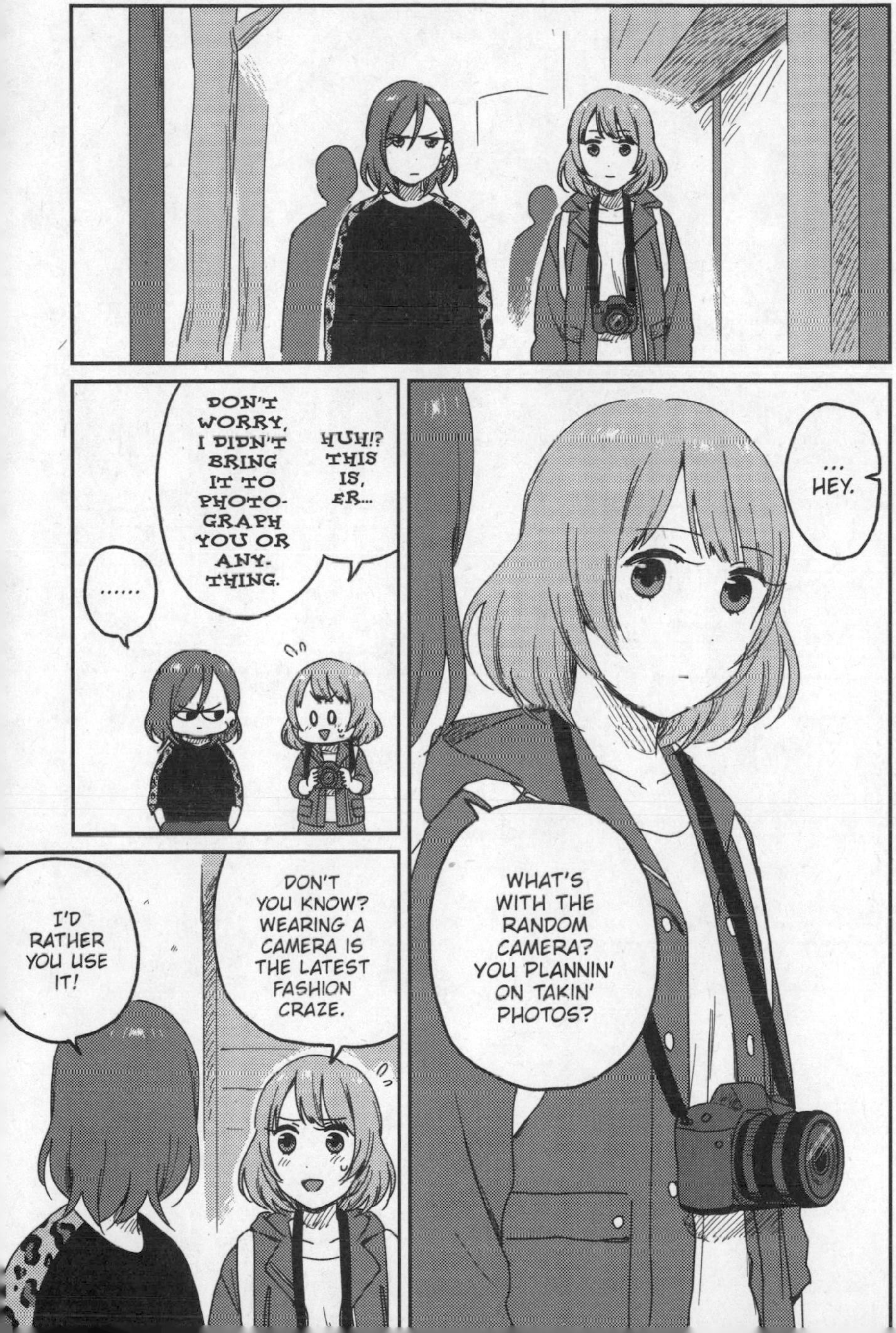
...HEY.
WHAT'S WITH THE RANDOM CAMERA? YOU PLANNIN' ON TAKIN' PHOTOS?
HUH!? THIS IS, ER...
DON'T WORRY, I DIDN'T BRING IT TO PHOTOGRAPH YOU OR ANYTHING.
......
DON'T YOU KNOW? WEARING A CAMERA IS THE LATEST FASHION CRAZE.
I'D RATHER YOU USE IT!

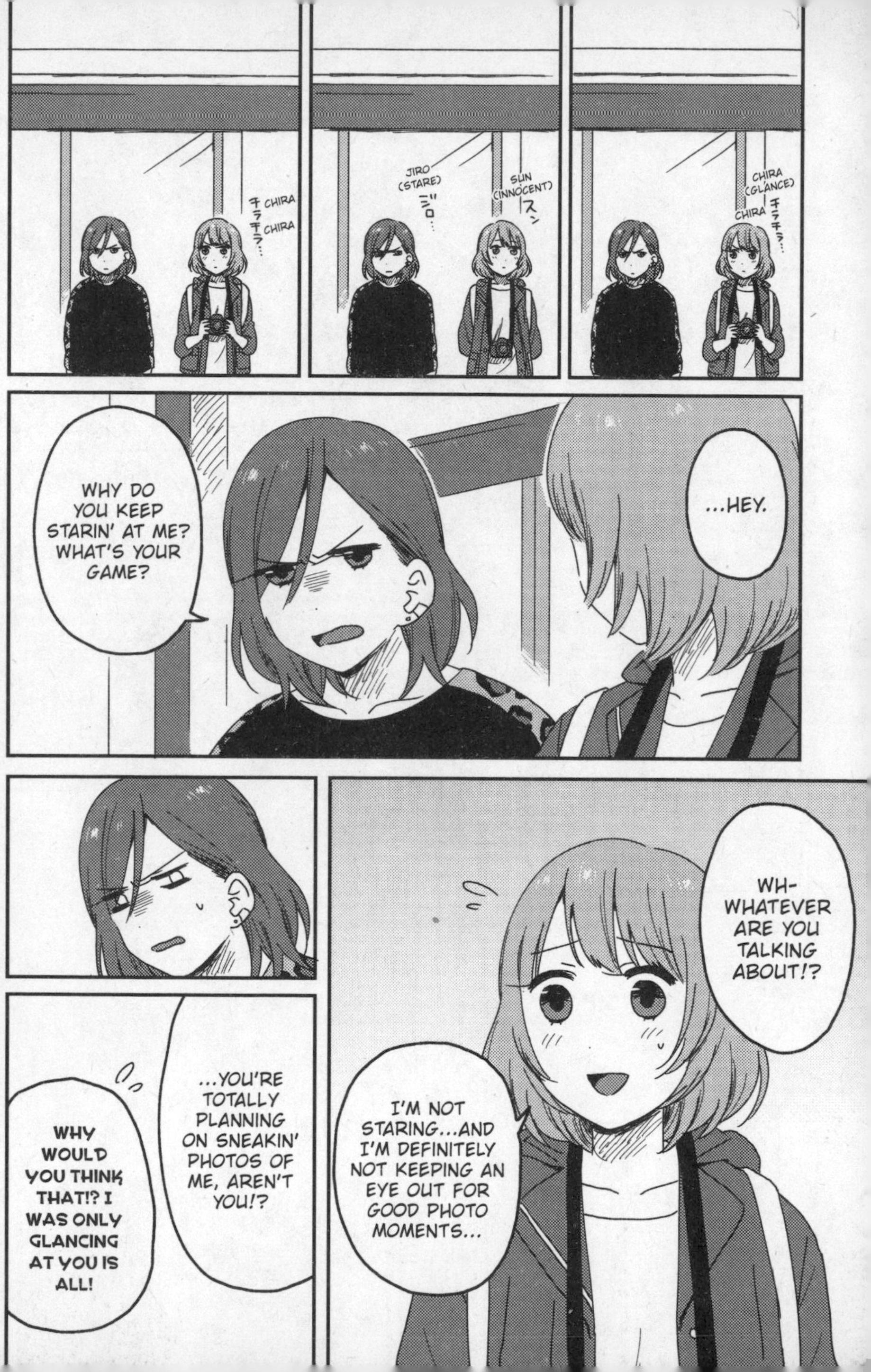
CHIRA (GLANCE)
CHIRA
チラチラ…
SUN (INNOCENT)
スン
JIRO (STARE)
ジロ…
CHIRA
CHIRA
チラチラ…
...HEY.
WHY DO YOU KEEP STARIN' AT ME? WHAT'S YOUR GAME?
WH-WHATEVER ARE YOU TALKING ABOUT!?
I'M NOT STARING...AND I'M DEFINITELY NOT KEEPING AN EYE OUT FOR GOOD PHOTO MOMENTS...
...YOU'RE TOTALLY PLANNING ON SNEAKIN' PHOTOS OF ME, AREN'T YOU!?
WHY WOULD YOU THINK THAT!? I WAS ONLY GLANCING AT YOU IS ALL!

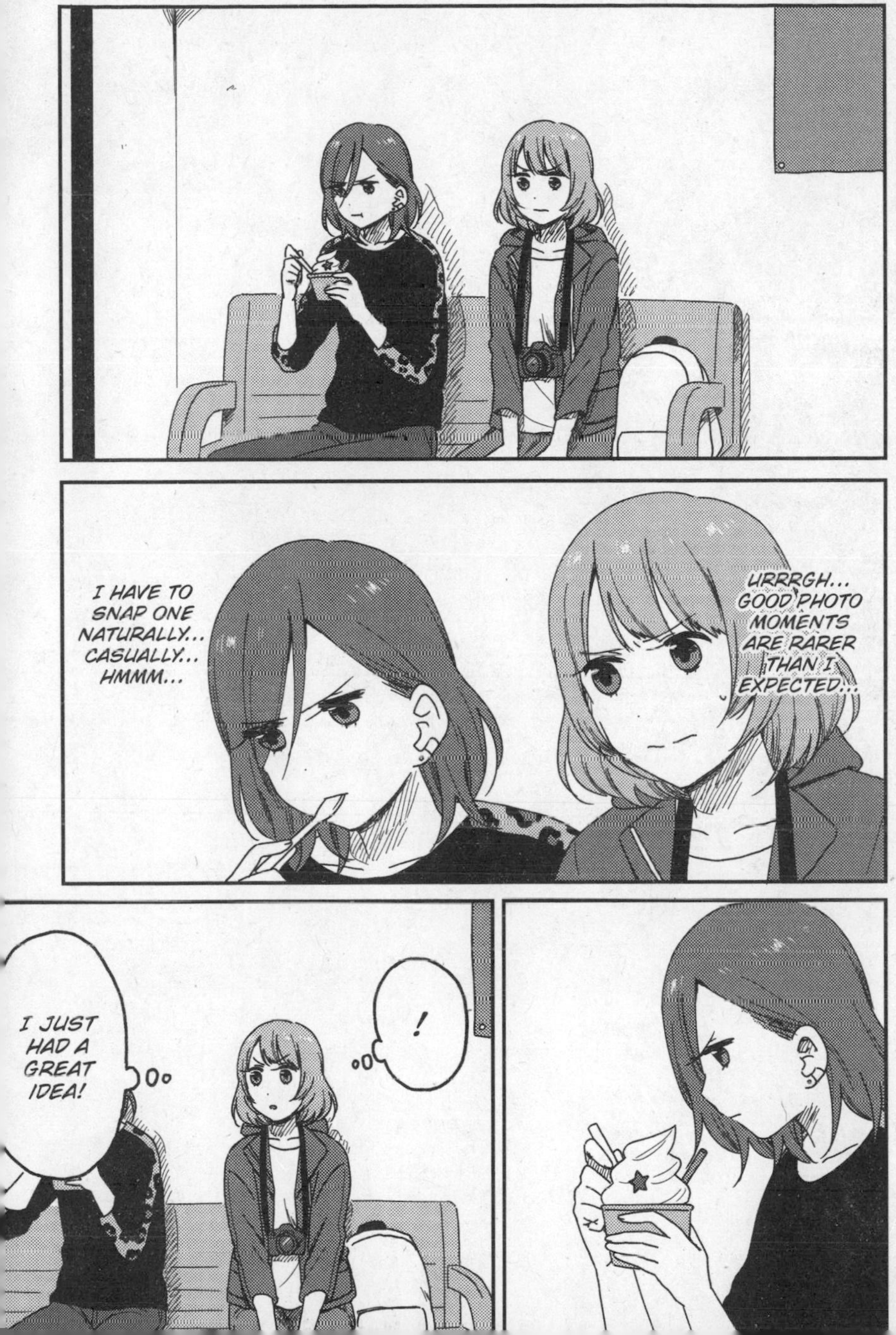
URRRGH... GOOD PHOTO MOMENTS ARE RARER THAN I EXPECTED...
I HAVE TO SNAP ONE NATURALLY... CASUALLY... HMMM...
!
I JUST HAD A GREAT IDEA!

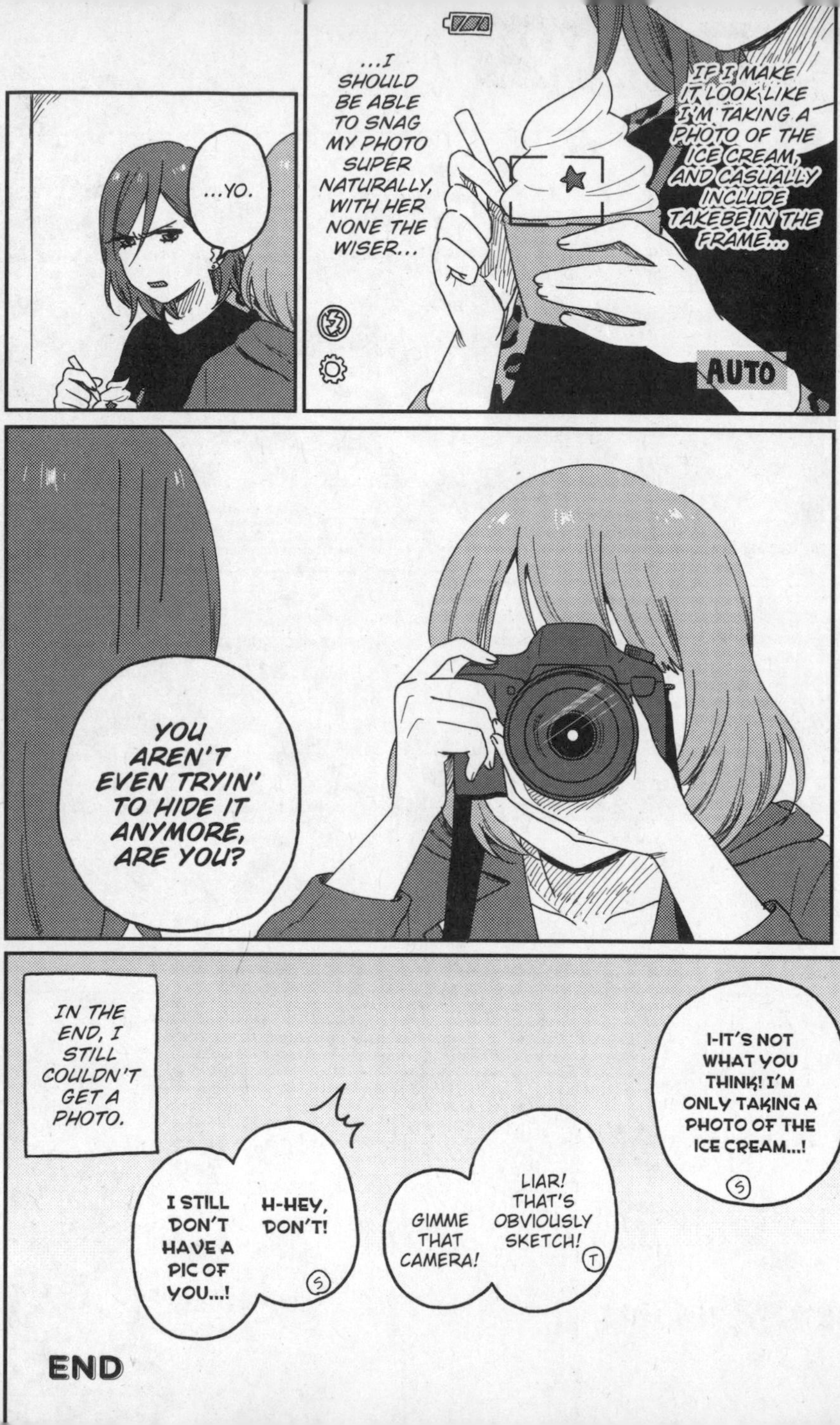
IF I MAKE IT LOOK LIKE I'M TAKING A PHOTO OF THE ICE CREAM, AND CASUALLY INCLUDE TAKEBE IN THE FRAME...
...I SHOULD BE ABLE TO SNAG MY PHOTO SUPER NATURALLY, WITH HER NONE THE WISER...
AUTO
...YO.
YOU AREN'T EVEN TRYIN' TO HIDE IT ANYMORE, ARE YOU?
I-IT'S NOT WHAT YOU THINK! I'M ONLY TAKING A PHOTO OF THE ICE CREAM...!
LIAR! THAT'S OBVIOUSLY SKETCH!
GIMME THAT CAMERA!
H-HEY, DON'T!
I STILL DON'T HAVE A PIC OF YOU...!
IN THE END, I STILL COULDN'T GET A PHOTO.
END

PREVIEW

THE ARCADE, THE MOVIE THEATER, THE ART MUSEUM...

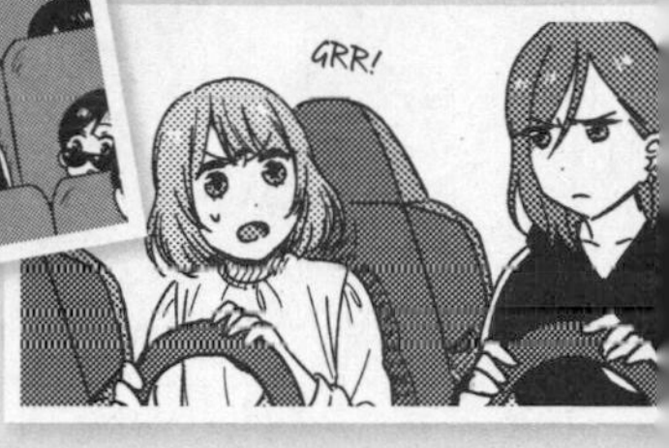
GRR!

SORAMORI TRIES ALL KINDS OF CLASSIC DATES, BUT WILL THEY WORK...?

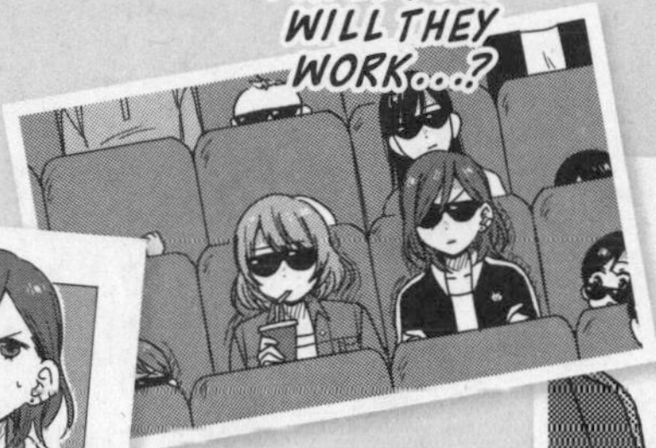

PLUS, SORAMORI GETS A CHANCE TO MEET THE PARENTS!?

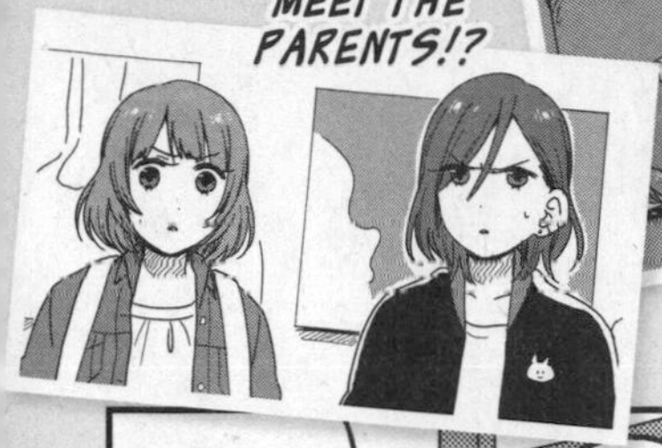

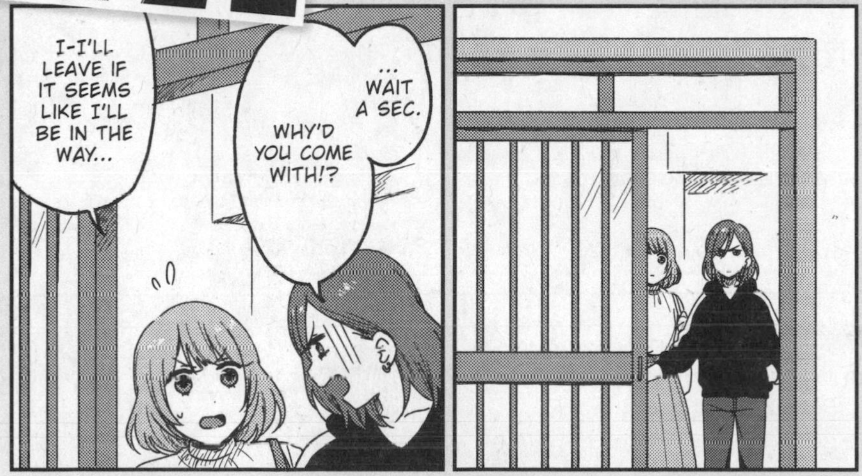
... WAIT A SEC.
WHY'D YOU COME WITH!?
I-I'LL LEAVE IF IT SEEMS LIKE I'LL BE IN THE WAY...

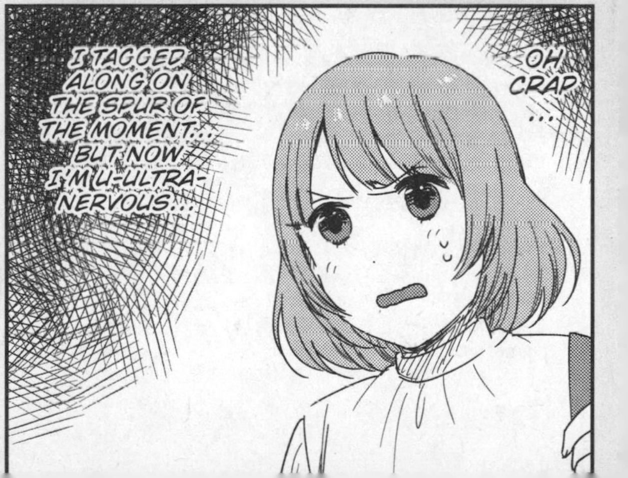
OH CRAP...
I TAGGED ALONG ON THE SPUR OF THE MOMENT... BUT NOW I'M U-ULTRA-NERVOUS...

CATCH THESE HANDS!

Volume 2

Coming Soon!!

Catch These Hands!

murata

Translation: AMANDA HALEY ✖ Lettering: BIANCA PISTILLO

This book is a work of fiction. Names, characters, places, and incidents are the product of the author's imagination or are used fictitiously. Any resemblance to actual events, locales, or persons, living or dead, is coincidental.

WATASHI NO KOBUSHI WO UKETOMETE! Vol. 1
©murata 2018
First published in Japan in 2018 by KADOKAWA CORPORATION, Tokyo.
English translation rights arranged with KADOKAWA CORPORATION, Tokyo through TUTTLE-MORI AGENCY, INC., Tokyo.

English translation © 2022 by Yen Press, LLC

Yen Press, LLC supports the right to free expression and the value of copyright. The purpose of copyright is to encourage writers and artists to produce the creative works that enrich our culture.

The scanning, uploading, and distribution of this book without permission is a theft of the author's intellectual property. If you would like permission to use material from the book (other than for review purposes), please contact the publisher. Thank you for your support of the author's rights.

Yen Press
150 West 30th Street, 19th Floor
New York, NY 10001

Visit us at yenpress.com
facebook.com/yenpress
twitter.com/yenpress
yenpress.tumblr.com
instagram.com/yenpress

First Yen Press Edition: March 2022

Yen Press is an imprint of Yen Press, LLC. The Yen Press name and logo are trademarks of Yen Press, LLC.

The publisher is not responsible for websites (or their content) that are not owned by the publisher.

Library of Congress Control Number: 2021950487

ISBNs: 978-1-9753-4005-6 (paperback)
       978-1-9753-4006-3 (ebook)

10 9 8 7 6 5 4 3 2 1

WOR

Printed in the United States of America